Two Thousand Years
of Coptic Christianity

Two Thousand Years of Coptic Christianity

Otto F.A. Meinardus

The American University in Cairo Press
Cairo • New York

Contents

Introduction

TODAY, the Coptic Church is experiencing an unprecedented renaissance. It is the purpose of this volume to unfold this story and acquaint the visitor to the land of the Nile with one of the most remarkable developments of world Christianity toward the end of the second millenium.

The history of Christian Egypt begins with the traditions of the visit of the holy family to Egypt, which were circulated to fulfill the Old Testament prophecy "When Israel was a child, then I loved him, and called my son out of Egypt" (Hos. 11:1). The feast of the coming of the Lord to Egypt (June 1) is one of the important feasts for many Egyptian Christians. Undoubtedly, Egyptians filled with the gifts of the Holy Spirit on the first day of Pentecost returned to their homes along the Nile Valley (Acts 2:10) and established there the first Christian communities. The Copts regard Saint Mark the Evangelist as the founder of their church. In Alexandria he preached and suffered martyrdom. The theology of the great Alexandrian doctors of the church, Clement, Origen, Athanasius, and Cyril, has had a profound influence on the development of Christian thought and piety. Both the eremitical and cenobitic forms of monasticism had their origin in Egypt: Saint Antony, the great hermit of the Eastern Desert, inspired thousands of Christians to follow his example; Pachomius became the founder of the Christian communal life.

At the same time, Coptic Christianity went through numerous trials, persecutions, and afflictions. The vast numbers of their martyrs are a testimony to their unshaken faith. During the Middle Ages, the Coptic Church kept the lamp of their faith burning amid trials and tribulations of all kinds.

With an ever increasing number of visitors to Egypt and greatly improved facilities for travel within the country, there is now an imperative need for an introductory volume to the history and theology of the Coptic Orthodox church and the topography of its principal churches, monasteries, and monuments. To this day, large numbers of visitors flock annually to the ancient pharaonic monuments in Luxor and Aswan to behold the magnificent achievements of the ancient Egyptians. Few of them realize, however, that

Egypt was once a great Christian nation, with its churches, monasteries, institutions, and culture established throughout the Nile Valley. Indeed, one of the objectives of the present volume is to encourage scholars and visitors to depart from the tracks beaten by tourists and to discover some of the ancient and modern Christian monuments for themselves.

This work combines in a single volume some of the specific Coptic material of my former studies *Christian Egypt, Ancient and Modern* (Cairo 1965, 1977) and *Christian Egypt, Faith and Life* (Cairo 1970). Due to the rapid and dynamic developments within the Coptic Orthodox Church during the last thirty years, numerous additions and corrections to the original texts became obligatory. Moreover, in view of the major theme of this book, it was necessary to limit a certain amount of the material. Therefore, descriptions and references to the other Christian communities in Egypt, along with the Greek, Armenian, and Syrian Orthodox churches, the various Catholic and Uniate churches, and the Episocopal and Protestant churches have been omitted; this should not be seen as an assessment of their religious importance in Egyptian society.

In duty bound I want to thank Zora O'Neill, who has carefully read the manuscript and offered many valuable suggestions. Her priceless computer expertise has made the publication of this volume possible. In conclusion, I should like to express my gratitude to the director and staff of the American University in Cairo Press, who have assisted me in the process of publication.

1

Toward the Third Millennium

❦

The Pontificate of Shenuda III

THE unprecedented revival of the Coptic Church toward the second half of the twentieth century is one of the great historical events of world Christianity. Whereas in many parts of the world, historians recognize a certain stagnation of the Christian witness, the sons and daughters of the pharaohs are filled with an unheard-of enthusiasm for the establishment of the kingdom of God and for evangelization through their Coptic Church.

This spiritual renaissance had its beginnings half a century ago—in the forties and fifties—in the Coptic Sunday School movements in Cairo, Giza, and Asyut. Inspired by the challenges they experienced in the Sunday School classes, young men consecrated their lives to God and joined the desert fathers. Especially in the Monastery of the Syrians under the able leadership of Anba Tawfilus (Bishop Theophilus), they were prepared for the work of rejuvenating their church.

Following the enthronement of Pope Cyril VI in 1959, some of the former Sunday School teachers and monks and hermits were called to the episcopacy in order to occupy responsible positions in the life and organization of the church. Among these young men was Nazir Gayyid, later known as Abuna Antonius al-Suriani (1954–62), then Shenuda, bishop for theological and educational institutions of the Coptic Church (1962–71), and now as Shenuda III, the present pope and patriarch.

Both the pontificate of Shenuda III and a dynamic, deeply spiritual, and capable episcopate have succeeded in providing an almost lifeless ecclesiastical institution with new visions and life, thereby retaining the much cherished and long established traditions of the church and filling them with a new sense of spirituality.

The spiritual and educational background of Pope Shenuda III has largely determined the direction of the present movements of the church. At the young age of sixteen he had joined the Sunday School at Saint Antony's Church in Shubra. Later he became its teacher and drew thousands of young Egyptians to faith in Jesus Christ.

In more than one way, Nazir Gayyid became the leader of an altogether new youth ministry in the Coptic Church. In 1947 he received his B.A. in English and history from Cairo University. To this day, his speeches, sermons, and books reflect his impeccable use of the English language. At the theological college he completed the course of studies with academic brilliance, which led to his appointment as lecturer in the Old and New Testaments. In 1953 he was appointed full-time lecturer at the monastic college in Helwan.

On July 19, 1954, he was made a monk by Bishop Tawfilus of the Monastery of the Syrians and received the name Antony. At this time young Nazir Gayyid offered the following pledge:

> I acknowledge that monasticism is a complete death to the world and all that is in it in the way of wealth and possessions, and in the way of relatives and friends, and in the way of appointments and occupations, and that it is a life of worship and dedication to God, a life of penitence and deprivation and perfect obedience and exclusion and poverty. And before God and his angels and his holy altar, and in the saintly presence of my father, the bishop, and of the assembly of my fathers, the monks, members of this holy congregation, I dedicate my life to God, that I may live in virginity and continency and estrangement from the world, promising that I will follow the life of true monasticism and obey its canons, even as our saintly Fathers have set for us, who have followed this angelic manner of life . . . .

A year later he was ordained priest. Throughout his life as priest, bishop, and patriarch, he has faithfully kept the monastic vows he made in the ancient Church of the Holy Virgin at the Syrian Monastery.

At the monastery he was placed in charge of the library. These duties enabled him to devote his studies to the reading of the church fathers and doctors. Meanwhile, though, his longing was for the solitary life. First he selected a cave three kilometers from the monastery. Later he exchanged this eremitical abode for a cave at Bahr al-Farigh, some ten kilometers from the monastery. As early as 1948 he had written a poem entitled "The Hermit," which was published in 1954 in the Sunday School magazine:

> Alone am I in the desert minding my own affairs,
> I have a cave in the crevasse of the hill where I have hidden
> And I will leave it one day, dwelling where I know not.

In 1959 Pope Cyril VI appointed him to be his personal secretary, but Abuna Antonius preferred the life of solitude. For several years

Abuna Antonius had successfully withstood all pressure to be consecrated to the episcopacy. Then, in September 1962, Cyril VI summoned the hermit to the patriarchate in Cairo because of some insignificant misunderstanding pertaining to the administrative affairs of the monastery. While kneeling in front of the patriarch apologizing and expecting to be forgiven and to be relieved from the administrative affairs in the monastery, the patriarch placed his hands on the head of the hermit, thereby consecrating him bishop of theological and educational institutions of the Coptic Church. The ordination took place in the patriarchate on September 30, 1962. In reply to my letter of congratulation, Bishop Shenuda wrote:

> Grace and peace from our Lord and Saviour Jesus Christ be upon you. I thank you for your gentle words of congratulation sent to me. I can never forget your friendship and love. As a matter of fact, however, a letter of consolation—not of congratulation—was fit for the occasion. How may a monk be congratulated on leaving the calmness of the wilderness and abiding again amidst the disturbance of the city? How can anyone congratulate Mary if she leaves her place at the feet of Christ and goes to labor with Martha in the kitchen? For me, it is, indeed, a matter of shame. I remember that day of my consecration to the Episcopacy in tears and lamentation. Indeed, the glory of solitude and contemplation is above measure. It may not be compared with that of the Episcopacy or even that of the Papacy. The true consecration, my dear friend, is the consecration of the heart as a holy temple for the Lord, Who on the Last Day will not ask us for our pastoral grade but for our purity of heart. I write this letter from my beloved cave at Bahr al-Faregh in Wadi al-Natrun, in which I expect to stay till Epiphany, and then return to Cairo . . . .

Nevertheless, whenever possible the bishop retired to the monastery.

His leadership in the field of Christian education was rewarded when he was elected president of the Association of Middle East Theological Colleges in 1969. An important aspect of his ministry was the innovation of his weekly sermons, in which he responded to theological and social questions. Thousands of young people attended these services. After lecturing and preaching for half of the week in Cairo or Alexandria, Bishop Shenuda would retire for the second half of the week to the monastery.

During these years one of the aims of the Coptic Church was to free itself from its century-old theological isolation. Bishop Shenuda represented his church at several ecumenical conferences. The last conference he attended as bishop for education was the First Pro Oriente Consultation between the Oriental Orthodox and the Catholic

Churches in Vienna in September 1971, just one month prior to his election as pope and patriarch of Alexandria. At this conference Bishop Shenuda espoused the christological formula of Saint Cyril of Alexandria. This was the text that was later officially accepted by Pope Paul VI and Pope Shenuda III:

> We all believe that Our Lord, God, and Saviour Jesus Christ is the Incarnate Word. We believe that He was perfect in His Divinity and perfect in His Humanity and that His Divinity never departed from His Humanity not even for a single instant. His Humanity is one with His Divinity without commixture, without confusion, without division, without separation.

Following the death of Pope Cyril VI on March 9, 1971, the Holy Synod decided on March 22 to prepare the election of a successor. On October 29, 1971 an official election reduced the five candidates to three. Then on October 31, young blindfolded Ayman Munir Kamil chose one of the pieces of paper with the names of the candidates and gave it to the locum tenens, the Metropolitan Antonius. He declared God's chosen shepherd for the Coptic Church: "Bishop Shenuda!" Two weeks later, on November 14, 1971 the bishop was enthroned as His Holiness Shenuda III, 117th pope and patriarch of the See of Saint Mark.

As pope and patriarch he continued lecturing at the theological college and the Higher Institute of Coptic Studies. An additional six branches of the theological college were established in Lower and Upper Egypt, and three more were founded in the United States and Australia.

As a scholar, Pope Shenuda III encouraged the various fields of Coptic studies, including the publication of the monumental *Coptic Encyclopedia*. In April 1988 he signed a contract with al-Ahram news agency to have the archives of the Coptic patriarchate put on microfilm.

As head of the church he has consecrated more than eighty bishops and over five hundred priests for the Coptic churches in Egypt and the diaspora. Through periodic seminars with members of the clergy, he has encouraged the pastoral, spiritual, and educational life of both bishops and priests. His special attention to young people has led to the establishment of a very dynamic youth ministry under Bishop Musa. Because of the unprecedented increase of churches, especially in the diaspora, Pope Shenuda III has consecrated large quantities of the holy myron, or sacramental oil, at Easter in 1981, 1987, 1993, and 1995 at the Monastery of Saint Bishoi.

Because of his deep commitment to Christian unity, he has invested much time and effort in creating better ecumenical understanding. His emphasis has always been that Christian unity should be founded on unity of faith rather than on jurisdiction. To this end he initiated the theological dialogue with the Eastern Orthodox, Roman Catholic, Anglican, Presbyterian, Swedish Lutheran, and Reformed Churches.

In May 1973 Pope Shenuda III was invited by Pope Paul VI to visit Rome, which was the first meeting between an Alexandrian and a Roman pontiff since 451. At this occasion they signed the confession of their common christological faith. In 1979, 1987, and 1995 Pope Shenuda III met with the archbishop of Canterbury to discuss their mutual understanding on the basis of the Scriptures. In November 1988 Shenuda initiated the Coptic-Presbyterian theological dialogue, which could pave the way for reconciling some of the theological problems between the Orthodox and the Protestants in the Middle East.

Regarding relations with the other Orthodox churches, Shenuda III visited the Orthodox patriarchates in Damascus, Istanbul, Moscow, Bucharest, and Sofia. As head of the largest church in the Middle East and the oldest church in Africa, he has given particular attention to his church's involvement in the Middle East Council of Churches and the All-African Council of Churches.

In February 1991 he led a delegation of eleven Copts to the Seventh Assembly of the World Council of Churches in Canberra, Australia. At the conclusion of the assembly he was elected one of the presidents of the World Council of Churches, representing the Oriental Orthodox Churches. In November 1994, at the assembly in Cyprus, he was elected one of the four presidents of the Middle East Council of Churches.

Although he has spent much time and effort serving world Christianity, in his heart Shenuda III remains a monk. As such he has been instrumental in rebuilding and renovating several deserted medieval Coptic monasteries. His pontifical residence is established at the rear of the Monastery of Saint Bishoi. This houses a chapel, conference and lecture halls, and guest houses. Here he spends half of each week in contemplation and reflection.

In 1971 there were only seven Coptic churches in the diaspora. Today there are almost eighty Coptic churches in the United States and Canada, about twenty-six churches in Australia, and almost thirty churches in Europe. Seven Coptic bishops serve the overseas congregations.

In 1994 the nineteen parishes of the Orthodox Church of the British Isles were received into full communion with the Coptic Orthodox Church. On Pentecost 1994 Anba Seraphim was consecrated metropolitan of Glastonbury. Following Eritrea's gaining political independence from Ethiopia, the president of Eritrea, Isayas Afewerki, requested from Shenuda III the establishment of an independent Eritrean Orthodox Church under the ecclesiastical juris-diction of the See of Alexandria. At the meeting of the Holy Synod of the Coptic Church on September 28, 1993, it was decided to accept the request of the Eritrean Christians. On Pentecost 1994 Pope Shenuda III consecrated five Eritrean bishops, thus laying the founda-tion for an independent Holy Synod of the Eritrean Orthodox Church. On May 7, 1998, the pope consecrated the 93-year-old Bishop Philippus as first Patriarch of the Orthodox Church of Eritrea. More than fifty Coptic bishops and seven Eritrean bishops participated in the ceremony in St. Mark's Cathedral in Cairo.

Meanwhile, due to several misunderstandings and accusations against Pope Shenuda III made by President Anwar al-Sadat, especially in his speech before Parliament on May 14, 1980, the polit-ical climate between the Coptic Church and the Egyptian state had seriously deteriorated. This tragic situation culminated in the presi-dental decree of Sepember 3, 1981, in which Sadat ordered the exile of Pope Shenuda III to the Monastery of Saint Bishoi, while at the same time imprisoning eight bishops and twenty-four priests, as well as numerous Coptic notables. Sadat then created an administrative committee of five bishops for the Coptic Orthodox Church. The Holy Synod, however, confirmed Pope Shenuda III as the head of the Coptic Church, although President Sadat continued to refer to him as the 'ex-pope.'

During his enforced exile in Saint Bishoi's Monastery, Amnesty International officially named him a 'Prisoner of Conscience' on August 26, 1983. Many Christians throughout the world expressed their deep concern. Special prayers for his release were organized in June 1982 and again in November 1984. Bishop Dumadius (formerly Abuna Mityas al-Suriani) visited his old friend every week. On January 2, 1985, President Mubarak revoked President Sadat's decree of 1981. Accompanied by fourteen bishops, Pope Shenuda III left his exile on January 4. The following day he celebrated Coptic Christmas at Saint Mark's Cathedral, where over ten thousand people welcomed him as pope.

In the meantime the relationship between the government and the church had significantly improved. As a small testimony of good relations with the Islamic majority, Shenuda III has regularly invited the leading personalities in religion and politics for the evening fast-breaking meal of *iftar* during Ramadan. Since 1986 the prime minister, the grand mufti, the *shaikh* of al-Azhar, and others have joined in this meaningful demonstration of goodwill. Shenuda III has repeatedly refused to be identified as the leader of a Christian minority. "As Copts," he has emphasized, "we are Egyptians, part of Egypt."

The Holy Synod of the Coptic Orthodox Church

The Holy Synod is the highest ecclesiastical body in the church and is responsible for the church's spiritual, ecclesiastical, structural, organizational, and economic affairs. From the beginning of the fourth century, the Holy Synod, made up of all the members of the Coptic episcopate, attended the important ecumenical councils and synods. The members of the Holy Synod are always expected to be present at the coction and consecration of the holy myron.

The historical data of the Holy Synod reflect both the spiritual and numerical strength of the church at any given time. When ninety-four bishops under the jurisdiction of Saint Athanasius attended the Council of Alexandria in 320, this number included not only the dioceses in the Nile Delta and the Nile Valley, but also those of Libya and the Pentapolis. At the time of the reign of Constantine the Great, the Egyptian episcopacy consisted of seventy sees. The First Ecumenical Council in Nicea in 325 was attended by a total of 318 bishops. There Saint Athanasius and fifteen bishops represented the Egyptian Church. In the following century, the Third Ecumenical Council convened in Ephesus in 431 and was attended by two hundred bishops under the chairmanship of Cyril I, the twenty-fourth patriarch of Alexandria, who was accompanied by forty Egyptian bishops. Eighteen years later, the Emperor Theodosius II called another council at Ephesus, in which fifteen bishops from Egypt participated. A total of five hundred bishops attended the Fourth Ecumenical Council at Chalcedon in 451, which led to the tragic schism with the Imperial Church. At the first session, Dioscorus, the twenty-fifth patriarch of Alexandria, was accompanied by sixteen bishops from Lower Egypt. At the fourth session on October 17, 451, thirteen Egyptian bishops presented their profession of faith to the Emperor Marcianus.

We do not know whether all bishops attended every local episcopal synod. For the election of Kha'il I in 744 as the forty-sixth patriarch of Alexandria, the episcopal synod was represented by merely eleven bishops. Thirteen bishops selected Cyril II (1078–92) to be the sixty-seventh patriarch of Alexandria.

When Badr al-Gamali, the commander of the armies, called an episcopal council in 1086 to settle certain ecclesiastical affairs, a total of forty-seven bishops attended, twenty-two each from Lower and Upper Egypt as well as those from Cairo, Giza, and al-Khandaq.

It is doubtful that the whole hierarchy of the Coptic Church participated in the ceremony of the consecration of the holy myron (*tabikh
al-mayrun*), which took place either in the Monastery of Saint
Macarius or in Cairo. In 1257, twelve bishops, eight from Lower and
four from Upper Egypt, were present, while in 1299 the same number
of bishops, this time five from Lower and seven from Upper Egypt,
gathered for the ceremony of the consecration of the holy myron in
the Church of Abu Saifain in Old Cairo. In 1305, the consecration of
the holy myron took place again at the Monastery of Saint Macarius
with eighteen bishops in attendance, while in 1320, one metropolitan,
from Damietta, and twenty-four bishops were present at the
ceremony.

In this respect it is noteworthy that Abu al-Makarim, known as Abu
Salih the Armenian, mentions in the thirteenth century "sixty bishops
in the two provinces of Northern and Southern Egypt." The Coptic
manuscript 53 of the John Rylands Library, Manchester (fourteenth
century), goes beyond that and enumerates ninety-five dioceses. This
represented the height of medieval Coptic church life.

By the seventeenth century, however, the number of bishoprics had
considerably decreased. In his *History of the Church of Alexandria* of
1672/73, Johann Michael Wansleben lists a mere seventeen dioceses,
and in 1714 the Jesuit C. Sicard refers to fifteen diocesan bishops,
including the bishop of Alexandria, who served as grand vicar of the
patriarchate and whose jurisdiction included the provinces of Sharqiya
and Buhayra and the towns of Mahalla, Mansura, Damietta, Rosetta,
and Damanhur. Throughout the following years the number of
dioceses remained more or less stable. R. Strothmann, writing in 1932,
lists eighteen bishoprics, including Jerusalem and the Sudan. My own
list of Coptic bishops in Egypt as of 1964 mentions thirty-one
episcopal sees, including the monasteries, six of which were temporarily
vacant. In my list of Coptic bishops in Egypt as of 1977 I provide the
names of thirty-two bishops and their respective diocesan sees.

Today, the Holy Synod includes seventy-eight metropolitans,
bishops, and the *wakil al-batrakiya*, an archpriest representing the
married clergy. In 1985 a constitution for the Holy Synod was
drafted, setting out its objectives, policies, and procedures. To facili-
tate more effective functioning, Pope Shenuda III divided the Holy
Synod into seven subcommittees dealing with pastoral affairs, liturgical affairs, ecumenical relations, monastic affairs, faith and ethics,
and diocesan affairs. The Holy Synod convenes annually on the
Saturday prior to Pentecost Sunday in the Chapel of Saint Antony in
the Pontifical Residence in Cairo. In 1994 Pope Shenuda III
conducted the inaugural seminar for the members of the Holy Synod.

The Members of the Holy Synod of 1998

The consecration date represents the most recent ordination.
Abbreviations: M=Metropolitan, DB=Diocesan Bishop,
MB=Monastic Bishop or Abbot, GB=General Bishop

Name	*Monastery*	*Diocese*	*Consecration*
1. Mikha'il (M)	Abu Maqar	Asyut	8/25/46
2. Mina (M)	Abu Maqar	Girga	8/7/60
3. Athanasius (M)	al-Surian	Beni Suef/Bahnasa	6/18/78
4. Dumadius (M)	al-Surian	Giza	6/2/85
5. Gregorius (GB)	al-Muharraq	Higher Studies	5/10/67
6. Daniel (M)	Antonius	Khartoum, Uganda	8/78
7. Philippus (M)	Antonius	Daqahliya	6/2/85
8. Pachomius (M)	al-Surian	Buhayra/Tahrir	9/2/90
9. Agathon (M)	al-Surian	Ismailia	11/17/91
10. Bishoi (M)	al-Surian	Damietta, Kafr al-Shaikh	9/2/90
11. Timotheus (GB)	Abu Maqar	General Bishop	6/17/73
12. Sarabamun (MB)	al-Surian	Dair Anba Bishoi	5/29/77
13. Murqus (M)	Bishoi	Marseilles, France	6/19/94
14. Athanasius (DB)	Bishoi	France	6/19/94
15. Hadra (DB)	al-Surian	Aswan, Edfu	6/22/75
16. Arsenius (DB)	al-Baramus	Minya, Abu Qurqas	6/13/76
17. Wisa (DB)	Bishoi	Balyana	6/22/75
18. Paphnutius (DB)	al-Surian	Samalut	6/13/76
19. Ammonius (DB)	Bishoi	Luxor, Armant, Esna	6/13/76
20. Banyamin (DB)	al-Baramus	Minufiya	6/13/76
21. Antonius Marcus (GB)	al-Baramus	Africa	6/13/76
22. Angelus (DB)	al-Surian	Sharqiya	11/14/76
23. Tadrus (DB)	Bishoi	Port Said	11/14/76
24. Ruwais (GB)	al-Surian	General Bishop	5/29/77
25. Ighnatius (DB)	Bishoi	Suez	5/29/77
26. Yakubus (DB)	al-Baramus	Zaqaziq, Minya al-Qamh	5/29/77
27. Kirillus (DB)	Bula	Nag' Hammadi	5/29/77
28. Sawirus (MB)	al-Muharraq	Dair al-Muharraq	6/2/85
29. Bula (DB)	al-Baramus	Tanta	6/18/89
30. Mattawus (MB)	al-Surian	Dair al-Surian	6/6/93
31. Bamwa (MB)	Bishoi	Dair Mari Girgis	6/11/95
32. Musa (GB)	al-Baramus	Youth Affairs	5/25/80
33. Murqus (DB)	Bishoi	Shubra al-Khayma	6/14/92
34. Diyusqurus (GB)	Antonius	General Bishop	5/25/80
35. Butrus (GB)	Bula	General Bishop	6/2/85
36. Misa'il (DB)	al-Surian	Birmingham, UK	5/26/91
37. Bisada (DB)	Bishoi	Akhmim, Saqulta	5/25/80
38. Andarawus (DB)	Bishoi	Abu Tig, Sidfa	5/25/80
39. Isha'iya (DB)	Bishoi	Tanta	5/25/80
40. Fam (DB)	Bishoi	Tima	5/25/80
41. Abra'am (DB)	Bishoi	Fayyum	6/2/85
42. Serapion (DB)	Bishoi	Los Angeles, Calif.	11/14/95
43. Bisanti (DB)	Bishoi	Helwan, Ma'asara	5/29/88
44. Kirillus (DB)	al-Baramus	Milan, Italy	6/2/96

Name	Monastery	Diocese	Consecration
45. Barsum (DB)	al-Surian	Dairut, Sanabu	6/22/86
46. Bakhum (DB)	Rizaiqat	Suhag	6/22/86
47. Luqa (DB)	Bishoi	Abnub	6/22/86
48. Demetrius (DB)	Abu Mina	Mallawi	6/22/86
49. Antonius (DB)	al-Surian	Manfalut	6/22/86
50. Aghabius (DB)	Bishoi	Dair Mawas	11/13/88
51. Tuma (DB)	Bakhum	al-Qusiya, Mayr	11/13/88
52. Matthias (DB)	al-Surian	al-Mahalla al-Kubra	6/18/89
53. Yuhanna (GB)	Bishoi	Old Cairo	5/26/91
54. Basilius (MB)	Samuel	Dair Anba Samuel	5/26/91
55. Daniel (GB)	al-Surian	Ma'adi, Dar al-Salam	5/26/91
56. Sharubim (DB)	Bishoi	Qina, Qift	5/26/91
57. Pimen (DB)	al-Muharraq	Naqada, Qus	5/26/91
58. Takla (DB)	Bakhum	Dishna	5/26/91
59. Abraham (M)	Bishoi	Jerusalem	11/17/91
60. Yustus (MB)	Antonius	Dair Anba Antonius	11/17/91
61. Isidorus (MB)	Baramus	Dair al-Baramus	6/14/92
62. Tawfilus (DB)	al-Surian	Hurghada, Red Sea	6/14/92
63. Samuel (DB)	al-Surian	Shibin al-Qanatir	6/14/92
64. Maximus (DB)	Bishoi	Banha, Quwaysna	6/14/92
65. Yusuf (DB)	al-Surian	South America	11/14/95
66. Karas (MB)	Bishoi	Saint Antony's, Calif.	6/6/93
67. Yu'annis (MB)	Bula	Dair Anba Bula	6/6/93
68. Sarabamun (DB)	al-Surian	Atbara, Umdurman	11/14/93
69. Seraphim (M)	al-Surian	Glastonbury, UK	6/16/94
70. Antony (DB)	Bishoi	Ireland, Scotland	6/11/95
71. Barnaba (DB)	al-Surian	Turin, Italy	6/2/96
72. Damian (GB)	Bishoi	Germany	6/11/95
73. Bulus (GB)	Bishoi	General Bishop	6/11/95
74. Macari (DB)	Bishoi	Sinai, al-'Arish	11/17/96
75. Ghubriyal (GB)	al-Muharraq	General Bishop	6/15/97
76. Suriel (GB)	Bishoi	General Bishop	6/15/97
77. Rufa'il (GB)	al-Baramus	Asst. Youth Affairs	6/15/97
78. Tawadrus (GB)	Bishoi	Asst. to Bishop Pachomius	6/15/97

2

The Coptic Church:
Its History, Traditions, Theology,
and Structure

✦

Traditions about the Flight of the
Holy Family into Egypt

THE visitor who passes through Cairo and studies the folders for the myriad tours offered by the various sightseeing agencies will notice that, in addition to the excursions to the pyramids and Saqqara and the trips to the Muhammad 'Ali Mosque and the Mosques of Sultan Hassan and Ibn Tulun, a visit to the ancient Coptic churches of Old Cairo is offered.

Many visitors are only now being exposed for the first time to Coptic Christianity, which represents one of the most ancient churches of Christendom. Those tourists who decide to take the tour to Old Cairo are singularly rewarded, for here they are confronted with some of the most ancient monuments of Christianity, dating as far back as the fifth century. Here, for example, they discover the Church of Saints Sergius and Bacchus, which was built on the traditional site of the visit of the holy family to Babylon, as Old Cairo was once called. To this day, thousands of pilgrims enter the church to offer prayers to Him who came to bless the land of the pharaohs. The flight of the holy family into Egypt is a significant, living tradition for the people of this land.

According to the Gospel of Saint Matthew, the holy family, fleeing from the wrath of Herod the Great, sought refuge in Egypt, where, according to local tradition, they stayed for a period of three years, until Herod's death in 4 B.C. Many Copts believe that even prior to the beginning of the public ministry of Jesus Christ, Egyptians accepted the Divine Child as Lord over their lives. In fact, a wealth of stories and legends has been transmitted to us about the wondrous works wrought by the Christ child in the Delta and the Valley of the Nile.

The Birth of Christ

"And it came to pass in those days, that there went out a decree from Caesar Augustus, that all the world should be taxed" (Luke 2:1). This general census took place every fourteen years throughout the Roman empire, which at that time included Egypt, Syria, and Palestine. As regards the Roman province of Syria, "this taxing was first made when Cyrenius was governor of Syria" (Luke 2:2). The governor was the well-known Roman senator Publius Sulpicius Quirinius, who during the period between 10 and 7 B.C. commanded the legions in the war against the Homonadenses, a tribe from the Taurus Mountains in Asia Minor. During these three years, Quirinius had his headquarters in Syria.

Quirinius was later appointed legatus of Syria, and a census was taken in A.D. 6 or 7. This census, however, cannot be the one referred to by Saint Luke, as the first census took place at the time of the birth of Christ, while King Herod was still living, that is to say, before 4 B.C.

In connection with this, it should be noted that in the change from the *ab urbe condita* (Roman era) to *anno Domini* (Christian era) dating made by Dionysius Exiguus in 526, an error of four years occurred in his calculations. He placed the birth of Christ in the year 754 A.U.C. But Herod the Great, who slew the innocents of Bethlehem, died in April of the year 750 A.U.C.

Now, if we add the three and a half years residence of the holy family in Egypt (according to Coptic tradition) to the date of the death of King Herod (4 B.C.), we arrive at the date of 7 B.C. for the birth of Christ, which was the very period when Quirinius first held office in Syria. Furthermore, if we count back fourteen years from the census made in A.D. 6 or 7, we discover the date of the first census to be 7 B.C., the year of the birth of Christ.

From Bethlehem to the Nile Delta

And when they [the wise men from the East] were departed, behold, the angel of the Lord appeareth to Joseph in a dream, saying, Arise, and take the young child and his mother, and flee into Egypt, and be thou there until I bring thee word: for Herod will seek the young child to destroy him. When he arose, he took the young child and his mother by night, and departed into Egypt: And was there until the death of Herod: that it might be fulfilled which was spoken of the Lord by the Prophet, saying, out of Egypt have I called my son (Matt. 2:13–15).

Before the holy family, together with Salome, the midwife, departed from Bethlehem, they remained for a while in a grotto situated south-east of the Basilica of the Nativity. This grotto, known to the Arabs as

Magharat al-Sayyida ('the grotto of the lady'), is an ancient sanctuary venerated by Christians and Muslims alike. An Armenian tradition relates that the Holy Virgin Mary stopped here and suckled her child. Some drops of her milk fell on the rock, and it immediately turned white. A church was built on this site by Saint Paula, who lived in Bethlehem and died there in 404. Though first dedicated to the Virgin Mother, the church was later known as that of Saint Paula. In the fourteenth century, it belonged to the Greeks and was dedicated to Saint Nicholas, and eventually it passed into Latin (Roman Catholic) hands. This grotto has supplied the soft white stones known as 'Virgin's Milk' that are found in many Latin churches throughout Europe. The present church built over the grotto was dedicated in 1872. The grotto is a favorite place of pilgrimage for women on account of the milk-white rock, which is prized for its healing power and as an aid for lactation. Women pilgrims take away pieces of this soft rock, which they grind into a powder, mix with water, and drink.

When the Russian abbot Daniel visited the Byzantine monasteries in the Plain of Jericho in 1106, he stayed in a monastery known as Kalamonia, for "here the Holy Virgin passed the night with Jesus Christ, Joseph, and James at the time of their flight into Egypt." It was then that the Holy Virgin named this place Kalamonia, which means 'good abode.' The laura built on this spot in the Middle Ages has been taken over by the Greek Orthodox Monastery of Saint Gerasimus in the Plain of Jericho, one kilometer southwest of the oasis of 'Ain Hagla. Here, on the ground floor, below the narthex of the Church of Saint Gerasimus, the tradition is still honored in the Church of the Holy Family, which commemorates their visit to this site.

According to the Armenian Infancy Gospel, the holy family went to the ancient city and seaport of Ashkelon, where Samson went to kill thirty Philistines (Judges 14:19). At the time of the visit of the holy family, Ashkelon was a strong and beautiful center of Hellenistic culture with a special cult to Dercetus, or Atargates, a goddess with the body of a fish and the face of a woman.

From Ashkelon the holy family proceeded in an easterly direction to Hebron, one of the oldest towns in the world. The city was founded seven years before Zoan (Num. 13:22), the present village of San al-Hagar in Lower Egypt. Hebron's chief interest is its *haram*, an enclosure built over the traditional site of the cave of Machpelah (Gen. 23). Within the enclosure is a mosque, formerly a twelfth-century Crusaders' church, which in its turn was built on the site of a basilica from Justinian's time. Within the mosque are the cenotaphs of Abraham, Isaac, Jacob, Sarah, Rebecca, and Leah. Since 1967 a synagogue has been built into the Islamic sanctuary. The Armenian Infancy Gospel informs us that the holy family remained here in hiding for a period of six months.

About forty kilometers further west is the site of the ancient Canaanite stronghold of Gaza (Gen. 10:19). If the holy family had followed the caravan route from Judea to Egypt, they would have passed this city, in which Samson was enticed and finally overcome by the beautiful Delilah (Judges 16:21–31). At the time of Christ, this city had acquired a certain amount of splendor and magnificence, as it had become a center of Hellenistic culture.

By taking the route that runs parallel to the shore of the Mediterranean Sea, the holy family must have crossed, after another two hours, Wadi Gaza. A day's journey from Gaza brought the holy family to the ancient township of Jenysos, which is mentioned by Herodotus. Today this village, which is part of the Gaza Strip, is known as Khan Yunis.

The next town on the holy family's path would have been Raphia (Rafah), at present the border town between the Gaza Strip and Egypt. Raphia, which had been the battle ground of the contending forces of Ptolemy IV and Antiochus the Great in 217 B.C., was conquered by Alexander Jannaeus the Maccabee and annexed to Judea. It was restored to Egypt, however, by Gabinus. During the Byzantine period, Raphia, like Gaza, was the seat of a bishop.

Continuing on the caravan route for another forty-four kilometers, the holy family crossed the river of Egypt, Wadi al-'Arish, which has always formed the natural boundary between Egypt and Palestine. What the ancients called the 'river of Egypt' was not the mighty Nile, but a small stream. By crossing this inconspicuous trickle, the holy family must have thought of the many occasions in the history of their people when this 'river of Egypt,' with its 'goings out' at the sea, served as the boundary, from the days of the conquest of Canaan (Num. 34:5) to the calling of Solomon's assembly (I Kings 8:65). A little further on, the holy family reached the city of Rhinocolura, the present al-'Arish. Criminals and those accused of high treason were sent to this city to receive their punishment, which consisted of their noses being cut off.

We possess no evidence, either written or oral, as to the exact route followed by the holy family in their flight from Bethlehem to Egypt. The particulars given about it are purely conjectural, but we may reasonably suppose that once the holy family was out of danger of pursuit, they would have traveled along the usual caravan route between Judea and Egypt, which passed through towns and villages where they could have obtained food and shelter.

Near the southwestern end of the caravan route was the celebrated city of Pelusium (Tell al-Farama), metropolis of the province of Augustamnica, a seaport and gateway to Egypt. To this city, which is identified with the biblical Tahpanhes, Johanan, the son of Kareah (588 B.C.), "took all the remnant of Judah . . . men, and women, and children, and the king's daughters, and every person that Nebuzaradan, the captain of the guard, had left with Gedaliah. . ., and Jeremiah the prophet" (Jer. 43:5–6). Sixty-three years later, in 525 B.C., Psammetichos III was defeated at Pelusium by Cambyses, the King of Persia, and Egypt became a Persian province. At the time of the holy family's visit, Pelusium was still an important city and seaport.

Both the Greek monk Epiphanius (ninth century) and Bernard the Wise (870) mention the tradition according to which the holy family visited this historical city, which Maqrizi (fifteenth century) reckoned among the wonders of Egypt. In 1994, archaeologists discovered among the medieval ruins of Pelusium the foundations of a "circular church," testimony to an early (fifth century) Christian community at this site.

That many of the pilgrims passed through Farama is attested to by the itineraries of travelers like Jacques de Vitry (1180) and Marino Sanuto (1321). Abu al-Makarim considered Farama "exceedingly wonderful, and one of the most ancient foundations of which there is a record. There were at Farama many churches and monasteries, which were wrecked by the Persians and the Arabs." In fact, this city was occupied by 'Amr ibn al-'As on his way to conquer Egypt. Subsequently, it was fortified again by al-Mutawakkil around 853. In 1117, Baldwin I, King of Jerusalem, occupied the city, but when he was unable to hold it, he laid it waste.

In the Nile Delta

When Gaius Turranius (7–4 B.C.) was Roman prefect of Egypt, the holy family crossed the narrow isthmus at al-Qantara ('the bridge'), which separates Lake Manzala from Lake Ballah. It was over this isthmus that the ancient caravan route from Judea to Egypt passed, a route that centuries before had been used by Abraham (Gen. 12:10) and Jacob and his sons (Gen. 16). In the steps of the patriarchs, the holy family entered the province of Goshen.

By the land of Goshen (Gen. 45:10) we are to understand approximately the triangle of land which has as its apex the modern town of Zaqaziq, and as its base Bilbais and Tell al-Kabir. However, as the city of Pithom, the site of which is marked by the mounds near al-Mahsama, was also in the land of Goshen, Wadi Tumilat must likewise have formed part of Goshen. Moreover, both the Septuagint and

Flavius Josephus include On, that is to say, Heliopolis, with Pithom and Rameses. If On really lay in Goshen, this would extend the district in which the Hebrews lived almost to the outskirts of the present city of Cairo. It should be remembered that it was Asenath, a daughter of a priest of On, whom Joseph married (Gen. 41:45).

There is good reason to assume that the holy family entered the Nile Delta through the Wadi Tumilat. One of the first towns they would have reached on their way would have been Pithom or Pi-tum, the abode of Tum, the setting sun. We read in Exodus 1:11 that the children of Israel built for Pharoah the treasure cities Pithom and Raamses (Rameses) in the land of Goshen. The construction of these military storehouses, of Nile mud mixed with chopped straw, was evidently ordered by Ramses II, the pharaoh of the oppression. The ruins of Tell al-Maskhuta, near al-Mahsama, mark the site of the biblical Pithom.

About fifteen kilometers west of the ancient Pithom was the township of Succoth, the first halt of the Israelites on their exodus from Egypt (Exod. 12:37, 13–20). This site is generally identified with the village of al-Qassasin. A day's journey from Succoth would have brought the holy family to the other treasure city built by the children of Israel, Rameses, the present village of Tell al-Kabir.

At Rameses, the holy family entered the fertile Nile Delta. Traveling further west, they passed the ancient city of Pi-Sopt, the present village of Saft al-Hinna, and thence to Bubastis, the Pi-Beseth of the Bible (Ezek. 30:17–18). Most probably, the court where Joseph had his headquarters was at Bubastis. This city, of which only the ruins remain today, must have been very important in the past. The deity of Bubastis was the great goddess Bast, who is represented with a disk encircled by a uraeus on her head and a lotus scepter in one hand.

According to the Coptic Synaxarion, the official calendar with the Lives of the Saints, Basata (Bubastis, Pi-Beseth, Basta, or Tell Basta), which is two kilometers southwest of Zaqaziq, was the first town in the Delta that the holy family and Salome visited. They were not, however, well received, despite the fact that they revealed a spring of water, which became a source of healing for all, except for the inhabitants of Basata.

Details of this story are given in the *Vision of Theophilus*, where we read that in Basata, the holy family met two brigands, Titus, an Egyptian, and Dumachus, a Syrian:

> And the Syrian brigand said to the Egyptian, "I should have liked to plunder the garments that are on this woman and her son, because they resemble the garments of kings." But the Egyptian brigand said to him,

"Let us proceed on our way. I have never seen a child like this since I was born."

When the brigands saw the Holy Virgin and her son entering Basata, they came back to Joseph, and while he was asleep, they absconded with Jesus' gold and silver sandals. When the Holy Virgin realized this, she was much distressed and wept. When Jesus saw his mother weeping, however, he wiped away her tears and stretched his small finger and made the sign of the cross on the earth, and instantly a spring of water jetted forth and flowed on the ground. And they drank this water, which was as sweet as honey and as white as snow. Then Jesus blessed this water and said, "Let this water help make whole and heal the souls and bodies of all those who shall drink of it, with the exception of this town's inhabitants, none of whom shall be healed by it."

According to Dr. Mahmud 'Amr of the University of Zaqaziq, archaeologists discovered in 1997 "the well in the Temple of al-Basta which the Lord Jesus blessed." This Roman well has a depth of four meters. The Coptic Church of Saint George in Zaqaziq is said to be built on the traditional site of the house of Klum and Sarah. According to a local tradition, the holy family turned to the house of Klum in dire need. When the Holy Virgin knocked at the door, Klum apologized, saying that his poor wife could not receive them because of an illness that had kept her in bed for many years. When the Christ child heard this, he said, "Thy wife Sarah is not ill," and immediately Klum's wife arose and welcomed the holy family, and Klum and Sarah served them for the time of their stay. Before the holy family departed, the Divine Child said to Sarah, "Blessed art thou and blessed is thy house."

The holy family went on a day's journey further south and reached the town of Bilbais, past which the modern Ismailia Canal flows. As the holy family entered the town, a funeral procession came out, and Jesus, who had compassion for the mourners, raised the dead man to life. He was the son of a widow and having been brought back to life, he declared, "This is the True God, the Savior of the world, who is born of the Holy Virgin, who accomplished a mystery the human intellect cannot comprehend." And all the inhabitants of Bilbais believed in Jesus.

During the Middle Ages, the pilgrims who passed through Egypt on their way to the holy places stopped at Bilbais to kneel at the foot of the great tree, which, according to both Christians and Muslims, commemorated the stay of the holy family at Bilbais. The Muslims called it the Tree of the Virgin, and they had such respect for it that they reserved the space around the tree as a necropolis for their venerated saints.

Today, there is only one Coptic church in Bilbais, the Church of Saint George, which is situated in the northeastern part of the town. The site that commemorates the visit of the holy family to Bilbais is the 'Uthman ibn al-Haris al-Ansari Mosque, in the center of the town, at the corner of Shari' al-Ansari and Shari' al-Baghdadi.

According to the Ethiopic and Coptic synaxaries, the holy family left the Sharqiya province and went on their way in a northerly direction until they reached the town of Samannud (Gamnudi), the ancient Sebennytos or Zeb-nuter, which is situated on the Damietta branch of the Nile. Here they crossed the river toward the west. A local tradition in Samannud relates that the present Church of Apa Nub was built on the ruins of an ancient church dedicated to the Holy Virgin, which, in its turn, was built on the site where the holy family stayed. The Christians of Samannud point to a place in the nave of the church where there was once a well, the water of which was blessed by Jesus.

Having crossed the Damietta branch of the Nile, the holy family traveled westward to al-Gharbiya, the province situated between the Rosetta and Damietta branches of the Nile. On the way, Jesus put his foot on a stone, imprinting it with the sole of his foot, and the place became known as Bikha Isous, that is to say, the footprint of Jesus. I have been unable to locate this place, which is mentioned by the Ethiopic and Coptic synaxaries. It has been suggested that Basus may be a contraction of the name Bikha Isous, but it is most unlikely that Bikha Isous should be identified with the village of Basus, which lies between Cairo and Qalyub.

Continuing their journey, they saw from afar the Desert of Scetis, or Wadi al-Natrun, and Jesus blessed it, saying to his mother, "Know, O my Mother, that in this desert there shall live many monks, ascetes, and spiritual fighters, and they shall serve God like angels."

Today, there are only four monasteries left in Wadi al-Natrun, namely, the Monastery of the Romans (Dair al-Baramus), the Monastery of the Syrians (Dair al-Surian), the Monastery of Saint Bishoi (Dair Anba Bishai), and the monastery of Saint Macarius (Dair Abu Maqar).

In the Nile Valley

Continuing their journey south, the holy family eventually reached the city of On, or Heliopolis (Jer. 43:13). At the time of Strabo, about sixteen years before the visit of the holy family to Heliopolis, the city was entirely deserted, not having recovered from the destruction incurred at the time of the Persian invasion in 525 B.C. Various temples and buildings of historical interest were still standing, however, and were pointed out to Strabo by a dragoman. The holy family naturally would have avoided lodging in this deserted pagan city, and consequently they sought some dwelling place nearby in which there would most likely have been Jewish families living, on account of its proximity to the Jewish center at Leontopolis. Thus they halted at the site of the present village of Matariya, now a suburb of Cairo. The visit to Matariya is not only well attested by the Apocryphal Gospel of Pseudo-Matthew and the Coptic and Ethiopic synaxaries, but it is also mentioned by medieval pilgrims to the Holy Land. According to the Ethiopic Synaxarion, when the holy family approached Matariya:

> There was a staff in the hand of Joseph wherewith he used to smite Jesus, but Joseph gave him the staff. Then said Jesus unto his mother: "We will tarry here" and that place and its desert and the well became known as Matariya. And Jesus took Joseph's staff, and broke it into little pieces, and planted these pieces in that place, and he dug with his own divine hands a well, and there flowed from it sweet water, which had an exceeding sweet odor. And Jesus took some of the water in his hands, and watered therewith the pieces of wood which he had planted, and straightaway they took root, and put forth leaves, and an exceedingly sweet perfume was emitted by them, which was sweeter than any other perfume. And these pieces of wood grew and increased, and they called them 'balsam.' And Jesus said unto his Mother, "O my Mother, these balsam, which I have planted, shall abide here forever, and from them shall be taken the oil for Christian baptism when they baptize in the name of the Father, the Son, and the Holy Ghost."

The Apocryphal Gospel of Pseudo-Matthew replaces the balsam with a palm tree, a tradition that is also preserved in the Quran. According to the Quranic version, the Holy Virgin saw a palm tree and wished to rest under it, and she said to Joseph that she would like to have some of its fruit. Then Jesus, sitting in his mother's lap, with a joyful countenance, bade the palm tree give his mother of its fruit. The tree bent as low as her feet, and she gathered as much as she wanted. He told it to rise again and give them the water concealed below its roots. A spring came forth, and all rejoiced and drank from it.

The village of Matariya enjoyed great popularity among pilgrims to the Holy Land. This site must have seemed like a paradise to these pilgrims who had crossed the desert from Mount Sinai, for the well, with its beautiful surroundings, was a resort for such wealthy Mamluks as the emir Yashbak, who built a domed house here in which, from time to time, he entertained his master and friend Qayt Bey (1467–96).

In 1480, the Dominican friar Felix Fabri made note of an immense fig tree close to the gate. In its hollow trunk two lamps hung, as in a small chapel, for the tree had once opened to provide refuge for the Holy Virgin. There is a tradition that the holy family was pursued by two brigands, and that the tree miraculously opened to conceal them.

The sycamore tree that now stands at Matariya was planted in 1672. Due to old age, this venerable tree fell on June 14, 1906, but fortunately a living shoot from it remains to this day.

From Matariya the holy family went to the place where the Church of the Holy Virgin now stands in Harat Zuwayla in Cairo. It is situated in the northeast district of Cairo, at the end of a lane leading off Shari' Bain al-Surayn, and was probably first erected in the tenth century. From the fourteenth century to the year 1660 it served as the patriarchal church in Cairo.

Annexed to the Church of the Holy Virgin of Harat Zuwayla is a convent. The nuns of this convent relate the tradition that when the holy family rested at this site, Jesus blessed the water of the well, and the Holy Virgin drank from it. This well is situated in the floor before the southern sanctuary of the lower church, and the water is still used for healing the sick.

Continuing southward, the holy family passed the Fortress of Babylon (now known as Old Cairo), which commanded the route to Upper Egypt and where they also halted on their return to Palestine. They would have certainly seen the pyramids of Giza, which may have seemed to them, as they did to pilgrims several centuries later, to be Joseph's granaries.

According to al-Hafiz Abu Bakr ibn Thabit al-Khatib, who received the tradition from Nabit ibn Sharit, there used to be at Giza the palm tree under which the Holy Virgin suckled Jesus, and this palm tree was said to have been the only one in the region that bore any fruit. On their way south, the holy family would have seen the site on the bank of the Nile where Moses was hidden in an ark of bulrushes and discovered by Pharaoh's daughter (Exod. 2:3–5).

Some twelve kilometers south of Cairo, in Ma'adi on the very bank of the Nile, is the Church of the Holy Virgin with its three cupolas. Here, according to an oral tradition, there was a synagogue that the holy family attended. Joseph became acquainted with the sailors of the Nile boats, and the holy family was offered to be taken south to Upper Egypt.

Al-Maqrizi, the fifteenth-century Muslim historian, mentions a palm tree in Ihnasya al-Madina, the ancient city of Heracleopolis, in the province of Beni Suef, which was seen there until the end of the Umayyad dynasty (A.D. 750). This palm tree is supposed to have been the one mentioned in the Quran:

And the pangs of childbirth drove her [the Holy Virgin] unto the trunk of the palm tree. She said, "O, would that I had died ere this, and had become a thing of naught, forgotten." Then [one] cried unto her from below her, saying, "Grieve not, thy Lord has placed a rivulet beneath thee. And shake the trunk of the palm tree toward thee, thou wilt cause ripe dates to fall upon thee" (XIX:23–25).

According to al-Maqrizi, the Copts are in agreement that the holy family visited al-Bahnasa, some fifty kilometers south of Ihnasya, and a commentator of the Quran asserts that the passage "and we have made the Son of Mary and His Mother a portent, and we gave them refuge on a height, a place of flocks and water-springs" (XXIII:50) refers to al-Bahnasa.

Another commentator adds that at the time of their arrival at al-Bahnasa, the holy family went to the place of the famous well, and Joseph returned, leaving the Holy Virgin near the well. Then Jesus asked for water, and he began to weep because of his thirst. There was no water at that time, but the level of the water rose, so that Jesus could drink, and since that day Christians have celebrated this event.

Muhammad al-Baqir (676–731), the Fifth Imam of the Shi'ites, says that when Jesus was nine months old, his mother took him to school in al-Bahnasa:

The teacher said to Jesus, "Say the alphabet." Jesus lifted up His head and said, "Dost thou know what these words mean?" The teacher wished to strike Him, but Jesus said, "Do not strike me, but if thou dost not know, ask me and I shall explain to thee." "Speak," said the teacher. "Come down from thy desk," answered Jesus. The teacher came down and Jesus took his place and began to say, "The *Alif* stands for the good deeds of God, the *Da* for the glory of God, the *Gim* for the splendor of God, the *Dal* for the religion of God, the *Ha* for the abyss of Hell, the *Wa* indicates the misery of those living in Hell, the *Ha* means the remission of sins of those who ask for forgiveness, the *Ka* is the word of God which will never change, the *Sad* is the measure for a measure, and the *Ta* stands for the serpents of hell." "Well," said the teacher to the Holy Virgin, "take thy Son and watch over Him, for God hath given to Him wisdom and He doth not need a teacher."

This tradition should be compared with the almost identical story in the Gospel of Thomas the Israelite (c. 140–60).

Wahb ibn Munabbih (d.728) relates that the holy family stayed at a hospice for the poor at al-Bahnasa, which was supported by a *diqhan*, a nobleman of the king. One day, an important part of the *diqhan*'s treasure was stolen, and the Holy Virgin was pained by the misfortune.

When Jesus realized His Mother's distress, He said to her, "Mother, dost thou wish me to show where the *diqhan*'s money is?" The Holy Virgin informed the *diqhan* of what Jesus had said. When they were all gathered together, Jesus approached two men, one of whom was blind and the other lame, the latter being carried by the blind man. Then Jesus said to the blind man, "Arise!" "This I cannot do," said the blind man. "How then was it possible for you to steal?" When they heard this, they struck the blind man until he showed Jesus where the treasure was. This then was their trick. The blind man used his strength and the lame man his eyes. The stolen treasure was restored to the *diqhan*.

Near the ancient Cynopolis, the present village of al-Qays, the holy family boarded a boat to travel south. After 35 kilometers they passed Gabal al-Tayr, which is almost opposite Samalut and Bayahu. Abu al-Makarim recalls that when the holy family passed this mountain, a large rock threatened to fall on the boat, and the Holy Virgin was very frightened. But Jesus extended his hand and prevented the rock from falling, and the imprint of his hand left a fine perforation, large enough to admit a collyrium needle. When the needle is inserted and pulled out, it brings upon it a black collyrium that makes an indelible mark.

According to the *Vision of Theophilus*, the holy family found images of horses at all four corners of the gate leading into Hermopolis Magna (present-day al-Ashmunain). But these fell down and broke when the holy family entered the city.

The Gospel of Pseudo-Matthew, which also attests the holy family's visit to Hermopolis Magna, mentions that when Aphrodosius, the governor of the city, saw that the idols were destroyed, he adored the child and said to those present, "Unless this were the God of our gods, they would not have fallen. If we do not adore Him, as they have done, we are in danger of such destruction as fell upon Pharaoh, who was drowned with his army." On the following day, great multitudes of sick people assembled around Jesus, and Jesus laid his hand on each of them and healed them of their infirmities.

Today, there is no trace left of the holy family's visit to al-Ashmunain, nor is there even a Coptic Orthodox church.

Two days further traveling south brought the holy family to the town of Kenis (Nikyas, Funkus), the present Dairut al-Sharif. The inhabitants of this town were very charitable, and the holy family remained there for several days. Jesus wrought innumerable miracles in that place, and all those who had diseases or afflictions came to him with faith to be healed. After this, Dianos, a carpenter who had known Joseph in Jerusalem, invited the holy family to stay with him. He had a son who was possessed by a devil. Then Jesus said, "O accursed devil, shut up thy mouth and come out of him." And the child was healed in that very hour, and many people believed in him. After Jesus had performed these miracles, the idols in the town were broken up and smashed to pieces.

Then the holy family entered the city of Cusae, now the town of al-Qusiya. At the time of the holy family's visit, there was a temple of idols surmounted by one idol covered in seven veils.

When Jesus reached the gate of Cusae, the seven veils were rent asunder, and the idol fell to the ground and was dashed to pieces. Then the devils who were in the idol threatened the priests and cried, "If you do not pursue that woman and the Child who is with her, they will put an end to your service, and we will leave the town." When the priests of the idols, who were a hundred in number, heard this speech of the idols, they pursued the holy family with rods and axes in order to strike them. Thereupon the holy family left the town, and after they had traveled a little distance, Jesus turned and cursed the town, saying, "Let its people be in an estate lower than that of all other people, and let them be more lowly and suppressed than all the inhabitants of the Land of Egypt."

After Jesus had cursed the town of Cusae and its inhabitants, the holy family went on a short distance south of the town.

That evening the holy family went up to a mountain, and the two brigands whom the holy family had met at Basata (Tell Basta) came toward them. They had followed them from one place to another, and when they saw the holy family in this deserted mountain, they approached them with drawn daggers, unsheathed swords, and their faces masked and said, "You have exhausted us, because we have pursued you for many days and have not found you. Today, we will strip you of your garments and rob you." And they snatched Jesus from the arm of his mother and stripped him of his garments. Then they took the garments of the Holy Virgin, and they even took her veil. Then they also stripped Joseph, who was standing by speechless as a lamb. As for Salome, when she perceived what was taking place, she threw her garments to them before they came to her.

While the Holy Virgin was lamenting and weeping, her tears streamed down her cheeks. Then one of the brigands looked toward her and saw her weeping, and he spoke to his companion who was a Syrian Jew and said to him, "O my companion, I beseech thee today not to take the garments of these strangers, because I perceive on their faces a light greater than that on all the faces of mankind. This child resembles a prince, the likes of whom I have never seen." The Jewish brigand said to the Egyptian brigand, "I will not listen to you this time. I will take their garments, because they are royal garments that will bring us much wealth for our living." Then the Egyptian brigand asked for his portion of the garments, for he was much distressed at the nakedness of the holy family, and he returned his portion of the garments to them. When Jesus had put on his garments, he looked at the brigand and stretched out his finger and made the sign of the cross over him, and said to his mother, "O Mary, the Jews will crucify me in Jerusalem. And these two brigands whom you see, one of them will be crucified on my right hand, and the other on my left hand. The Egyptian will be crucified on my right hand, and the Jew on my left, and the brigand who has returned our garments will confess to me and believe in me on the cross, and he will be the first to enter Paradise, even before Adam and all his descendants."

Not far away, about eight kilometers south of Meir, the holy family discovered a well, though it was dried up. But when the Holy Virgin took Jesus to the well and he stretched out his finger and blessed it, it became full. While searching around, Salome came upon a wash basin and a water jug, as if they had been placed there specifically for them. It was always Salome who bathed Jesus and his mother who gave him milk. And often while her nipple was in the mouth of Jesus, she saw the angels and celestial beings prostrating themselves and worshiping Jesus.

The holy family sojourned for six months in this house. Then Jesus said to his mother, "This house in which we are shall contain holy monks on whom no rule in this world shall be able to inflict any injury, because it has been a refuge to us. Any barren woman who beseecheth me with a pure heart and calleth to mind this house, unto her will I give sons. There shall, moreover, be in this place a blessed congregation who shall remember and bless my Name, and pray unto me at all times, and so gain strength against all their adversaries. Those women in travail who shall be mindful of me and of the labor which thou didst endure with me, their prayers will I hear, and they shall be relieved."

This holy place, blessed on account of the holy family's presence in it, was dedicated to the Holy Virgin and became known as Dair al-Muharraq, or the Monastery of the Holy Virgin. Pilgrimages to this church have been made by multitudes of people from all districts of Egypt from ancient times to the present day, due to the signs and wonders manifested here.

According to tradition, the Church of the Holy Virgin at the Monastery of the Holy Virgin in al-Qusiya was the first church built in Egypt, and the monks believe that this church was built immediately after Saint Mark the Evangelist's arrival in Egypt, sometime around A.D. 60. The present church may be assigned to the twelfth or thirteenth century. It lies about 1.2 meters below the present ground level of the inner court of the monastery, and it is used for the daily celebration of the Divine Liturgy.

An oral tradition in Asyut, the ancient Lycopolis, asserts that the southernmost place visited by the holy family in Egypt was ten kilometers southwest of Asyut. Today, about eighty thousand pilgrims assemble annually at the foot of Istabl 'Antar ('Antar's stable,' a mountain range west of Asyut) to commemorate and celebrate the stay of the holy family in the large rock tombs dating from the Ninth to the Twelfth dynasties.

The Church of the Holy Virgin at Dair al-'Adhra' at Durunka was built by Bishop Michael in 1955. The church is situated east of the cave in which the holy family supposedly rested.

The Return of the Holy Family to Palestine

And it came to pass that during their sojourn at the place where the Monastery of the Holy Virgin now stands, the Angel of the Lord appeared unto Joseph in a dream and said, "Arise, and take the young child and his mother, and go into the land of Israel, for they are dead which sought the young child's life (Matt. 2:20).

Obeying the voice of the angel, the holy family thereupon returned to Palestine.

There is good reason to believe that the holy family returned to Palestine by the same way they had come. According to the Coptic Synaxarion, on their return the holy family lodged in a cave situated beneath what is today the Church of Saints Sergius and Bacchus (Abu Sarga) in Old Cairo, the ancient Babylon of Egypt.

For the medieval pilgrims to the Holy Land, a visit to the Cave of the Holy Family was included in their itineraries. In 1421, John Poloner went out of his way to visit the underground chapel, where he saw a cross over the place where the Christ child had slept. At the time of Poloner's visit, the church was called the Church of Our Lady of Cana in Babylon. That western Christians also accepted this tradition is confirmed by the fact that until the eighteenth century, the Franciscan friars used to celebrate mass on the altar in the crypt.

In the Church of the Holy Virgin at Musturud, about three kilometers west of Matariya, on the western bank of the Ismailia Canal, there is to this day a well blessed by the holy family. The well is situated in the northeast corner of the church, east of a cave where the holy family found shelter. Stairs from the east and the west lead down to the cave, to which thousands of people come for the annual fair (*mulid*) held August 7–22.

From al-Mahamma, the holy family's next halting place was Leontopolis, known today as the ruins of Tell al-Yahudiya and referred to in old Roman maps as Vicus Judaeorum. An oral tradition of the Christians of Shibin al-Qanatir (two kilometers northwest of the ancient Leontopolis) states that the holy family visited their countrymen, who had settled around the Temple of Onias. The high priest Onias IV went to Egypt in 154 B.C. to seek aid against the tyranny of the Seleucids at the court of the Ptolemies, who were their political enemies. With the permission of Ptolemy IV (Philometer), he built at Leontopolis a temple modeled on the one in Jerusalem, though it was relatively small.

When the holy family entered Palestine, Joseph heard "that Archelaus did reign in Judea in the room of his father Herod, he was afraid to go thither: notwithstanding, being warned of God in a dream, he turned aside into the parts of Galilee: and he came and dwelt in a city called Nazareth, that it might be fulfilled which was spoken by the prophets, He shall be called a Nazarene" (Matt. 2:22–23).

Saint Mark the Evangelist and the Founding of the Church in Egypt

The Preaching and Martyrdom of Mark

According to a longstanding tradition, Saint Mark the Evangelist visited Alexandria, where he preached the gospel, founded the See of Alexandria, and on May 8, A.D. 68, received the crown of martyrdom.

Eusebius, who wrote his *Ecclesiastical History* in the first quarter of the fourth century, records this tradition and states that Mark came to Egypt in the first or third year of the reign of the Roman emperor Claudius, in A.D. 41/42 or 43/44. If these dates are correct, Mark's stay at Alexandria could not have been a long one, for in 46 he was at Antioch and the following year in Cyprus. From 49 to 50 he was again at Antioch, and from 58 to 62 at Rome with Saint Paul. For the intervening period between 50 and 62, however, the New Testament is silent in regard to Mark, and, therefore, it is quite possible that the Evangelist may have visited Alexandria at this time. It is generally held that when Paul was released from his first captivity in Rome in 62, Mark did not accompany him on his new missionary journey, and this being the case, the Evangelist could very well have left Rome for Alexandria.

The Copts pride themselves on the apostolicity of their national church, whose founder was none other than St. Mark, the author of the oldest canonical Gospel used by both St. Matthew and St. Luke, and probably also by St. John. Mark is regarded by the Coptic hierarchy as the first in their unbroken chain of 117 patriarchs. The apocryphal *Acta Marci* record that after setting sail from Cyprus he came to the Pentapolis and from there proceeded to Alexandria; other sources inform us that he went first to the land of Egypt before he began his missionary work in Alexandria. The chronology of the apostolic age is so uncertain that no final decision on the travels of Mark can be offered.

The Coptic tradition states that the first Egyptian to be converted by the Evangelist was Anianus, and the story of his conversion is told by the different Coptic sources with almost no variation. As the Evangelist entered Rhakotis and walked along its stony paths, the strap of his shoe was torn, and he went to a cobbler by the name of Anianus to have it fixed. When the cobbler took an awl to work on it, he accidentally pierced his hand and cried aloud, "God is one." Mark rejoiced at this utterance, and after miraculously healing the cobbler's hand, preached the gospel to him and his whole household. They were ignorant of the Old Testament prophecies that Mark quoted, and the only books they knew were those of the Greek philosophers.

Anianus and all his household believed and were baptized. The Christians in Egypt multiplied in number, and the pagans took notice of them and sought to lay hands on the Evangelist. Sensing danger, Mark ordained Anianus bishop, together with three priests and seven deacons. Afterward, he seems to have undertaken a missionary journey to Rome, whence he proceeded to Aquileia and later to the Pentapolis, where he spent two years performing miracles, ordaining bishops and elders, and winning more converts. When at last he returned to Alexandria, he was overjoyed to find that the church had increased in numbers.

Rumors that the Christians threatened to overthrow the pagan deities infuriated the people of Alexandria. On Easter Sunday of the year 68, the pagans celebrated the festival of Serapis. Searching for the Evangelist, they found him in the church at Bucolia where the Christians celebrated the Easter service. Mark was seized, dragged through the streets by a rope around his neck, and then incarcerated for the night. Around midnight, an angel appeared to him, strengthening him and promising him the crown of martyrdom. On the following day, the idolatrous populace of Alexandria again dragged him through the streets, until he finally gave up the ghost. But they were not satisfied, and prepared to light a great fire, on which they placed the body to burn. But nature would not permit disrespect to the body of the saint, for it thundered and rained heavily, and the fire was put out. Then the faithful assembled and took the body of Mark from the ashes, and nothing in it had been changed. They carried it to the church in which they celebrated the liturgy and enshrouded it and prayed over it according to the established rites. Then they dug a place for him and buried his holy body there that they might preserve his memory. And finally they placed him in the eastern part of the church, on the day on which his martyrdom was accomplished.

The History of the Relics of Mark

According to Coptic tradition, the body of the Evangelist still reposed in the Church of Saint Mark at Bucolia at the time of the martyrdom of Peter I, the seventeenth patriarch of Alexandria, in 311. There is no question that this site was highly venerated by the Christians of Alexandria. Patriarchs were enthroned here, and pilgrims from all over the ancient world repaired to the holy relics of Saint Mark. Following the schism that separated the Chalcedonians, or Melkites, from the non-Chalcedonians, or Copts, in 451, the church in which the body of the Evangelist reposed remained in the hands of the Melkites. At the time of the Arab conquest, the Church of Saint Mark escaped destruction. It was only during the recapture of Alexandria from Manuel and his troops in the summer of 646 that the Arabs destroyed, plundered, and burned a great part of Alexandria, including the Church of Saint Mark. The account in the *History of the Patriarchs* describes the event as follows:

> In the year 646, the Muslims captured Alexandria, and they burned the Church of St. Mark, which was built by the sea where his body was laid, and this was the place to which the father, the patriarch Peter the Martyr, went before his martyrdom and blessed St. Mark. At the burning of said church a miracle took place which was performed and that was that one of the captains of the ships, namely the captain of the ship of the duke Sanutius, climbed over the wall and descended into the church and came to the shrine, where he found that the coverings had been taken, for the plunderers thought that there was money in the chest. But when they found nothing there, they took away the covering from the body of St. Mark, but his bones were left in their place. So the captain put his hand into the shrine and there he found the head of the holy Mark, which he took. Then he returned to his ship secretly and told no one of it, and hid the head in the hold among his baggage . . . . The ship in which the head of the Evangelist was hidden was miraculously prevented from leaving the harbour of Alexandria. Therefore, the duke returned the head of St. Mark to Benjamin the Patriarch, and as soon as he had received the pure head, the ship got under sail at once and departed in a straight course. The patriarch returned to the city, carrying the head in his bosom, and the priests went

before him with chanting and singing as befitted the reception of that sacred and glorious head. And he made a chest of plain wood with a padlock on it, and placed the head therein, and he waited for a time in which he might find means to build a church.

The narrative of this miracle should be assigned to a considerably later date than the theft of the body of the Evangelist by the Venetians in the ninth century. The account seems to indicate that the body perished with the destruction of the church and that the head was saved from destruction by being stolen and later returned, not to the original owners, the Melkites, but to the Coptic patriarch Benjamin I. The narrative of the manufacture of the wooden reliquary for the head reflects a period in the history of the Coptic Church when, indeed, the head was actually carried from person to person and used for the ceremony of the consecration of the Coptic patriarchs. In this context it is interesting that in the year 700 a tradition was still maintained that the whole body of the Evangelist reposed in Alexandria. Bishop Arculf's account written from his dictation by Adamnan, abbot of Iona, states explicitly that "there [in Alexandria] is a large church in which St. Mark the Evangelist is interred. The body is buried in the eastern part of the church, before the altar, with a monument of squared marble over it."

The translation of the body of Saint Mark from Alexandria to Venice was a well-known fact in Alexandria in the ninth century, as is evident from the report of Bernard the Wise, who visited the city in 869 and recorded his impressions:

The city of Alexandria is adjacent to the sea. It was here that St. Mark, preaching the gospel, bore the episcopal dignity, and outside the eastern gate of the city is the monastery of the saint, with the church in which he formerly reposed. But the Venetians coming there obtained his body by stealth, and, carrying it on shipboard, sailed home with it.

Neither Bernard the Wise nor the Venetians refer to the translation of a body without a head. We must assume, therefore, that the tradition pertaining to the severing of the head from the body developed at a time when a relic of the Evangelist became important for functional or liturgical purposes, in this case probably the consecration of the patriarchs of the Coptic church, who used to take the apostolic head of the divinely inspired Mark in their bosoms at the end of the rite of consecration. From the *History of the Patriarchs of the Coptic Church*, we learn that from the eleventh to the fourteenth centuries, the head of Mark played an increasingly important part in the history and the tradition of the Coptic Church. It is in this period, therefore, that we should place the emergence of the tradition of the above-mentioned miracle of the manifestation of the head.

The eleventh-century Bishop Michael of Tinnis, compiler of the biographies of the patriarchs from Kha'il III (880–907) to Shenute II (1032–46), implies that during the eleventh century, the head of the Evangelist reposed in the desert of Wadi al-Natrun, undoubtedly in the Monastery of Saint Macarius. Shortly after Zacharias (1004–32), the sixty-fourth patriarch of Alexandria, retired to Wadi al-Natrun, a Turkish amir obtained the head of Mark. It was said to him, "The Christians will pay to thee whatsoever thou desirest for it." Then he carried the head to Misr (Cairo). When Buqayra al-Rashidi, known as 'the Crossbearer,' was informed of this, he took the head from the Turk for three hundred dinars and carried it to the father, the patriarch, who was at that time in the Monastery of Saint Macarius, where most of the bishops were dwelling. In the middle of the eleventh century, the head of the Evangelist was translated from the Monastery of Saint Macarius in Wadi al-Natrun to Alexandria. During the patriarchate of Christodoulus (1047–77), the sixty-sixth patriarch of Alexandria, the head of Mark was in Alexandria.

A very significant reference to the head of the Evangelist appears in the biography of Cyril III (1235–43), the seventy-fifth patriarch of Alexandria, where it is stated that the head reposed in the house of Ibn al-Shukri:

> And it is said that it was the head of Peter the beatified martyr, because the head of the Apostle, the Evangelist, was with his body when the Ventians transported him to Venice.

Undoubtedly, Venetian merchants must have spread in Alexandria their local tradition that the whole body reposed in Venice. Yet a head did exist, a head that had been used for some time in the rite of consecration of the patriarchs of the Coptic Church. It is interesting that the chronicler should include the tradition that it was the head of Peter. The possibility of this being the head of the beatified 'Seal of the Martyrs' is increased by the tradition that states that his martyrdom in 311 took place at Bucolia near the tomb where Mark was beheaded.

Yet doubt and uncertainty about this relic, so important for the liturgical life of the Coptic hierarchy, had to be dispelled. Numerous stories and traditions must have circulated in Cairo and Alexandria, and some of the more thoughtful theologians must have wondered about the truth. In the fourteenth century, Abu al-Barakat ibn Kabar, the most distinguished of the medieval Coptic theologians, wrote an account of the head of the Evangelist, which was to become the standard version for the Coptic church, often repeated and believed to this day:

> And his [Mark's] martyrdom was at the end of Baramuda, Nisan 27, in the reign of Tiberius, and it is said that it was still buried in the eastern church on the shore of Alexandria up to the time when it was taken by craft by some Franks [*al-Farang*], those of Venice, where it is now. And it [the head] was transferred to a house in Alexandria and it is still in it now.

Regarding the relic's location, Abu al-Barakat merely confirms the statement of the biographer of Cyril III; otherwise he clearly assigns the body to Venice, and the head to Alexandria!

The Return of the Relics of Mark

The recent translation of several holy relics inaugurated by the See of Rome has renewed the interest of clerics and historians in long-forgotten traditions pertaining to these relics. With genuine gratitude and jubilation, Christians of the eastern churches have welcomed the return of the relics of their patrons.

It is within this context that we should place the request of Pope Cyril VI of Alexandria to Pope Paul VI of Rome to "return to the Coptic Church the relics of Saint Mark which repose in the Cathedral in Venice." On March 29, 1967, it was announced in Cairo that once these relics were returned, they would be buried with the head of the Evangelist together with the relics of forty-two popes of the Coptic Church in the Cathedral of Saint Mark in Alexandria. In fact, the Copts requested the return of the whole body so as "to join the head with the body of the Evangelist as a tribute to the African Church."

On June 20, 1968, a delegation of bishops and notables of the Coptic and Ethiopian churches left Cairo for Rome to receive the relics of the Evangelist. The delegation consisted of the Metropolitan Mark of Abu Tig, Tima, and Tahta; the Metropolitan Michael of Asyut and the Monastery of Saint Macarius; the Metropolitan Antonius of Suhag; the Metropolitan Peter of Akhmim and Saqulta; the Metropolitan Domitius of Giza; the Metropolitan Paul of Helwan; Gregorius, Bishop of Theological Studies; Archbishop Luke of Arusi; Archbishop Peter of Bagemder ; Archbishop John of Tegre; ten priests; and some seventy Coptic notables. On June 22, 1968, Pope Paul VI presented to the delegation an alleged relic of Saint Mark—a small particle of bone, which had been a gift from Cardinal Giovanni Urbani, the patriarch of Venice, to the pope of Rome. This relic had reposed in a reliquary in the treasury of the Cathedral of Saint Mark in Venice, for the martyrium of the Evangelist was not opened for this purpose.

Late in the evening of June 24, the delegation, accompanied by the papal delegation, arrived at Cairo Airport. The papal delegation consisted of Cardinal Leon Etienne Duval, the archbishop of Algiers; Cardinal Willebrands, Secretary of the Secretariat for Christian Unity; Monsignor Olivotti, Coadjutor to Cardinal Urbani; Pierre Duprey; Abbé Teissie; and Monsignor Nicotra, representing the Oriental Congregation. Upon the plane's arrival, the relic was personally carried by Pope Cyril VI of Alexandria to the car. The same night, the relic was translated to the patriarchate at Azbakiya. The small particle, lying in a magnificent silver reliquary, was placed in a wooden box covered with a rich green velvet and fastened with golden cords in the form of a cross.

On June 26, the day following the inauguration of the new Cathedral of Saint Mark in 'Abbasiya, Cairo, a Divine Liturgy was celebrated by Cyril VI in commemoration of the 1,900th anniversary of the martyrdom of the Evangelist in Alexandria. Afterward, Cyril VI offered the relic to H.I.M. Haile Selassie I, Emperor of Ethiopia, for veneration. Then Cyril VI carried the relic to the crypt beneath the high altar. Here the reliquary was solemnly lowered into a cavity in a square block of polished Aswan granite. As the heavy granite lid was placed on the cavity, the choirs of the Coptic Catholic and Coptic Evangelical Churches sang to the glory of God.

In spite of the previous pronouncements by the Coptic hierarchy, the relic was not joined to the head, which was believed to repose in Alexandria. On the contrary, a new cult center was created in Cairo. Moreover, instead of the whole body of the Evangelist, only a small particle of a relic was returned. Neither the box with the head nor the reliquary containing the other relic was opened for veneration or inspection, thereby either intentionally, or, more likely, unintentionally perpetuating the mystery of the relics of the Evangelist.

On June 27, the representatives of the Vatican proceeded to Alexandria, where they were received by His Most Divine Beatitude Nicholas VI, the Greek Orthodox patriarch of Alexandria; the Reverend Father Nicholas Tenedios, the recorder of the patriarchate; and Dr. Theodore D. Moschonas, the remembrancer and librarian. Then, while the members of the delegations stood reverently, Cardinal Duval offered the Greek Orthodox patriarch a precious, dark-colored reliquary containing a part of the relics of the Evangelist. The cardinal said:

When in 1952 the urn was opened, they took reverently and for a future blessing the holy fragments, and the urn of the patron of Venice was closed. Now, on our coming to Cairo, His Holiness the Pope gave to us also the present reliquary specially for the Greek Orthodox Church of Alexandria, which is also a daughter of Saint Mark.

Having kissed the holy relics enclosed in the silver reliquary, the patriarch thanked them with words of brotherliness, saying, "The Church of Alexandria receives joyfully for blessing and strengthening the reliquary of her holy founder, and she will guard it as the apple of her eye.

On July 7, these relics of Saint Mark were exhibited for veneration by the faithful in the Greek Orthodox Cathedral of Saint Sabas in Alexandria. Since 1970, some relics of the Evangelist repose in the crypt of the new Coptic Cathedral of St. Mark in Alexandria. Other relics of St. Mark are kept together with those of St. Anianus in the reliquary chapel north of the altar.

The Theological Contributions of the See of Alexandria

The Spread of Coptic Monasticism to the Orient and the Occident

The outstanding contribution of the Egyptian Church to world Christianity was the monastic movement, which received its impetus from men like Saints Antony, Paul of Thebes, Macarius, and others. Saint Antony's name became known and associated with a new way of life leading to salvation. His disciple Saint Macarius, who stayed with Saint Antony at least twice, established Antonian monasticism in the Desert of Scetis, where several thousand monks imitated and even surpassed the rigor and austerity of their founder. Saint Amon, the father of Nitrian monasticism, had been inspired by Saint Antony just as Saint Isaac and Saint Pelusian had upheld the Antonian tradition at Mount Clysma.

Two types of Christian asceticism arose in response to the words of Jesus, who said, "If you would be perfect, go sell what you possess and give to the poor and you will have treasure in heaven; and come, follow me" (Mt 19:21). The anchorite or hermit withdrew to the inner desert, "wandering over deserts and mountains, and in dens and caves of the earth" (Heb 11:38); extreme examples of such hermits were Sts. Onuphrius and Timothy. The coenobites practised their ascetic virtues within a community of like-minded men and followed certain rules and regulations. These were enforced by an abbot. A well-known abbot of the Scetis was St. John the Hegumen.

Saint Hilarion, the originator of Palestinian monasticism, derived his ascetic enthusiasm from the Great Hermit, as Saint Antony was called. Born in 291 in the vicinity of Gaza, Saint Hilarion made a pilgrimage to the South Qalala mountain range for the purpose of learning the angelic life from Saint Antony. After staying two months with him, he could no longer endure the crowds that came to visit the hermit. On his return to his native land, Saint Hilarion lived in a tiny cell near Gaza, which he made his abode for fifty years. Within a few years of his death, laurae and monasteries were to be found in all parts of Palestine.

Johannes Cassianus (360–435) of Dobrudsha visited the east with his friend Germanus. At Bethlehem he entered a monastery, but his desire to visit the Egyptian hermits of the Desert of Scetis inspired him to leave Palestine. For seven years he lived with the Egyptian desert fathers. Afterward he went to Constantinople, where he became a pupil of Saint John Chrysostom.

At Marseille, Cassianus founded a monastery where the Egyptian rule was followed. Nearby, Saint Honoratus founded in 400 the Monastery of Lerinum (Lerins), where the Egyptian system was followed until the introduction of the Benedictine rule in the sixth century.

One of the leaders of Christian monasticism in Mesopotamia was Saint Eugenius, an Egyptian pearl diver who had worked at Clysma. Following his call to the ascetic life, he entered a monastery. Then he chose a number of Egyptian monks to go with him to Mesopotamia to build a monastery near Nisibis. He died around 363.

Soon after Saint Antony's death, people from all over the Levant came to Egypt to see and study the monasticism of which they had heard so much. Saint Epiphanius, bishop of Constantia (Salamis) in Cyprus, visited Egypt, and after his return to Palestine, he became hegumen of a monastery that he founded near Eleutheropolis in Judea. Saint Basil the Great, bishop of Caesarea and founder of many monastic institutions in Asia Minor, derived his knowledge of monasticism from the monks and hermits he visited in Syria and Egypt.

Like Christianity, monasticism was introduced into Ethiopia from Egypt. In 480, Saint Aragawi, who is said to have received his habit from Saint Pachomius, founded the celebrated monastery at Debra Damo. With him came eight other monks from the Monastery of Saint Antony; together they are known in the Ethiopian Church as the 'Nine Saints.'

In 385, Saint Jerome traveled to Palestine in the company of two Roman women, Saint Paula and her daughter Eustochium. From the Holy Land, Saint Jerome and his companions continued their journey to Egypt, where they visited the monasteries of the Scetis (Wadi al-Natrun). After their return to Palestine they settled at Bethlehem, where Saint Paula founded four monasteries, three for nuns and one for monks. It was the latter monastery over which Saint Jerome presided and where he was engaged in most of his literary work.

The part played by early Egyptian monasticism in the conversion of England is a matter that has yet to be determined. Writes Stanley Lane-Poole:

> It is more than probable that we are indebted to the remote hermits for the first preaching of the Gospel in England, where, till the coming of Saint Augustine, the Egyptian monastic rule prevailed. But more important is the belief that Irish Christianity, the great civilizing agent of the early Middle Ages among the northern nations, was the child of the Egyptian Church.

The Irish Stowe Missal, which is the oldest missal of the Irish Church, refers to the Egyptian anchorites of the fourth century. The text is in four columns and consists mostly of single words; the second column of folio 32, verso, reads: "Pauli, Antoni, et ceterorum patrum heremi sciti." This clearly shows that the ascetic examples of the Egyptian hermits were well known throughout northern Europe.

There is no question that the Church of Egypt and the Church of Ireland had rather intimate relations with each other. The Irish monk and geographer Dicuil referred to Egypt in his 825 text, *De mensura orbis terrae.* Seven Coptic monks were buried at Disert Ulidh in Ulster, and we find their names invoked in the litany attributed to Saint Oengus.

Both Saint Antony and Celtic and Irish monks are often portrayed with little bells in Celtic art. Portable clochettes, whether of iron or bronze, have played an important role in the Celtic countries of Ireland, Scotland, and Gaul. It seems likely that, with the increase of Saint Antony's popularity in the western world, religious art bestowed upon him the same insignia with which the Irish monks were represented.

Even in Switzerland, the city seal of Uznach shows Saint Antony in prayer, with a staff and clochettes, while the city seal of Saint Antoni/Freiburg has the Coptic tau cross with two clochettes.

Furthermore, in the ninth-century *Vita Bonifatii* attributed to Radbodo, bishop of Utrecht, we discover a significant reference to the very illustrious company of anchorites and monks in Egypt.

The Catechetical School and Theological Controversies

After the infant Christ visited the land of the pharoahs, Saint Luke informs us that Egyptians were present in Jerusalem on the Day of Pentecost, when the Holy Spirit descended upon the faithful.

These Egyptians returned to their homeland, where they established

Christian congregations. The Christians of Egypt are convinced that
Saint Mark the Evangelist visited Alexandria, where he preached the
gospel, founded the See of Alexandria, and received the crown of
martyrdom.

The apostolic foundation of the Coptic Church is both glorious and
tragic: glorious in the number of its illustrious leaders such as Saint
Athanasius, Saint Cyril, Saint Antony, and Saint Pachomius, to
mention but a few, and tragic in the vast number of its followers who
suffered martyrdom in the various persecutions for their adherence to
the Christian faith. These are commemorated to this day by the
Coptic calendar, in which the years are dated from *anno martyrum,*
the 'year of the martyrs' (A.M.), which recalls the great persecution of
the Christians that began in Egypt in 303. The era of the martyrs
actually commenced on August 29, 284, the year in which Diocletian
became emperor. Following the Diocletian persecution in Egypt from
303 to 305, Egyptian Christianity emerged victorious and dynamic, so
much so that its theology and Christology were to leave a lasting
impression on the whole church.

The Catechetical School of Alexandria

The outstanding contribution of Alexandrian Christianity to world
Christianity was the Didascalia, the famous catechetical school where
Christian scholars labored to prove that reason and revelation, philosophy and theology were not only compatible but also essential for
each other's comprehension. The first great scholar who served as
head of the Didascalia was Pantaenus. Authorities say that Pantaenus
most probably came to Alexandria around the year 180, when he was
appointed head of the school of catechumens, and remained there
until he died, shortly before 200.

Upon the death of Pantaenus, Clement became the head of the
catechetical school. When the severe persecutions by Septimius
Severus compelled him to leave Egypt, he sought refuge in
Cappadocia. Clement asserted that the ancient Greeks recognized the
spirituality of the Divine, which was further illuminated through the
message of the Hebrew prophets.

The most important theologian and prolific author was Origen,
who at an early age joined the catechetical school, where he listened to
the lectures of Pantaenus and Clement. Intensely ascetic by nature, he
observed the most rigorous vigils. Four *oboli* (meager coins) a day
earned by copying manuscripts sufficed for his bodily sustenance. A
rash decision led him to apply to himself the evangelical injunction of
Matthew 19:12 (". . . and there be eunuchs which have made
themselves eunuchs for the kingdom of heaven's sake"). From 204

until 230, Origen worked in Alexandria. In 230, after having settled in Caesarea, Origen established a flourishing school, and some of his pupils, such as Gregory Thaumaturgus, later bishop of Neocaesarea, rose to important positions in the hierarchy.

Among his exegetical and theological writings is the Hexapla, in which he placed the Hebrew text of the Old Testament side by side with the various Greek versions. His principal apologetic work is his book *Against Celsus*, a second century pagan philosopher. This work, written in Caesarea, has been completely preserved.

Origen was succeeded as head of the Catechetical School of Alexandria by Heracles, his former pupil. Heracles' successor was another famous pupil of Origen, Dionysius of Alexandria, later surnamed the Great. In 231, he was head of the school, and in 248 he became bishop of Alexandria.

Dionysius was succeeded by Theognostus, who administered the school from 265 to 282 and wrote the *Hypotyposes*. Little is known about him beyond the testimony of Photius. He was followed by Prierus, Achillas, and Peter of Alexandria before he was elected patriarch around 300.

Theological Controversies

During the fourth and fifth centuries, theological and christological controversies dominated the course of the history of the Egyptian Church. The significance of the Arian controversy, particularly within Egypt, is seen in two Egyptians: Meletius, the Arian bishop of Lycopolis, and Saint Athanasius, who emerged from the Arian controversy not merely as the Orthodox patriarch of the Church of Alexandria, but also as the universally accepted and revered doctor of the Catholic Church.

The Chalcedonian controversy, with Cyril I and Dioscorus I as the two principal personalities on the miaphysitic side, eventually led to the tragic schism that alienated the Church of Egypt from both the Byzantine and Roman Catholic Churches.

Egyptian national sentiment—a non-theological factor—may well have been an important issue in the unfortunate division over the subject of the body of Christ. The post-Chalcedonian developments only led to further schisms, particularly because of the struggle for supremacy between Dyophysites and Miaphysites in Alexandria, and the emperor Zeno's attempt to settle the theological estrangement by omitting the word 'nature' from the text of his *Henoticon* ("Instrument of Union"). At any rate, by the fifth century, the church was divided into Dyophysites, Miaphysites, Arians, and Nestorians.

By the beginning of the sixth century, several further divisions emerged among the non-Chalcedonians, and thus weakened even further the witness of the Coptic, or Egyptian Church. Moreover, the Miaphysite leadership passed to the Syrian Church, which determined the theological thinking of the Non-Chalcedonians for centuries to come.

The Canon of the Holy Scriptures

The religious and moral norms of the Copts are largely determined by three different forms of authority: the legal authority, the traditional authority, and the charismatic authority. The legal authority includes the canon of holy scripture, the writings of the church fathers, and the canons of the church. These sources were and still are the most imporant criteria for the religious and moral life of the Coptic Church. The traditional authorities are considered to be the statements and attitudes of the ecclesiastical hierarchy, as well as certain ways of thinking and patterns of behavior adopted from pre-Christian times and subsequently adapted and transformed so as to correspond with the Christian ethos. The charismatic authority normally depends on the extraordinary qualities of a person, whether a gifted anchorite or a patriarch, whose legitimacy rests on supernatural gifts, which are demonstrated through miracles or other extraordinary deeds. In reality, however, we discover a constant overlapping and intermingling of these three authorities, and it is important that theologians and sociologists are aware of the interaction of these authoritative criteria, which determine so much of the personal and the social life of the Copts.

Egypt's role in the formation of the canon of the Scriptures was of the utmost importance, owing to the natural advantages of its position and the conspicuous eminence of its great teachers during the third century, particularly Clement of Alexandria and Origen. The testimony of the Alexandrian Church to the New Testament canon is generally uniform. In addition to the acknowledged books, the Epistle to the Hebrews and the Apocalypse were received there as divine scripture, even by those who doubted their immediate apostolic origin. The two shorter Epistles of Saint John were well known and commonly received, but no one except Origen, so far as can be discovered, was acquainted with the Second Epistle of Peter.

The first reference to the complete canon, however, is found in the Thirty-ninth Festal Letter of Saint Athanasius (fourth century), where the books are listed in the following order:

Old Testament: the Pentateuch, Joshua, Judges, Ruth, four Kings, two Chronicles, Esdras (I and II), Psalms, Proverbs, Ecclesiastes, Song of Songs, Job, twelve Prophets, Isaiah, Jeremiah, Baruch, Lamentations, Ezekiel, and Daniel.

New Testament: Matthew, Mark, Luke, John, Acts, seven Catholic Epistles (James; I and II Peter; I, II, and III John; Jude), fourteen Pauline Epistles (Romans, I and II Corinthians, Hebrews, Galatians, Ephesians, Philippians, Colossians, I and II Thessalonians, I and II Timothy, Titus, Philemon), and the Apocalypse.

For profitable reading, Saint Athanasius listed the following Old and New Testament books: the Wisdom of Solomon, Ecclesiasticus or the Wisdom of Jesus Son of Sirach, Esther, Judith, Tobit, the Acts of the Apostles, and the Shepherd of Hermes.

At the beginning of the twentieth century, the question of the canon was discussed again in the Coptic Church, and by order of Cyril V, the 112th patriarch, the following books were removed from the canon: Tobit, Judith, the Complement of Esther, the Wisdom of Solomon, Ecclesiasticus, the Epistle of Jeremiah, Baruch, the Complement of Daniel (Susanna and the three youths in the fire), and the Books of Maccabees. No changes, however, were made regarding the New Testament canon. In 1928, Habib Girgis published his *Catechism for Youth*, which lists the following Old Testament books as canonical: the Pentateuch, Joshua, Judges, Ruth, I and II Samuel, I and II Kings, I and II Chronicles, Ezra, Nehemiah, Esther, Job, Psalms, Proverbs, Ecclesiastes, Song of Songs, and the four major and twelve minor Prophets.

The Arabic Bible

A translation of the Scriptures into Arabic became imperative with the decline of the Coptic language. Contemporaneous with the beginning of the use of bilingual (Bohairic and Arabic) liturgical books in the tenth century, there were bilingual texts of the various books of the Scriptures. According to al-Mas'udi (d.957), Hunayn ibn Ishaq, the Nestorian philosopher, translated the whole Septuagint into Arabic. By the thirteenth century, the Copts had several translations of certain books of the Scriptures in Arabic, although an Arabic text of the complete canon translated by the Copts was not finished until the second part of the eleventh century. The Arabic version of the psalter used by the Copts was based on the eleventh-century translation by the Antiochene deacon Abu al-Fath 'Abd Allah ibn Fadl. With regard to the Arabic texts of the Prophets, the Coptic Church used the tenth-century Egyptian Melkite recension of al-'Alam, which includes all the Prophets and is based on the Septuagint. As with the Old Testament, we discover that neither was the complete canon of the New Testament translated much before the sixteenth century. The tenth-century Arabic text of the Gospels, known as the Egyptian or the Alexandrian

Vulgate, was based on a Bohairic text. In addition to this translation, there existed in the Coptic Church a second translation of the Gospels by al-As'ad Abu al-Farag Hibat Allah made in the thirteenth century, which was a linguistic improvement on the previous text. The Arabic text of the epistular literature was also based on a Bohairic text. Noteworthy in this context is an Arabic collection of the Pauline epistles from the thirteenth century, which was the work of al-Wagih Yuhanna al-Qalyubi, a contemporary of the 'Assalides. With respect to the Apocalypse, we must remember that in the Coptic Church this book seldom appeared in connection with the New Testament. It constituted an independent part, and was used and commented on as such.

The first printed Arabic Bibles were the Arabic versions of the Paris and London Polyglots. The Arabic Old Testament of the Paris Polyglot followed closely Paris arab.1, which was secured by Francis Savary de Brèves in Cairo in 1606; the Arabic New Testament generally followed the Arabic edition of the Gospels printed by Giovanni Battista Rainmundi in Rome in 1590, which in turn was based on Vatican copt. 9. The London Polyglot appeared almost two decades later, and the text of the Arabic version is almost a transcript of the Paris Polyglot, with some additions in the Prophetic literature. The Congregatio de Propaganda Fide published a *Biblia Sacra Arabica* in three volumes in 1671, which was followed by the Smith-Van Dyck version of 1865. In 1876 and 1878, the Jesuit version, *al-Kitab al-muqaddas*, was published in Beirut. The Smith-Van Dyck and the Jesuit version are both used by the Copts. The former is more widely distributed, and, therefore, more widely read in Egypt. Moreover, whereas the Jesuit Version is admired by the learned, the Smith-Van Dyck Version is more easily understandable to the lay reader.

The Writings of the Church Fathers

In addition to the canon of the Scriptures, the Coptic Church, like all other churches of apostolic origin, relies on the writings of the church fathers as authorities in matters of faith and morals. Generally speaking, the writings of all church fathers prior to the Fourth Ecumenical Council of Chalcedon in 451, as well as those of non-Chalcedonian fathers, are considered authoritative. At the same time, it must be added that there is no consensus of opinion on the writings of those fathers, who are accepted or rejected by various authorities. The following list represents those writings that are accepted by most Coptic theologians.

The Pre-Chalcedonian Fathers

In the sixth chapter of his fourteenth-century work *The Lamp of Darkness*, Abu al-Barakat makes a list of the canonical books of the Scriptures that includes the two epistles attributed to Clement (c.96), a disciple of Peter and a pope of Rome. In his *Book on the Councils*, Sawirus ibn al-Muqaffa', bishop of al-Ashmunain, quoted the *Epistle to the Smyrnaeans* by Saint Ignatius of Antioch (98–117). The two epistles of Saint Polycarp (69–155) are accepted, although they are not well known. The same is true of the *First Apology to the Emperor Antoninus Pius*, the *Dialogue with Trypho*, and the *Second Apology addressed to the Roman Senate* by Saint Justin Martyr (100–165). Justin was the first Christian theologian to reconcile the claims of faith and reason, since he held that traces of truth were to be found even in the pagan philosophers. Irenaeus of Lyons (130–200) is listed among the fathers of the Coptic Church, although his *Adversus omnes haereses*, a detailed attack on Gnosticism, is not well known among the Copts. The writings of the Athenian Clement of Alexandria (150–215), head of the Catechetichal School of Alexandria from 190 to 202, are accepted and known among the Copts, especially the *Paedagogus* and the *Stromata*.

As for the person and the writings of Origen (185–254), there exists no consensus among the Copts. On the one hand, Origen was placed with the sanction of Demetrius of Alexandria at the head of the Catechetichal School of Alexandria, where he labored from 204 to 230. On the other hand, Demetrius later convened a synod at which it was resolved to banish Origen from Alexandria. A second synod, composed entirely of bishops, determined that Origen must be deprived of his rank as presbyter. Today, the Coptic Theological Seminary in Cairo considers Origen one of the great teachers of the church.

Tertullian of Carthage (166–220), the first Christian theologian to write in Latin, is accepted by some Coptic theologians, yet rejected by others on account of his montanistic tenets (Montanus, d.179, claimed to be the Paraclete mentioned in the New Testament and proclaimed the imminent end of the world). The writings of Hippolytus of Rome (d.230), and those attributed to him, are well known in the Coptic Church. The canons attributed to him are accepted as canon law, and quotations from him appear in the thirteenth-century *Commentary on the Apocalypse* by Ibn Katib Qaysar. The *Expositio fidei* by Gregory of Neocaesarea, known as Thaumaturgus (c.213–70) is mentioned by Abu al-Barakat. Ephraem Syrus (306–73), known as the Prophet of the Syrians, wrote a large number of homilies and hagiological and eschatological discourses, which have been translated into Arabic and circulated among the Copts.

The epistle of Dionysius of Alexandria (d.264), the penitential canons of Peter of Alexandria (d.310), and the writings of Alexander of Alexandria (d.328) are all known and accepted by the Copts.

The writings of Cyprian of Carthage (200–58) are also accepted. They include such works as *De habitu virginum* ('In praise of virginity'), *De lapsis*, which deals with the conditions for reconciling the lapsed, and *De catholicae ecclesiae unitate*, a treatise on the nature of the true unity in the church. Saint Athanasius the Apostolic, known as al-Rasuli, (328–73) is one of the principal authorities of the Coptic Church. Abu al-Barakat knows his *Commentary on the Psalms*, his *Vita Antonii* and the *Apophthegmata* are well known to the Coptic monks; and the 107 canons attributed to Saint Athanasius are accepted as canon law. Saint Theophilus of Alexandria (384–412) is another important theologian of the Coptic Church, whose *Homilies* are well known.

Although mentioned by Abu al-Barakat, the writings of Eusebius of Caesarea (260–340), founder of a theological school there, are not so well known. The ascetic writings, epistles, and homilies of Basil the Great of Caesarea (330–79), as well as the two series of canons attributed to him, are accepted and known. The same pertains to the Arabic collection of *Thirty Discourses* and the homilies by Gregory of Nyssa (d.390). Cyril of Jerusalem (315–86) wrote eighteen exhortations and several homilies for the church, all of which are accepted. John Chrysostom, or Yuhanna Fam al-Dahab, (354–407) is one of the principal church fathers, and his discourses and homilies are known among the Copts. Epiphanius of Cyprus (d.403) wrote the *Ancoratus* (*al-Marsa*), which is accepted, but hardly known.

Cyril of Alexandria (376–444), the great champion of Orthodoxy, taught the personal, or hypostatic union of the two natures of Jesus Christ. Cyril's antagonism to the Antiochene School is shown in his opposition to John Chrysostom. His *Thesaurus de sancta et consubstantiali Trinitate* is a treatise in dialogue form on the Trinity. Other writings include his *Dialogue with Nestorius* and his *Twelve Anathematisms*.

Whereas the Alexandrian theologians composed their writings in Greek, Shenute (d.466) was the first and most prominent Coptic writer and theologian; he is best known for his homilies. His vita was written by his disciple Besa (Wisa). Finally, the discourse attributed to Dioscorus (444–54) is hardly known among the Copts.

The Post-Chalcedonian Fathers

By the beginning of the sixth century, several internal divisions had emerged within the Coptic Church, and the theological leadership of the non-Chalcedonian, or Miaphysite Churches moved from Alexandria to Antioch, which determined the theological thinking of the non-Chalcedonians for the following centuries.

The most important theologian of the sixth century was Severus of Antioch (512–38), whose dogmatic and liturgical discourses, homilies, and epistles, mentioned by Abu al-Barakat, are known among the Copts. Less known are the sixth-century polemic writings by John Philoponus.

Also from the sixth century are the homilies of James of Sarug, published by Michael Athanasius in Cairo in 1905, and the *Commentary on the Psalter* by Daniel of Salah, published by Yusuf Manqariyus and Habib Girgis in Cairo in 1902.

Among the writings of the post-Chalcedonian Coptic fathers are the homilies of Theodosius I of Alexandria (536–67) and the homilies and apologetic works of John, bishop of Burullus (sixth century). Benjamin I (623–62) wrote several Easter epistles and a collection of replies to some forty biblical and liturgical questions. *The Questions of Theodore,* also dealing with theological issues, were answered by John III (680–89).

Other important statements of the non-Chalcedonian faith are the *Synodica,* confessional writings, that the Antiochene patriarchs exchanged with the Alexandrian patriarchs at their enthronement.

The Canons of the Coptic Church

Only fifteen years after its foundation, the church was already faced with the need to enact certain regulations for the Gentile converts to Christianity. These enactments, made at the Council of the Apostles at Jerusalem in 48 (Acts 15), may be regarded as the beginning of what was known later as canon law, and, in the centuries that followed, the church was forced on many occasions to enact such laws to establish correct belief, to regulate the performance of the Divine Liturgy and the administration of the sacraments, and to control the conduct of the clergy and laity alike.

These laws, or canons, are of two kinds, those that may be called 'general' and those that may be termed 'local,' depending on whether they were applicable to the church as a whole or only to a restricted part of it. Up to the middle of the fifth century, the general canons were received everywhere by the church, and even some of the local canons were also accepted as being suitable for general application.

The Pre-Nicene Canons

The *Didascalia*, or the *Teachings of the Apostles*, which is the earliest attempt at forming a corpus of canon law, belongs to the second half of the third century. This corpus is based in part on an earlier canon, the *Didache*, or the *Teachings of the Twelve Apostles*, which belongs to the second century at least. The *Didascalia* provides disciplinary measures as well as spiritual and moral precepts for the clergy and the laity. It also contains regulations relating to liturgical questions, such as the canonical hours and the periods of fasting.

The 127 Canons of the Apostles are divided into two books, the first of which contains seventy-one canons and is derived in part from the *Apostolic Church Order* (canons 1–20), the *Apostolic Tradition of Hippolytus*, also known as the *Egyptian Church Order* (canons 21–47), and excerpts from the *Apostolic Constitutions*, Book VIII (canons 48–71), which are attributed to Clement of Rome (c.95). The second book, with fifty-six canons, is based on the *Apostolic Constitutions*, Book VIII, 47.

The Thirty Canons of the Apostles contain regulations regarding the order of the service, the hierarchy, the feasts of our Lord, and the congregational life. The introduction gives an account of the laying on of hands that the apostles received prior to the Ascension of our Lord. Furthermore, the canons offer admonitions for the spiritual life.

The Canons of the Councils and the Synods

The Ecumenical Councils

Nicea (325). The First Ecumenical Council assembled at Nicea in Bithynia. The twenty canons of the 318 holy fathers are of greatest importance for the study of canon law. After the *Confessio fidei*, the creed promulgated by the council, there follow the canons. These canons state that pagans are not to be ordained, unless they have been well instructed in the Christian faith; that members of the clergy should not castrate themselves; and that they should not live with women, except those belonging to their families. Furthermore, those who have been excommunicated should not be restored to communion by another bishop, and those who engage in usury shall be cast forth. Canon six states, "Let the ancient customs which are observed in Egypt, Libya, and the Pentapolis prevail, so that the Bishop of Alexandria may have jurisdiction over all these [nomes], since this is also customary with the Bishop at Rome." Special requirements are set forth for those who lapsed during the persecutions.

The Eighty-Four Oriental Canons of Nicea may have been the work of Maruta, bishop of Mayafarqin (Martyropolis) in Syria in 400. These canons contain regulations for bishops, priests, and monks, and also rules for those who return to the Orthodox faith after having left the sects of Paul of Samosata and the Cathari. Fellowship with sorcerers is prohibited. The canons also deal with the relationship among the heads of the churches in Persia, Ethiopia, and Cyprus, and with the duties of metropolitans and bishops. The thirty-seventh canon recognizes the primacy of the pope of Rome, based on apostolic order.

Constantinople (381). The canons of the 150 fathers who assembled at the Second Ecumenical Council, held in Constantinople during the consulate of Flavius Eucherius and Flavius Evagrius, are seven in number. These canons are a reaffirmation of the Nicene canons, laying emphasis on the rule that bishops may not ordain outside their dioceses. Canon three grants the prerogatives of honor after the bishop of Rome to Constantinople because it is the New Rome.

Ephesus (431). The Third Ecumenical Council promulgated eight canons, all of which deal with the Nestorian heresy. Furthermore, we find among the literature of the Council the Twelve Anathemas of Saint Cyril against Nestorius. The Council gave formal approval to the term Theotokos ('Godbearer') as a title of the Holy Virgin Mary.

The Canons of the Synods

Ancyra (314). The first nine canons of the synod held at Ancyra in Galatia deal with the disciplinary measures to be taken against Christians who had lapsed during the persecutions. The remaining canons (10–25) form the basis of the penitential system to be followed for other offenses.

Neocaesarea (probably early fourth century, before 352). The fifteen canons of the synod held at Neocaesarea in Pontus contain disciplinary measures dealing with the clergy and the penance to be imposed for polygamy, especially for digamists and trigamists. These canons permitted pregnant women to be baptized and prohibited a priest from being ordained before thirty years of age.

Gangra (c.345). The twenty canons of the synod held at Gangra in Paphlagonia were directed against the false asceticism of Eustathius, which condemned marriage, the eating of meat, etc. These canons reaffirm that presbyters may be married before ordination and state that those who hesitate to receive communion from a married priest are condemned. Those who live in virginity should not be boastful and arrogant. If a woman under pretense of asceticism should change her apparel and, instead of a woman's customary clothing, should put on that of a man, then let her be anathema. Those who forsake their children and do not nurture them under the pretense of asceticism are likewise anathematized. Finally, women should not shave off their hair, pretending to do so out of reverence for God. The epilogue, often called Canon Twenty-One, explains the true nature of asceticism.

Antioch (341). The synod held at Antioch in Encaeniis was attended by ninety-seven bishops, as well as the emperor Constantius. The twenty-five canons of this assembly deal with ecclesiastical discipline, such as the obedience of all clergy to the canons of the council; that bishops and presbyters are not to go to the emperor without notifying their respective metropolitans; that bishops should ordain only within their diocese; and that bishops are to be judged by a council of bishops.

Laodicea (between 343 and 381). For the synod held at Laodicea in Phrygia Pacatiana we have no exact date. The forty canons of this synod are also of a disciplinary nature, dealing with matters such as the prohibition of usury by priests and the use of holy places by heretics. Furthermore, it is stated that digamists shall be held blameless; that no one should marry heretics; that the lessons in the service shall be interspersed with psalms; that the clergy should not enter taverns; and that beds should not be set up in churches. Other statements include a prohibition to bathe with women or to have love feasts in church buildings. The blessings of heretics are regarded as a curse, and priests ought not to engage in magic. The last canons deal with matters concerning Lent and prohibit the celebration of marriage during this season.

Sardica (343 or 344). The twenty canons of the Synod of Sardica (modern Sofia) are a reaffirmation of previous disciplinary canons, chief among which are the provisions that allow the bishop of Rome to act as a court of appeal for accused bishops in certain circumstances. It also forbids the translation of a bishop to another see. Candidates for the office of bishop must have received all the holy orders of the church. The last canons deal with disciplinary matters in regard to communion with heretics.

Carthage (419). The 137 canons of the synod held at Carthage reaffirm the canons of the Council of Nicea. Thus we read that usury by priests and laymen is condemned; that those who communicate with those who are excommunicated, are excommunicated by their act; that three bishops are required for the consecration of a bishop; that heretics should not be helped by the clergy; that only canonical scripture should be read in the churches; and that the Eucharist should be administered only to those who are fasting. The last canons prohibit the practice of rebaptism and reordination. There are to be no theatrical representations on the Lord's Day, and all remains of idolatry are to be abolished. The canons close with statements concerning the relationship with the Donatists.

The Canons of the Doctors of the Church

Athanasius
The 107 canons attributed to Athanasius (295–373) contain regulations for the higher and lower clergy, matters concerning the Liturgy, the administration of the church treasury, extra-ecclesiastical functions of the clergy, and a discipline for monks and laymen, especially for virgins. The canons may belong to the fourth century.

Basil
Two series of canons are attributed to Basil (330–79). The first series of thirteen canons includes penalties for immoral priests and deacons as well as prohibitions for the burning of relics. The second series of 106 canons deals with matters concerning the conjugal life, penance, prayer, and fasting, and the ascetic life in general. Warnings are given against all kinds of superstitions. Other canons include the duties of widows, orphans, and virgins, as well as the duties of the clergy, and the celebration of the Eucharist and the sacrament of baptism.

Hippolytus
The thirty-eight canons attributed to Hippolytus (c.325) are dependent on the *Apostolic Tradition* of Hippolytus as well as on the *Apostolic Constitutions*. The canons may belong to the beginning of the sixth century.

Gregory of Nyssa
The four canons attributed to Gregory of Nyssa (330–95) are, in fact, moral pronouncements of unknown origin. Another series of canons attributed to Gregory of Nyssa, dealing with the clergy's attitude to the altar, is used by Michael of Damietta.

Cyril
The twelve anathemas of Cyril (d.444) are a defense of the Orthodox faith against the Nestorian heresy.

John Chrysostom
The twelve canons of John Chrysostom (347–407) are excerpts from the treatise *On the Priesthood, II, III*. These canons are included by al-Safi ibn al-'Assal in his collection of canons.

Peter of Alexandria
The fourteen penitential canons of Peter (302–10), seventeenth patriarch of Alexandria, pertain to Christian discipline at the time of persecution by the state.

Timothy of Alexandria
The seventeen *Responsa Canonica* of Timothy (d.477) contain

matters relating to marital problems, sexual abstinence before the reception of the Sacrament, and other matters.

The Canons of the Middle Ages

Christodoulus
The thirty-one canons of Christodoulus (1047–77), sixty-sixth patriarch of Alexandria, deal with liturgical observances, the feasts of the year, the behavior of the congregation while at church, and the conduct of the clergy toward their superiors. Furthermore, it is stated that male and female infants shall not be baptized in the same baptismal water and that no one shall talk or converse at the time of prayer and during the Divine Liturgy. The canons list numerous feasts to be observed by the faithful and state that fasting on Wednesdays and Fridays is obligatory throughout the year, except during Paschaltide. The canons are used by al-Safi ibn al-'Assal.

Cyril II
The thirty-four canons are the result of conferences between Cyril II (1078–92), sixty-seventh patriarch of Alexandria, and the bishops, at which the vizier assisted. The canons prohibit simony and declare that anathemas should be pronounced only for necessary reasons. Bishops ought to visit their churches and monasteries and be attentive to their cleanliness. Further, the bishops should examine the Divine Liturgies and thus ascertain that they are not abridged. Those in attendance to the bishop should be honest and clean-living persons. There should be neither selling nor buying on Sundays. In case of disputes, priests and laity should not resort to the government authorities, but turn to their bishop. Those desiring their children to be circumcised should have this performed before baptism. Christian women should not dye the underparts of their hands and feet with henna. Christians should not sell their slaves to dissidents.

Gabriel II
The first series of thirty-two canons of Gabriel II (1131–45), seventieth patriarch of Alexandria, deals with matters of conduct, the duties of bishops and priests, and such matters as circumcision, marriage, and burials. Those who practice simony shall be anathematized. Priests and monks shall not indulge in drinking. None shall marry during the forty days of the Holy Fast, or at Easter, or on the Eve of Pentecost. Families, children, and servants should not use the churches as dwelling places. Monks shall not leave their monasteries except with special permission. Only the Liturgies of Saint Basil, Saint Gregory, and Saint Cyril shall be used. Bishops and monks shall not have female servants in their service. The second series of ten canons is mainly concerned with

regulating the duties of the various ranks of the clergy and with their conduct in civil life. Priests shall not be present at banquets and wedding feasts where there are jestings and amusements.

The Laws of Inheritance are a part of the Canons of Gabriel and are based on the Scriptures, the *Canons of the Kings*, the *Didascalia*, and the *Ecclesiastical Canons*.

Cyril III

These canons furnish us with a complete record of the canon law of the Coptic Church. They relate to betrothals, marriages, wills, inheritance, and the precedence of clergy. The canons open with a profession of the Coptic faith, the election and consecration of bishops, the ordination of priests, fasting, the suspension of the clergy, and the rights and privileges of the hegumen. The canons are divided into five chapters: On Baptism, On Marriage, On Wills, On Inheritance, and On the Priesthood.

A second series of canons of Cyril III (1235–43), seventy-fifth patriarch of Alexandria, dates from 1240. These canons are arranged in eighteen sections and are an attempt to restrict even further the power of the patriarch. The canons state that a bishop shall be consecrated for the See of Cairo, and that the patriarch has no right to solicit anything whatsoever from the bishops, priests, monks, and laity. Among the bishops there shall be equality in rights and responsibilities, and the bishops shall assemble once every year to hold a synod. In addition to these canons, Cyril III laid down six conditions under which pious foundations *(awqaf)* might be made. The last part of this series is concerned with ten questions propounded by Christodoulus, bishop of Damietta, and answered by Cyril III. These answers, which are accepted as canon law, pertain to legal matters.

Use of Coptic Canon Law Today

In theory, all the canons set forth in the preceding chapter are accepted and applied, except those prescribing ecclesiastical penalties, which under the circumstances cannot be enforced. In practice, however, there are discrepancies as to the application of the various canons. Again, we must admit that it is difficult to find a consensus of opinion among the theologians of the Coptic Church with regard to the applicability of the canons of the church.

Among the pre-Nicene canons, the *Didascalia* is widely used in the Arabic recension. With regard to the canons of the councils and synods, their application and use depends largely on their availability in Arabic. Thus, for example, the Twelve Canons of Nicea are accepted, although they are not very well known. The Eighty-Four

Canons of Nicea, on the other hand, are rejected by some Coptic theologians. The Canons of Constantinople and Ephesus are accepted, although they are not very well known. Concerning the canons of the synods, those of Ancyra, Neocaesarea, and Laodicea are in use, while those of Gangra, Sardica, and Carthage are not applied. The same rather arbitrary selection with regard to their application pertains to the canons of the doctors of the church. The canons attributed to Athanasius, Hippolytus, Gregory of Nyssa, Cyril, Peter of Alexandria, and Timothy of Alexandria are rarely applied, whereas the canons of Basil are used. About the canons of the Middle Ages, there exists a general feeling that they were written in response to particular historical circumstances and, therefore, that they are not applicable for all times. An exception are the Canons of Cyril III, which form the foundation for the personal status law.

The History of Coptic Theology from the Fifth to the Twentieth Century

The Pre-Chalcedonian Theology

Prior to the Council of Chalcedon, there existed no theological differences between the Church of Alexandria and the Churches of Rome, Constantinople, Antioch, and Jerusalem. The patriarchate of Alexandria had provided the Church with Athanasius, the great champion of Orthodoxy, who was instrumental in the defeat of Arianism at the Ecumenical Council of Nicea in 325. The teachings of Athanasius were upheld, declaring Christ to be consubstantial and co-eternal with God the Father. Cyril of Alexandria, the defender of the use of the title Theotokos, took considerable measures in the excommunication of Nestorius at the Ecumenical Council of Ephesus in 431. Cyril taught the personal, or hypostatic union of the two natures in Christ, holding to the view that after the union, the Logos formed but one nature with the body (*Mia physis tou Logou sesarkomene*). Accompanying Cyril to Ephesus was Shenute, the first and greatest of all the Coptic theologians of the pre-Chalcedonian Church. Shenute of Atripe, a theologian of distinction and originality, was abbot of the large White Monastery west of Suhag, where over two thousand monks lived in the fourth and fifth centuries. He succeeded in making the Coptic dialect of Atripe the literary medium of Egypt for the following centuries. As a theologian, preacher, and abbot, Shenute left a profound mark on Coptic theology and institutions. His literary efforts, namely his letters, ordinances, and sermons, influenced the religious life of the Copts to such an extent that he became known as the great religious reformer of the Coptic Church.

The Council of Chalcedon

Historically speaking, the decisions of the Council of Chalcedon have caused the division of Christianity into Chalcedonian and non-Chalcedonian Churches. The former ones adhered and still adhere to the *Tome of Leo*, the letter sent by Pope Leo I to Flavian, patriarch of Constantinople, in which the pope of Rome sets forth the christological doctrine, according to which Jesus Christ is one person in whom there are two natures, the divine and the human, permanently united, though unconfused and unmixed. In the name of the teachings of Athanasius and Cyril, Dioscorus, patriarch of Alexandria, felt himself unable to accept the christological teachings of the *Tome of Leo* and was exiled to Gangra in Paphlagonia as a result. Consequences of the Chalcedonian schism were serious for the Egyptian Church, for in the wake of the Council, two parties, the Chalcedonians, or Melkites, and the non-Chalcedonians, or Miaphysites, both claimed authority over the Egyptian Church. To this very day, there are two Alexandrian patriarchates, the Greek Orthodox patriarchate (Chalcedonian) and the Coptic patriarchate (non-Chalcedonian).

After having rejected the decrees of Chalcedon, the Egyptian, or Coptic Church condemned the Eutychian and Nestorian heresies and committed itself solely to the first three Ecumenical Councils: Nicea, Constantinople, and Ephesus. Ever since, the Coptic Church has upheld the Miaphysite doctrine against the Melkites, or Chalcedonians. Throughout the ages, the Copts have felt that the definition of Chalcedon contradicted the faith expressed at the Council of Ephesus, wherein a perfect union of Christ's divinity and humanity was determined against the Nestorian heresy. Moreover, it has been felt by several Miaphysite theologians that the duality of natures as expressed in the *Tome of Leo* and affirmed by the Council of Chalcedon has significantly tended to the very Nestorianism condemned at the Council of Ephesus.

Coptic theology has seen in the *Chalcedonense* a statement of belief that expresses the two natures of Christ, each left as separate entities rather than united.

The issue, therefore, that separates the Coptic and other non-Chalcedonian Churches from the Chalcedonians is not so much the case of the 'two natures.' The Copts believe that Christ is of two natures. These, however, became united in the mystery of the Incarnation:

The Incarnation as explained by Miaphysite theologians is the mutual permeation of two natures, appropriation of our nature and the communi-cation of His; in one Person, the Son of God appropriated the human nature to Himself and communicated Himself to man. All that concerns Christ should be applied not to the one or the other nature, but to His entire Person in its unity. All that concerns the human and the divine nature must be referred to that Person of unity.

To sum up, the Coptic Church believes in one nature of the Logos Incarnate. They testify that Jesus Christ is one, true God and true man, possessing the divine as well as the human natures, united in him without confusion and without division. It is this profession that is made by the Coptic Orthodox priest when he celebrates the Divine Liturgy:

> I believe, I believe, I believe, I confess unto my last breath, that this is the life-giving flesh which Thou tookest, O Christ our God, from the Lady of us all, Mary the Mother of God, Thou madest it one with Thy Godhead, without mixture or change; . . . I believe that Thy Godhead was not severed from Thy manhood for one moment, not even for the twinkling of an eye, to give it for us; the redemption and the forgiveness of our sins, and life everlasting, to those who shall partake of it. I believe that it is so in truth. Amen.

The Post-Chalcedonian Theology

The theological efforts after Chalcedon were largely determined by the desire of the Chalcedonians to bring the non-Chalcedonian Churches back into the fold of 'Orthodoxy,' and various methods were used to reach this goal. In the course of his reign, the emperor Zeno issued his famous *Henoticon*, or the "Instrument of Union," a theological treatise addressed to the most reverend bishops and clergy and to the monks and laity throughout Alexandria, Egypt, Libya, and the Pentapolis. This document was carefully drawn up to secure a union between the Miaphysites and the Chalcedonians insofar as it condemned Eutyches and Nestorius and asserted that the Orthodox faith was epitomized in the Nicene-Constantinopolitan Creed together with the Twelve Anathematisms of Saint Cyril. The *Henoticon* omitted all reference to the number of the 'natures' of Christ and made some important concessions to Miaphysitism. Though widely accepted in the east, this document was never counte-nanced in the west.

During the reign of Justinian, all available methods were employed to impose the Chalcedonian decrees on the Copts, yet without any significant success. National feeling in Egypt was so intensely opposed to the *Chalcedonense*, which had become the Imperial Creed, that shortly before the Arab conquest in the seventh century, the Melkite or Chalcedonian patriarch of Alexandria had but two hundred thousand Greeks and officials for his adherents, whereas as many as six million Egyptians acknowledged the non-Chalcedonian faith.

Meanwhile, theological debate concerning the nature of Christ was still carried on within the realm of Egyptian Miaphysitism. There were the Phantasiasts, or Aphthartodocetae, represented by Julian, bishop of Halicarnassus, who maintained that Christ's body from the moment of its conception was endowed with divine attributes, and, therefore, was incorruptible, not of itself liable to death, but liable only as and when he willed. The followers of Severus of Antioch, on the other hand, maintained that the corruptibility of the body of Christ was an essential doctrine of faith, for otherwise the truth of Christ's Passion would be denied.

It is beyond the scope of this chapter to describe all of the many theological divergencies that emerged following Chalcedon. Miaphysite authors reckon there were as many as ten of these miserable sects that continued for more than two hundred years until they were brought back to the Coptic Church by Alexander II (704–29).

Important Coptic theologians of the post-Chalcedonian period were Timothy II (457–77), twenty-sixth patriarch of Alexandria, whose *Responsa Canonica* dealing with disciplinary issues were later incorporated into the set of canon law of the Coptic Church. Pisentius, bishop of Qift and a contemporary of the patriarch Damian (576–605), is alleged to have written a "Letter to the Faithful," which prophesied the Arab conquest. More of an apologetic nature dealing with contemporary heretics are the writings of John, bishop of Burullus. His main concern was the preservation of the pure Miaphysite faith by pointing out the numerous heretical teachings in Egypt that emerged after Chalcedon.

The Theology of the Middle Ages

Little is known about the theological developments in Egypt immediately following the Arab conquest, and whatever we know comes from the literature of isolated theologians rather than from any theological school of thought.

In the seventh century, about a generation after the Arab conquest, a certain priest named Theodore addressed some twenty-three questions to John III, patriarch of Alexandria (680–89). These questions, concerned with speculative and moral theology as well as with biblical exegesis and eschatology, reflect the theological concerns of the seventh century. Interestingly enough, these questions were not of simply an academic nature. Rather, they centered around biblical passages that obviously puzzled the mind of an ordinary priest who sought enlightenment from his patriarch. Interesting for us is the eschatological comment of the patriarch with reference to the fate of the sinners in the Hereafter. While eternal damnation is reserved for the unbaptized, the soul of the Christian who has sinned will be purifed in the purgatorial fire of Hades according to the measure of it sins. This concept of purgatory, though prevalent in the seventh century, has been long abandoned by the Coptic Church. For that matter, one of the distinguishing marks of the Copts, eschatologically speaking, is this non-acceptance of the idea of purgatory.

With the early Middle Ages, Coptic theology changed its language of communication. Whereas Greek and Coptic were commonly used prior to and even for a few centuries after the Arab conquest, by the tenth and eleventh centuries, Arabic became more and more predominant as the *lingua theologica*, though the Coptic language still retained its importance for liturgical purposes. The patriarchs Benjamin I (626–665) and even Alexander II (705–730) sent their Easter messages to the Egyptian churches in Upper and Lower Egypt in Greek.

Coptic theology of the Middle Ages commenced with the writings of Sawirus ibn al-Muqaffa', bishop of al-Ashmunain (tenth century), whose main interest and concern was the religious education of his people in matters pertaining to the Scriptures, Christian doctrine and morals, and the liturgical life. Best known for his *History of the Patriarchs of Alexandria*, Sawirus is the author of some twenty-six theological and historical works in which, among other things, he restates the biblical foundations of the Miaphysite doctrine and the theological issues leading up to the Council of Chalcedon. Aware of the theological ignorance and illiteracy of the Christians of his time, which he explains as due to the decline of the Coptic language as the popular means of communication, the bishop of al-Ashmunain felt himself compelled to write theology for the masses, that is, treatises in the form of articles stating the fundamentals of the Christian faith. In the *Second Book of the Council*, Sawirus engaged in apologetics against the Nestorians and the Mu'tazilites, the latter being an Islamic rationalist movement.

A contemporary and friend of Sawirus ibn al-Muqaffa' who shared his apologetic interests was al-Wadih ibn Raja, a Muslim convert to Christianity who wrote three apologetic works against the teachings of Islam. Some decades later, another convert, 'Abd al-Masih al-Isra'ili, produced three books purposely written to convert his former Jewish fellow believers to Christianity.

An important position in the history of the medieval theology of the

Coptic Church is taken by the three eleventh- and twelfth-century patriarchs, whose writings are considered canonical to this day. These are the thirty-two disciplinary canons of Christodoulus (1047–77), which deal with moral theology, that is, intermarriage with Chalcedonians, the relationship among the ecclesiastical offices, etc. Christodoulus was followed by Cyril II (1078–92), a deeply pious and ascetic patriarch who issued thirty-four canons dealing with contemporary ethical issues. Commencing with a prohibition of simony, the patriarch admonished the members of the clergy to lead a morally exemplary life. More important because of their inclusiveness even than the canonical writings of Christodoulus and Cyril II are the canonical contributions of Gabriel II (1131–45), the seventieth patriarch of Alexandria. Gabriel II issued two series of canons.

The theological contributions of the latter part of the twelfth century were largely determined by the reformatory attempts of Murqus al-Darir ibn Mawhub ibn al-Qanbar. A contemporary of John V, Murqus ibn al-Qanbar instigated numerous reforms, such as the reintroduction of the auricular confession in the Coptic Church and a more frequent participation in the Divine Mysteries. Opposed to the common practice of circumcision prior to baptism, Murqus was determined to change many other traditionally well-established customs. Soon, however, replies to the reformatory zeal of Murqus came forth, most importantly those of the twelfth-century theologian Michael, bishop of Damietta, who is best known for his nomocanon of seventy-two sections, in which he discussed theological, ethical, and administrative problems of his day. A cultural conservative, Michael defended the traditional customs and considered them important criteria by which the Copts distinguish themselves from other Christians and heretics.

During the latter part of the twelfth century and the beginning of the thirteenth century, Butrus Sawirus al-Gamali, bishop of Malig, engaged in polemics and apologetics against the Chalcedonian churches, especially with reference to their theology and practices. In his *Book of the Sunrise*, he attacked the heretical practices of the Franks (Catholics) and other non-Miaphysite Christians. In a second volume, Butrus engaged in a polemic against the teachings of Islam in which the bishop argued for the superiority of Christianity over the faith of the prophet Muhammad. His most important contribution, however, was not so much in the field of theology as in hagiography and liturgiology, for Butrus, together with Mikha'il, bishop of Atrib and Malig, is considered the co-editor of the Coptic Synaxarion.

The thirteenth century is generally considered the age of Coptic theology and Coptic dogmatics, and one of the greatest theologians of the Coptic Church in this period is al-Rashid Abu al-Khayr ibn al-Tayyib. In addition to being both a priest and a physician, Abu al-Khayr also served as a secretary to Taqi al-Din 'Umar al-Muzaffar al-Qadi al-Fadl, who was vizier under Salah al-Din (1193–98). A contemporary of and theological collaborator with Abu Ishaq ibn al-'Assal, Abu al-Khayr's works are predominantly of a polemic nature. His objective is to obtain the sympathy of the infidels and impress them with an admiration for the Christian faith. His most important writings are the *Theriac of Understanding*, the *Summa of the Faith of the Christian Confession and the Reply to the Muslims and Jews*, and finally, the *Demonstration of the Free Will*. His method of argumentation is neither violent nor aggressive, and his procedure is quite different from that of the Jacobite theologian Yahya ibn 'Adi, whose influence on Abu al-Khayr, however, is undeniable. With Abu al-Khayr, philosophy plays a secondary role; it only confirms the established truth. Truth is found in holy scripture, which testifies to its own veracity. The apologetics of Abu al-Khayr are considered the most complete and original contribution by a Coptic theologian writing in Arabic.

A biblical theologian of the thirteenth century was the Armenian monk Butrus al-Sadamanti al-Armani, who lived in the Coptic Monastery of Saint George in Sadamant. Important is his *Commentary on the Gospels*, in which the author discusses the various types of exegesis, including metaphysical, literal, and mystical exegesis. His own method is that of the literal type, insofar as he refuses to accept the allegorical interpretation. On the other hand, his exegesis is largely determined by dogmatic and ethical explanations. A *Discourse on the Faith*, which is a simple statement of the Miaphysite doctrine, was written by the monk at the request of Yusab, bishop of Akhmim. Less significant than Butrus, yet also engaged in exegesis, was Bulus al-Bushi, bishop of Misr. Bulus al-Bushi's major literary contribution was his *Commentary on the Apocalypse*.

The fourth medieval patriarch to participate in the studies of the canon law of the Coptic Church was Cyril III, the seventy-fifth patriarch of Alexandria. His canons furnish us with a complete record of the canon law of the Coptic Church. A collaborator in this work was Bulus al-Bushi, who was a friend of the patriarch.

The thirteenth century produced two other Coptic biblical theologians who contributed in the field of biblical exegesis. Al-Wagih Yuhanna al-Qalyubi wrote a commentary on the Epistle to the Romans, in which he attempted to discover the literal meaning of the text. Ibn Katib Qaysar, generally known as a prominent philologist, is the most important and greatest of all Coptic exegetes, and his interpretations include the whole of the New Testament. Best known is his *Commentary on the Apocalypse.*

The nucleus of thirteenth-century Coptic theology is composed of the three brothers with the family name of Ibn al-'Assal. Al-Safi Abu al-Fada'il ibn al-'Assal, the oldest of the three, was primarily engaged in polemics against Islam and the study of canon law. In apologetic commentaries, al-Safi testifed to the deity of Christ, based on personal experience, the witness of the gospel, the miraculous power of Christ, and the miracles wrought by the apostles in the name of Christ. Another volume is an apology of the New Testament Revelation in which he defends the canon of holy scripture against Islamic reproaches of scriptural forgeries. The apologetic method used by al-Safi is that of the classical dialogue. Well known for his nomocanon, al-Safi's collection of Coptic canon law is considered to be his major contribution. According to al-Safi, human knowledge is twofold: primarily, it is knowledge based on the teachings of the Scriptures; secondly, it is the knowledge based on the deductions of the Scriptures, which are the canons of the church.

Al-Safi's brother Abu al-Farag Hibat Allah ibn al-'Assal wrote between 1231 and 1253. His literary efforts stand out because of his versatility. His *Treatise on the Soul* discusses the psychological and eschatological nature of the soul. The author advocated the belief that souls, though conscious of their destiny during the period between death and resurrection, enter the final state of blessedness or punishment only after reunion with the body. The *Compendium of Inheritance Law* provided a survey of permissible and prohibited marriage relations.

The younger stepbrother of al-Safi and Abu al-Farag was al-Mu'taman Abu Ishaq Ibrahim al-'Assal, a student of philosophy, theology, linguistics, exegesis, homiletics, and liturgies. Abu Ishaq's major effort was his theological *summa*, the *Compendium of the Foundations of Religion*, in five parts and seventy chapters. Written around 1260, this major work of Coptic theology distinguishes itself not only through its systematic structure, but also through its omission of church-historical material. In his approach, Abu Ishaq was strongly influenced by the philosophical-rational presentation of Yahya ibn 'Adi. In addition to his *Compendium*, Abu Ishaq wrote the *Introduction to the Pauline Epistles*, with a concordance and cross-references regarding theology and ethics.

Well known for his contribution to the collection of material for the Synaxarion, Michael, Bishop of Atrib and Malig, also worked in the field of polemics and apologetics. In twelve treatises, Michael provided enlightenment for Muslims in matters concerning predestination, soteriology, and the doctrine of the Eucharist. Moreover, he wrote the *Book on the Religion of Christendom with a Refutation of Islam.*

Also belonging to the middle of the thirteenth century are the writings of al-Nushu' Abu Shakir ibn Butrus al-Rahib, at one time deacon at al-Mu'allaqa, the Church of the Holy Virgin, in Old Cairo. Like many of his predecessors, Abu Shakir centered his attention on the Christology of his church, which he developed from Old and New Testament sources.

Shams al-Ri'asa Abu al-Barakat ibn Kabar, commonly known as Abu al-Barakat, is without a doubt the most prominent and last of the great Coptic-Arabic theologians of the Middle Ages. In his day, the great catastrophe of 1321 occurred, which gave the finishing blow to the Copts. Abu al-Barakat, who had served as secretary to Rukn al-Din Baybars al-Mansuri al-Khitayi, was seized by Muslim authorities, but fortunately protected by the Mamluk prince in whose service he was. After his death (between 1323 and 1335), his writings were largely forgotten, until they were rediscovered by Kircher and Wansleben in the seventeenth century. As a theologian and priest at al-Mu'allaqa Church, Abu al-Barakat wrote the *Lamp of Darkness,* a monumental encyclopedia of theology and ecclesiastical knowledge in twenty-four chapters. Commencing with the central doctrines of the church, that is, the doctrine of the Trinity and the Incarnation, Abu al-Barakat listed the various historical heresies. Helpful to the church historian and theologian was his list of the Coptic canon of holy scripture and his appraisal of Coptic canon law. The latter included a number of spurious documents. As a collection of theological information, Abu al-Barakat's *summa* transcended any previous attempt; indeed, it was the crown of medieval Coptic theology.

A contemporary of Abu al-Barakat, Yuhanna ibn Zachariah ibn Saba' was the author of a textbook of Coptic theology, which may have been used by the candidates for holy orders. His work *The Precious Pearl, the Sciences of the Church* is a theological compendium of 112 chapters dealing with dogmatic and moral theology, as well as liturgical and disciplinary questions.

Then, for about three hundred years, there appeared to be an almost complete silence in the field of Coptic theology, which was interrupted in the eighteenth century by the literary contributions of Ibrahim al-Gawhari (d.1795). As a layman and head of the chancery in Cairo, Ibrahim became well known as a philanthropic and literary contributor to the Coptic Church, especially with regard to the restoration of ancient churches and monasteries and the collection of ancient manuscripts. His major literary production was the *Commentary on the Major and Minor Prophets.*

By the eighteenth century, Coptic theology and apologetics became more and more concerned with the proselytizing work of the Catholic Church. Ever since the seventeenth century, the Catholic Church had worked among the Copts with the purpose of uniting the See of Alexandria with the See of Rome. Thus, Murqus al-Mashriqi answered a letter by a certain Girgis al-Qibti, a Catholic convert, in such a manner that he even influenced Girgis to return to the Miaphysite faith of the Copts. Still more important than this letter are the polemic writings of Yusab, bishop of Girga and Akhmim, a contemporary of John XVIII (1769–96). Condemning the theology and practices of the Catholics, Yusab invited those who had accepted the Catholic faith to return to the teachings of their own church.

During the latter part of the nineteenth century, anti-Catholic polemics gained a new impetus through the writings of Afram 'Adad, known under the pseudonym of the "Monk of Baramus." In addition to a theological compendium, Afraam wrote *A Handbook of Religion* in the form of a dialogue of questions and answers with special reference to the Miaphysite Christology. The same material was later published in a two-volume textbook of Coptic dogmatics. Other writings by the "Monk of Baramus" include a pastoral theology, a church history, and an introduction to the Scriptures.

Coptic Theologians of the Nineteenth and Twentieth Centuries

After the introduction of the printing press by Cyril IV, there emerged an increased and rather intense literary activity among the Copts. Qummus Butrus Muftah (d.1875), a monk of the Monastery of Saint Antony, advocated disciplinary reforms within the church, especially with regard to the practice of excessive fasting, and laid down his arguments in the order of the church and monasticism. 'Aryan Girgis Muftah (d.1886) was one of the principal promoters of the Coptic language in the nineteenth century and wrote two volumes on dogmatics, *The Mystery of the Incarnation* and *The Glittering Pearl of the Divine Mysteries.* The latter study was written in conjunction with Ibrahim Rufa'il al-Tukhi (d.1904), a layman, and attacked the Protestant theology of the American Presbyterian Mission in Egypt, especially with regard to the ministry and the sacraments. Ibrahim Rufa'il al-Tukhi was an active member of several Coptic societies. His book *The Nature of Faith* is an apology of the Miaphysitic dogma, and his *Proofs of the Gospel* upholds the dogma of the perpetual virginity of the Theotokos.

Probably the most important theologian of the nineteenth century was the hegumen Filuthawus Ibrahim (1837–1904). From Tanta, his place of birth, he was called to be a teacher first at Mansura, then in the Coptic College in the Harat al-Saqqa'in. As priest at the patriar-chal cathedral he became well known for his homiletical abilities. He participated in the foundation of the Gami'at al-Tawfiq, was a member of the *Maglis al-milli* (community council), and played a leading role in the banishment of Cyril V in 1892. In his polemics, Filuthawus Ibrahim attacked the Catholic Church, especially in *The Orthodox Evidence against Roman Talk*, in which he discussed the spiritual equality of the apostles and consequently that of the patriarchs. His *Refutation of the Missionary* defends the dogma of the consubstan-tiality of Christ. He was commissioned by 'Ali Mubarak, the founder of the National Library in Cairo, to continue writing the *History of the Patriarchs*, from Athanasius III, the seventy-sixth patriarch, to Cyril V, the 112th patriarch. Thereby he carried on the work begun by Sawirus ibn al-Muqaffa'. Other publications by Filuthawus Ibrahim include his public speeches and sermons and his important studies on personal status laws, as well as his *Catechism of the Coptic Church*. The latter is largely based on the fourteenth-century text *The Precious Pearl* by Yuhanna ibn Zachariah, known as Ibn Saba'. Following the literary example of Filuthawus Ibrahim, Qummus Yuhanna Girgis and Gibran Ni'mat Allah engaged in the composition of liturgical hymnology.

As important as the writings of Filuthawus Ibrahim were the critical and polemical contributions of Girgis Filuthawus 'Awad, an indepen-dent Coptic scholar and author who was deeply concerned with certain reformatory measures within the Coptic Church. In his commentary *A True Word, that the bishops are to be elected from the married clergy*, he questioned the reasons for episcopal celibacy. In other volumes of his *Awakening*, he dealt with practical issues pertaining to the history and programs of the *Maglis al-milli*. His sharp criticisms are principally directed against Cyril V and Anba Yuhanna of Alexandria. In addition to his *Awakening*, he published annually the *Coptic Almanac*. In his crusade against the monastic monopolies within the Coptic Church, Filuthawus 'Awad studied and published the Canons of Cyril III.

In the realm of church history, the nineteenth and twentieth centuries proved to be exceptionally creative. Mikha'il Sharubim (d.1918), a *mufattish*, or inspector in the Ministry of Finance, wrote a comprehensive *Ancient and New History of Egypt* in four volumes (Bulaq, 1889–1900), which was largely inspired by the new era of Muhammad 'Ali and the political developments during the patriar-chate of Cyril IV. *A History of the Coptic Community* (Cairo, 1898) was written by Ya'qub Nakhla Rufa'il (d.1905), who was one of the teachers of Butrus Ghali Pasha. In many ways heavily dependent on Sawirus ibn al-Muqaffa' is the *Summary of the History of the Coptic*

Community (Cairo, 1914) by Salim Sulaiman and the *History of the Coptic Church* (Cairo, 1924) by the deacon Manassa Yuhanna Qummus (d.1930). On the other hand, *The Precious Pearl: A Church History* (2 volumes, Cairo, 1923) by Na'um Efra'im Isidur, a monk of the Monastery of al-Baramus, is a general history of the Christian Church, although seen from a distinctly Coptic perspective. A collection of biographies in *Illustrious and Famous Copts of the Nineteenth Century* (2 volumes, Cairo, 1910, 1913) was composed by Tawfiq Iskarus, the librarian of the National Library and a member of the *Maglis al-milli*. *The Truth about the Copts* is a factual account of the Coptic problem by Yusuf Manqariyus, the director of the Coptic Theological Seminary from 1893 to 1918.

In the beginning of the twentieth century, we notice also a distinct revival of spiritual literature in the Coptic Church. In 1909, there appears the *Precious Pearls: Commentary on the Ecclesiastical Rites and Doctrines of the Faith* by Ibn Shuga' and edited by Ikladiyus Labib (d.1918). The latter had contributed distinct services to the revival of the Coptic language, especially on account of his Coptic editions of the lectionary and the Divine Liturgy. In 1922, Hafiz Dawud, secretary of the Society of the Friends of the Bible, published a commentary on the Divine Liturgy, while Girgis Hanna al-Sharuni and Hanna 'Atiya 'Atallah issued a collection of homilies entitled *Spiritual Sunday Sermons*. Habib Girgis, who succeeded Yusuf Manqariyus as director of the Coptic Theological Seminary in Cairo, wrote altogether more than thirty books, the best known of which are his *Dogmatic Theology, The Mystery of Godliness, The Seven Sacraments of the Church*, and *Practical Ways to Reform the Coptic Church*. Through his religious education lessons for primary and secondary schools, he left a lasting impression on the Coptic Church, especially because of his religious poetry and hymns, some of which are even sung in the Coptic Evangelical Church.

Qummus Mikha'il Mina, the director of the Theological Seminary for Monks at Helwan, is the author of *A Systematic Theology* in three volumes (Cairo, 1933–38). Bishop Gregorius, the foremost theologian of the Coptic Church in the middle of the twentieth century, has published many books. *Spiritual Values in the Dogmas and Rituals of the Orthodox Church* in four volumes (1964–66), *Christological Teaching, The Importance of the Orthodox Dogma to the Spiritual Life, A Plea for the Christians (Apology by Athenagoras)*, and *An Introduction to the Study of Athenagoras* are some of the earlier volumes.

The theological and liturgical studies by Salib Suryal include the *Didascalia, The Canons of the Apostles, The Canons of the Pre-Nicene Church, Engagement, Marriage, and Divorce*, and a study, *On the*

Liturgy. Banua 'Abduh published a commentary on the lectionary of the church, which appeared in 1953, 1954, and 1958.

Abuna Matta al-Maskin, spiritual father of the Monastery of Saint Macarius, is one of the most prolific authors of ascetic, dogmatic, and spiritual Coptic literature. His *Communion of Love* (USA, 1984) presents a non-critical biblicism and is one of his major English works. He has written more than fifty books and brochures on theological, spiritual, and pastoral issues. Pope Shenuda III began publishing Coptic dogmatic and pastoral theology while still bishop for educational institutions. More than ninety titles in spiritual and pastoral theology carry the name of the pope.

The Copts from the Seventh to the Twentieth Century

The Copts and the Arab Conquest

The Arab conquest under 'Amr ibn al-'As, begun in 639, introduced a radically different situation for the Copts, and though at first the Muslim Arabs displayed an appreciable amount of tolerance, soon increasing numbers of Christians accepted the new religion. In this context, the role of Benjamin I, the thirty-eighth patriarch of Alexandria, is a rather significant one, for not only was he the first patriarch who embodied the isolation and self-sufficiency of the Coptic Church, it occurred also during his patriarchate that Islam penetrated into the Nile Valley. By the beginning of the eight century, Arabic became the official language; the first Arabic document of the Nile Valley dates from 709.

One of the most serious consequences of the Arab conquest was the increasing taxation of the Copts by their Muslim rulers. While churches were occasionally destroyed, the religious life as such suffered relatively little. Indeed, it is significant that the Coptic Synaxarion records considerably fewer martyrs for the Islamic period than for the pre-Nicene era. Still, Islamic pressure evoked Coptic resentment, which expressed itself in at least six Coptic insurrections between 725 and 773. The political failure of these revolutions only increased the prestige of the conquerors, so that from that time on, even more Copts accepted the faith of Islam. At any rate, by the ninth century, the Muslims had gained the majority in Egypt, and the decrease in the numbers of Christians caused a parallel decline in the number of dioceses.

The financial pressure exerted on the Copts, the confiscation of ecclesiastical treasures, and the temporary imprisonment of members of the hierarchy were largely responsible for the introduction of the *cheirotonia*, or the payment of sums of money for an ecclesiastical position.

The Copts in the Middle Ages

During the reign of the Tulunids (868–905), the Ikhshidids (935–960), and the Fatimids (969–1171), the Copts experienced a general attitude of tolerance, which, however, was unfortunately interrupted by the violent persecutions of the caliph al-Hakim bi-Amr Allah. Thus during the years 1012–15, many churches and monasteries were destroyed, Christians were persecuted, and Christian public servants were expelled from their government offices. Al-Hakim's successor al-Zahir, however, permitted those who were forced to accept Islam to return to their original faith.

The patriarchate of Christodoulus (1047–77) constituted one of the more significant periods in the history of the Coptic Church. During this period, the Coptic patriarchate was moved from Alexandria to Cairo, a transfer that on the one hand symbolized a certain accommodation to the Fatimid rulers, while on the other hand isolated the Coptic Church even more from the other Oriental churches. The sympathetic attitude of the Fatimids toward the Copts, expressed in their participation in Christian feasts and their unprejudiced employment of Copts in the government, was largely due to their Isma'ili faith, which Egyptian Sunni Muslims never accepted. Both Isma'ilis and Copts represented a religious minority.

With the invasion of Egypt by Shirkuh, Fatimid rule ended and the Ayyubid dynasty came to power, ruling from 1171 to 1250. Although this period is not marked by major persecutions and violence, none of the Ayyubids shared any particularly sympathetic feelings for the Copts. Whereas the Crusaders had challenged the supremacy of Islam, the Copts, as well as the other Oriental Christians, had accepted their minority position, and thus, they had little choice but to play the role of the loyal Christian subject. During the thirteenth century, a brief Christian Arabic renaissance flared in the fields of theology, apologetics, ecclesiastical history, and canon law, yet its impact on the church was hardly noticeable, and Christianity in Egypt rapidly declined under the new rulers, the Mamluks, who took power in 1250 and who had little or no understanding or sympathy for the Christians. Between 1279 and 1447, the Mamluks attempted altogether eight times to expel all Coptic civil servants from government posts. By the fourteenth century, the number of Copts in Egypt had significantly decreased. Moreover, recorded Coptic history came to an end by the fourteenth century. This means that between the fourteenth and the nineteenth centuries we are dependent largely on occasional references by Muslim authors or observations by Western pilgrims and travelers.

The impression one receives during this period from the study of the history of the monasteries, which no doubt reflects in some measure the general conditions of the church, is that the Coptic Church declined sadly and that it had lost almost all of its former spiritual vitality. This spiritual paucity is also reflected in the almost complete absence of theological creativity from the thirteenth to the twentieth century. True, there were no longer any serious persecutions and devastations of Coptic properties, and the Church as a whole was tolerated, yet the *jizya* (poll tax) was collected from the Copts until 1815.

The French Invasion

When Napoleon Bonaparte and his thirty-seven thousand soldiers disembarked in Alexandria on July 1, 1798, the Coptic Church had reached its lowest ebb, both in numbers and in spiritual strength, and, paradoxically enough, for most Christians the situation steadily deteriorated during the three years of French occupation. In order to win the favor of his new subjects, Napoleon proclaimed himself a Muslim, though not a single Egyptian could possibly have trusted his profession of faith. When the news of the French invasion reached Cairo, Copts and European Christians were in great danger. In fact, the suggestion was made in the Ottoman Divan that one of the first measures to be taken should be the extermination of all Christians in Cairo, and it was only the favorable intervention of Ibrahim Bey that saved the Christians from a general massacre. Having taken Alexandria, Napoleon marched toward Cairo, where he defeated the Mamluk forces in the Battle of the Pyramids. Once established in Cairo, he commenced his administration by creating a General Divan, thus securing at least the outward support of the most influential and stable elements in Egyptian society. For the collection of taxes, he retained the hierarchy of the Coptic fiscal agents, which was headed by al-Mu'allim Girgis al-Gawhari. For a brief period, so al-Gabarti points out, Christians and Jews were even seen riding on horseback, though the complaints of the Muslims forced Napoleon to order the Copts and Jews to resume wearing their distinctive turbans, belts, and shoes and to ride donkeys.

The most outstanding Copt during Napoleon's stay in Egypt was Mu'allam Ya'qub Tadrus, who was officially in charge of tax collection in Upper Egypt, but served as the joint commander with General Desaix's expeditionary force in the Upper Egyptian campaign against Murad Bey's Mamluks. In fact, there was hardly a decision Desaix made throughout the campaign without first consulting Ya'qub. And when in the spring of 1800 portions of the Turkish forces under Nasif Pasha overwhelmed the few French troops stationed in Cairo and plunged the city into chaos, only the Coptic quarter, under the capable leadership of al-Mu'allim Ya'qub, held out and thus evaded the invaders' looting and raping. After Napoleon's departure from Egypt, a Coptic legion was formed, and al-Mu'allim Ya'qub became its commanding general. On his way to France, however, the Coptic general died.

Among the most outstanding Copts during the Napoleonic period was Girgis al-Gawhari, who served as minister of finance. Among other accomplishments, he gave the land in Azbakiya to the Coptic Church for the building of the patriarchal cathedral and residence. Another important person was Yusuf Malati, who served in the court. Ilyas Buqtur, who was born in 1774 in Asyut, left a marked impression on learning. At the age of twenty, he joined his uncle, General Ya'qub, and went first to Beni Suef and then to Cairo. After learning French, Buqtur became Napoleon's private secretary and the official interpreter for the French army. He worked with members of the Institut Français, where he was in charge of translations. When the French troops left Egypt, he joined them and became a professor at the National Library in Paris. In 1805, the first French-Arabic dictionary was published, a work in which Ilyas Buqtur had participated. He died in 1811. Antun Abu Taqiya was a wealthy Copt who financed several government projects and served as a government representative in the province of Sharqiya. Filuthawus Hanna occupied the same post in the province of Gharbiya, as did Wasif al-Masri in the province of Minufiya.

Among the Coptic military leaders of the Napoleonic era was General Ya'qub Tadrus, who was born in Asyut in 1761. He was the organizer of the Coptic Legion in Napoleon's army. Commandant 'Abd Allah Mansur was born in Cairo in 1772. He was educated by his father, and when he was old enough, he joined the Coptic Legion. Very soon he was promoted to officer's rank. He participated in Napoleon's European campaigns and was promoted to commandant in 1807. In 1809 he participated in the Paris parade. After the dissolution of the Coptic Legion in 1814, he continued to reside in Paris, where he died in 1831. Colonel Makaryus Hinayn was born in Cairo in 1773. As a youth he worked in his father's jewelry shop. Later, he became an interpreter in the Coptic Legion. He joined the French forces when they left Egypt in August 1801. Promoted to captain and later colonel, he too participated in Napoleon's European campaigns. He was killed in the Battle of Austerlitz in 1805. Colonel Hanna

Hiral, born in Manfalut in 1776, was another officer in the Coptic Legion. In the European wars, Colonel Hiral fought alongside Colonel Gabriel Sidarus. He was awarded the Legion of Honor and killed in the Battle of Austerlitz.

The Reign of Muhammad 'Ali

In the wake of the departure of the French, the Turks seized control of Egypt, and again, as in the case of any governmental change in Egypt, the unfortunate Christians suffered severely. Turkish troops were stationed in the Christian quarters, where they were given the liberty to plunder and seduce. Many Christians were accused of cooperating with the French, and several Copts were put to the sword by the Turkish pasha. Then, in 1805, Muhammad 'Ali rose to power.Through a well-prepared revolt in favor of the Albanian usurper, the *shaikhs* of Cairo elected him pasha and implored him to assume the government, in the hope of putting a stop to the intolerable anarchy that prevailed. A year later an imperial decree confirmed the choice.

During the reign of Muhammad 'Ali, many Christians, Greeks, Armenians, and Copts reached high positions. He chose the most qualified men for his administrative posts regardless of their religion and nationality, and even bestowed upon several Christians the honorary titles of 'bey' and 'pasha.' For many years, his financial adviser was al-Mu'allim Ghali, a Christian who at one time had served as secretary to Alfi Bey. Either because of false accusations or because of Ghali's truthful report on the financial state of Egypt, Muhammad 'Ali issued an order for his assassination. In 1821, in the presence of his son Tobias Bey and Ibrahim Pasha, al-Mu'allim Ghali was executed.

Muhammad 'Ali's knowledge of Turkish led him to employ many Armenian Christians in his government. Boghos Bey Yousoufian, an immigrant from Izmir, first served as economic advisor, later as minister of foreign affairs. Many other advisers to the ruler were Armenians, the most noteworthy of whom were Artin Bey Cherakian, Garabed Noubarian, and Arisdages Altoune Duri; one of the important financiers was Yeghiazar Amira.

For the first half of the nineteenth century, the throne of Saint Mark was occupied by Peter VII (1809–52), the 109th patriarch, who had one of the longest patriarchal reigns. Elected from the monks of the fifth-century Red Sea Monastery of Saint Antony, Peter VII displayed a high character. As patriarch he was much interested in the new developments of his time, always trying to raise the standard of his clergy and laity. The Coptic desert monasteries, which by this time had decreased to seven, welcomed the rule of Muhammad 'Ali, who stabilized the internal situation and restored order to the desert.

Many stories are still related about Peter VII and Muhammad 'Ali. Muhammad 'Ali had a daughter named Zuhra who suffered from a devil. The physicians who had been consulted were unable to do anything for her, and so Muhammad 'Ali approached the patriarch with a request to heal his daughter. Peter recalled that he had a bishop, John of Minufiya, who had the power to cast out devils. Bishop John was delegated to go to Muhammad 'Ali's palace to pray over Zuhra, and while he prayed, the devil came out of her toe in the form of a drop of blood. Then Muhammad 'Ali turned to the bishop and said, "What art thou in need of for thy troubles?" But the bishop replied, "I am not in need of anything." The pasha, however, insisted on repaying the bishop. Then the bishop said, "If thou art really willing to give me what I ask, then I beseech thee that we may build our churches as we please, and that thou mayest treat our Christian sons equally in all positions of government and public life."

During the reign of Muhammad 'Ali the Copts gained an increasing sense of identity, and many Christians were able to develop their skills in business, commerce, and other professions. Though they remained a beleaguered minority, the proportion of Copts among the wealthy and the educated far surpassed their previous numbers.

The Coptic Enlightenment

Following the death of Muhammad 'Ali and his son Ibrahim Pasha in 1848, 'Abbas I, the grandson of Muhammad 'Ali, succeeded his uncle Ibrahim. 'Abbas Pasha ruled for only six years. When he was strangled to death in his own harem in 1854, he was succeeded by Sa'id Pasha, and at least outwardly, the Copts continued to enjoy the same freedom and tolerance accorded them by Muhammad 'Ali. In many respects, the Copts were placed on the same level as the Muslims. Thus, for example, Sa'id Pasha ordered that all Egyptians without distinction of religion should be liable to military service. This meant that for the first time since the Arab conquest Christians were allowed to bear arms. In Asyut, a largely Christian town, all males were conscripted, and not one was left to support his family. Though Sa'id Pasha had intended with his proclamation to put an end to discriminatory legislations, in actuality the decree was used as an instrument of pressure. So uncomfortable was the situation for many Copts that Cyril IV, the 110th patriarch, intervened to have the Copts exempted from military service.

The patriarchate of Cyril IV, who was also known as the Reformer, was one of the most significant milestones in the history of the Coptic

Church. Committed to raising the educational standard of the Copts, he spent his short reign as patriarch establishing schools. At the age of twenty-three, he had entered the Monastery of Saint Antony, where he was known as Abuna Dawud al-Antuni. After two years, he was elected hegumen, and soon afterward he inaugurated a school for monks at the Antonian dependency in Bush near Beni Suef. In 1853, Dawud was consecrated metropolitan of Babylon (Cairo) on the understanding that if he proved himself worthy, he would be shortly afterward elected to the patriarchate. In 1854, Cyril ascended the patriarchal throne, and though his pontificate lasted only seven years, more than two of which he spent in Ethiopia, he initiated lasting reforms. In 1855, the Coptic Patriarchal College was opened, followed by two girls' schools in Azbakiya and in Harat al-Saqqa'in and a boys' school in the latter district. In addition to arithmetic, geography, and science, special attention was paid to the study of languages, which included Arabic, Coptic, Turkish, French, Italian, and English. Moreover, Cyril was responsible for one of the first private Arabic printing presses in Egypt. The candidates for the Coptic priesthood were summoned by Cyril to the patriarchate, where either he or Qummus Girgis, his assistant, taught them.

In addition to establishing schools, Cyril IV also rebuilt the patriarchal cathedral in Azbakiya. At this time, an iconoclastic controversy emerged within the Coptic Church, and Cyril, who considered his people guilty of idolatry, prohibited the display of icons in the cathedral. In Cairo and Asyut many Coptic icons were publicly burned, whereby no doubt many valuable objects of medieval Christian art were destroyed.

Throughout his pontificate, Cyril consolidated the Christian communities in Egypt, thus effecting some understanding between the Greek, Coptic, and Anglican communions. His dynamic character and his efficient thoroughness soon attracted the attention of the authorities, who had him quietly removed. He died on January 31, 1861.

Cyril IV was succeeded by Demetrius II (1862–70), at one time hegumen of the Monastery of Saint Macarius in Wadi al-Natrun. His pontificate was uneventful, except for the rather widespread Coptic response to the American United Presbyterian Mission in the Nile Valley, especially in Asyut and Minya. Dissatisfied with the spiritual laxity and political intrigues within the Coptic Church, many educated Copts joined the Protestant Mission churches. Demetrius, realizing the potential danger in the rapid growth of the Protestants, excommunicated the members of the heretical church, thereby creating a most unfortunate ecclesiastical atmosphere, which to some extent has prevailed to this day.

Demetrius II entertained very cordial relations with the respective heads of state, Saʻid Pasha, the khedive Ismaʻil, and the sultan ʻAbd al-ʻAziz. On the occasion of the visit of the sultan, the patriarch kissed the sultan's breast. Questioned about it later, he replied, "The king's heart is in the hand of the Lord" (Prov. 21:1). The sultan bestowed upon him one thousand feddans, and the khedive added another five hundred feddans.

The Emergence of the Laymen's Movement

The *Maglis al-milli* ('religious council') is the general council of the Coptic Church, which corresponds in structure and function to the idea of a general church community council. The first *Maglis al-milli* was elected in 1874 to share with the patriarchate the burden of supervising the financial and civil affairs of the Copts. The *Maglis al-milli* consisted of twelve lay members and twelve submembers, to be elected by the people every five years.

Throughout its existence, however, the organization of the *Maglis al-milli* was the subject of many disputes between the laity, the clergy, and the patriarch. Whereas some considered the council an auxiliary organization to the patriarchate, which would not necessarily conflict with the canon law of the Coptic Church, others rejected this idea and held that such a council would constitute an interference of the laity in the authority vested in the clergy or the patriarch.

The Coptic *Maglis al-milli* was organized with the permission of the government with which the council's constitution was registered. This constitution, however, has undergone many changes. Thus, the original constitution, which was accepted on May 14, 1885, was changed on December 31, 1908; on February 12, 1912; and on June 22, 1927.

In 1874, Egypt was ruled by the khedive Ismaʻil. The laws in force in Egypt gave all non-Muslims the right to apply their own laws pertaining to personal status. This right gave the Copts the opportunity to have their own courts in which their canon law could be applied. This then demanded a council with jurisdictional powers that could apply the canon law in such personal affairs as marriage, divorce, adoption, and inheritance.

When the idea of a *Maglis al-milli* crystallized, Butrus Ghali Pasha wrote a letter to the khedive on February 2, 1874, asking for his permission. The letter said that the Coptic community felt that in order to improve its affairs, a council of laymen should be elected to supervise the Coptic *awqaf,* churches, schools, press, and benevolences, and that this council was to consist of twelve members and twelve submembers, who would be elected by general suffrage. A letter of acceptance of those proposals by the khedive (February 5, 1874) was received, and the first *Maglis al-milli* was elected in November 1874. But unfortunately, this council did not function for a long time, for it was soon dissolved on account of disputes that arose between the members of the clergy and the laity.

In 1883, the Coptic community requested that Cyril V, the 112th patriarch of Alexandria, and the government permit them to elect a new *Maglis al-milli*, which subsequently was reorganized on March 22, 1883. The first constitution of the *Maglis al-milli* was passed on May 14, 1883, by the order of the khedive. This constitution dealt with the organization of the council and its respective functions and settled its relationship with the patriarchate.

Cyril V (1875–1927)

Immediately following his enthronement, the patriarch rejected the idea of having a *Maglis al-milli*, and since he intended to be the sole authority in all matters pertaining to the Coptic Church, the council was dissolved. The council members were able to strive for their rights and responsibilities, however, and the *Maglis al-milli* was reinstated on March 22, 1883. At the time of the re-election of the *Maglis al-milli* on June 30, 1892, it faced many disputes with the patriarch and the clergy, who did not approve its election. As a result, the members of the *Maglis al-milli* requested the government to intervene and force the patriarch to resign from the chairmanship of the council. The patriarch, however, insisted on his rights, and, as a consequence, he was exiled by the Holy Synod and the *Maglis al-milli* to the Monastery of al-Baramus for a period of five months, after which he returned to Cairo. Yet disputes between the patriarch and the laity continued. The patriarch, however, was able to regain some of his prerogatives by having the changes to the 1883 constitution passed by the government in the new constitutions of 1908 and 1912. But the laity struggled until their rights were restored by the constitution of 1927. The heads of the respective monasteries had refused to allow the monastic *awqaf* to be administered by the *Maglis al-milli*, whereupon the *Maglis al-milli* eventually resorted to filing suit against the head of each monastery, which culminated in the 1927 constitution's reinstating the *Maglis al-milli* to its previously established functions.

Cyril V died on August 7, 1927, at the time of the passing of the new constitution.

John XIX (1928–42)

John XIX, the 113th patriarch of Alexandria, was first appointed in 1927 as *locum tenens*. He issued an effective system for the *awqaf*, which, at least in the beginning, satisfied both the members of the clergy and the *Maglis al-milli.* His idea was to establish a committee to supervise the *awqaf,* which in turn should be responsible to the patriarch and the *Maglis al-milli.* This committee was to consist of three laymembers of the *Maglis al-milli* and two bishops. In 1932, however, the committee was abandoned.

Macarius III (1942–45)

Macarius III, the 114th patriarch of Alexandria, was much interested in improving relations with the members of the *Maglis al-milli.* On February 22, 1944, he sent a report to the council containing several suggestions for reform. His reforms were mainly concerned with administrative improvements of the *awqaf.*

He suggested that a committee should be elected by the *Maglis al-milli* and approved by the patriarch and that the committee should present a report on the budget of the *awqaf* to the patriarch. According to this system, the income of the *awqaf* was to be distributed among the monasteries for the education of the monks. The members of the council, however, rejected this proposal because it was believed that this system of administration would give all authority to the patriarch.

Joseph II (1946–56)

At the time of his election, Joseph II promised the members of the *Maglis al-milli* that he would give them the supervision of the monastic *awqaf* without any interference by the clergy. But the patriarch did not fulfill his promises and renounced the rights of the council to supervise the monastic *awqaf.*

The Coptic community grew more and more rebellious against the patriarch, demanding that he resign. Finally, after pressure by the Holy Synod and the *Maglis al-milli,* the patriarch was deposed. At the same time, however, the responsibilities for personal status law passed from the *Maglis al-milli* to the government. On September 20, 1955, an attempt on the life of the patriarch was made by a certain 'Abd al-Masih Basha, a member of the Society of the Coptic Nation. On November 13, 1956, Joseph II died.

Cyril VI (1959–71)

Following his election to the patriarchate, Cyril VI declared in his message to the Coptic Church that he was determined to cooperate with the *Maglis al-milli* for the good of the people and the clergy. By this time, however, the *Maglis al-milli* no longer enjoyed its initial rights and responsibilites. In 1960, a law was passed by the government that stated that all Coptic *awqaf* were to be placed under the supervision of a special committee.

The importance of the *Maglis al-milli* decreased, as many of the original functions of the council had become obsolete on account of the policies of the Arab Socialist Union, which was constituted on December 7, 1962. Four years later, Pope Cyril VI issued a decree for all Coptic priests to attend the seminars on Arab Socialism. In May 1968 the Arab Socialist Congress was held in the al-Mu'allaqa Church of the Holy Virgin in Old Cairo. Cyril VI and the members of the Coptic hierarchy supported the Arab Socialist Manifest of March 30, 1968. Upon presidential order the *Maglis al-milli* was dissolved in 1962.

Shenuda III (1971–)

Two years after his enthronement, Shenuda III resolved the conflict between the *Maglis al-milli* and the church administration. He ensured that the monthly meetings of the *Maglis al-milli* were to be chaired by him. To encourage efficient operation of the council he divided its responsibilities into six subcommittees: public relations, construction works, legal affairs, financial affairs, rural development, and education. Moreover, he encouraged women to be candidates for the *Maglis al-milli*, and since 1991 several women have been elected to participate in the work of the council. Shenuda III also ordered that the laity be actively involved in the administration of each parish. He proclaimed, "The laity have the right to air their views, but not to govern the church!"

The British Occupation: Expectations and Frustrations

In order to evaluate and appreciate the situation of the Coptic Church in the mid-twentieth century, it is imperative to understand the contributions its members have made to the cause of freedom and independence. Throughout the nineteenth century and the first decades of the twentieth century, Coptic notables played an important role in political developments in Egypt. The history of the Coptic Church in this period was largely determined by the devoted laymen rather than by the patriarchate.

In the summer of 1882, the British under Sir Garnet Wolsely landed their troops at Ismailia, and soon afterward they defeated the rebellious Egyptian forces under the fellah officer Ahmad 'Urabi in the battle of Tell al-Kabir. The Copts, who anticipated a new era of freedom, rejoiced at the coming of the British, a Christian nation. The financial chaos, the agitation and disorder under the reign of Isma'il Pasha, and 'Urabi Pasha's proclamation that Islam in Egypt was endangered by the increasing foreign participation in government all caused the Copts to be well disposed towards the arrival of the British. The Copts had hoped that the British would represent and safeguard their interests in the political field, thus providing here and there favorable treatment for their fellow believers. The Egyptian Christians were soon to realize, however, that the British were more concerned with a just and impartial administration than in engaging in a nineteenth-century crusade. Aware of the explosive atmosphere, the British felt that they had to pacify the demands of the Muslim majority, even at the expense of the Copts. The British government officials who administered Egypt were not zealous missionaries, and while they were manipulating for the preservation of internal peace, Muslim demands were frequently granted. In return, the Copts became more and more impatient as they saw their position and influence deteriorating, in spite of the fact that their country was occupied by fellow Christians. The Coptic grievances under Lord Cromer's and, later, under Sir Eldon Gorst's administration increased to the point that a Coptic congress was held in Asyut in 1911. The government, fearing that the meeting might agitate the public, advised Cyril V to publish a patriarchal proclamation suggesting moderation and counseling the inadvisability of the meeting in Asyut. Notwithstanding all difficulties, the congress was held as originally intended. A committee of seventy representatives of the different provinces was formed, and George Bey Wisa was chosen president, Khalil Bey Ibrahim and Dr. Akhnukh Fanus vice presidents, and Mr. Andarawus Bishara treasurer. Other notables participating in the executive committee were Bushra Hanna Pasha, Tawfiq Bey Doss, Ilyas Bey 'Awad, Mikha'il Effendi Fanus, Fakhri Bey 'Abd al-Nur, 'Abd al-Masih Bey Musa, Murqus Effendi Fahmi, and Murqus Hanna Pasha. The grievances were discussed under the following headings:

1. As a Christian body of people, the Copts are forced to violate the commandments of their religion by Sunday labor. The Congress requests that government officials be exempted from duty and students from study on the Sabbath.
2. A large number of administrative posts in government service are entirely closed to Copts, and it is felt that in general they are not promoted in accordance with their capabilities and merit.
3. Under the existing electoral system in Egypt, the Copts are left unrepresented on the provincial councils.
4. The Copts have no equal right to take advantage of the educational facilites provided by the new provincial councils.
5. The Copts claim that government grants should be bestowed upon deserving institutions without invidious distinctions on the basis of race or creed.

Throughout the first decade of the twentieth century, nationalist and anti-British feelings increased steadily. The Nationalist Party under Mustafa Kamil (1874–1908) claimed that Egypt was ready for self-government. In 1907, Lord Cromer resigned from his post as British consul-general, leaving Egypt in a state of unexampled material prosperity. He was succeeded by Sir Eldon Gorst, whose installation of political freedom, however, was regarded as negligible. During the British administration, one of the most brilliant sons of the Coptic nation, Butrus Ghali Pasha, served his country. Following the resignation of Mustafa Fahmi, Butrus Pasha assumed the post of prime minister. Though accused of pro-British sympathies, he is considered by the Copts to have had only Egyptian interests in mind in all of his principal policy decisions, such as the Sudan question, the Dinshaway incident, and the Suez Canal concessions.

Toward Independence: The Wafd

The desire to have 'Egypt for the Egyptians' was always a cherished dream among the Copts. Inspired by the nationalistic sentiments of Mustafa Kamil and later by Sa'd Zaghlul, Copts and Muslims joined in common purpose against the British administration. It was the first time in the history of Egypt that cross and crescent appeared on the same flag. Coptic priests paraded arm in arm with the Muslim ulema through the streets of Cairo, while Abuna Sargius, one of the most dynamic Coptic priests of the time, preached regularly from the pulpit of the tenth-century mosque at the University of al-Azhar, the center of Islamic learning and orthodoxy.

Again it should suffice to mention some of the most outstanding Copts who actively participated in the Wafd. Most prominent were Wasif Ghali, Wisa Wasif, George Bey Khayyat, and Murqus Hanna. Other important Copts serving in the Wafd included Yusuf Sulaiman Pasha, Sinut Bey Hanna, and 'Aziz Antun. For many years, the Wafd was led by Nahhas Pasha, a Muslim notable, who, together with the Copt Makram 'Ubayd Pasha, emerged as the leader of the nationalist movement. In 1922, Egyptian independence was proclaimed, and in January 1924 Zaghlul Pasha formed his cabinet, in which two Copts served: Murqus Hanna, as minister of public works, and Wasif Ghali, as foreign minister. By 1940 Nahhas Pasha and Makram 'Ubayd Pasha faced insurmountable difficulties in the leadership of the party, which subsequently led to its general disintegration.

The Wafd was a short-lived yet highly significant movement, in which for the first time since the seventh century, the Copts could openly manifest their nationalist feelings and play a decisive role in the patriotic struggle for freedom and independence.

The Patriarchates of Joseph II and Cyril VI

The middle of the twentieth century saw one of the major crises in the Coptic Church. From 1942 to 1944, Joseph II, at one time bishop of Girga in Upper Egypt, served as *locum tenens*, or acting patriarch. In May 1946 he ascended the patriarchal throne, beginning a pontificate as turbulent and restless as his political environment. Often indecisive and weak, Joseph II was unable to settle the many feuds and power struggles within the Coptic Church. Corruption within the hierarchy had reached an unbelievable height. In the shadow of the patriarch, there always stood Malik, an unlettered but shrewd Upper Egyptian fellah who served as the patriarch's valet. His political power increased as he managed all relations between the bishops, priests, and laity on one hand, and the feeble patriarch on the other hand. For all intents and purposes, Malik was the *eminence grise*, who, so it is reported, sold at least sixteen of the nineteen episcopal appointments made during the pontificate of Joseph II.

Accusations against the patriarch for his practices of simony and immorality appeared repeatedly in the local press, and in July 1954, a group from the *Umma Qibtiya* (Society of the Coptic Nation) demanded the patriarch's resignation. On July 25, 1954, the Coptic protest culminated in the kidnapping of the 115th successor of Saint Mark. When he refused to abandon his throne, he was forced into a taxi and driven to the Coptic Convent of Saint George in Old Cairo. The police intervened, however, and the patriarch returned to the patriarchal residence. Fourteen months later, Joseph II narrowly escaped assassination, and shortly afterward, the patriarch was officially banished by the Holy Synod and the *Maglis al-milli*. On September 21, 1955, Gindi 'Abd al-Malik, the Coptic minister of supply, announced that the government had agreed to relieve the patriarch of his powers in response to the wishes of the Coptic people; the leaders of the church, after all, agreed that His Holiness was not fit to execute his duties. A few days later, the sickly and disabled patriarch was sent to the al-Muharraq Monastery of the Holy Virgin in al-Qusiya, and a triumvirate of bishops was elected to administer the affairs of the patriarchate. On November 14, 1956, Joseph II died, and Bishop Athanasius of Beni Suef was elected *locum tenens*.

Several times the Copts had nominated candidates for the position of the patriarch, but each and every time the candidates did not meet some of the stipulated requirements. Thus, the patriarchal See of Saint Mark had remained vacant for two and a half years when on Sunday, April 19, 1959, the altar lot was cast in favor of Abuna Mina Mutawahhid al-Baramusi, who became Cyril VI.

Cyril VI was born in 1902 in Tukh al-Nasara, a small village in the Delta province of Gharbiya, where the Monastery of al-Baramus has its dependency. As a young boy, he attended the primary school at Damanhur and a secondary school in Alexandria. It was during his days in Alexandria, while working for Thomas Cook and Sons, that he began reading *The Lives of the Desert Fathers*, an experience that determined the course of his life. At the age of twenty-five, he approached John XIX, the 113th patriarch of Alexandria, with the request to enter the Monastery of al-Baramus. Here he became attached to and influenced by the famous monk Abuna 'Abd al-Malik al-Mas'udi, who became his spiritual father. In 1931, he was ordained and assumed the monastic name of Mina al-Mutawahhid al-Baramusi. For two years, he attended the Theological Seminary for Monks at Helwan. Believing that he was called to the solitary life, Abuna Mina again visited the patriarch with the request to be permitted to restore the ancient White Monastery near Suhag in Upper Egypt. But after a short stay, he was ordered to return, and so he moved to a cave in the vicinity of the Monastery of al-Baramus, where he spent his most formative years. This cave previously had been occupied by Abuna Sarabamun, who was well known for his strict ascetic practices and who had died just before Abuna Mina's arrival. In the desert, miles away from civilization, the man who would be patriarch met with the prophet of the desert, Abuna 'Abd al-Masih al-Habashi.

In 1936, the anchorite again approached the patriarch, this time asking his permission to rebuild the ancient Shrine of Saint Menas in the Desert of Mareotis. Permission was refused, and from 1936 to 1942, Abuna Mina retreated to Gabal al-Guyushi, east of Old Cairo, where he inhabited one of the deserted Napoleonic windmills. The first few months he spent building his cell and a small church. Nights he slept on the floor in coarse sackcloth. One day, Pope John XIX climbed up the mountain to visit the hermit in his deserted windmill. On his way to the anchorite, he broke his patriarchal staff, the symbol of his office. As he arrived at the abode of Abuna Mina, the hermit offered to repair the staff. But the patriarch gave his staff to the monk and refused to take it back, indicating that this staff would now be his.

During the Second World War, the British, believing the desert monk to be a spy, forced him to leave his solitary abode. Abuna Mina came down from the hills, and for the following years he stayed in one room in Old Cairo. It was during this time that he was appointed hegumen of the Monastery of Saint Samuel at al-Qalamun.

In April 1959, the electors of the Coptic Church from Egypt, Ethiopia, Jerusalem, and the Sudan gathered in Cairo to elect three of the five candidates for the patriarchal throne. Disagreement and disappointment with the candidates caused considerable uneasiness among the electors, and twenty-two of the twenty-four members of the *Maglis al-milli* as well as five bishops abstained from voting. Damian al-Muharraqi, Angelus al-Muharraqi, and Mina were the three candidates whose names were placed on the altar of Saint Mark's Cathedral. On April 19, 1959, a five-year-old deacon was led to the altar to select the name of the future patriarch. According to apostolic practice (Acts 1:26), the law of chance and a child's hand were about to end several years of turmoil for the Copts by electing a new patriarch. Immediately after his election and enthronement, Cyril VI devoted his attention to several major problems in the church: the Ethiopian problem, the quest for greater unity among the Copts, and the issue of the *awqaf*, which had been a stumbling block in the life of the church for seventy years. Moreover, a dream the patriarch had entertained for many years was fulfilled when on November 27, 1959, he laid the cornerstone to the ninth monastery of the Coptic Church, the Monastery of Saint Menas at Maryut.

Cyril VI enjoyed good relations with the government. During his pontificate the religious courts for Muslims and Copts were abolished. While he was pope and patriarch, Cyril VI remained a monk and depended on the advice of Bishop Samuel, Bishop Shenuda, and Bishop Gregorius for his administrative duties.

Four important events occurred during his pontificate. On July 24, 1965, President Nasser laid the cornerstone for the Cathedral of Saint Mark in 'Abbasiya. Beginning on April 2, 1968, and continuing for several months after, the Holy Virgin Mary appeared on the roof of the Church of Saint Mary in Zaytun. On July 24, 1968, the relics of Saint Mark the Evangelist, a gift of the Roman Catholic Church, arrived in Cairo. On the following day the Cathedral of Saint Mark was ceremoniously dedicated and consecrated. The political and economic consequences of the Six-Day War of 1967 united Copts and Muslims against the threat of foreign aggression. The relations of Cyril VI with Shaikh Hasan Ma'mun, the rector of al-Azhar University, were very cordial. During Lent of 1967 the pope consecrated the holy myron for the twenty-sixth time in the history of the Coptic Church. On March 9, 1971, at the age of sixty-nine, Cyril VI died. His body reposes in the crypt of the Cathedral of Saint Menas in Maryut.

The Patriarchate of Shenuda III

Born in Abnub on August 3, 1923, Shenuda III was baptized Nazir Gayyid. Shortly after his birth, his mother died, leaving him with five sisters and two brothers. He attended school in Damanhur, Banha, and Cairo. From Cairo University he received a B.A. in history and English. He graduated from the Theological Seminary with a B.D. and was appointed there as a lecturer in the Old and New Testaments. While the archdeacon Habib Girgis was the founder of the Coptic Sunday Schools, Nazir Gayyid extended this ministry and became the founder of the youth meetings of the Coptic Church. He regularly provided articles for the Sunday School magazine; they were later published in *The Release of the Spirit*.

On July 18, 1954, he joined the Monastery of the Syrians in Wadi al-Natrun, where Anba Tawfilus, the abbot, gave him the name Antonius. Here he spent his days reading patristics and church history. For several years he lived in a cave three kilometers from the monastery. In 1959, Cyril VI appointed him to be his personal secretary. He returned to the desert, however, this time choosing a cave some ten kilometers from the monastery.

In September 1962, Cyril VI summoned him to the patriarchate in Cairo. As he bowed his head to receive the blessings, Cyril VI laid his hands on him and consecrated him bishop for theological education and Sunday schools. By 1969, the number of full-time students at the Theological College had increased from one hundred to 207. As bishop for education, Shenuda began his weekly spiritual meetings answering questions on theological and social topics. As he was still attached to the monastic life, Bishop Shenuda spent half the week in Cairo lecturing and preaching, and the other half in the desert in prayer.

Following the death of Cyril VI on March 9, 1971, the Holy Synod planned on March 22 for the election of a successor. On October 29 the names of three candidates were presented. On Sunday, October 31, after the Divine Liturgy, young, blindfolded Ayman Munir Kamil selected one of the three names from a small box on the altar and presented the paper to Metropolitan Antonius. He unfolded it and declared God's chosen shepherd to be Shenuda, who was proclaimed the 117th successor of Saint Mark. On November 14, 1971, Shenuda was enthroned as pope and patriarch of the See of Saint Mark. As a result of the unprecedented increase in the number of churches and their geographical expansion in the past three decades, Shenuda III consecrated large quantities of the holy myron during Lent in 1981, 1987, 1993, and 1995. These ceremonies took place in the Monastery of Saint Bishoi.

Political agitation and misunderstandings led President Sadat to issue a presidential decree on September 3, 1981, discharging Shenuda III of his pontifical duties and ordering his exile to the Monastery of Saint Bishoi. On January 2, 1985, President Mubarak revoked Sadat's decree, and Shenuda III returned to Cairo.

The ecumenical discussions with the Roman Catholic, Eastern Orthodox, and Oriental Churches led to a general acceptance of Cyril of Alexandria's christological confession, the 'one nature of the incarnate Word.' Realizing that the renaissance of the church depended on the rejuvenation of monasticism, Shenuda III ordered the rebuilding and occupation of the formerly deserted monasteries and convents in the Nile Valley. His desert pontifical residence was established at the rear of Saint Bishoi's Monastery, where he still spends half of the week in contemplation and reflection.

On account of the massive exodus of Copts to Europe, America, and Australia, Shenuda III responded with an extensive overseas ministry. There are over eighty Coptic churches, two theological colleges, and a monastery in the United States and Canada; twenty-five churches, a theological college, three schools, and two monasteries in Australia; and thirty churches and two monasteries in Europe. Seven bishops have been consecrated for the overseas dioceses. In order to retain relations with the overseas Copts, Shenuda III has regularly visited the Coptic churches all over the world. In the course of his pontificate, the Holy Synod has increased to almost eighty metropolitans and bishops.

The Copts and the National Struggle

The Copts considered themselves very loyal and nationalist Egyptians, and there are still many Copts who point with pride to their pharaonic ancestry. Whereas for many centuries there was little or no opportunity for the Copts to demonstrate their patriotic convictions, the twentieth century has provided many occasions for individual Copts as well as for the Coptic community to identify with the national struggle and aspirations. In the fight against the British occupation, which started in 1882, the Copts played a significant role. The principal party to uphold the banner of cross and crescent against the British was the Wafd, a truly nationalist movement in which both Muslims and Christians joined. Nationalist demonstrators marched behind banners displaying the cross and crescent, and in the final phases of resistance against the British from 1919 to 1920, Muslim-Christian rapprochement was greater than it had ever been before.

Thirty years later, Egypt was again passing through critical moments in the struggle for national sovereignty, and again, the Christians of Egypt did not hesitate to join with their Muslim fellow citizens in loyalty for their homeland. With the revolution of July 23, 1952, religious liberty was officially proclaimed. The leaders of the new regime were determined to abolish all kinds of discrimination on the basis of race, language, and religion. On October 15, 1952, the president declared: "the minorities are like jewels, which are rare and therefore they are precious. It is the unity of all elements of the nation that constitutes its power." On September 10, 1952, Coptic New Year's Day, the commander-in-chief insisted on personally presiding at the celebrations conducted at the Coptic patriarchate, and very soon these festivities were transformed into a patriotic manifestation of understanding and harmony.

In the same year, Dr. Mahmud 'Azmi, the Egyptian delegate to the United Nations, stated in connection with the United Nations Charter:

> Islamic law rejects all kinds of religious persecution. By participating in the elaboration of this text [the charter], Egypt wishes to safeguard most fully religious liberty. Article Twelve of the last Egyptian Constitution, which sanctions the liberty of religion, does not merely mean that every individual can embrace any religion, but that he can freely pass from one religion to another.

On the occasion of Coptic Christmas in January 1953, the Egyptian president addressed the Christians of Egypt with the following message:

> It is particularly agreeable to me on this feast to present to the members of the Christian community of Egypt and to the Christians of the whole world my best wishes of happiness and prosperity. While hearing today the sound of the bells recalling the eternal message of Christ, I express the wish to see peace and prosperity rule amongst peoples, and I beseech the Almighty that He may make this message come true, because more than ever, the present world is in need of goodwill and peace . . . .

Two years later, Shaikh Ahmad H. al-Baquri sent the following Christmas message to the Copts:

> All citizens, whether Muslims or Christians, have the right to celebrate this feast with joy and respect. They must seek in this feast an example which incites them to work and an impulse which pushes them to peace in the heart, to its purification from all feelings of hatred, to love and harmony instead of competition and war. The Lord Christ had an abhorrence of all racial fanaticism and spirit of castes. Opposed to such sentiments, He called on all men to approach one another in kindness and friendship, to unite in love and humility, and to live in understanding and peace. Such is the appeal of God to men through the voice of His prophets.

At the time of the Suez War in October and November of 1956, the Copts rallied again to express their loyalty to their homeland, which was threatened by the enemy. On October 4, 1956, a large public demonstration took place in the Coptic Orthodox patriarchate, at which both Islamic and Christian leaders proclaimed an 'Islamic-Christian union' in the face of the grave situation following the nationalization of the Suez Canal. The Christian minority, representing all denominations, affirmed its patriotism through official spokespersons. The meeting was held under the sign of the crescent surmounted by the cross. Again, many *shaikhs* could be seen together with members of the clergy. The meeting was opened with the Lord's Prayer, followed by speeches by Mr. Iskandar Damian, vice president of the *Maglis al-milli*; Shaikh al-Baquri, the minister of *awqaf* at that time; and the Reverend Father Henri Ayrout s.j., who declared:

Today there are no more foreign influences to trouble relations between Egyptians. We are members of the same family; the time has come to establish a dialogue between brothers in order to eliminate the griefs, misunderstandings, and quarrels which exist between Christians and Muslims, as those which can exist in the best families and which are simply caused by selfishness, ambitions, and fears, three elements which are inherent in human nature. The Egyptian nation must neither be a gathering of dispersed elements nor the kind of unity in which the strong swallows up the weak, but rather a living and harmonious body where everyone knows his duties and his rights under the same sun which God created. A Christian must remain a Christian, so must the Muslim remain a Muslim. Everybody must enter deeply into his religion, but with trust and sincerity, like the black and red are united by the symbolic white color in the flag of the revolution.

From 1956 onward, the identification of the aspirations of the Coptic hierarchy with those of the government became increasingly pronounced. Official statements by the patriarch and the bishops with respect to their support of the internal and foreign policies of the government could be read regularly in the newspapers. On July 24, 1965, President Nasser laid the cornerstone of the new Cathedral of Saint Mark in 'Abbasiya, Cairo. In his speech, the president said, "Christians and Muslims have always lived as brothers, and the Quran referred to this fact." Moreover, he pointed out that "when Islam came to Egypt, amity continued to prevail among Christians and Muslims." Repeatedly, the president emphasized that there is "no distinction between a Muslim and a Christian, and that everyone has the same opportunities and responsibilities offered to him." In reply, Cyril VI, pope and patriarch of Alexandria, pledged his full allegiance to the government, and the official proclamations of the patriarch became more numerous. In them he condemned the American involvement in Vietnam, imperialism and colonialism in Africa, and racism in Israel. He also decreed the introduction of studies in socialism for the Coptic clergy.

At the occasion of the third Arab-Israeli war in June 1967, jubilant masses assembled in the Cathedral of Saint Mark in Cairo and in other Coptic churches. Islamic and Coptic dignitaries jointly hailed the 'holy war' as willed by God and therefore destined to be crowned by victory. These religious-political demonstrations for national solidarity should not be regarded simply as unpremeditated, spontaneous acts produced by the crisis. For several months, Cyril VI had proclaimed the basic identity of the goals of the Christian Gospel with the aspirations of the Arab Socialist Union. For years, the Christmas and Easter messages of Cyril VI upheld the right and the responsibility of the Arabs to liberate Palestine from the imperialists and the Zionists. As in every national crisis, the Copts stood solidly behind the government.

Ever since the military catastrophe of the Six-Day War of 1967, the Coptic leadership under Bishop Samuel increased its antisemitic pronouncements at every possible occasion. The Jews, as "murderers of God," would eventually experience the same fate as that of the Roman emperor Julian (363), who died fighting against the Persians! Problems arose for the Copts in their use of the term 'Israel,' since the Arabic language lacks the distinction between the modern inhabitants of Israel and their biblical predecessors. The *Isra'iliyun* are the Old Testament Jews as well as the inhabitants of the Zionist State. Because of this problem, Copts tried for several years in the 1960s to avoid the use of the word *Isra'iliyun* in their religious services.

The declarations of the Second Vatican Council (October 11, 1962–December 8, 1965) about the role of the Jews in the crucifixion of Christ caused a major political crisis between the Coptic Church and the Vatican. The fact that the document absolved the Jews from guilt was considered an act of treachery against the teachings of the Bible and the Christian traditions. Repeatedly, Cyril VI condemned the Vatican statement as an imperialist-Zionist plot against the Arab nations and the Arab Christians.

The pontificate of Shenuda III was seriously troubled by violent attacks and encroachments in Upper Egypt and the Delta. Islamic fundamentalists had used their anti-Coptic campaign to debilitate the government. Churches were destroyed and Coptic priests and businessmen were assassinated. In order to retain national unity, President Sadat condemned the Islamic fanatics. At the same time he expressed his displeasure with the Coptic reactions. The president's anti-Coptic pronouncements climaxed in his speech on May 14, 1980, before the parliament. He accused the Coptic leadership of trying to undermine the stability and unity of the Egyptian state by planning a secession, with a Coptic capital in the Upper Egyptian town of Asyut. The climate between pope and president had deteriorated to a point of no return. On September 3, 1980, President Sadat removed Shenuda III from his pontifical responsibilities and exiled him to his desert monastery of Saint Bishoi. At the same time, 150 Coptic bishops, priests, notables, and others were arrested.

On January 2, 1985, President Mubarak revoked Sadat's decree of September 1981. Accompanied by fourteen bishops, Shenuda III left Saint Bishoi's Monastery on January 4. Over ten thousand people filled the cathedral of Saint Mark to welcome the pope. Upon his return he said, "I would like to do my best to deepen love, peace, and reconciliation between the church and the state, between the church and our Muslim brothers. We are like organs in the one body, which is Egypt."

Following his return from exile, Coptic-Muslim relations have significantly improved as a result of his efforts in promoting the spirit of love and unity. Since 1986, Pope Shenuda III has hosted a dinner and reception (*iftar*) for Muslim leaders at the end of the Muslim fasting month of Ramadan. This function has been attended by leading Muslim *shaikhs*, the prime minister, the speaker of the national assembly, and senior government ministers. This practice has also been adopted in all dioceses as a symbol of genuine love and goodwill.

In a press release at the time of the 1994 UN-sponsored conference on minorities in Cyprus, Shenuda III dismissed the notion that the Copts are a minority in Egypt. "We do not accept being distinguished from other Egyptians. We do not accept the word 'minority' in such a meaning of claiming political rights or foreign help. We are Egyptians, part of Egypt, of the same nation."

Shenuda periodically confirms his basic anti-Israel policy insofar as he has threatened Copts with excommunication if they should visit Israel while the Zionist state occupies the Arab territories, especially the Old City of Jerusalem.

Some Notable Coptic Families of the Nineteenth and Twentieth Centuries

In spite of the fact that since the seventh century the political leadership, and thus also a great deal of the social and economic life, has been in the hands of Muslims, Copts have made significant contributions to the national life of Egypt. This list does not claim to be inclusive; on the contrary, only a few families can be mentioned in this context.

Butrus Ghali Pasha. One of his first public contributions was connected with the liquidation of the wealth of the *Da'ira al-Saniya* (for the payment of the khedive Ismail's debts). In 1882, he served as the intermediary between Ahmad 'Urabi and the khedive after the former's defeat. As undersecretary of state in the Ministry of Justice, he reorganized the judiciary system of Egypt. In 1893, he was appointed minister of finance, and in 1894, minister of foreign affairs. In 1908, he was appointed prime minister, becoming the first Coptic Egyptian to have risen to the highest position in his country. There had not even been an Egyptian Muslim prime minister since the British occupation in 1882. One was an Armenian, while four were Turkish Muslims. Among Ghali's famous contributions were the Convention of the Sudan of 1899, his diplomacy in the Dinshaway incident of June 1906, and his negotiations pertaining to the prolongation of the Suez Canal concession. On Sunday morning, February 20, 1910, Butrus Ghali Pasha was entering his carriage when a young pharmacist shot him to death.

Qalini Fahmi Pasha, the son of Yusuf Bey 'Abd al-Shahid, was born in a small village near Minya in 1860. Educated in the Coptic College in Cairo, he was appointed in 1875 as Secretary of the *Da'ira al-Saniya.* He was known for his concern for the poor, especially the ditch diggers and the Upper Egyptian fellahin who came to work in Cairo. Later, he was promoted to the office of representative of the Divan. At the time of the 'Urabi Revolt in 1882, Qalini participated in restoring order. In March 1887, Tawfiq Pasha, the khedive, bestowed upon him the title 'pasha.' In January 1888, he was appointed general inspector of the *Da'ira.* Decorated with the highest insignia, he participated in various aspects of political life. At the time of the Coptic crisis in the last decade of the nineteenth century, Qalini Pasha, with the help of the prime minister Riyad Pasha, reconciled the alienated parties. Qalini Fahmi Pasha is remembered by many Egyptians for his genuine concern for the economic welfare of the poor.

Makram 'Ubayd Pasha was born in 1888 in Qina. After his mother's death, he studied at the American Mission School in Asyut. He completed his studies at Oxford and returned to Egypt in 1906, when he became the private secretary to the British counsellor in the Ministry of Justice. In 1919 he participated in the general strike of the Egyptian laborers. As a member of the Wafd Party, he left for London, where he led a movement of protest against the signing of a treaty with England. In December 1921, he was arrested and exiled to the Seychelles Islands. After his return in 1924, he was elected deputy of Qina, and in September 1927, after the death of Sa'd Zaghlul, he became the general secretary of the Wafd Party. In 1928, he was appointed minister of communication in the cabinet of Mustafa al-Nahhas. In 1930 and again in 1936 he served as minister of finance. He became the principal promoter of the Anglo-Egyptian Treaty, which terminated the British occupation of Egypt and made the complete independence of the country definite. His disputes with Nahhas Pasha led to the dissolution of the Wafd Party. In 1944, he was again appointed minister of finance, though in 1946 he resigned from the ministry and joined the opposition from 1946 to 1952. After 1953 he retired from the political life and died in June 1961.

Murqus Hanna Pasha was born in Cairo in 1872. His father, Qummus Yuhanna, was the *wakil* of the Coptic legislature at Tanta. Murqus Hanna was educated in the Tawfiqiya School and in France. He returned to Egypt in 1892, and in 1893, he was appointed by the Ministry of Justice to the position of assistant deputy in the court of Asyut. He resigned in 1898 to work as a lawyer and published several volumes on the practice of law in Egypt. In 1905, he became a member of the *Maglis al-milli*, and in 1912 he received his title of 'pasha.' In 1914, he was elected a representative of the lawyer's syndicate and appointed professor at Cairo University. He also served on the board of the Tawfiq Benevolent Society. As a member of the Wafd Party, he was among the seven sentenced to death for their activities on behalf of political independence. The sentence was not carried out, however, and instead he was sentenced to penal servitude and the payment of five thousand pounds. After his release he served for an interim period as chairman of the Wafd Party. In November 1923 he was elected to the Egyptian parliament and then appointed minister of public works.

Sinut Bey Hanna was born in Asyut in 1880 as the son of Hanna Mikha'il. He was educated in Asyut and later in the School of the Christian Brothers in Alexandria. From 1918 onward he participated in the movement for Egypt's independence. In April 1919, he joined Zaghlul on his trip to Paris, where their hopes of obtaining a hearing at the peace conference were disappointed. During his stay in Europe he worked as a journalist. Upon his return to Egypt, Sinut Bey Hanna participated in the popular and diplomatic affairs against the Milner Mission, which had been sent to Egypt to inquire into the causes of the recent disorders and to report on the existing situation in the country and the form of the constitution that would best promote peace and prosperity under the protectorate. Sinut wrote innumerable letters and resolutions denouncing the protectorate. As a result, he was exiled to his farm in al-Fashn, south of Beni Suef, but he continued to write from there and fight for his country's independence. In December 1921 he was deported to Aden and later to the

Seychelles Islands. In November 1922 he was released and returned to Egypt, whereupon he was elected to Parliament.

Dr. Nagib Iskandar Bey was the son of Iskandar Bey Masiha and the grandson of Hanna Bey Masiha. Nagib was born in 1887. In his youth he learned Coptic and Amharic, and in 1904 he received his high school diploma and entered the faculty of medicine. From 1910 to 1912 he studied in France. At the end of the First World War, Dr. Nagib joined the Wafd Party and went to France to attend the peace conference. When Sa'd Zaghlul was exiled to the Seychelles, Dr. Nagib Iskandar Bey served as the interim chairman of the Wafd. Dr. Nagib was also an outstanding physician. In 1924 he was elected to the Royal Medical Association. Later, he served as deputy of the district of Shubra and became minister of public health.

Raghib Iskandar Bey was born in 1888 and educated in the Coptic College, then later in the Amariya and Tawfiqiya schools. In 1910 he received his degree from the faculty of law. In 1918 he joined the national independence movement and worked with Sa'd Zaghlul in the Wafd Party. Committed to promoting help for the poor, he established an association for the education of the poor. He published numerous articles and several books, including a work on Butrus Ghali Pasha. He served on the board of administration of the Coptic College for Girls, as well as on the board of the Tawfiq Benevolent Society and other philanthropic societies.

Wasif Ghali Pasha, the son of Butrus Ghali Pasha, was born in Cairo in 1878. In 1919 he joined the Wafd Party and was commissioned to go to London in connection with the Milner Mission. In 1921 he issued the declaration calling for the boycott of English goods. He was imprisoned, but released a month later. In 1922 he wrote in favor of forming a new Wafd, and again he was imprisoned when he led a group of militant Wafdists, to whom Wisa Wasif, Hamad al-Bassal, Eloni al-Gazzar, Ahmad al-Ser'i, George Khayyat, and Murqus Hanna belonged. Accused of plotting, the members of the group were sentenced to death, though they were not executed. In 1923, Wasif Ghali Pasha was elected deputy of Beni Suef. Following the death of Sa'd Zaghlul, he continued to support Mustafa al-Nahhas. In 1937 he resigned from the Wafd and was elected to represent Egypt in the League of Nations. In 1950, he was nominated senator, but he resigned after the burning of Cairo in 1952. 'Ali Mahir, then prime minister, offered him the foreign ministry, but in vain. In 1956, one month before the nationalization of the Suez Canal, he resigned from the Suez Canal Company's council of administration. He died in 1958.

Murqus Simayka Pasha served his nation as minister, and he was a member of the *Maglis al-milli*. He is best known, however, for his interest in Coptic art and archaeology. He contributed the money for the building of the Coptic Museum in Old Cairo and offered many antiquities from his private collection. The Coptic Museum was inaugurated in 1926.

Shafiq Bey Mikha'il Sharubim was born in Cairo in 1895. He was educated in the School of the Christian Brothers. In 1914 he joined the Ministry of Public Works. After a while, he resigned and commenced his studies of art, first in Egypt and later in Italy, where he was the first Egyptian to be awarded a diploma from the Higher Institute of Art. His artwork became internationally known. Shafiq Bey was one of the greatest Egyptian artists of the 1920s.

Tadrus Bey Shenuda al-Manqabadi was born in Asyut in 1859. In 1862, the patriarch Demetrius II visited Asyut to inaugurate the new Coptic school there. Tadrus attended the first class of this school. After graduation he became inspector in Armant, and later he worked for the postal department and the police in Asyut. He retired from his government posts in 1895. His principal contribution to his country was his founding of the daily newspaper *Misr*, the first copy of which appeared in 1895. He invested the profits in welfare agencies. In 1884, he founded the Association for Coptic History as well as the Coptic Trading Company. The profits of the company were invested in the building of a Coptic school in Asyut. He purchased desert land and cultivated it and also started the first savings bank in Asyut. In 1892 he was elected a member of the *Maglis al-milli*. He is best known for his philanthropic works and his generous contributions to the Upper Egyptian churches.

Mikha'il Bey Sharubim was born in Sayyida Zaynab, Cairo in 1860. As a youth he was appointed to the Ministry of Finance to write for the European section. At the age of sixteen he became the private secretary of the minister, Isma'il Siddiq Pasha, where he remained until Isma'il's death in 1876. In 1877 he was elected director of customs at Damietta and later promoted to the same office at Port Said. In 1882 he assisted in the administration of the British Army in Cairo. In 1884 he was appointed judge in Mansura. He was decorated by the king of Greece and knighted by the king of Spain. In 1899 he was appointed the director of the national treasury. He died in 1917

Khalil Ibrahim Pasha was born in 1832. Having studied on his own for ten years, he completed his studies in Cairo. In 1880 he became a lawyer, though he retained his interest in agriculture. He founded the Tawfiq Benevolent Society and the Coptic Benevolent Association. He is best known for his untiring concern for the emancipation and education of women.

Iskandar Bey Masiha, son of Masiha Effendi, was born in 1864. In 1875 he joined the Ministry of Finance, where he remained until 1915. In 1916, he was elected to the *Maglis al-milli* and entrusted with the financial affairs of the patriarchate. In 1919 he resigned from the *Maglis al-milli* and joined the board of directors of Bank Misr. Altogether he was elected three times to serve on the *Maglis al-milli*. The title 'bey' was bestowed upon him by King Fu'ad in 1924.

Dr. Akhnukh Fanus, son of Fanus Rufa'il, was born in Abnub in 1856. Educated in Asyut, he went with Wasif Khayyat to Cairo, then completed his studies at the American University of Beirut. In 1883 he was elected representative of Abnub, and a year later he became a lawyer. For several years he served as president of the Coptic Evangelical *Maglis al-milli*. The American University of Beirut granted him an honorary degree.

Ya'qub Bey Nakhla Rufa'il was born in 1847. He excelled in the knowledge of several foreign languages and served in the Ministry of Finance, where he became head of a department. Later, he worked with the Fayyum railroad. He is known for his work with the Coptic benevolent societies. He published several books, including the *History of the Coptic Community* (1898). He died in 1905.

Gindi Bey Ibrahim was born in 1864 in Girga. Educated in a Coptic school, he continued his education at al-Azhar University, where he was known as Shaikh Ibrahim al-Gindi. In 1883 he joined the Ministry of Finance and later the Egyptian Supreme Court. He worked with the Tawfiq Benevolent Society from its beginnings and eventually became its director. He also worked in journalism and established the newspaper *al-Watan*.

Girgis Bey 'Abd al-Shahid was born in Biba. He was a successful businessman, known for his philanthropic concerns for the needy and for the establishment of benevolent societies in Upper Egypt.

Bushra Hanna Mikha'il Pasha was born in 1866 in Asyut. He was a member of Parliament and was elected to the Council of Agriculture. He contributed generously to various benevolent societies and hospitals.

Amin Ghali Pasha, brother of Butrus Ghali Pasha, was born in 1865. He studied law, and in 1885 he became district attorney, in 1893 director of the mixed courts. In 1908, 'Abbas Hilmi Pasha bestowed upon him the title 'pasha.' He transformed one thousand feddans of uncultivated land into mango plantations.

Wisa Wasif came from a middle-class family in Tahta, Upper Egypt. At first a teacher in Alexandria, he continued his studies at the École Normale in Paris. Upon his return, he served as barrister in the mixed courts. In 1920 he joined the Wafd Party, and in 1922 he was arrested. He became vice president, and later president of Parliament.

He died in 1931 under mysterious circumstances.

Sadiq Hinayn was born in Cairo in 1882. He joined the Ministry of Agriculture, where he became director of the department of statistics. In 1921, he participated in the general strike. In 1924 he was appointed undersecretary of finance, and from 1925 to 1929 he served as ambassador in Madrid and in Rome. In 1932, he represented the government in the stock exchange. After he left political life he became director of the national water company.

Tawfiq Bey Khalil was born in Cairo in 1880. He was educated in the Jesuit College in Cairo and later in Paris. Upon his return he worked as a businessman and later in the Ministry of Communication and in the Egyptian diplomatic service in Switzerland.

Niqula Bey Khalil was born in Cairo in 1885. He was a distinguished lawyer and was appointed to the Egyptian diplomatic service, where he served in Washingon, Prague, and Rome.

Wahbi Bey was born in Cairo in 1860. He was educated in Armenian and Coptic schools. He served as an interpreter in the Ministry of Education and published several historical books. He is best known for his contribution to the field of poetry.

Nagib Ghali Pasha was another son of Butrus Ghali Pasha. He was educated in Cairo and Toulouse. He served as undersecretary in the Ministry of Foreign Affairs and later in the Ministry of Agriculture. He bestowed large sums of money for work among the poor. He died in 1932.

Hanna Bey 'Ayyad was born in Rashid (Rosetta) in October 1861 and received his education in Alexandria. From 1876 to 1877 he was employed by the Alexandria Customs Department; subsequently he transferred to the Ministry of Finance. In 1894, he was promoted to the rank of secretary in the Ministry of Finance, and eventually he rose to be director in the same ministry. He was retired in 1921.

Murqus Sadiq, son of Girgis Effendi Matta, was a famous lawyer who was born in 1882 in the village of Fisha, south of Minuf, in the province of Minufiya. He was educated in the Husayniya Public School and the Coptic School in Cairo. In 1902 he entered the Faculty of Law in Cairo. In 1905, he received his diploma and in 1908 his doctorate. Two years later he began work as a lawyer and gained international fame. He was awarded numerous honors and degrees from European universities.

Ibrahim Bey Rufa'il al-Tukhi was born in 1831 in the village of Tukh between Banha and Qalyub in the province of Qalyubiya. He received his education in Cairo, and in 1850 he began working as a clerk in the Ministry of Finance. In 1873, he was promoted to chief of the Department of the Sudan. From 1882 to 1884 he worked as clerk in the Sudanese *hikimdariya*, or police force. Later he was called back to work in the Ministry of Justice, and after having attained the office of judge, he retired in 1892. Among his literary contributions are six volumes on theology. He died in 1904.

Yusuf Sulaiman Pasha was born in 1862. He attended the Coptic School in Cairo and then continued his studies at the Faculty of Law. He worked as a clerk in the Mixed Courts (1882–84) until he was promoted to serve as *wakil na'ib* (deputy agent). In 1890 he was advanced to *na'ib* (agent) of the Supreme Court. In 1902, he became *ra'is niyaba* (chief prosecutor) of the court of appeals. In 1906, he went to the Mixed Court of Mansura, and in 1916, he was promoted to the position of counsellor of the national court of appeals. Along with Yusuf Wahba and Murqus Simayka Pasha he founded the Egyptian Magistracy. In 1920, he became minister of agriculture, and in 1922 he was appointed minister of finance. He resigned in 1923. Yusuf Pasha was an active member of the Wafd Party and for many years participated in the deliberations of the *Maglis al-milli*, from 1890 to 1892, and from 1892 to 1912; later he became a permanent member.

Girgis Antun Pasha was the principal collaborator with Butrus Ghali Pasha in the establishment of the Coptic Hospital and the Coptic Welfare Society.

In the Egyptian feminist movement, Coptic women have contributed significantly to further the cause of women's rights, and the names of Esther Fahmi Wisa, Mathilda Greiss, Lisa Milad, and Lily Doss are intimately connected with the movement.

Some of the more influential Coptic families in the beginning of the twentieth century were the following: Wisa Buqtur (Asyut), Butrus (Balyana), 'Ubayd (Qina), Khalil Pasha Ibrahim (Cairo), Bushra Bey, Sinut Bey, Raghib Bey Hanna (Asyut), Andarawus Bishara (Luxor), Bulus Bey Hanna (Armant), Butrus Pasha and Amin Ghali Pasha (Cairo, Beni Suef, Ekiad), Girgis Bey Ya'qub (Beni Suef), Sa'id Bey 'Abd al-Masih (Minya), Ikladiyus, 'Abd al-Nur, Mashriqi (Girga), Hanna Salih Nasim (Fayyum), Shenuda al-Manqabadi (Fayyum), Suryal (Sharqiya), 'Abd al-Masih Bey Musa (Ekiad), Wasif Girgis (Mansura), 'Abd al-Shahid (Nazlat al-Fallahin), Ilyas Bishai (Asyut), Mikha'il Faltas (Sanabu), Habib Suryal (Maghagha), Zaqlama (Nakhla), Mikha'il Athanasiyus al-Ashrubi (Minya), Hanna Mikha'il (Asyut), Butrus Batarsa (Girga), Rizq Agha (Sharqiya), Makram (Giza), Bakhit (Beni Suef).

The Coptic Sunday Schools, Cradle of the Twentieth-Century Renaissance

The members of the Coptic Sunday schools of the middle of the twentieth century emerged from the so-called 'Takris Movement,' in which the participants had consecrated their lives to the service of the church. Whereas from 1948 to 1962 most of the members of the *takris* were laymen, after 1962 many of them had joined the Coptic monasteries, especially the Monastery of the Syrians, or they had been ordained parish priests.

In 1918 Habib Girgis, director of the first Coptic Institute of Higher Theological Learning, realized the need for religious instruction of young Copts. A general Sunday school committee provided a coordinated religious education program for the Coptic churches in Cairo as well as for those in the Delta and Upper Egypt. One of the first Sunday schools was established in the thirties in Asyut, undoubtedly motivated by the successful missionary and educational work of the American Presbyterians in Upper Egypt.

For our understanding of the Coptic renaissance toward the latter part of the twentieth century we must examine the work of the four major Sunday schools in Cairo. The men of these centers left a lasting impression upon the theology and piety, the spiritual and educational climate of the Coptic Church. The Sunday school center of the Church of Saint Antony is situated in the eastern part of Shubra behind the well-known Kitchener Hospital. This Sunday school grew out of the Shikolany Society, a fellowship founded in 1934 by Sidrak Tadrus, a Coptic notable. Its principal aim was to support the preaching ministry and the religious education of the clergy and laity. The school building was officially consecrated on April 24, 1935 by Anba Abram, the metropolitan of Giza, Fayyum, and Qalyubiya. The spiritual pioneers of this school were Zarif 'Abdallah Iskander, Dr. Raghib 'Abd al-Nur, Labib Raghib, 'Awad Farag, Michael Wahba, Malak Mikhail, and Abuna Butrus 'Atallah al-Gawhari. Spiritual growth through prayer and ascetic practices were the main concern of the founding fathers of Saint Antony's Sunday school. The examples of the saints, martyrs, and confessors played an important educational role. The leaders of this Sunday school had to accept a strict and coherent spiritual life of prayer as well as ascetic disciplines over a prolonged period extending up to two years. In the fifties and sixties several pioneers of this Sunday school had joined the monasteries, and others were ordained parish priests or even consecrated to the episcopacy. The most important member of the Sunday school of Saint

Antony was Nazir Gayyid—Pope Shenuda III, who joined the school at the age of seventeen. Anba Athanasius, metropolitan of Beni Suef and al-Bahnasa, was an active member of Saint Antony's before he moved to the Church of the Holy Virgin in Faggala. Anba Gregorius, Bishop for Higher Theological Studies, had joined the Sunday school of Saint Antony in 1936. For at least twelve years he remained an active member of this center. Other church leaders of this particular school were Anba Yuannis, bishop of Gharbiya and Anba Bakhumius, bishop of Buhayra and the Pentapolis.

The Sunday school center of Giza was located in the Coptic Church of St. Mark where Abuna Ibrahim Basilius used to serve as parish priest. Some of the pioneers of this center were the law students Sa'd 'Aziz, Wahib Zaki, and Grant Khalil. Also Zarif 'Abdallah, later known as Abuna Bulus Bulus of Damanhur, was one of the founders of this Sunday school, which saw its vocation in Bible study as well as in social activities and service. Another person who determined the spiritual direction of this center was Wahib Zaki, later known as Abuna Salib Surial. He was to play a significant role in the discussions pertaining to personal status legislation for the Copts. Together with Sa'd 'Aziz—later Abuna Makari al-Suriani and since 1962 Bishop Samuel—and Zarif 'Abdallah, he shared his deep concern for the Copts in the diaspora parishes. Service for the less fortunate in city and country was the principal concept of this Sunday school. The creation of good and solid relationships with the Muslim majority was an integral part of the Giza Sunday school center. With respect to the overall expansion of the Sunday school movement throughout Egypt, the ecumenical and social concerns of the Giza project could be credited as having been the most successful of the four centers. The establishment of the bishopric of social services and ecumenical affairs under Bishop Samuel and the involvement in the interreligious dialogue with the representatives of Islam were undoubtedly some of the permanent fruits of the Giza Sunday school.

The Sunday school center of Gazirat Badran was situated close to the Center of Saint Antony in east Shubra, not far from the Center of the Archangel Michael in the northwestern section of the district. The Sunday school center in Gazirat Badran was located in the Church of Saint George, which was consecrated in May 1936 also by Anba Abram. Though founded by the al-Khuli family, the leadership of the Sunday school remained in the hands of Abuna Girgis Butrus, parish priest of the Church of Saint George. The principal educational purpose of this center aimed at the total involvement of members in the social and religious projects of the church. In addition to the traditional educational program, the members of this center participated in excursions, study trips to the churches and monasteries, camps, and celebrations of religious and social festivities. A new aspect of the Gazirat Badran school was the religious and social education of girls. This was begun in 1937 by Madelaine al-Khuli. Some of the important personalities who were influenced by the activities of this school included Dr. William Sulaiman, historian, educator, and author; Dr. Maurice Assad, ecumenical advisor and theologian; and Kamal Habib, later Bishop Bimen of Mallawi (d.1986).

The Sunday school center of the Church of Saint Michael in Tusun is also situated in Shubra, northwest of the main railroad station. The beginnings of the work of this center are associated with Henry al-Khuli and Edward Banyamin. Abuna Girgis Ibrahim and Abuna Murqus Ghali have significantly assisted the educational and social activities of this school. The program benefited undoubtedly from the experiences of Edward Banyamin, Louis Zikri, Zarif 'Abdallah, and Nagib Zaki, which they had gained from the Sunday school work in Asyut.

Almost all of the young men who joined the monasteries in the Wadi al-Natrun, the Monastery of Saint Samuel at Qalamun, or the hermitages in the Wadi al-Rayyan had originated in one of these four Sunday schools. The character of the Sunday schools had impressed itself so strongly upon its members that their future roles as church leaders were largely determined by the theology and piety of their Sunday schools. This is evident in the lives of Pope Shenuda III (Nazir Gayyid) from Saint Antony's Sunday school and Abuna Matta al-Maskin (Yusuf Iskander) from the Sunday school in Giza.

The Folk Religion of the Copts

The Coptic Mulid, Its Origins and Functions

In sharp contrast to the official cultus, the folk religion of the Copts is very inclusive, since it touches every aspect of the personal and social life of the people. The folk religious attitudes and practices, which have their roots in the religious heritage of pharaonic Egypt, should be distinguished from the attitudes and practices of the official cultus as set forth in the dogmatic and catechetical treatises of the church. At the same time, however, we notice a good deal of overlap between the two spheres of religious experience.

The masses are unable to comprehend and understand the revealed truth, couched as it is in abstract thought, so they have no other alternative but to follow the more primitive religious patterns of their ancestors, which adopted a Christian garb from the fourth century onward.

The religion of the masses, or the folk religion, has expressed itself in many instances in sub-Christian forms, tenuously maintaining the cultus and the institutions of the past. Thus we discover many cases in which, one or two centuries after the process of Christianization, forms and patterns borrowed from the 'official' religion of the old, pre-Christian cultus were being filled with new religious content. Thus, for example, the *crux ansata* or ankh, originally the pharaonic symbol of life, was not employed in a specifically Christian context, that is, representing salvation through the vicarious death of the Christ, before the fifth or sixth century, or one or two centuries after the Christianization of the Nile Valley.

In some instances it has been well illustrated that the Christian saint, martyr, or confessor occupied the role of a pharaonic deity. With the advent of Christianity in the Nile Delta and valley, the masses soon replaced the cult of the pharaonic deities with historical or fictitious accounts of saints and martyrs. Historical and legendary personages and events, locally identified in either the Nile Valley or the Delta region, increasingly became objects of veneration and worship. Thus, the *vita* of a saint, related to a certain community and pregnant with the miraculous, provided a significantly more tangible object of religious identification than the abstract dogmas of the 'official' religion. This practice was very widespread in the fifth and sixth centuries.

It is very likely that the Egyptian Horus spearing the crocodile is not only the prototype of Saint George spearing the dragon, but also the inspiration for many of the warrior saints, such as Saint Mercurius, Saint Theodore, and Saint Menas, who are also popular among the Copts. Thus, the pharaonic deity, retaining the characteristics of its original cultus, merely adopted a Hellenistic-Christian garb. The fact that this process of cult transference continued well into the Islamic era is illustrated by the transformation of certain Christian cults into Islamic ones, so that the Muslim *shaikh* has now taken the place of the Christian saint or confessor.

About two centuries after the evangelization of the Nile Valley, evidence of this practice can be clearly seen from Shenute's outspoken and harsh words of rebuke and condemnation, as he severely criticized the Christian villagers for inventing patron saints and erecting shrines for the bones assumed to be relics of martyrs.

At one time, almost every settlement along the Nile had its local shrine or shrines to which believers made their annual or semiannual pilgrimages. These pilgrimages were made in commemoration of the 'birthday' of a saint or some other historical event related to the particular locality. With regard to the birthday, or *mulid*, of the saint, it is important to remember that the religious attitudes of the Egyptians were and still are fundamentally eschatologically directed, a factor that no doubt was instrumental in the ready acceptance of an eschatologically accentuated religion like Christianity. Therefore, the Coptic Church, like other churches throughout the ancient world, saw a saint's martyrdom as a 'birthday,' the *natalitia* or *genethlion*, and it was only in the fourth century or even later that the idea of martyrdom was transformed into a *depositio*, or burial. For that matter, the Copts still interpret the *mulids* of their saints as a 'second birth,' or birth into the Life Everlasting. In this respect, the commemoration of the Coptic *mulid* differs from that of the Islamic *mulid*, which is held in honor of the natural birth of a *shaikh*.

Among the essential characteristics of the Coptic *mulid* are certain miraculous manifestations that assure the pilgrims of the supernatural nature of the feast. These phenomena have a long history and are expected to occur annually. They are regarded as proof of divine approval of the feast, and as such they are considered to be of the greatest importance. Generally speaking, these miraculous displays can be divided into two categories: those pertaining to individual pilgrims, such as therapies, exorcisms, the granting of fertility to barren women, and the restoration of lost or stolen objects to the owner; and those that are shared by all and are of an impersonal nature.

In the second category, the most frequent expectation is the annual apparition of the saint at the time of the *mulid*. Many pilgrims, both educated and illiterate, have testified to having seen visions of Saint George on his horse at the Churches of Saint George at Mit Damsis in the Nile Delta and at Biba in the Nile Valley on his *mulid* on Baramuda 23.

At the Monastery of Saint George west of Dimuqrat near Asfun, I was told by the local priests that every year at the time of the *mulid* a large number of pigeons fly in the form of the cross over the monastery and that this phenomenon is regarded as proof of divine pleasure with the celebrations and festivities of the pilgrims. At the famous Church of the Holy Virgin at Gabal al-Tayr, pilgrims relate many accounts of supernatural and sensational events.

In addition, every year the Coptic *mulids* attract large numbers of psychoneurotics, epileptics, hysterical paralytics, and mentally disturbed pilgrims who come to the feasts expecting to be healed. It is believed that on account of the merits acquired by the saints, God will accept the saints' intercessions and restore the sick to health.

Generally speaking, the Copts turn to Saint George or any other warrior-saint to cast out evil spirits, and to the Holy Virgin or Saint Damiana to grant fruitfulness to barren women and blessings upon children. Saint Damiana is also believed to be able to prevent thieves from stealing and to return stolen goods to their rightful owners.

In this context it should be remembered that the Copts venerate only a very few saints. The Holy Virgin and Saint George are implored throughout Egypt, from Alexandria to Aswan. Indeed, devotion to the Holy Virgin is very marked among the Copts, with thirty-two feasts in her honor and a service known as the Theotokia, which calls for a special prayer for each day of the week, although it is now performed only in the month of Kiyahk. Moreover, the dedication of churches to the Holy Virgin was and still is more frequent in Egypt than any other dedication. Next in popularity is Saint George.

An important aspect of the Coptic *mulid* is the pilgrims' presentation of certain votive offerings, which are attached to the principal object of veneration, either the tomb of the saint or the most venerated icon. These votive offerings may consist of a handkerchief, a tie, or any other small patch of cloth. In some cases, the first fruits of the fields, bracelets, rings, or jewelry are also offered, in which case they are hung up in gratitude for the fulfillment of certain prayers. Thus women in particular will adorn sacred sites and icons with votive offerings in gratitude for healings or the restoration of stolen or lost objects. Often candles are used as votive offerings, and at some *mulids*, one can see large numbers of candles burning in front of the icon of the patron saint or in the caves blessed by Christ and the holy family on their flight into Egypt.

Furthermore, *mulids* afford an occasion for certain rites and ceremonies that are part of the 'official' religion. Thus, the pilgrims take their infants to *mulids* for the purpose of baptism and chrismation, which, according to the doctrines of the Coptic Church, are sacraments of regeneration and sanctification. At a recent *mulid* of the Holy Virgin on Ba'una 21 at the al-Muharraq Monastery of the Holy Virgin in al-Qusiya, over three hundred infants were baptized.

A common sight at the Coptic *mulid* is the village barber, whose function is to circumcise boys prior to baptism. The Copts strongly prohibit the circumcision to be performed after baptism, except in the case of girls, who are circumcised before the age of twelve or so. I have even heard it said that the sacrament of baptism would actually be annulled by the operation. The practice of circumcision prior to baptism was laid down in the eleventh-century canons of Cyril II, sixty-seventh patriarch of Alexandria. In some instances, the Coptic priest officiates as barber.

Whenever a *mulid* is in the vicinity of a cemetery, the women use this occasion to visit the tombs of their ancestors. These cemeteries, which are just outside the church or the abandoned monastery on the edge of the desert, become places of mass lamentation at the time of the *mulid*. Women address their dead relatives, and often other women will join those mourning in their lamentations. Offerings are made, and the blood of the animals is smeared over the tombs and the meat distributed among the poor. "Happy are the dead who are remembered, and happier still those for whom prayers are said," as the common saying has it.

One of the interesting qualities of the folk religion is its highly inclusive nature with regard to so-called schismatic Christians, as well as Muslims. Whereas the 'official' religion carefully specifies that only the orthodox are eligible to participate in the official cultus, the folk religion knows no excluding criteria. On the contrary, the folk religion is very inclusive. Indeed, many a Coptic *mulid* is attended by as many Muslims as Copts nowadays. This is especially true in the Nile Delta at the *mulid* of Saint Damiana near Bilqas and at the *mulid* of Saint George at Mit Damsis, but it is also true of the *mulid*s in the Nile Valley.

At the level of the folk religion, there exists a great deal of social interaction between Muslims and Christians, and only those rituals of the 'official' religion, that is, the sacraments celebrated at the *mulid* separate the orthodox from the schismatics and Muslims.

The Healing Ministry of the Coptic Church

Long before anything that could be called 'medical science' was born, men were healed of their diseases by certain methods directed toward their minds rather than their bodies. In fact, it was religion that first attacked the misery of disease and tackled the problem of pain. The various methods of healing the sick practiced in the Coptic Church can be traced to ancient Egyptian as well as to Judeo-Christian traditions, though in many instances it is difficult to determine whether this or that particular method had its origin in the magical texts of pharaonic Egypt or in the pages of the New Testament and the writings of the church fathers.

From time immemorial, the wide open desert of Egypt was thought of as the land of the afreet and the djinn, the evil spirits that were and still are held responsible for many physiological and psychological ailments.

The ancient Egyptians addressed their prayers for healing to many different gods and never designated a single god of medicine, as the Greeks did with Aesculapius. In the eighth century B.C., popular devotion raised Imhotep to the status of a demigod, and finally, during the Hellenistic era, he became fully deified under the name of Imouthes and identified with Aesculapius. He was invoked as a god and was believed to visit suffering people during their sleep and heal their diseases.

In its theology, the Coptic Church, like all Christian churches, traces its healing ministry to Jesus Christ and the Apostolic Church. Whatever Jesus did, his apostles and his church were to accomplish as well, and thus, to this day we discover many of the New Testament healing methods practiced in the Coptic Church.

However, we must make an important distinction between the official, or sacramental healing ministry of the Coptic Church, and the popular healing ministry of the Coptic Church. The sacramental healing ministry follows the healing practice as set forth by James:

> Is any among you afflicted? Let him pray. Is any merry? Let him sing psalms. Is any sick among you? Let him call for the elders of the church; and let them pray over him, anointing him with oil in the name of the Lord: And the prayer of faith will save the sick, and the Lord shall raise him up; and if he have committed sins, they shall be forgiven him (James 5:13–15).

On the other hand, in the popular healing ministry of the Coptic Church we recognize certain healing methods that were employed by Jesus Christ as well as by the early church. In large sections of the Christian Church, however, many of these apostolic methods of healing were lost, largely on account of controversy, heresy, and apostasy, which lowered the church's spiritual power.

The Sacramental Healing Ministry

The official or sacramental healing ministry is conducted through the administration of the sacrament of Anointing of the Sick and the service of Abu Tarbu.

The Sacrament of Anointing of the Sick

The administration of the sacrament of Anointing of the Sick is not only supported by primitive practice, but, as we have seen, it was also advised by the apostle James. The disciples of Jesus Christ used oil, for Mark reports, "And they cast out many devils and anointed with oil many that were sick, and healed them" (Mark 6:13). Jesus Christ probably initiated or at least approved this method, and anointing, together with prayer and the laying on of hands, was one of the principal healing methods of the early church.

In the Coptic Church, the application of holy oil has always been used for the restoration of health. The sacrament of Anointing of the Sick is administered for those who are sick as well as for all believers once a year on the Friday preceding the Saturday of Lazarus, at the conclusion of the service of the morning offering of incense and immediately before the commencement of the Divine Liturgy. On this occasion, all the members present are anointed on the forehead, throat, and both wrists.

The Service of Abu Tarbu

The service of Abu Tarbu is performed for one who has been bitten by a rabid dog. The service is to be understood, therefore, as a remedy against hydrophobia. After the reading of certain Old and New Testament passages and the offering of supplications, the priest reads the biography of Abu Tarbu (Therapon), followed by the recitation of several psalms. Then the priest assembles seven children, who join hands and go around in a circle seven times while saying a prayer. After this, one of these children asks for healing and health from God and from Abu Tarbu. The priest then holds out a piece of unleavened bread, and this child takes it in his mouth. The priest then takes the piece of bread out of the child's mouth and places it in the lap of the one the dog has bitten. The same procedure is followed with the other six children. Then the sick person receives the pieces of bread to eat, together with some water and wine, and the priest anoints him with oil over which prayers have been said.

The Popular Healing Ministry

Demon Possession

The majority of healings effected by popular methods occur at the annual Coptic *mulid*s. To this day, the Copts attribute many of their diseases to demon possession, and thus we find various methods of exorcism still widely practiced by the officiating clergy at Coptic *mulid*s in Lower and Upper Egypt.

Throughout Coptic church history, there are many examples of Coptic patriarchs, bishops, and priests who cast out demons, and it is quite impossible to list all the names of even the better-known exorcists. Kha'il I (743–67), the forty-sixth patriarch, was a famous exorcist who was called to heal the governor's daughter. After he prayed over her, the demon went out of her and she recuperated.

One of the very famous exorcists of the nineteenth century was John, the bishop of Minufiya. During the patriarchate of Peter VII (1809–52), Bishop John cast out many demons. On one occasion, Muhammad 'Ali consulted the patriarch about the sickness of his daughter Zuhra. After being approached by the viceroy, the patriarch asked Bishop John to proceed to Muhammad 'Ali's palace. He did as he was ordered and prayed over Zuhra until the demons left her and she recovered. As a reward for the cure, Muhammad 'Ali promised that the Copts would be treated equally in all positions of government and public life.

Exorcism

The exorcisms, which take place at a Coptic *mulid*, are very similar to some of the experiences related in the New Testament. The Gospels portray Jesus as an exorcist (Mark 1:23–28; 5:1–5; 9:17–27) and suggest that the practice of casting out demons was not only apostolic but also a highly reputable profession. The exorcist employs techniques and methods adapted to the mood of the time and the environment, and thus serves as a physician by curing dumbness, lameness, epilepsy, and other diseases attributed to demons. In fact, it is very questionable whether all the cases of demon possession recorded in the New Testament or occuring at Coptic *mulid*s can be completely explained in purely psychiatric terms.

Many Copts conceive of demons as entities that invade a person and take over most conscious and some unconscious functions, though, at the same time, reason is not altogether dethroned. The case of the "man with an unclean spirit" at Capernaum (Mark 1:23–28) serves as a prototype for many possessed Coptic men and women whom I have observed at Coptic *mulid*s. Repeatedly I have noticed the reluctance of the demons to leave the body of the possessed and the heightened state of mental conflict, culminating in a convulsive seizure that appears to be a violent abreaction, or discharge of emotions long repressed in the unconscious mind. Leeder, in his book *Modern Sons of the Pharaohs*, relates the following case study:

> A young woman suffered from acute convulsions and was lying on the floor of the Church of St. George at Mit Damsis. With her hands, her legs and her head she was constantly beating the cement floor of the nave, shouting: "I am the emperor of . . . . how can I leave her body? . . . his sword is piercing me . . . his horse is kicking me . . . he is choking me." Finally through the help of the priest, who identified the demon with a pagan emperor, the situation was brought under control. He called upon St. George, the mightly warrior, to kill the demon, but the demon, causing intense reactions, left the young woman through her toe. A few minutes later, she opened her eyes and breathed heavily. Then she fell into a long sleep. When she awoke, she thanked St. George for the blessings.

Suggestion

The method used by most exorcists—certainly not by all—is that of suggestion, especially when the patient demonstrates a high degree of suggestibility; nervous and neurotic patients are generally more suggestible than other people. Still, it is important that some form of rapport between the exorcist and the patient is established. The danger of this method is that it merely deals with the symptoms rather than with the causes, and this is the main objection of psychotherapists to many of the exorcisms performed by the Coptic clergy.

Another important factor in the ministry of exorcism is the discovery of the name of the demon. In the story of the Gerasene demoniac, Jesus asks the patient, "What is thy name?" The man answers, "My name is Legion: for we are many" (Mark 5:9). First Jesus tries the method of suggestion, but this method fails, and so he uses a more powerful method to cast out the demons. In Egypt, but also elsewhere in the east, to surrender one's name to a person is to give that person power over oneself. In the Genesis narrative, the angel asks Jacob his name, and Jacob gives it. But when Jacob asks the angel, "Tell me, I pray thee, thy name," the angel refuses (Gen. 32:27–29). The angel has power over Jacob, but Jacob has no power over the angel. The fact that in some exorcisms the priest asks for the name of the demon means merely that the priest is seeking power over the demon.

The Copts believe demons to be of a tangible nature; therefore, they have to leave the body through some opening. Often the demon chooses to depart through the eyes, which is believed to result in blindness. So as to prevent this and force the demon to leave from the part of the body furthest from the eyes, the priest or someone standing by makes a small cut in the big toe, which causes some minor bleeding. The blood stains the white robe or sheet placed over the patient, and this section of the robe is often cut off and kept as a blessing.

The Laying on of Hands
The laying on of hands is widely practiced in the Coptic Church. Jesus Christ practiced it, and the early church continued it. Ananias used it in the case of Saul (Acts 9:17), as did Paul in the case of Publius (Acts 28:8). The laying on of hands, however, is not only used in the case of sick people; it is also part of the ceremonies observed in the adminis-tration of baptism, anointing the sick, and holy orders. When people visit with a priest, he normally blesses them by laying his hands on their heads.

Actually, the act of touching has not a magical, but rather a sacra-mental significance, and in cases where illness is a byproduct of the disunity of the soul with God—and there are many such illnesses—the laying on of hands plays an important part in the ministry of healing.

The Use of Charms and Relics
The use of religious charms is widespread among the Copts. Many

diseases are believed to be caused by the evil eye. A prophylactic charm is used as a safeguard as well as a means of treatment. The charms worn by the Copts are preferably crosses. The cross contains the mystical force that is behind the *ankh*, or the sign of life, as well as the power of forgiveness and the promise of the Life Everlasting. Religious objects that have been blessed or acquired in Jerusalem are held in especially high esteem. I have seen Copts using the Scriptures for healing purposes, laying the book on the forehead and expecting the patient to be healed. Again, the suggestive nature of the patient may well remove the symptoms of the ailment.

From ancient times, the Christians have venerated the bodily remains of their saints and martyrs, to whom they attribute supernatural and healing powers. There are many stories in the annals of the Coptic Church that relate how people have received blessings and healing from the relics of the saints. They used to cut off pieces of the garments of Michael I (743–67) for the sake of a blessing. The most valuable relics for the Copts have always been those of Saint Mark the Evangelist. Already during the patriarchate of Peter I (d.310), the faithful resorted to the relics of the Evangelist for blessings. In the biography of Christodoulus, the sixty-sixth patriarch of Alexandria, the head of Mark is mentioned twice, and the spiritual powers attributed to these relics are well attested.

In the ninth century, the Coptic Church was still in possession of a large number of relics, as is clear from the detailed inventory of relics compiled by the biographer of Cyril II, the sixty-seventh patriarch of Alexandria. Over the centuries, however, many Coptic churches were demolished, which resulted in the disappearance of such relics as were kept there. Most of the relics that have survived the vicissitudes of the preceding centuries are now kept in the Coptic Churches of Cairo and in the desert monasteries of Wadi al-Natrun. The faithful who turn to these relics for blessings and healing are predominantly women. The relics are always kept in long cylindrical boxes covered with silk or other stuff, so that they look like bolsters. Generally the bolsters may be found in a locker in the wall of the church under the principal icon, where anyone can take them out.

Mystical Phenomena among the Copts

In view of the steadily increasing interest in the study of mystical phenomena throughout the centuries in the Orient and the Occident, this chapter provides some selected case studies from the history of the Coptic Church. In all instances, the particular physical manifestations are visible demonstrations of intense religious experiences of one form or another. From the very beginning, however, it should be borne in mind that mystical phenomena, though universal in their variety of types and forms, are, nevertheless, colored and to some extent even determined by the cultural environment, and especially by the religious traditions in which they occur.

We have selected four mystical phenomena, which for the purpose of typological clarification are described independently. The paragraph 'The Human Salamander' consists of a series of case studies of persons who, being exposed to the natural elements, suffered no harm. The second study, 'Miraculous Multiplication of Food,' deals with the phenomenon of the multiplication of certain necessities effected either by the prayers or by the ascetic way of devout persons. The third discussion, 'Appearances of Light,' describes a variety of mystical light phenomena as recorded in the annals of the Coptic Church. The paragraph entitled 'The Miraculous Icons' is a descriptive study of some human characteristics attributed to certain icons.

In our evaluation of the following stories it is important for us to remember that both the narrator and the listener belong to an era of faith, in which many stories were reported for the glorification of God rather than for the purpose of giving an accurate scientific account of a particular psychic or parapsychological phenomenon. Moreover, the Copts, like all members of the Oriental churches, have never accepted the criterion of scholarly self-criticism, largely on account of fear of falling into the worst of all sins, that of heresy.

Certain mystical phenomena traditionally assigned to the realm of the supernatural belonged until very recently exclusively to the sphere of faith; thus, many miracles were either blindly accepted or categorically rejected as pious fraud. Yet the recent investigations into the realm of paranormal phenomena promise a new conceptual understanding of the miraculous. Whereas at one time scientists and historians readily dismissed all stories and traditions dealing with the supernatural as mere delusion, and whereas saints or those who wrote about them were regarded as outright liars, today scientists are no longer so dogmatic in their condemnation of these stories. On the contrary, it is hoped that the following study may add to our knowledge of mystical manifestations, so as to gain a better and more mature understanding of the operations of these phenomena, which clearly fall into the realm of the paranormal.

The Human Salamander

The hagiographies of the Occidental and Oriental Churches list numerous authenticated instances in which believers have withstood contact with fire unharmed. With regard to Coptic hagiography, we can clearly distinguish between two categories of manifestations of the human salamander. On the one hand, there are the numerous third to fifth century martyrdoms, many of which actually belong to the Greek world, and therefore have little if anything in common with ancient Egypt. On the other hand, the *History of the Patriarchs of the Egyptian Church* records a few isolated medieval accounts. Yet for both categories the Scriptures provide the prototype.

For the early church, and especially for the Coptic Church, the account of the three confessors in the fiery furnace (Dan. 3:1–30) served theological as well as moral purposes by illustrating how martyrdom is preferable to apostasy. On the one hand, the angel of God's protection of Shadrach, Mesach, and Abednego was interpreted in terms of a preincarnation appearance of the Redeemer; on the other hand, if God had saved the three confessors, why should he not also protect those who were confronted with the pagan idolatry of the Roman emperors?

For our study of human salamanders, the following selection of stories related in the Coptic Synaxarion are of interest for comparing certain typological similarities in the respective 'salamander-like' manifestations.

In one case, Abakradion was tied to a mast, but the cords burst; then he was cast into the sea, but brought safely to land. The governor Justus, his wife, and all the soldiers were converted. Finally, another governor executed him (Abib 25). In another story, Alladius was cast into a fiery furnace but escaped unharmed, which led to the conversion of many bystanders. Then the emperor Julian ordered that he was to be beheaded (Ba'una 3). The eparch Ptolemy tried to burn Apoli, but instead the fire consumed the priests of Apollo who stood around him, and left Apoli unharmed (Misra 1). Banikarus was put on a pyre, and soldiers set it alight, but an angel extinguished the flames and Banikarus was unharmed. Eventually he was executed (Tuba 5). The seven ascetes of Tuna were burned and found without injury, a miracle that caused the conversion of 130 people (Ba'una 29). Bassilissa was cast into fire, but at her prayer water gushed out and extinguished the fire. Finally, she was beheaded (Tut 6). Batra was cast into a furnace, but preserved unhurt; then his feet and hands were cut off, and finally he was beheaded (Misra 10). Heavy stones were tied to the necks of Benjamin and Eudoxia, and they were cast into the river, but an angel cut loose the stones, and they swam to the shore (Misra 28). Chanazhum and Sophronius suffered tortures from boiling water but suffered no ill effect (Hatur 20). Decius had Christophorus put in a cauldron beneath which a fire was lighted, but he suffered no harm; then a heavy stone was hung from his neck, and he was cast into a cistern, but he was preserved from all harm. Finally he was beheaded

(Baramuda 2). For three days, Cosmas and Damian were burned in the furnace used to heat the baths, but they were preserved from all injury; then they were roasted on iron grids, but again God protected them. They were finally beheaded (Hatur 22). The governor Lucas placed fire underneath Epime, but Christ protected him from suffering any harm. Later, he was put into a furnace used to heat the baths, but again he was preserved by Christ. Then a heavy stone was tied to his neck, and he was cast into the sea, yet he was thrown back safely onto the shore. Finally he was beheaded (Abib 8). Hor was dragged through Alexandria by a bull, and plates of hot iron were laid on him, but in all this he sustained no injury (Ba'una 29). After having confessed her faith, Julietta was cast into a fire, but escaped unhurt. Finally she was beheaded (Misra 6). Paphnutius of Dandara had a heavy stone hung from his neck and was cast into the river, but he was borne in safety on the waves; then he was hung from a palm tree, but remained unhurt (Baramuda 20). Maximian ordered Shenute to be hanged and a fire lighted beneath him, but this had no effect. Later he was cut into pieces (Baramhat 14). In the case of Timothy of Memphis, the governor Arianus hanged him, boiled his body, and cast it out. God restored him to life, and he came back and confronted Arianus. This caused the conversion of many onlookers. Finally he was beheaded (Ba'una 21).

With reference to Egypt, the persecutions following the edict of Decius in 250 supply us with the first series of authenticated martyrdoms, though even here we notice certain borrowings from both the Roman and Greek martyrologies. The majority of the Egyptian martyrdoms, however, fall into the period of the Diocletian persecution. In general, these martyrdoms follow a certain recurring pattern:

1. The saint is called by Christ or by an angel to bear witness to his faith.
2. The saint responds and fearlessly makes his confession of faith.
3. The saint is arrested and invited to worship the idol.
4. The saint refuses and suffers the consequences; however, either Christ or an angel comforts him.
5. The saint is either delivered to the fire, from which he emerges uninjured, or he is cast into the river, and again he suffers no harm.
6. The witnesses are converted by the steadfastness of the saint and the miraculous protection offered by God.
7. Finally the saint is beheaded.

Many of the Coptic martyrologies, which betray so much uniformity of pattern and content, are the product of a school of scribes devoted to the manufacture of these passions, which would be read at the martyr's feast. Nevertheless there still remains the Christian martyr, who, like the three confessors in the fiery furnace, is miraculously protected. We do not know their names, nor do we know the circumstances of their martyrdoms. But there is no doubt that there were saints, perhaps only very few, who were neither touched by the flames of fire nor drowned in the waves of the water. For although the whole body of Coptic martyrologies of the Diocletian era is highly apocryphal, and though the characters may be utterly fictitious, there still remains the historical fact of the violent madness and harshness of the persecution as such. Apart from the rather spurious hagiologies of the third to the fifth centuries, there are several well-authenticated accounts referring to certain people who have withstood unharmed extreme heat and fire. The *History of the Patriarchs of the Egyptian Church* records altogether three instances that fall into the category of the human salamander.

The legendary *vita* of Demetrius I (189–230), the twelfth patriarch of Alexandria, includes an account in which both the patriarch and his wife handled blazing logs, yet remained unharmed. The occasion was the Feast of Pentecost. After the patriarch had celebrated the Divine Liturgy, he bid the brethren collect much fuel and they did so. Then, after praying, he introduced his wife to the believers so that she could receive their blessings:

> So the holy woman entered, and stood in the midst of the congregation. And her husband, the patriarch, arose, where they could all behold him, and stood by the blazing logs, which had already been lighted, and spread out his cloak, and took burning embers from the fire with his hand and put them in his cloak; and all the spectators were astonished at the quantity of burning fuel in his garment, and yet it was not burned. Then he said to his wife: "Spread out thy woollen pallium which thou hast upon thee." So she spread it out; and the patriarch transferred the embers to it while she stood there; and he put incense on the fire, and commanded her to incense all the congregation; and she did so, and yet her pallium was not burned. Then the patriarch said again: "Let us pray" while the embers were blazing in his wife's pallium, which yet was not burned.

This miracle was attributed to the fact that Demetrius had made himself a eunuch of his own free will, so that he was more glorious than those that are born eunuchs, and therefore, the fire had no effect on him, nor on his garments, nor on his wife, because he had extinguished the flames of lust.

The second story is reported in the *vita* of Zacharias (1004–32), the sixty-fourth patriarch of Alexandria, and reflects the cruel persecutions of the Copts by the Fatimid caliph al-Hakim bi-Amr Allah (996–1021). Having killed the notables of his state and his secretaries, al-Hakim turned to the Christian notables, from whom he selected ten. Among these, there was one known as Fahd ibn Ibrahim:

> Al-Hakim had set him over all the secretaries and chiefs of the diwans. He caused him to be brought into his presence and he said to him: "Thou knowest that I chose thee and set thee over all those who are in my state. Hearken to me and join me in my religion and I will exalt thee higher than thou art, and thou shalt be to me as a brother," but he did not answer his words. Al-Hakim ordered that he should be beheaded and that his body should be burned with fire. The fire remained alight upon him for three days, but he was not burned. His right hand remained as if the fire had not approached it at all.

The reason for this unusual phenomenon is supplied by the chronicler, who states that with his right hand Fahd ibn Ibrahim had dealt compassionately by bestowing alms upon the poor and needy: "Wherefore this miracle was manifested in his right hand, which he used to stretch out for almsgiving at all times, for he performed very kind deeds through God."

Again, a moral virtue, in this case charity rather than chastity, is seen as the determining cause for the preservation of human tissue. This case, however, is somewhat different from the normal 'salamander types,' for Fahd ibn Ibrahim was beheaded first. This means that the account of the "charitable hand which did not burn" really falls into the category of the miracle-working relics, of which there are many parallels in the hagiologies of the Occidental and Oriental Churches.

The last reference to the phenomenon of the human salamander is reported in the *vita* of Christodoulus (1047–77), the sixty-sixth patriarch of Alexandria. Bessus (Bisus), the saintly monk of the Monastery of Saint John Kame in Wadi al-Natrun, received a request to pray for the deliverance of the oppressive measures inflicted by the Muslims. Thereupon, in the morning of the first day of the Nativity, which is the twenty-eighth of the month of Kiyahk, "Bessus took a burning coal and stood upon it and prayed for us." In this instance, there is no reference that Bessus remained unharmed, although we may assume that this was the case. Bessus' performance was to demonstrate the intensity and earnestness of his supplications, which did indeed result in the deliverance of the Copts from their immediate sufferings.

Regarding the cases recorded in the *History of the Patriarchs*, the persons' spirituality in terms of their asceticism, charity, and piety is intimately linked to their immunity to excessive heat and their ability to withstand unharmed the natural consequences of being exposed to fire.

Miraculous Multiplications of Food

The phenomenon of the multiplication of food, of which there are numerous well-documented accounts in the Occidental and in the Oriental Churches, finds its typological model in the Old and New Testaments. With regard to the Old Testament, we refer to the narratives of the miraculous multiplication of the widow of Zarephath's meal and oil in the Elijah cycle (1 Kings 17:8–16), and the miraculous multiplication of the oil of the widow (2 Kings 4:1–7) and the story of the twenty loaves (2 Kings 4:42–44), both in the Elisha cycle. For the establishment of our typology, however, we must also turn to the gospel narratives of the miraculous feeding of the five thousand Jews at Bethsaida (Mark 6:30–46) and of the four thousand Gentiles at Decapolis (Mark 8:1–9), though the Synoptic accounts in particular have been interpreted in terms of the messianic banquet. In fact, Christians believed that whatever Elijah and Elisha did, Jesus Christ could also do. Moreover, it was felt that whatever their Lord accomplished, they, following the counsels of perfection, were to do as well.

Generally, the process of the multiplication of food passes through four stages, which appear in different forms according to the circumstances. Stage one is normally characterized by a definite need on the part of the faithful. In every case, we notice that a minimum of food is available, which proves to be insufficient to nourish everybody. This means that in all cases we are dealing with multiplication rather than with creation *ex nihilo*. The second stage normally reflects various degrees of doubt or unbelief on the part of the faithful. The third stage, the miraculous multiplication, for which God employs one of his 'elect,' includes prayers, processions, blessings, etc. The fourth and final stage culminates in the realization of God's concern for humankind, and in devout manifestations, the faithful express their gratitude for the miraculous salvation from their economic misery. In some instances the multiplication even results in an economic abundance.

In terms of purpose, the phenomena clearly show three criteria. Certainly, like all miracles, the multiplication of food testifies to the omnipotence of God; however, it also bears witness to God's compassion and concern for humankind. And lastly, the emphasis on food demonstrates that God's blessings also include objects that cause certain physical joys and satisfaction.

In the annals of the Copts there are only few instances of miraculous multiplication of food. The first case is recorded by Palladius with respect to the blessed Apollo, who lived in the Thebaid, on the borders of Hermopolis, "whereunto our Redeemer went with Mary and Joseph:"

> There was a great famine in the district of the Thebaid, and when the people of the country who were dwelling in that place heard that the monks who were with the blessed man [Apollo] were living without labour, they gathered themselves together, and came to him with their wives and children, and asked him for alms and for food, and he, like a man who did not fear that peradventure food would be wanting for himself and those who were with him, gave unto all those who had come to him that which was sufficient for each one of them from day to day. And when three baskets full of bread were all that remained, and the famine was still severe, he commanded and they brought these baskets into the midst of them, and he found that they would only suffice for one day's food for the monks and those who were with them; and in the presence of all the crowds, who were listening, and the whole brotherhood of monks, he said with a loud voice, "Is not the hand of the Lord able to increase these? For thus saith the Holy Spirit, 'Bread shall not be wanting in these baskets until we all eat new bread.'" And all those who were near him said, "In very truth the bread was sufficient to feed them for four months." And he was in the habit of doing thus from time to time in respect of oil and wheat.

All of the other cases fall into the eleventh century and are recorded in the *vita* of Christodoulus:

> In the year A.H. 404 [A.D. 1013–14], there was a great dearth, so that wheat was sold on the eve of the Feast of the Olive-branches for a dinar and a half a waiba. Then the Christians went out with the olive-branches on that eve, and it happened that fresh barley arrived early in the morning from al-Buhaira, and wheat was sold at a dinar for a waiba and a half. On the next day, two waibahs were sold for a dinar, and after ten days, more than one ardab was sold for a dinar. Abundance increased and God in His mercy and His compassion removed the dearth. The Muslim inhabitants of Alexandria were certain that this was through the blessing of the bringing out of the olive-branches and the going with them in procession through the city, and they used to rejoice at the going-out with the olive-branches every year on the eve of the Feast of the Olive-branches.

In this case, the Muslims rather than the Copts attributed the miraculous multiplication of food in time of dearth to the prayers and the Palm Sunday procession of the Copts. In the strictest sense, however, this account does not really fall into our frame of reference, for here the source of supply is clearly stated ("barley arrived from al-Buhaira"), and the problems of the critical shortage and the high price were solved.

It is an altogether different matter, however, with the miracles recorded of Bessus (Bisus). In the first instance, we hear of a visit of eleven Copts, who in the month of Tuba of the year A.M. 778 (A.D. 1062) went to the desert of Wadi al-Natrun to visit the saintly Bessus. There they passed the night with the monks, and they ate what he presented to them. He brought them a small jar, which he blessed, and they all drank of it until they were nearly intoxicated, but the jar was only diminished by half its amount.

The following story of the miraculous provision of food should be seen in light of the parable of the feeding of the five thousand Jews. John (Yu'annis), one of the sons of the saintly Bessus, related to the chronicler that in a hard year the monastery was much frequented by the Arabs and others besides them. The monastery used to supply biscuits *(ka'k)* and wheat to everyone who knocked at its door, until nothing remained for the monks, save food for one day only. The monks were determined to eat it, and when it was morning, to go forth from the monastery and wander aimlessly. Then some people visited them and asked them for something to eat.

> Bessus said to the monks, "Give them what ye have." The monks murmured and became furious on account of this, but Bessus said to them in calmness and tranquility, "At the end of the day there will reach you from Christ what will be sufficient for you for many days. Let not your breasts be straitened." Then they gave to the people the wheat they had. The people said to Bessus, "O monk, we have no mill." There was in the monastery only one mill, but Bessus gave it to them. And again the monks murmured, but Bessus said, "Do not despair, for the Lord will bring us what we need, for his name is great and he knows everything. Comfort yourselves." John swore that he ascended the keep when Bessus had said this to them, and he saw two camels laden with wheat. On the back of one of the two camels, there was a sound, new Persian mill larger than the mill that he had given away. We praised God and glorified him who revealed to this saint what was hidden from others.

It should be noted, however, that these accounts of the miraculous provision of food are isolated instances in the Coptic ecclesiastical tradition. They occurred within the frame of the monastic life and at a time when Christians were severely persecuted by the Muslims.

Appearances of Light

Throughout the centuries some devout Christians have emanated rays of light, which either descended upon them or which radiated from them on account of their distinguished spirituality. From the early apostolic days onward, light has been identified with holiness, purity, and truth. The New Testament bears witness to the duality of light and darkness denoting good and evil (John 3:19). Not only is light a gift of God, but God by nature is light: "This then is the message which we have heard of him, and declare unto you, that God is light, and in him is no darkness at all" (1 John 1:5). God is "the Father of lights, with whom is no variableness, neither shadow of turning" (James 1:17). The attribute of light is also ascribed to Christ, and the fourth evangelist records Jesus as saying, "I am the light of the world: he that followeth me shall not walk in darkness, but shall have the light of life" (John 8:12). Paul speaks of the "armour of light" (Rom. 13:12) and the fruits of the Spirit that are manifest by the light (Eph. 5:13). In an inferior sense, the servants, the disciples are also lights. Saint John the Baptist is referred to as "a burning and a shining light" (John 5:35), and in an inclusive sense, all Christians are the lights of the world (Matt. 5:14). The angels also are of the light, and in their appearance they emanate light.

The fact that the early church clearly identified light with holiness and purity is also attested by the artistic representations of the saints. Although inherited from the Hellenistic period, the halo or nimbus became the distinguishing mark of holiness. At first, the halo was restricted to Christ and the Lamb; later, however, the halo was bestowed upon the Holy Virgin, the angels, the martyrs, and the saints.

In the Coptic traditions, there are also some cases of the appearance of light, and the following selection merely illustrates some of the various types of phenomena. Palladius, the fourth- and fifth-century bishop of Helenopolis, begins his *Histories of the Holy Men* with a description of Abba Isidore, the bishop of Hermopolis Parva. Toward the end of his life, "Isidore never washed, never ate flesh, and he never ate a full meal seated comfortably at a table; and yet, through Divine Grace, his body shone."

The phenomenon of the appearance of light as a visible manifestation of God's blessings and confirmation of his grace is well attested in the lives of the desert fathers. There was a certain distinguished wandering monk who lived a life of great sanctity in the mountains and who despaired of his repentance. And thus he prayed unto God, "Show compassion upon me, O Merciful One, and kindle this lamp by thy light, so that I by means thereof may receive the encouragement of thy mercy, and may pass the remainder of my life which thou wilt bestow upon me in the way which shall please thee . . . ."

And the monk prayed in this manner three times, and then he was heard by God, for when he went back the fourth time to see if the lamp had been lighted, he found it burning brightly; and he was strengthened with hope, and rejoiced and wept abundantly, and he marveled at divine grace.

They used to say about a certain monk who lived in a monastery of the brotherhood that although he kept frequent vigil and prayed, he was neglectful about praying with the congregation. One night there appeared unto him a glorious pillar of brilliant light from the place where the brethren were congregated, and it reached up into heaven. He saw a small spark that flew about the pillar, and sometimes it shone brightly, and sometimes it was extinguished. While he was wondering at the vision, it was explained to him by God, who said, "The pillar which thou seest is the prayer of the many brethren who gather together and go up to God and gratify Him; and the spark is the prayers of those who dwell among the congregation, and who despise the appointed services of the brotherhood."

The Coptic Synaxarion records the story of Athanasia of Minuf (Misra 2), who had offered her home as a shelter for monks and wayfarers. But soon her hospitality was misused for sinful purposes, in which Athanasia also became gradually involved. When John, the seventh-century hegumen of the Monastery of Saint Macarius, heard of this scandal, he decided to visit her and to admonish her. Then he guided her to the desert, and during the night, while John offered supplications for the sinful woman, he saw a pillar of light standing over Athanasia and heard a voice saying that she was forgiven. Here the pillar of light demonstrates in a visible manner the confirmation of God's pardon.

In the *vita* of Christodoulus, we read of Phoebammon (Abi Fam ibn Bakura al-Sawwaf), who suffered martyrdom during the reign of al-Mustansir bi-Llah (1036–94). After his execution, four men were placed to watch over him that night, and they saw a great and fearful light descend upon Phoebammon, so that two of them became mad, and the other two departed from Cairo, and nothing was heard of them again.

In addition to the rays of light emanated by devout persons, there are recorded instances of light appearing in churches and emanating from icons. In connection with this, it should be borne in mind that the Copts attribute certain personality characteristics to their representations of the Holy Virgin and the saints. For among the Copts as well as the Byzantine Orthodox it is believed that the icon represents in a mystical sense the virtues and properties of the person portrayed.

It is in this context that we should read the account of Abba Elijah (Ilya), the bishop of Tammua. On the feast of Saint Victor, the illustrious martyr Elijah celebrated the Divine Liturgy in the Church of Saint Victor at Giza, and "when the middle of the Liturgy was reached, I saw a great light upon the picture of the Mistress, the Lady, my Lady Mary, the Pure Virgin, which is in the niche of the sanctuary, and light remained upon it for a long while, and all the people present at the feast witnessed it."

Stories of miraculous ignitions and light appearing in icons or sanctuary lamps are even more frequent. In the *History of the Patriarchs* we read of the miraculous ignition of an icon lamp in the Church of Saint George at Qutur. 'Abd al-Masih, the priest of Dahshur, related that he went to the icon of Saint George to cut off the top of the wick of the icon lamp. While he was waiting for the sacristan to bring him a lamp to light the wick, there descended upon the church a white light in three places, and the light lighted the wick.

In the Coptic Church, especially in the desert monasteries, many stories are related by the monks about miraculous ignitions of sanctuary lamps. Thus, for example, in the Red Sea Monastery of Saint Antony the monks frequently refer to the miraculous ignition of the sanctuary lamp suspended above the feretory of Saint Mark in the Church of Saint Mark. For many years, Abuna Yustus al-Antuni has taken care of the sanctuary lamp, cutting its wick and providing the oil. On certain occasions, however, other monks have noticed that the extinguished sanctuary lamp ignites spontaneously without any of the monks lighting it.

Another common phenomenon among the Copts is the miraculous illumination of churches reported throughout Egypt. Moreover, these phenomena are not limited to Coptic Orthodox Churches. At the beginning of this century, in the Coptic Catholic Church of the Holy Virgin at al-Sanayna, east of Tima in the province of Asyut, a bright light illuminated the whole sanctuary, and the light was so glaring that one could not identify its source. The parish priest did not believe it at first, when he was called to his church, but then he saw the light appearance. Gradually, the light disappeared and remained for a while on the icon of the Holy Virgin, until finally it disappeared altogether. After some time, the icon of the Holy Virgin oozed a certain liquid.

With electric light now widespread in Coptic churches, the light appearances have somehow changed their phenomenal characteristics. Qummus Shenuda Hanna of the al-Mu'allaqa Church of the Holy Virgin related that on December 6, 1965, at 4:30 p.m. a group of Copts assembled in his church to invoke the blessings of the Holy Virgin, Saint George, and Saint Michael. They lighted the candles in front of the icons, when suddenly, without anyone touching the switch, the electric light went on. I have heard similar stories pertaining to the Church of Saint Damiana near Bilqas, the Church of Saint George at Biba, the Church of the Holy Virgin at Musturud, and the Church of the Holy Virgin at Gabal al-Tayr. In the case of the church at Gabal al-Tayr, many pilgrims have assured me that on the day of the *mulid*, the church is illuminated without anyone switching on the electric light, a sign that God wants the church to appear in all its splendor.

In April and May 1968, tens of thousands of Copts and Muslims went to the Church of the Holy Virgin in Shari' Tuman Bey, Zaytun, a suburb of Cairo, to behold the apparition of the Holy Virgin, who had been seen in and around this church. More than a month after the first apparition on April 2, the Coptic Orthodox patriarchate issued an official statement by Bishop Athanasius of the diocese of Beni Suef, a member of the committee appointed by Cyril VI to investigate and determine whether or not the Virgin had been appearing at Zaytun Church.

Reading out the statement at a press conference to which more than 150 local and foreign correspondents were invited, the bishop said that he had personally seen the apparition:

> The apparition was seen on various nights and is still being seen. Sometimes the Virgin Mary appeared in full form, while on other occasions, only the Virgin's bust, surrounded by a glorious halo of shining light, appeared. Occasionally, the apparition came through the opening in the church's domes, and sometimes it appeared outside the domes. The apparition walked above the altar and bowed before the upper cross of the church. On many occasions, the apparition faced the people, blessed them and moved its head as a sign of greeting. The apparition also took the form of a nimbus preceded by a shining, quick-moving white cloud. Sometimes it stayed for periods as long as two and a quarter hours. The longest period was on April 30, 1968, when the shining full-size apparition of the Virgin Mary appeared from 2:45 a.m. until 5:00 a.m. The apparition has been followed by two important factors: a revival of faith in God, as many people became true Christian believers after witnessing the apparition; and the occurrence of a number of miracles, as several people suffering from incurable diseases were healed after seeing the apparition of the Virgin.

In the evening hours of Tuesday, March 25, 1986, numerous people of the district of Ard Baba Dublu (Papadopolus) in Shubra, Cairo saw bright lights around the Coptic Orthodox Church of Saint Damiana and Her Forty Virgins. This church, with its two bell towers, is situated on Shari' Muhammad 'Abd al-Muta'il. On April 9, 1986, Pope Shenuda III appointed a committee to ascertain details about the occurrences. The members of the committee, including three bishops, several priests, and laymen, who saw the Holy Virgin appear within a bright aureole between the two belltowers for approximately one hour. This happened on Thursday, April 10 and on Friday, April 11. The Holy Virgin appeared again on Monday, April 14 and every day until May 13, 1986.

Again on August 16, 1997, and for many evenings thereafter the Holy Virgin appeared in and outside the Church of the Holy Virgin in the Nile Delta village of Shentana al-Hagar between Quweisna and Tanta. The patriarchal committee of Metropolitan Bishoi and the bishops Banyamin, Sarabamun, Ghubriyal, and Yu'annis watched an apparition of the Holy Virgin on the roof of the church. With outstretched arms she blessed the people.

In spite of the fact that thousands of people from all walks of life, including both Egyptians and foreigners of various nationalities, have seen the Holy Virgin and that the apparitions were officially confirmed by the Coptic Patriarchal Commission, we shall classify these particular phenomena as light appearances rather than as 'apparitions' in the strict sense of the term. In this context, we must distinguish between the phenomenological manifestation of a light appearance and an apparition.

With regard to apparitions, the traditions of the Coptic Church supply numerous instances in which some person has appeared to individuals or a small group of believers. These apparitions are normally related to times of intense personal suffering and anxiety, when the apparition fulfills the role of the healer or the comforter and offers counsel and advice or makes eschatological promises. Thus, for example, Christ is said to have appeared to Saints Mercurius (Hatur 25), Cyrus (Amshir 6), Shamul (Bashans 16), Epime (Abib 8), Abamun (Abib 27), and Didymus (Tut 8), while the angel of God or Saints Michael, Gabriel, or Raphael are said to have appeared to Saints Dioscorus and Aesculapius (Tuba 1), Ezekiel of Armant (Kiyahk 14), George of Damira (Ba'una 19), Isaac of Tiphre (Bashans 6), John of Sanhut (Bashans 8), John Kame (Kiyahk 25), Hilaria (Abib 25), Kaou (Tuba 28), Macarius the Great (Baramhat 27), Warshenufa (Abib 29), Paphnutius of Dandara (Baramuda 20) and Pidjimi (Kiyahk 11).

Apparitions of St. Michael occurred in 1995 and 1996 in the Church of the Archangel in Kafr Yusuf Samri in the diocese of Zaqaziq and Minya al-Qamh, Sharqiya. The archangel was seen dressed in a white gallabiya, and some people even saw his wings outside the sanctuary, according to the published report by Abuna Samwil Zakaria of Kafr Yusuf Samri. No doubt the present social and political situation of the Copts leads to an increased confidence in the biblical promises: "At that time shall arise Michael . . . and there shall be a time of trouble, such as never has been . . . but at that time your people shall be delivered" (Dan 12,1).

In comparison to the number of traditional accounts of apparitions of Christ or the angels, we notice that Coptic hagiography has very little to say about apparitions of the Holy Virgin. True, in the *vita* of Ammonius (Kiyahk 14) we read that the Holy Virgin appeared to Sarus, Hennan, Banuf, and Bistai in prison and comforted them. Phoebammon (Tuba 27) had a vision of Christ with the Holy Virgin and Saints Michael and Gabriel, while James, the fiftieth patriarch of Alexandria (Amshir 14), was instructed by the Holy Virgin to rebuild the monasteries of Wadi al-Natrun.

It is noteworthy that the attitude of Cyril VI, pope and patriarch of Alexandria, to this phenomenon has been less enthusiastic than that of most Copts. More than a month after the first 'apparition' in May 1968 Cyril VI finally paid a visit to the church. Asked why he had not gone before, the patriarch said that he had been seeing visions of the Virgin Mary since his early childhood. He added that the vision had appeared in 1910 at his family home in Alexandria, and that the appearance had cured a member of the family who had been sick for some time.

The Miraculous Icons

In comparison to the large number of Byzantine and Russian miraculous icons, which have influenced the destiny of individuals and nations, the Copts have only a few icons to which believers have attributed miraculous powers. From both a theological and an aesthetic point of view, Coptic iconography never developed in the same proportions as the iconography in the Byzantine and Russian Churches. To some extent, Islam's iconoclastic attitude prevented the Copts from creating their own indigenous rich iconography. In addition, the Copts lacked the solid theological framework for icon veneration that the Byzantine Church acquired in response to the eighth-and ninth-century iconoclastic controversies.

For the Copts the veneration of icons is based largely on the traditions of Abgar, the legendary prince of Osrhoene, and the traditions of Luke, the first Christian iconographer. In *The Precious Pearl, the Sciences of the Church*, Yuhanna ibn Zachariah ibn Saba', a contemporary of the fourteenth-century theologian Abu al-Barakat, devotes a chapter to icons, in which he says:

> There should be in the church painted images in colour representing the martyrs and the saints, whose lives are read to the people in order to provoke emulation of them and to imitate their [the saints] conduct. The reason is that Abgar, King of Edessa, on account of the impossibility to reach our Lord Christ, of Whom he had heard [people] speak, sent a letter

through which he made known to Him that he earnestly desired to contemplate His Divine Countenance. And our Lord Christ, having washed His Divine Countenance, took a towel, called a *sabaniya*, with which He wiped it, and His Holy Countenance remained printed thereon. Then He had this towel sent to Abgar, King of Edessa. Likewise, the Lady our Virgin, before leaving this world, said to Saint Luke the Evangelist: "Make my portrait for you so that you should never forget me." And Saint Luke painted her in several colours on a board of wood with her beloved Son at her breast. This pleased the Virgin very much. After her Assumption and to this day, these pictures succeeded one another in the churches.

Generally speaking, the Copts make no distinction between the qualities and characteristics of the icon and those of the person represented by the icon. Whatever the person could perform in his or her lifetime or post mortem, the icon representing the person could do as well. For that matter, the icon is the artistic 'incarnation' of the person, and as such it is subject to as much veneration as the person represented. Therefore, it is not surprising that the Copts, like the Greeks and the Russians, ascribe human qualities such as weeping, sweating, and bleeding to their icons. In this context, it is interesting to note that among the miraculous manifestations of an oozing liquid, tears, sweat, and blood are more frequent than any other signs. Indeed, it is entirely possible that on occasion the wood or the paint oozed a certain liquid, which the believers interpreted as a human liquid.

The following illustrations merely demonstrate some typical manifestations. It is impossible to describe all the miraculous signs connected with Coptic icons, yet it might be helpful to list some of the most widely venerated icons in the Coptic Church: the icon of Saint Damiana and her forty virgins in the Shrine of Saint Damiana, near Bilqas, Mansura; the icon of Saint George in the old Church of Saint George, Mit Damsis, near Mit Ghamr; the icon of the Holy Virgin in the Church of the Holy Virgin, Musturud; the icon of the Holy Virgin of the Tree of Jesse in the Church of the Holy Virgin, Harat Zuwayla, Cairo; the icon of the Holy Virgin in the al-Mu'allaqa Church of the Holy Virgin, Old Cairo; the icon of Saint Barsum al-'Aryan in the Church of Saint Barsum, Ma'sara, near Helwan; the icon of Saint George in the Church of Saint George, Biba, Beni Suef; the icon of Saint Theodore in Dair al-Sanquriya, Bani Mazar; the icon of the Holy Virgin in the Church of the Holy Virgin, Gabal al-Tayr; the icon of the Holy Virgin in the al-Muharraq Monastery of the Holy Virgin, al-Qusiya; the icon of Saint Mercurius at the Monastery of Saint Mercurius, Qamula; and the icon of Saint George at the Monastery of Saint George, Dimuqrat, Asfun. Except for the icon of the Holy Virgin in the Harat Zuwayla (fourteenth century), the other icons belong to the eighteenth and nineteenth centuries.

In terms of the miraculous functions, we can distinguish five different forms of manifestations that have occurred repeatedly throughout the centuries: the fertility-granting icon, the healing icon, the weeping icon, the bleeding icon, and the light-emanating icon.

The Fertility-Granting Icon

Some of the earliest references to the miraculous powers of icons are intimately related to the problem of fertility. There is no doubt that the narratives of the two following incidents were written at a much later date; nevertheless, it is of interest to note that the chroniclers ascribed such powers to their icons.

It was through the intercessions of Peter and Paul as they were portrayed on an icon that the mother of Peter I (d.310), who was barren, conceived. On the Feast of Saints Peter and Paul, when all the people were present in the church, the mother of Peter I, who was near the icon of the two saints, saw the faithful bringing their children forward and anointing them with the oil of the lamp that was lighted before the two pictures. She prayed to the two saints to intercede with the Lord for her. A short time after that she conceived and brought forth a son, and Theonas, the sixteenth patriarch of Alexandria, told her to name him Peter.

According to the *Coptic Synaxarium*, Saint Menas was miraculously conceived. Menas of Nikiu was the son of Eudoxius, the governor of Pentapolis. His wife, who desired a son, was praying before the icon of the Holy Virgin when a voice from the icon answered her, saying, "Amin." When the child was born, the boy was called Mina.

The Healing Icon

In times of sickness and emotional distress, Copts have turned to their icons to seek therapeutical help from those saints who are portrayed. To this day, thousands of Copts suffering from various ailments visit the icons of the Holy Virgin, Saint George, Saint Damiana and her forty virgins, Saint Theodore, and Saint Menas in hopes of being cured through the intercessions of the saints.

The *History of the Patriarchs* records the healing of Bishop Mercurius (Makura) of Tilbana, who shone with leprosy, and an awful whiteness appeared in him. After having consulted Zacharias (1004–32), the sixty-fourth patriarch of Alexandria, Bishop Mercurius went to the Church of the Holy Virgin in the village of Tima and prayed for three days in front of the icon, beseeching the Holy Virgin to examine the leprosy and remove it from him. In the ninth hour of the third day, the bishop became dazed from fasting and fatigue, and he leaned, dozing, against the wall on which the picture hung. Then he saw the hand of this picture reach out as if to wipe his body, and he woke up and was cured of his sickness.

The Weeping Icon

In times of persecution and oppression by the Muslims, the Copts were eager to demonstrate and publish their trials and tribulations by attributing the emotion of sorrow to the saints portrayed on icons. Moreover, it is believed that the saints, who constitute the church triumphant, participate in the sufferings of the church militant. Thus, in the days of Cosmas II (851–58), the fifty-fourth patriarch of Alexandria, the eyes of all the pictures in Wadi Habib at the Monastery of Saint Macarius and elsewhere gushed with tears like fountains. They knew that this was on account of the evil and unjust Muslim rulers' hiding away the cross. These miracles caused them to be patient and strengthened them against all that befell them at the hands of the Muslim rulers and judges.

Another account of weeping icons is given in the *vita* of Christodoulus. This time the sins and the transgressions of the Copts led to these unusual manifestations:

> Our sins and transgressions were multiplied, and our gluttony and our pride increased, so that a number of trustworthy people among the Muslims and the Christians saw with their own eyes tears flowing from the eyes of some of the pictures which were in the churches, among which was the picture of my Lord George in the church of a village called Dimul, one of the villages of Abwan, and the picture of the Mistress and the picture of the Angel Michael in the church of Tuna.

The Bleeding Icon

Similar to the reports of the weeping icon, accounts of the bleeding icon also appear in times of trial and tribulation, when it is held that the saints declare their spiritual solidarity with the suffering of the believers. In terms of this manifestation, the 'bleeding' of the icon is considered to demonstrate intense sorrow.

All the monks who dwelt in the Monastery of Saint Macarius observed the picture of the Lord Christ, the Merciful One, which is in the Church of Saint Severus on the rock, and how its side opened and blood came forth from it. All who saw this blood feared and glorified God for his marvelous works.

Many miracles were manifested in the day of Christodoulus, among them that the picture of Saint Menas the martyr, which is in the Monastery of Saint Macarius, exuded from it blood, and its mark remains till now. The congregation of the fathers, the saintly monks, witnessed this, and among them was the saintly Macarius, the doorkeeper, who fled from the election to the patriarchate.

The weeping *Mater Dolorosa* in the Church of Saint George in the village of Wadi al-Natrun has attracted many Coptic pilgrims from Cairo and Lower Egypt. The Church of Saint George, consecrated in 1987, is situated in the southeastern part of the village. In the northern apse is a large color print of the *Mater Dolorosa* by the Florentine master Carlo Dolci (1616–86). On Wednesday, May 17, 1989 the image began weeping blood. This continued for about a fortnight. It is said that the blood ran out of her right eye and trickled down her right cheek. Traces of the flow of blood are still noticeable on the picture. Copts have come to this picture to find answers to their problems, and testimonies of actual healings have caused others to visit this church.

The Light-Emanating Icon

As in the case of devout Christians who have emanated rays of light, so we hear of icons that manifest the same phenomenon. Again, the properties and the characteristics of the person are transferred to his image, and whatever has been said regarding the appearance of light in connection with the saints also applies to their representations on icons.

The appearance of light is interpreted as a sign of confirmation of the presence of God or of a particular saint. It is also considered as a visible demonstration of the blessings that the saint bestows upon the believers; thus, this sign is greeted with expressions of profound joy.

On the evening of Friday, September 23, 1988, five Coptic girls witnessed a bright light emanating from an icon of Jesus Christ in the Coptic Orthodox Church of Saint Mark in Agincourt, Toronto, Canada. To the amazement of the five girls, the icon of the Lord was gradually transfigured and bathed in a dazzling flood of light. The whole scene looked three-dimensional, and Christ's right hand also moved up and down in the the sign of the cross.

From a National to an International Christian Community

Four important concerns have determined recent developments within the Coptic Church. First, Pope Shenuda III holds a deep and profound interest in erasing the stains of heterodoxy, even heresy, from the historical and popular anathematizations of Western and Byzantine Christians. The numerous christological and theological debates, conferences, and communiqués with the Roman Catholic, non-Chalcedonian, and Byzantine Orthodox hierarchs and theologians are clear evidence of the desire of the Copts to be fully and unequivocally accepted as orthodox Christians by all members of world Christianity.

Moreover, the Coptic Church of the diaspora is a new and dynamic development of the second half of the twentieth century. In addition, recent missionary efforts of the Coptic Church in Africa have led to the establishment of numerous churches in Zambia, Kenya, Zaire, Zimbabwe, Namibia, and South Africa. The historic connections to the Church of Ethiopia have undergone recent reassessments. Finally, the thorny questions of Coptic property rights and claims in Jerusalem belong to those issues that remain unresolved.

Toward the Mia Physis, the One Nature of the Incarnate Word

Pope Shenuda III instigated the recent theological activities of the hierarchs and theologians of the Coptic Church for the purpose of discussing mainly christological but also ecclesiastical issues with members of the Western and Byzantine Churches. Motivated by the desire to enter into a meaningful dialogue with the other churches, Pope Shenuda III expected from these meetings and conferences a better understanding of the historical, theological, and non-theological factors that have led to the Coptic position.

Beginning in the 1970s, these theological discussions were conducted for twenty years with representatives of the Roman Catholic Church, the Greek Orthodox Church, and the non-Chalcedonian, or Oriental Orthodox Churches.

The relationship of the Roman Catholic Church to the Coptic Church can be traced to the fifteenth century. Throughout the past centuries it was the aim of the Catholic See of Saint Peter to unite the so-called 'schismatic' Copts with the 'Mother' Church of Rome. The first approach toward union with the Church of Rome was made in 1439. The Coptic pope John XI (1427–51) had commissioned Yuhanna, hegumen of the Red Sea Monastery of Saint Antony, to attend the Council of Florence as an observer. Although the Greek delegates had already departed, a decree was issued stating the reunion of the Coptic Church with the other churches. The desert father from Mount Clysma signed the 'Act of Union,' which united Latins (Roman Catholics), Greeks, and Jacobites. For a few days, at least, the whole of Christendom was united. In 1561, during the patriarchate of Gabriel VII (1525–68), Pope Pius IV sent two Jesuits, Christopher Rodriguez and John Baptist Eliano, to negotiate the submission of the Coptic Church to the See of Rome. The attempt failed, although the issue was taken up again in 1582 by the Coptic pope John XIV.

In 1630 a Capuchin mission was established in Cairo. The purpose was to penetrate the Coptic desert monasteries, especially the Monastery of Saint Antony and the Monastery of Saint Macarius. The strategy was to bring the Coptic desert fathers to accept the teachings of the Roman Catholic Church, thereby automatically effecting the union with the See of Rome, since the leadership, the bishops, and the pope were chosen from the desert monks. In 1636, the Franciscan Father Agathangelus stayed for a period of four months in the Monastery of Saint Antony, where two of the fifteen Coptic monks are said to have become Roman Catholics. But the prospect of reconciliation with the Coptic Church was wrecked by the evil conduct of the Catholic residents in Egypt in general and the Consul of France in particular. In 1741, Athanasius, the Coptic archbishop of Jerusalem (1725–66), accepted the teachings of the Roman Catholic Church; thereupon, Pope Benedict XIV consecrated him the first Coptic Catholic metropolitan of Egypt. Athanasius continued his residence in Jerusalem, however, and appointed a priest named Yustus Maraglic as his vicar general in Egypt. In the eighteenth century, Raphael Tukhi of Girga edited and published Coptic liturgical texts in Rome and was awarded the titular bishopric of Antinoe. In 1824, Maximus Joed was nominated Catholic patriarch of Alexandria, but the nomination was not put into effect. Thirty years later, in 1854, Pope Pius IX nominated Athanasius Khusam as administrator of the Catholic Copts.

The Coptic Catholic patriarchate of Alexandria was finally established in 1895 by the apostolic letter "Christi Domini." In 1908 the Coptic Catholic patriarch Cyril II Macarius resigned, and the patriarchal throne remained vacant until the nomination of Patriarch Marcus Khusam in 1947. He was followed in 1958 by Anba Stephanus I Sidarus, who occupied the throne until 1986. Presently the Coptic Catholic patriarch is Anba Stephanus II Ghattas. In comparison to the Orthodox Copts, the number of Coptic Catholic members is almost negligible: The church claims 147,000 members in seven dioceses. At the same time, the influence of this church is considerably more significant than mere numbers would indicate.

In view of the rather ambivalent history of Roman Catholic–Coptic Orthodox relationships, the recent ecumenical developments are remarkable and should be evaluated as a serious theological effort on the part of both parties. Special mention must be made of the pioneer work of the ecclesiastical foundation Pro Oriente under the chairmanship of Franz Cardinal König of Vienna and Professor Philipp Harnoncourt. Since 1971 Roman Catholic and Coptic Orthodox theologians have regularly convened to discuss the theological issues that have separated the two churches since the decisions of the Fourth

Ecumenical Council of Chalcedon in 451. Between 1971 and 1988 these theologians, hierarchs, and professors have met five times.

From May 4 to 10, 1973, Pope Shenuda III, accompanied by eight Egyptian and two Ethiopian metropolitans, visited the Vatican, where they were graciously received by Pope Paul VI. At this occasion the two pontiffs signed the document agreeing to the meaning of the christological formula of Saint Cyril of Alexandria, the famous "one nature of the incarnate Word." This was the first time since 451 that an Egyptian pope had visited the Holy See of Rome. During the celebrations in commemoration of the 1,600th anniversary of the death of Saint Athanasius the Great, Pope Paul VI presented Pope Shenuda III with a relic of the finger of the great church father and twenty-fifth Egyptian pope of Alexandria. This precious relic reposes on the ground floor of the Coptic Cathedral of Saint Mark in 'Abbasiya, Cairo. At the same time, the two pontiffs initiated a theological study commission to support the Roman Catholic and Coptic Orthodox consultations of Pro Oriente. This new commission met in Cairo from March 26 to 30, 1974, to study and debate the issues of the creedal statements of the early church.

Following up on these initial contacts and discussions, Franz Cardinal König visited Pope Shenuda III in Cairo in November 1975. Problems pertaining to the relationship between the Orthodox Copts and the Catholic Copts were discussed by a joint committee October 27–November 1, 1975, in the patriarchate in 'Abbasiya. A year later, in August 1976, three Coptic bishops met with Roman Catholic theologians in Vienna for the third Pro Oriente conference. After having reached a consensus on an acceptable christological formula, discussions were held in 1978 between Orthodox and Catholic Copts about the theology of the means of grace, the holy sacraments, and their relation to a believer's salvation. The September 1978 meeting under the aegis of Pro Oriente was primarily concerned with ecclesiastical questions of church leadership in the East and in the West. A delegation of Coptic bishops met with Roman Catholic theologians in Rome in June 1979.

The Dialogue Commission, consisting of eight Coptic Orthodox bishops, two lay-theologians, and five delegates each from the Coptic Catholic and the Roman Catholic Church, convened for the seventh time in April 1991 in the Monastery of Saint Bishoi under the joint chairmanship of Metropolitan Bishoi of Damietta, Secretary of the Holy Synod, and Monsignor Pierre Duprey, Secretary of the Pontifical Council for Christian Unity. On the agenda were such pressing theological issues as the different views regarding purgatory, the *filioque* (the procession of the Holy Spirit), the Immaculate Conception, and the sinlessness of the Holy Virgin. In the fall of 1991, on the occasion of the twentieth anniversary of Pope Shenuda's accession to the throne of Saint Mark, Franz Cardinal König conferred upon him the honorary title of protector of Pro Oriente.

One hundred and twenty Roman Catholic, Greek Orthodox, Coptic, Armenian, Ethiopian, Syrian, and Indian bishops and theologians followed the invitation of Pope Shenuda III to come to the Monastery of Saint Bishoi in October 1991 to clarify the terminology and content of the fifth century statements, to agree on the *Mia physis* Christology, and to end once and for all the historic polemic that for centuries had mistakenly accused the Copts of denying the human nature of Jesus Christ. In an attempt to remove mutual anathemas, an agreement was reached that the christological mystery was expressed in different words and in different traditions, though adhering to the same fundamental faith. They also discussed the questions of mixed marriages and rebaptisms for those changing their ecclesiastical affiliation. It was agreed that these consultations should continue on an annual basis for the next few years.

By contrast, the relationship of the Coptic Church with other non-Chalcedonian churches, including the Ethiopians, Armenians, Indians, and Syrians, are neither strained nor clouded by christological or theological issues. On the contrary, non-Chalcedonian ecumenicity used to be practiced in the Desert of Scetis (Wadi al-Natrun) from the eleventh to the thirteenth centuries, when Nubians and Ethiopians at the Monastery of Saint Elias, Syrians at the Monastery of the Syrians, and Armenians, with the visit of Gregory II, lived in harmony with the Coptic desert fathers.

In January 1959 Anba Ighnatius XXXIX Ya'qub III Sawirus, patriarch of the Syrian Orthodox Church, visited Pope Cyril VI and the Monastery of the Syrians. Two years later, in May 1961, Pope Cyril VI followed an invitation by the Syrian Orthodox patriarch to visit Damascus. In Addis Ababa in 1965, at the first conference of the non-Chalcedonian churches, under the chairmanship of Pope Cyril VI, it was agreed among other things that the Coptic Church should increase all efforts for missionary work among the new nations of the African continent. A follow-up conference of the non-Chalcedonian churches was held in Cairo in January 1966.

Relations with the Syrian Orthodox Church have always been friendly. The practice of exchanging synodical letters between Alexandria and Antioch can be traced back to the third century, when Dionysius the Wise of Alexandria sent a letter to Fabius of Antioch informing him of the stories of the martyrs during the persecutions of the emperor Decius in 250. Apart from a small number of Syrians who came to Egypt in the third and fourth centuries, a Syrian colony emerged in the seventh century in and around Alexandria, especially at the famous Ennaton Monastery. Today, the Syrian Orthodox community in Egypt is very small. The Syrian bishop in Cairo is Anba Sawirus Hara. In 1972, Pope Shenuda III adopted for the Coptic monks and nuns the *qalansuwa*, the traditional Syrian clerical black cap with thirteen yellow or white embroidered crosses symbolizing Christ and the twelve apostles.

The relationship of the Egyptians with the Armenians can be traced to the era of the emperor Justinian, when an Armenian general, Nerseh Pasentzi, is said to have conquered parts of Africa (sixth century). During the Fatimid period, the Armenian community spread from one part of the country to the other, and Armenian churches were built throughout the Nile Valley. Today, the Armenian community has significantly decreased in numbers and in influence, but the Armenians have actively participated in the conferences of the non-Chalcedonian churches. In February 1967 in Beirut, the Armenian catholicus of Sis (Antelias) convened a general synod of all non-Chalcedonian churches, where the principal christological and ecclesiastical issues were discussed.

The relationship of the Coptic Church with the Greek Orthodox Church in Egypt is somewhat complicated on account of a long history of distrust, antagonisms, and mutual prejudices and rebukes. As a result of the decisions of the Fourth Ecumenical Council in 451, the Egyptians appointed their own pope of Alexandria. Meanwhile, the Byzantines consecrated a successor to Dioscorus, who had been deposed by the Council. Thus it came about that since the fifth century there have been two lines of popes in Alexandria, one Chalcedonian, or Byzantine, and one non-Chalcedonian, or Egyptian (Coptic). For many centuries, especially during the early Middle Ages, these two Alexandrian sees competed with each other to be the legitimate Christian representative at the Islamic courts.

At present, the Greek Orthodox patriarchate of Alexandria comprises twelve metropolitans and one bishop. The head of the Alexandrian patriarchate is Peter VII, the Most Blessed, Most Divine and All-Holy, Pope and Patriarch of the Great City of Alexandria, of Libya, the Pentapolis, Ethiopia and all the Land of Egypt, Father of fathers, Shepherd of shepherds, Thirteenth Apostle and Judge of All the Earth. Once numerous and influential, the Greek community in Egypt has been considerably reduced through the exodus of large numbers of Greeks to other countries.

During the past thirty years there have been numerous meetings and conferences of Coptic churchmen with the hierarchs of the

Byzantine Orthodox churches. A Coptic delegation was invited to observe at the Pan-Orthodox Conference at Rhodes in September 1961. For the millenial celebrations of the monastic Republic of Haghion Oros, Pope Cyril VI sent Bishop Shenuda to represent the Coptic Church. In October 1972, Shenuda III, now pope, paid a visit to the orthodox patriarchs of Moscow, Constantinople, Bucharest, Tbilisi, and the Armenian catholicus in Yerevan.

Important for the ecumenical dialogue between the Coptic Church and the Byzantine churches were the four unofficial consultations of theologians of the two Orthodox families in Århus (1964), Bristol (1967), Geneva (1970), and Addis Ababa (1971). The first official Joint Commission for Theological Dialogue between the Orthodox Church and the Oriental Orthodox Churches took place in Chambésy, near Geneva, December 10–15, 1985. Co-presidents of the commission were Metropolitan Bishoi of Damietta for the Coptic Church and Dr. Chrysostomos Konstantinides, metropolitan of Myra for the ecumenical patriarchate. The second meeting of the Joint Commission took place at the Monastery of Saint Bishoi from June 20 to June 24, 1989. The twenty-three participants came from thirteen countries and represented thirteen churches. The meetings were co-chaired by Metropolitan Bishoi and Metropolitan Damaskinos of Switzerland. Agreement was reached on the christological formula of Saint Cyril of Alexandria, the famous "one nature of the incarnate Word." Moreover, they agreed on the use of the four following adverbs to qualify the mystery of the hypostatic union belonging to a shared faith: without confusion, without change, without separation, and without division. "Those among us who speak of two natures in Christ do not thereby deny their inseparable, indivisable union; those among us who speak of one united divine-human nature in Christ do not thereby deny the continuing dynamic presence in Christ of the divine and the human, without change, without confusion. We are agreed also in our understanding of the Person and Work of God the Holy Spirit, who proceeds from the Father alone, and is always adored with the Father and the Son."

The third meeting of the Joint Commission of Theological Dialogue between the Orthodox Church and the Oriental Orthodox Churches took place September 23–28, 1990 at the Orthodox Center of the Ecumenical Patriarchate in Geneva. At this meeting a report was received from the Joint Pastoral Subcommittee, which had met at the Monastery of Saint Bishoi from January 31 to February 4, 1990. The declarations were signed by Metropolitan Damaskinos of Switzerland, Metropolitan Bishoi of Damietta, Metropolitan Petros of Axum, Mar Yuhanna Ibrahim of Aleppo, Professor V. Phidas, and Mr. Joseph

M. Faltas. On the agenda were discussions pertaining to the preparation for unity, the relations to the World Council of Churches and the other Christian churches, cooperation in the propagation of the common faith and tradition, and service to the social and economic issues of the world.

The Coptic Diaspora

The Coptic diaspora during the second half of the twentieth century is undoubtedly one of the most significant demographic movements in the history of the Coptic Church. The exodus had already begun in the late fifties, then continued in the sixties, seventies, and eighties on account of the repressive political and economic measures by the Egyptian government. In 1963 Edward Wakin was already describing this trend:

> The attachment of the Copts to their Egyptian homeland is dramatized in the small-scale diaspora of the young, the educated and the qualified who have begun to leave Egypt. They leave with reluctance, talking not of greener pastures elsewhere but of closed doors at home. Feeling deprived of the traditional Coptic right to market their skills at a reasonably high price, they turn to the last resort of departure and dispersion.
>
> Yet the trappings of the Coptic identity are not suited to long journeys. Its symbols and ceremonies need the church and clergy which are left behind, while departure breaks the closed circle of community life.

Many Copts left for the United States, Canada, Australia, and Europe, while others found attractive economic possibilities to the east, in Lebanon, Jordan, or in the Gulf states and the Emirates. Wakin describes the situation of the emigrant Copt in the late fifties:

> Copts, already Westernized, become invisible in a Western country. In another Middle East country, they blend into the mosaic of Arab Christian minorities. If the Copt continues to attend church abroad, he will go to a Greek Orthodox Church or an Eastern Orthodox Church. Sometimes he chooses a Protestant church. It's a matter of personal predilection.

This was the situation to which Pope Cyril VI responded when he authorized Anba Samuel, bishop of social and public affairs, to consider and plan the establishment of Coptic churches overseas to serve the Copts in their new environment. In the mid-sixties the first Coptic churches were founded in the United States. Abuna Ghubriyal Amin was sent to Jersey City in 1965, Abuna Rufa'il Yunan to Montreal in 1967, and Abuna Bishai Kamil to Los Angeles in 1969. The demand for more Coptic churches increased incessantly throughout the seventies and eighties. Today, there are more than seventy Coptic congregations in the United States and Canada. Most of these congregations are served by married Coptic priests. In many cities the Copts have acquired their own church building, as in Detroit, Chicago, Washington, East Brunswick, Thornton, and Los Angeles. A Coptic monastery dedicated to Saint Antony was founded in Los Angeles, and Coptic theological seminaries staffed with Egyptian professors were opened in Jersey City and California. A special pontifical residence in the United States was established in Jersey City.

Due to the expanding nature of the Coptic emigration, there is naturally a great deal of fluctuation. The clerical appointments to the overseas Coptic churches are generally made by Pope Shenuda III in accordance with the recommendations of Metropolitan Bishoi, General Secretary of the Holy Synod.

The first Coptic church in Australia, dedicated to Saint Mary, was established by Abuna Mina Labib Ni'mat Allah in Sydenham, Sydney in 1970. One year later another Coptic Church of Saint Mary was opened by Abuna Buqtur Rufa'il in Melbourne. Today, there are twenty-five Coptic churches, two Coptic monasteries, one theological college, two secondary schools, and a nursing home in Australia.

According to Coptic tradition, the relationship of the Egyptian Church to Europe can be traced to the period of the Diocletian persecutions in the latter part of the third century. Tradition has associated Saints Maurice, Verena, Cassius, and Florentius with the martyrs of the Theban Legion, an Egyptian military unit that served under the emperors Diocletian and Maximianus in Switzerland and in the Rhine Valley.

The part played by early Egyptian monasticism in the conversion of England is a matter that has yet to be determined. As Stanley Lane-Poole writes:

> It is more than probable that we are indebted to the remote hermits for the first preaching of the Gospel in England, where, until the coming of St. Augustine, the Egyptian monastic rule prevailed. But more important is the belief that Irish Christianity, the great civilizing agent of the early Middle Ages among the northern nations, was the child of the Egyptian Church.

The extreme asceticism of Irish monasticism was inspired by the example of their Egyptian brethren. Saint Columban (seventh century), who retired into solitude was connected with his monastery merely by a 'minister.' The Irish double monasteries had their origin in Egyptian monasticism. Pachomius, the founder of the first coenobium in Upper Egypt, was also the first abbot of a double monastery, a monastery for monks and nuns.

One of the first Coptic overseas churches in Europe was the Coptic Church of Saint Mark in London. Today, there are ten Coptic churches in Great Britain and Ireland. In 1993 the British Orthodox Church, under the leadership of Metropolitan Seraphim, requested to be received into full communion with the See of Alexandria. The British Orthodox Church, which originated in 1866 with the consecration of Jules Ferrette as Bishop of Iona, has nineteen parishes in the United Kingdom, the Republic of Ireland, and the Isle of Man. On Pentecost Sunday, 1994, Pope Shenuda III consecrated Anba Seraphim as metropolitan of Glastonbury.

For the francophone Copts in Europe Pope Shenuda III consecrated on June 2, 1974, Anba Murqus as bishop of Marseille, Toulon, and All France and Anba Athanasius as suffragan bishop for Paris. Anba Murqus, who is Dutch, is also responsible for the two congregations in the Netherlands, the Coptic Church of Saint Athanasius and the church in the Hague, as well as for the Coptic Church of Saint Mary in Brussels. Anba Murqus resides in the Ermitage Saint Marc, Reveste-les-Eaux, Toulon. On June 27, 1981, the Church of Saint Mary of Zaytun in Reveste-les-Eaux was consecrated.

The first services for resident Copts in Germany were periodically celebrated in Wiesbaden in 1964 and in Mainz in 1969. The establishment of a Coptic church in Germany is intimately related to the pastoral work of Qummus Salib Suryal, who served for many years as a parish priest in Frankfurt. Today, there are nine Coptic churches in Germany.

In March 1988 Metropolitan Bishoi and Bishop Banyamin were present at the laying of the cornerstone for the Coptic Church of Saint Antony at the Monastery of Saint Antony in Waldsolms-Kröffelbach in the Taunus mountains in Germany. The church was consecrated on November 18, 1990, by Pope Shenuda III. In 1993 the Coptic Church acquired the Monastery of the Holy Virgin and Saint Maurice in Hoexter-Brenkhausen, which serves as residence of Anba Damian, the bishop in Germany.

The six Coptic congregations in Austria (in Vienna, Graz, Klagenfurt, Linz, Bischofshofen, and Innsbruck) are served by Qummus Yuhanna al-Baramusi and Abuna Rufa'il al-Baramusi. Both priests reside in Vienna. In Italy, Coptic services are conducted in Rome, Milan, and Turin, and in Venice, a Coptic cultural center, the Centro Culturale Copte Ortodosse, was ceremoniously inaugurated on September 16, 1980. For the Copts in Switzerland, Coptic services are offered in Geneva, Zurich, Soluthurn, and Wetzikon.

The Coptic African Mission

The history of the relationship of the See of Alexandria with Africa can be traced to the fourth century. According to Rufinus Tyrannius (340–410), a Syrian merchant named Meropius and his two sons, Frumentius and Aedesius, set out in a ship for India intending to open up business connections with the Indians. While sailing through the Red Sea, Meropius was forced to land on the coast of Ethiopia. The ship was attacked by the natives, and Meropius and the crew were put to the sword. The boys, however, were spared and sent to the king 'Ella 'Alada, whose capital was in Aksum. Greatly impressed by the two boys, the king freed them from slavery and made Frumentius his chancellor and Aedesius his cupbearer. Frumentius went to Alexandria, where he approached the newly elected patriarch Athanasius I (328–73) to look for some worthy man to be sent to Ethiopia as bishop. Thereupon, Athanasius consecrated Frumentius as bishop of Aksum. Following his return to Ethiopia, Frumentius is said to have converted the two kings 'Abreha and 'Asbeha, the sons of Senfa 'Ar'ad.

The consecration of Frumentius by Athanasius was an important event for the future development of Egyptian-Ethiopian ecclesiastical relations. By this act, a precedent was set on the basis of which, among other things, the patriarchate of Alexandria based its claims of superiority over the Ethiopian church. The Copts based their right to nominate and consecrate the abuna, or head of the Ethiopian Church, on the Eighty Disciplinary Canons of Nicea.

At the time of the controversies pertaining to the natures of Jesus Christ, the Ethiopian Church, having received its Christian faith from the Alexandrians, and being under the special suzerainty of the See of Saint Mark, supported the anti-Chalcedonian party in 451.

According to the annals of the Coptic Church, the popes of Alexandria continued throughout the centuries to consecrate the abuna for the Ethiopian Church. In 1268 a treaty was signed by the last Zagwe king Na'akueto La'ab that stipulated that one third of the kingdom should be ceded absolutely to the abuna for the maintenance of his state and dignity, as well as for the support of the churches, the clergy, the monasteries, and the monks. Furthermore, no native Ethiopian was to be chosen as abuna, even though he may have been selected by the pope of Alexandria.

In 1483, the first Portuguese expedition reached Ethiopia; it was led by the Franciscan Father J. Battista da Imola, who was accompanied by twelve other Franciscans. During the sixteenth century the relations between the Ethiopian abunate and the Alexandrian see were temporarily cut off. John Bermudez advised King Lebna Dengel to convert to Roman Catholicism and to sever relations with the Alexandrian Church. One year later, Murqus, the Coptic abuna, expressed his desire to be united with the Roman Catholic Church. Seventeen years later, Murqus abdicated, and John Bermudez was appointed abuna at the express desire of the Ethiopian king. Bermudez went to Rome, and Pope Paul III (1524–49) not only consecrated him as abuna of Ethiopia, but also as patriarch of Alexandria, a schismatic act accepted neither in Alexandria nor in Constantinople. In return for the ecclesiastical submission to Rome, a force of 450 Portuguese soldiers under the command of Christophe de Gama was sent to Ethiopia, where they defeated and killed Grañ, the emir of Harar, and his Muslim troops in 1543.

The king Galawdewos (Claudius, 1540–59) refused to acknowledge the religious supremacy of the pope of Rome and dispatched a mission to Gabriel VII (1525–70) with a request to send an abuna. The king published his *confessio fidei*, a theological statement of his belief in the doctrines of the Church of Alexandria.

Though the original Catholic mission to Ethiopia had failed, Ethiopia was not abandoned as far as the Church of Rome was concerned. In 1603, Father Pietro Paez, s.j., arrived in Fremona. Soon after his arrival, Father Paez preached in the presence of Za Dengel (1597–1607), who declared himself ready to adopt the Roman Catholic faith.

During the reign of Susenyos (1607–32), the Jesuits reached their greatest and most profound influence in Ethiopia. But revolution and civil war eventually led to the abdication of Susenyos in favor of his son Fasiladas (1632–67). Fasiladas announced the reestablishment of the Alexandrian faith, and dispatched a mission to Cairo with a request for a new abuna. For the following centuries the succession of the Ethiopian abunate remained more or less uninterrupted.

After the Italian occupation of Ethiopia in 1935, the Italian government attempted to detach the Church of Ethiopia from the See of Alexandria. The actions of the Italians, however, met with little success. The discussions for gaining ecclesiastical independence from the See of Alexandria coincided with Ethiopian independence in 1942. By 1942 Ethiopian priests had already been consecrated by the Ethiopian echegé. Thus, for all practical purposes the function of the Coptic abuna became obsolete.

In June 1947, Emperor Haile Selassie I made known his wish to settle the ecclesiastical conflict with the Coptic Church once and for all. The following proposition was offered: the Ethiopians would be granted the right to have an Ethiopian abuna with the power to consecrate Ethiopian bishops, on the condition that every decision of the Ethiopian Synod with regard to the consecration of bishops be presented to the pope of Alexandria with a list of the possible candidates. This, then, would enable the Coptic pope to delegate to the Ethiopian abuna, by special order, the power of consecration.

On October 22, 1950, Kirillus, the last Coptic abuna of Ethiopia, died. On January 13, 1951, Anba Basilius, Ethiopian bishop of Shoa, was consecrated by Joseph II (1946–56) as the abuna of Ethiopia. On September 2, 1951, five Ethiopian bishops were consecrated by Anba Basilius in accordance with the Coptic stipulations.

Following the enthronement of Cyril VI as the 116th successor to the See of Saint Mark in 1959, the Ethiopian question was the first item on his agenda. A joint statement was issued on June 29, 1959, that stipulated that the pope of Alexandria is the supreme head of the Church of Ethiopia; that representatives of the Ethiopian Church shall participate in the election of the successor of Saint Mark; that the archbishop of the Ethiopian Church, the successor of Saint Takla Haymanot, has been advanced to the dignity of patriarch-catholicus, or chief of the Church of Ethiopia; that after his election and confirmation he shall be consecrated by the pope of Alexandria; and that the patriarch-catholicus is authorized to consecrate metropolitans and bishops.

On June 20, 1959, the abuna Anba Basilius arrived in Egypt. On June 28, 1959 in the presence of Emperor Haile Selassie and Dr. Mahmud Fawzi, the minister of foreign affairs of the United Arab Republic, Cyril VI, pope of Alexandria, enthroned Anba Basilius as the first patriarch-catholicus of the Church of Ethiopia.

From September 25 to September 30, 1973, Pope Shenuda III visited Ethiopia with the aim of normalizing relations. Problems arose in 1976 on the occasion of the dismissal of Abuna Theophilus by the Communist government and the subsequent election of his successor Abuna Takla Haymanot in July 1976. The Coptic Church did not recognize the patriarchal election and anathematized the procedure and the persons involved. Abuna Takla Haymanot died on May 28, 1988.

From 1988 to 1991 the Ethiopian head of the church was Abuna Mercurius, who had very close relations to the Marxist government of Mengistu Haile Mariam. Following his dismissal, the same problems arose as in 1976 with Abuna Theophilus, namely the coexistence of two consecrated patriarchs. The Holy Synod called an electorate of approximately 360 persons, and Abuna Pawlos Gabre Yohannes was elected fifth patriarch. On July 12, 1992, he was enthroned in the Cathedral of the Holy Trinity in Addis Ababa.

After Eritrea gained its independence from Ethiopia, the Eritrean president, Mr. Isayas Afewerki, requested from Pope Shenuda III the establishment of an Eritrean Orthodox Church under the jurisdiction of the See of Alexandria. In June 1991 Pope Shenuda III ordained two Eritrean bishops for service in the United States and the United Kingdom. On September 28, 1993, the Holy Synod convened and decided on the establishment of an autocephalus Eritrean Orthodox Church. On Pentecost 1994 (June 9), Pope Shenuda III consecrated five Eritrean bishops, thus forming a Holy Synod for the Eritrean Orthodox Church. This action has led to serious judicial problems between the Coptic and Ethiopian churches. The latter claim to have sole ecclesiastical jurisdiction over Eritrea, as it used to be an Ethiopian province. On May 7, 1998, Pope Shenuda III consecrated Philippus patriarch of the Orthodox Church of Eritrea. Anba Philippus was one of eighteen priests ordained by Pope John XIX (1928–43). For many years he served as abbot of Debre Bijarou in Eritrea. The Holy Synod of the Eritrean Church consists of eight bishops.

While the relations of the Coptic Church with its Ethiopian counterpart are saddened and tarnished on account of the complicated Dair al-Sultan situation in Jerusalem (discussed below), the recent patriarchal developments in Addis Ababa and the judicial problems pertaining to the autocephalus Eritrean Orthodox Church have only increased the tensions between the orthodox churches of Egypt and Ethiopia.

Meanwhile, the Coptic Church has succeeded in penetrating with its ecclesiastical mission into regions in the south, east, and west of the African continent. In 1962, the Institute of Coptic Studies in 'Abbasiya established a department of African studies for the training of Copts to serve as missionaries. This constitutes the first attempt since the seventh century to think in terms of missions. In a press release of July 20, 1962, Pope Cyril VI declared that "final measures are now being taken to comply with the desire of the Christian inhabitants of Uganda, Kenya, and Tanganyika to join the Coptic Church. The Africa project of the Coptic Church is given priority over any other project."

In the beginning of 1965, a significant addition to the official ecclesiastical title of Cyril VI was adopted: in the local and international press he began to be referred to as "His Holiness Patriarch Cyril VI, Pope of Alexandria and of All Africa."

The actual missionary engagement of the Coptic Church began with the consecration of Abuna Antonius al-Baramusi in June 1976 as bishop for African missions. Just a year later the Coptic Church was already officially recognized and registered in Kenya. A number of heretical and schismatic congregations were dissolved. Today, the Coptic Church is well represented among the Kikuyu, Akamba, Luo, and Abaluya tribes. More than eight thousand people have been baptized in the past fourteen years. In October 1979 Pope Shenuda III visited Nairobi and laid the cornerstone for the Coptic Monastery of Saint Antony, which is situated next to the Coptic Church of Saint Antony. There are three large Coptic congregations in Ukambani: in Kinuyui (Saint Mark), in Katheka (Saint Damiana), and in Misslenni (Saint George). In Kisumu, province of Nyanza, the Copts have assembled since 1982 in the Church of Saint Mary. In Zambia, services commenced in 1984, with Saint Mark's Center in Lusaka established in 1990. In Zimbabwe Saint Antony's Monastery was opened in Harare in 1988 and Saint Mark's Church was completed in 1993. In Namibia, the monastery of Saint Antony was established in 1990 in Windhoek. In June 1995 Pope Shenuda III consecrated Bishop Bulus as bishop for missions and evangelism. He is a medical graduate with experience in missionary work.

The two Sudanese dioceses of Khartoum and Omdurman are well established. On February 16 and 17, 1978, Pope Shenuda III visited the Sudan accompanied by nine metropolitans and bishops. This was the first visit of a Coptic pope since the visit of Cyril V in 1909.

The Copts in the Holy Land and the Question of the Holy Places

Whoever visits Jerusalem, Bethlehem, Jericho, or Nazareth cannot help but notice the Coptic desert fathers among the clerics of the various Christian communities. They are easily distinguished by their *qalansuwa*s. Originally from Antioch, the headdress is a tight-fitting cap covering the head and neck embroidered with thirteen yellow or white crosses representing Christ and the apostles. Around their necks they wear large black-and-white leather Coptic crosses. They are the representatives of the Coptic Orthodox Church and His Holiness Anba Shenuda III, the 117th successor of Saint Mark the Evangelist.

Since the enthronement of Anba Abra'am I as the twentieth Coptic *mutran* (metropolitan) of Jerusalem and the Middle East in November 1991, the Coptic presence in Israel in general and Jerusalem in particular has acquired a new quality. In addition to some major restorations of old buildings—the Church of Saint Antony, the Church of Saint Helena, and the passage to the large subterranean cistern, to name a few—new social and educational projects like the new College of Saint Antony at Bet Hanina are tangible evidence of the Coptic renaissance that has overflowed to the Holy Land. At the same time, the age-old question pertaining to the jurisdiction of some of the holy places—namely, Dair al-Sultan on the roof of the Armenian Church of Saint Helena, the Chapel of the Four Creatures, the Chapel of the Archangel Michael—is presently being discussed again.

In view of these recent developments, some of the principal historical notes on the presence of the Copts in the Holy City should be restated. In the New Testament the relationship of the Egyptians to Jerusalem can be traced to the first Pentecost, when Jews from "Egypt and . . . the parts of Libya about Cyrene" were speaking in their own tongues the mighty works of God (Acts 2:10–11).

The "Letter of Paula and Eustachium to Marcella" (386) mentions monks coming from Egypt among those of various nations who visited Jerusalem, and the Spanish abbess, the fourth-century pilgrim of Etheria, refers very clearly to the monks of Egypt, or the Thebaid, who used to come to the Holy City. The Copts are mentioned as pilgrims to Jerusalem in the so-called "Letter of Guarantee" attributed to the caliph 'Umar and dated A.H. 15 (A.D. 637). According to tradition, this covenant is said to have been made between the caliph and the Greek patriarch Sophronius: "And in order that the Georgians and Abyssinians depending on the Greek Nation be well established, let all other nations that go there on pilgrimage, Latins, Copts, Syrians, Armenians, Nestorians, Jacobites, and Maronites, submit to the patriarch Sophronius of Jerusalem."

From then on, there are not many references to Coptic monks in or Coptic pilgrims to Jerusalem prior to the Crusades in the eleventh century, but from the beginning of the twelfth century, the Church and Monastery of Saint Mary Magdalene served as the spiritual center for the Jacobites, Syrian and Egyptian. The church was situated in the vicinity of the Gate of Herod, north of the Franciscan Via Dolorosa.

Following Salah al-Din's victory over the Crusader forces in the battle of the Horns of Hattin on July 4, 1187, the number of pilgrims from the various eastern Christian communities increased, and many of the churches felt the need to establish themselves on a permanent basis in the Holy City. In 1187, Sultan Salah al-Din granted exemption from taxes to the Greeks, Georgians, Copts, and Ethiopians who came to Jerusalem on pilgrimage. In the same ordinance the Sultan also confirmed the privilege of the Copts to own certain sites in the Church of the Resurrection.

In the middle of the thirteenth century tensions and misunderstandings emerged between the two non-Chalcedonian communities, the Syrians and the Copts. Thus, when it was discovered that the Syrians had added some properties of the Copts to their own and had wasted others, Cyril III (1235–43) appointed an Egyptian archbishop of

Jerusalem in 1238. He succeeded after much trouble in regaining the Coptic chapel in the Church of the Resurrection as well as the Church of Saint Mary Magdalene reconstructed by Mansur al-Tilbani. The first Coptic archbishop of Jerusalem was Anba Basilius I (1238–60). During the latter part of the thirteenth century the Copts had not only a resident archbishop, but also monks in the Holy City.

In 1537, the Copts possessed the small chapel behind the Holy Sepulcher of Christ, the altar of which they still possess. It is difficult to know when they acquired this site. An interesting transaction must have taken place before the sixteenth century, for by that time the Franciscan friars in Egypt had the right to say mass in the crypt of the Coptic Church of Saints Sergius and Bacchus in Old Cairo. R. Fedden maintains that it was quid pro quo for permission granted to the Coptic Church to maintain a small room or chapel in the Church of the Resurrection.

During the seventeenth century, the various Christian communities in the Church of the Resurrection suffered somewhat severely from the heavy taxes that they had to pay to their Muslim rulers. Yet, in spite of their poverty, the Copts retained their holy places.

Throughout the eighteenth century the small Coptic chapel behind the Holy Sepulcher is mentioned by pilgrims and travelers. In 1808, all but the eastern part of the Church of the Resurrection was destroyed by fire. The dome fell in, crushing the Tomb of Christ, altars and icons were consumed in the general conflagration, and the mass of ruin extended from the Chapel of Saint Helena to the rock-hewn tomb of Joseph of Arimathea. In the intrigues that followed at Jerusalem and Constantinople in connection with the rebuilding of the church, the Greeks secured for themselves the greater portion of the building. The Copts, however, retained their sites.

Some Copts were undoubtedly attached to the Monastery of Saint George, or Dair Mari Girgis, in Jerusalem, which the Copts had acquired in the middle of the eighteenth century. We know for certain that by 1720 the monastery was situated in the same location as today. Moreover, the monastery seems to have possessed at that time the right arm of Saint George and part of the chain used to torture him, relics that attract pilgrims and visitors to this day.

In 1806 Ulrich Seetzen visited the Holy Land and mentioned in his description the Copts, who had an unattractive and poor monastery called "Mar Dshurdschus," and furthermore, they possessed in Dair al-Sultan a courtyard next to the Church of the Resurrection, where several married priests lived. In a legal document of December 10th, 1820, it is stated, among other things, that the Monastery of Saint George belongs to the Copts. In 1782, the Copts had already enlarged their holdings in Jerusalem by buying some houses from al-Hajj 'Abd Allah Effendi, but it was not until 1837 that the Copts obtained permission to build the large Coptic *khan*, or caravansary, in the immediate vicinity of the Monastery of Saint George.

The Copts consider the Coptic chapel in the Church of the Resurrection, which is dedicated to the Holy Virgin, the holiest of all the sacred sites, for the Coptic altar is believed to be erected against the place where Christ's head rested at the time of his burial. Twenty-four lamps are suspended from the ceiling of the chapel. The cells of the Copts in the Church of the Resurrection are situated between the columns in the western part of the rotunda. The doors west of the Holy Sepulcher lead to the lodgings of the Coptic monks on the first and second floors. Generally, four or five monks keep vigil in the Church of the Resurrection, though during the feasts, this number increases to ten or twelve.

Though the Copts do not have the right to celebrate the Divine Liturgy in the Holy Sepulcher itself (the Greeks, Latins, and Armenians alone have this right), they own four sanctuary lamps, which hang in the second row from the east. The other lamps in the Holy Sepulcher belong to the Greeks, the Latins, and the Armenians, each of whom own thirteen. In the Chapel of the Angel east of the Holy Sepulcher, the Copts own one lamp, which hangs on the south side of the eastern row. Above the Stone of Unction are eight lamps, and the third from the left belongs to the Copts.

The Copts process four times a year around the Holy Sepulcher. On Palm Sunday, after the celebration of the Divine Liturgy, the Copts join the Greeks, Armenians, and Syrians in a procession three times around the Holy Sepulcher. On Good Friday between 5:00 and 7:00 p.m., only the Copts make a procession through the whole Church of the Resurrection, offering prayers at every altar (Greek, Latin, Armenian, Coptic, and Syrian). On the eve of Easter, about 1:30 p.m., the Greek Orthodox patriarch, accompanied by an Armenian archimandrite, enters the Holy Sepulcher for the ceremony of the holy fire. From the Chapel of the Angel, the holy fire is passed through the southern and northern opening to the pilgrims. The Copts also receive the holy fire through the southern opening. Then the holy fire is taken to the Coptic archbishop, who during the ceremony has remained in the Coptic Chapel of the Holy Virgin west of the Holy Sepulcher. After receiving the holy fire, the Coptic archbishop gives it to the Coptic pilgrims there. Then the Greeks, Armenians, Syrians, and Copts make a procession three times around the Holy Sepulcher. This same procession is repeated at 4:00 a.m. on Easter Sunday.

Northeast of the Holy Sepulcher, the Copts own Dair Mar

Antonius, the Monastery of Saint Antony. This monastery, which in previous centuries was considered part of Dair al-Sultan, was restored in 1875.

The Monastery of Saint Antony has three churches. On the ground level is the Church of Saint Helena. The narthex of this church leads to a large cistern, which is normally filled with water. The main church is dedicated to Saint Antony. It was built by Archbishop Basilius II (1856–99) and dedicated in 1903 by Archbishop Timothy (1899–1925), who also redecorated the chapel. The icons from north to south represent the Crucifixion, Christ's entry into Jerusalem, the Resurrection, the Last Supper, and Christ in the Garden of Gethsemane. Above the center icon of the Holy Virgin is another icon of the Resurrection. This church is adorned with numerous wall paintings showing biblical scenes such as the Last Supper, the stilling of the storm, the Nativity, the Baptism, the Annunciation, the Ascension, Christ's entry into Jerusalem, and the Via Dolorosa. The third church is dedicated to the Holy Virgin in commemoration of her appearing to the students of the Coptic College on June 21, 1954. According to the students, the Holy Virgin with the infant Christ, Saint Joseph, and two angels appeared for seven consecutive Mondays at 11:30 a.m. in the study of Dr. Shakir. Out of gratitude for this event Archbishop Jacob of Jerusalem (1946–56) had this room converted into a church. In commemoration of this apparition, the Coptic monks celebrate the Divine Liturgy in this church every Monday morning.

A survey of the Copts in the Holy Land and the question of the holy places would be incomplete without a reference to the thorny problem of the jurisdiction over Dair al-Sultan, the property on the roof of the Armenian Church of Saint Helena, and the two chapels leading to the parvis of the Church of the Resurrection.

The precarious ecclesiastical situation pertaining to Dair al-Sultan has always reflected the delicate political climate between the Egyptians and the government responsible for Jerusalem. This was the case during the reigns of the various sultans and viziers of the Ottoman empire. The cessation of diplomatic relations between the Arab Republic of Egypt and the Hashemite Kingdom of Jordan in 1958 led to the expulsion of the Coptic metropolitan and eleven Coptic priests and monks from Jerusalem in the same year. After diplomatic intervention, the Coptic members of the clergy were given tourist visas for three months with the possibility of renewal. In February 1959 the tensions between the Copts and the Ethiopian residents of the site in question increased. Subsequently, the Jordanian government ordered that Dair al-Sultan be handed over to the Ethiopians. "When the Copts did not follow the dictates of the authorities, the Jordanians changed the locks and handed the new keys to the Ethiopians. But their joy over the recuperation of their ancient place of worship was to be short-lived only."

On April 2, 1961, Dair al-Sultan was returned to the original owners, the Copts. In May 1965 structural alterations to Dair al-Sultan carried out by the Copts led to new deliberations between the Egyptians and the Jordanian government.

During the Easter celebrations of 1970, serious confrontations between the Coptic and Ethiopian monks on the roof of the Church of the Holy Sepulcher led to the Ethiopians' unlawfully and forcefully acquiring the keys to the chapels of the Four Creatures and the Archangel Saint Michael. The seizure of the keys by the Ethiopians was possible again because Ethiopia had full diplomatic relations with Israel from 1956 to 1973. These relations were broken when Ethiopia followed the policy of the rest of the African nations after the Yom Kippur War.

For the first time, an Israeli judge entered into a conflict between two Christian communities. The Israeli High Court of Justice announced a verdict on March 16, 1971, that actually ordered the Ethiopians to hand over the keys to the Copts, *unless* the Israeli government preferred to set up a commission to look into the question of ownership in this particular holy place. The government of Golda Meir decided to use this prerogative. Coptic appeals in 1977 and 1980 have only made the Israeli High Court confirm its original decision of 1971, while an Israeli arbitration attempt led by retired High Court Judge David Bacher in February 1982 produced no agreement. On April 3, 1981, the Israeli High Court again declined to intervene on behalf of the Copts for the return of the two chapels in the Church of the Resurrection. In December 1981 Pope Shenuda III reiterated his prohibition of Coptic pilgrimages to the Holy Land as long as the Israeli government would not intervene for the rightful return of Dair al-Sultan to its legitimate owners.

On January 14, 1993, the Israeli government finally decided to form a ministerial commission to study again the Coptic claims to Dair al-Sultan. The Coptic archbishop Anba Abra'am I stated that the relationship with the Ethiopians was excellent; instead, his rebuke was directed to the Israeli Government. Millions of Copts throughout Egypt—in the words of Anba Abra'am—eagerly awaited the very moment of the possibility to visit Jerusalem, once the situation between the two communities was solved. As long as the conflict remained, however, the Coptic patriarchate in Cairo would not support pilgrimages to the Holy Land.

3

The Coptic Church: Its Churches and Monasteries, Ancient and Modern

꒰꒱

Early Christianity in Alexandria

During the first century and the first half of the second century, the spread of Christianity in Alexandria and in Egypt had not been considerable. It appears that Alexandrian Christianity was rather syncretistic. Hadrian, according to a letter to Servianus in 134, saw Christians who worshiped Serapis and those who called themselves bishops of Christ devoting themselves to Serapis. Thus, Alexandrians prostrated themselves before Serapis or Christ impartially. From the beginning of the reign of Commodus in 180, the Christian religion appeared firmly established in Alexandria, almost completely purified of its gnostic doctrines and all traces of paganism. By the time of Septimius Severus (193–211), Christianity had begun to make history, and from this period onward its development was very rapid. The founding of the Catechetical School of Alexandria took place in this period. It will suffice to mention only three of the most celebrated scholars of this school: Pantaenus, Clement of Alexandria, and Origen.

Until the beginning of Constantine's Christian rule in 313, the Church in Egypt encountered many obstacles in the course of its existence. The conflict between church and state came to its height in Alexandria, which, more than any other city in the empire, may claim to have won the battle for Christianity. But in the meantime, the Christians suffered severe persecutions under the rule of Septimius Severus (204), Decius (250), Valerian (251), and Diocletian (303).

From the fourth century onward, Egyptian Christianity was characterized by its emphasis on the ascetic life, and the neighborhood of Alexandria was soon covered with monasteries, which grew more numerous as time went on. In the fifth and sixth centuries, we are told, there were no less than six hundred of them, all built like fortresses. The most famous group of monasteries is at the Ennaton, or ninth milestone on the road from Alexandria.

Likewise, the churches in Alexandria were fairly numerous in the fourth century, and in the course of the fifth and sixth centuries their numbers steadily increased. The most celebrated churches of this period were:

The Church of Saint Mark

The Church of Saint Mark, which commemorates the martyrdom of the Evangelist, must have been near the shore of the eastern harbor.

According to an early tradition, the Alexandrian Christians built a church in a place called Bucolia ('cattleshed') near the sea, beside a rock from which stone was hewn. In 311, at the time of the martyrdom of Peter, the seventeenth patriarch of Alexandria, the relics of Saint Mark were kept at Bucolia because that was reputedly where the Evangelist was martyred. In the first half of the fifth century, a new church was constructed by Saint Cyril to replace the one at Bucolia. This church was destroyed by the Arabs in the middle of the seventh century, and although Benjamin I (623–62) had received permission to restore the church, it was not rebuilt until the time of the patriarch Isaac (690–92). In 828, two Venetian merchants removed the relics of the Evangelist and carried them to Venice. A few years later, the church must have fallen into ruin, only to be rebuilt by Patriarch Shenute I (859–80). In 912, during the reign of al-Muqtadir, the church was destroyed again. Christodoulus, the sixty-sixth patriarch of Alexandria, rebuilt and consecrated the new Church of Saint Mark, which was finally destroyed by the sultan Malik al-Kamil when the Crusaders were approaching in 1218. As the sea encroached at this part of the coast, the foundations of this church were probably submerged.

The Church of Saint Michael

The Church of Saint Michael, also known as the Church of Saint Alexander, is considered to have once been the Temple of Saturn. Some archaeologists have placed the original site in the vicinity of the present municipality of Alexandria.

The patriarch Zacharias (1004–32) served as priest of this church prior to his enthronement.

The Great Church

The Megale Ecclesia, Kyriakon, or Dominicium took the place of the Caesareum. The Caesareum or Sebasteum was a temple begun by Cleopatra in honor of Antony, but completed by Octavian and dedicated to the worship of the emperors. In 354, Constantius II intended to present it to the church, but before the transfer could be effected, Athanasius I, the twentieth patriarch, held an Easter service in it. The emperor was offended. Two years later, his troops nearly killed Athanasius inside the building, and the emperor handed over the church to the Arians. In the following years, Arians and Orthodox fought about the sanctuary. The Caesareum was eventually dismantled and converted into a cathedral known as the Megale Ecclesia. The church was plundered and restored many times. In 368 it was reconstructed by Athanasius and dedicated to Saint Michael. It became the Cathedral of Alexandria, superseding that of Saint Theonas. Here, in 640, the Melkite patriarch Cyrus held a solemn service before surrendering the city to the Arabs. Later, Copts and Melkites disputed its possession until 912, at which time it disappeared in a conflagration, and its ruins were never restored.

The Church of Saint Athanasius

The Church of Saint Athanasius was constructed by the patriarch of the same name in the Bendideion quarter and consecrated in 370. At the time of the Arab conquest, the church was transformed into a large square mosque like the Mosque of Ibn Tulun in Cairo. The 'Attarin Mosque, as it is now called, is situated in the immediate vicinity of the Square of Saint Catherine, in Suq al-'Attarin.

The Church of the Holy Virgin

The oratory, known as the Theometor, was built by Patriarch Theonas (282–300) near the shore of the Eunostos harbor and reconstructed and enlarged by the patriarch Alexander I (d.328). The sanctuary was used as the Cathedral of Saint Mary until the end of the fourth century, when the Caesareum became the cathedral. The church built by Theonas served for many years as the palace of the bishops. Here Athanasius was brought up. Under early Muslim rule, this church was turned into a mosque. The Arabs gave it the name of the Western Mosque, or the Mosque of a Thousand Pillars. Now this historical site is reoccupied by the church and school of the Franciscan fathers at Rue Karam.

The Church of Saints Cyrus and John

Following the suppression of the Serapis and Isis cults by the patriarch Cyril I, the relics of the saints Cyrus and John were deposited at a locality now known as Abuqir. The relics were so intermingled, however, that they could not be separated. A church was built here in honor of the relics. The two saints remained quiet for two hundred years, but then began to disentangle themselves and work miracles. With the Arab conquest, their church vanished, but Saint Cyrus has given his name to the modern town of Abu Qir ('Father Cyr').

The Church of Saint John the Baptist

The small hill on which stands Pompey's Pillar, or more correctly, Diocletian's Pillar, marks the site of the Serapeum, the temple dedicated to the worship of Serapis. Following the destruction of the Serapeum by the patriarch Theophilus in 391, a monastery was installed on the plateau, and a church was dedicated to Saint John the Baptist. Theodosius (536–67) built the church, also known as the Angelion; Anastasius (605–16), the thirty-sixth patriarch, was a priest there; and Andronicus (616–23), the thirty-seventh patriarch, served as a deacon. The church was destroyed in the tenth century.

The Church of Saint Theodore

This church was in the eastern part of the city, that is, in the Brucheion.

The Church of Saint Peter the Martyr

This church was built opposite the Serapeum.

The Church of the Archangel Raphael

This church was situated on the Island of Pharos. There were two other churches on or near Pharos; one was the Church of Saint Faustus and the other that of Saint Sophia.

Some Coptic Churches in Modern Alexandria

The Patriarchal Church of Saint Mark

The Coptic Orthodox patriarchate, which includes the Cathedral of Saint Mark and the patriarchal offices, is situated at 19, Rue de l'Eglise Copte. One approaches the cathedral through a large courtyard surrounded by a school and the offices of the patriarchate.

The cathedral, which was reconstructed between 1950 and 1952, has three altars, which are dedicated to Saint Michael (north), Saint Mark (center), and Saint George (south). The iconostasis is adorned with the following icons, which show hints of Greco-Syrian origin: Saint Michael, Saint Paul the Theban, Saint Damiana, the Holy Virgin, Christ, Saint Mark, Saint Antony, and Saint George. The dome above the apsis is decorated with stained-glass windows of Christ and the evangelists. The stained-glass window of the Crucifixion shows the western inscription I.N.R.I. on the cross.

To the north of the three altars is the chapel of the relics, with those of Saint Apollo, Saint Mark, Saint Anianus (the patriarchal successor of the Evangelist), the martyrs of the Fayyum, Saints Dioscorus and Aesculapius, and parts of the 8,140 martyrs of Akhmim. The new prayer-room of Saint Mark, with a staircase leading to the subterranean reliquary of the Evangelist, is situated to the south of the nave. The walls of the prayer-room are adorned with a series of eleven mosaics by Mansur Farag and Isaac Fanus (1970) depicting the Coptic version of the life of Saint Mark: 1. The Evangelist with his gospel between two columns; 2. Saint Mark as one of the servants at the wedding of Cana (Jn 2:1–11); 3. Saint Mark leaving his linen cloth behind in the Garden of Gethsemane (Mk 14:51); 4. The descent of the Holy Spirit; 5. Saint Mark and the cobbler Anianus; 6. The confession of Anianus "God is one"; 7. Saint Mark consecrates Anianus bishop of Alexandria; 8. The martyrdom of Saint Mark; 9. The apparition of the Angel of the Lord to Saint Mark in prison; 10. The Catechetical School of Alexandria; 11. The return of the relics of Saint Mark from Venice to Cairo. The necrology in the southern part of the nave includes the names of forty-seven popes of Alexandria who were buried on the site of the cathedral.

The Church of Saint Menas

The Church of Saint Menas is situated at Rue al-Hurriya in the district of Fleming. The large basilican-style church was built in the first part of the twentieth century by Dr. Sami Bey Sabungi. The church is impressive on account of its simplicity. The altar is mounted on four different Greco-Roman columns. A series of beautiful stained-glass windows adorns the apse. The baptistery is situated on the northern side of the church.

Below the central altar, which is dedicated to Saint Menas, is the tomb of Dr. Sami Bey Sabungi (d.1943).

Other Coptic Orthodox Churches

The other Coptic Orthodox Churches of Alexandria are: The Church of the Holy Virgin (1935), Rue Radi, Muharram Bey; the church of Saint Michael (1939), Rue Shagarat al-Durr; the Church of Saints George and Antony (1951), 71, Rue Muharram Bey; the Church of Saint Mercurius (1952), 52, Rue al-Hilmiya; the Church of Saint George (1937), 64, Rue al-Anhar; the Church of the Holy Virgin (1956), 83, Rue al-Fawakih; the Church of Saint George (1944), Rue Canal al-Suways, Shatbi; the Church of Saint Theodore (1950), Rue Canal al-Suways; the Church of Saints Mary and Joseph (1956), 35, Rue Simuha; the Church of Saint George (1960), 126, Rue Amir Ibrahim, Sporting; the Church of Saint Shenute (1953), Rue al-Maks;

the Church of Saint Damiana (1953), Rue 'Arif Bey; the Church of
Saint George (1951), Rue al-Saqf, Maks; the Church of Saint George
(1959), Rue al-Mattaqi, Bakus; the Church of Saint George (1958),
Rue al-Sabba'i 'Abd al-Salam, Mandara; the Church of Saint Menas
(1952), 706, Rue al-Gaysh, Mandara; and the summer Church of
Saint George (1959), Abu Qir.

The Ancient Churches and Monasteries around Alexandria

The monasteries, and sometimes even their ruins, around Alexandria
have almost completely vanished. In many cases, nothing remains
except for their names, which have lingered on in the minds of the
people. Unfortunately, it is virtually impossible to identify with
certainty any of the numerous ruins around Alexandria with the
monasteries that played such an important role in the history of the
Egyptian Church from the fifth to the ninth centuries.

Southwest of Alexandria, on the way to the Desert of Scetis (Wadi
al-Natrun), there used to be several monasteries that were known by
the distance that separated them from Alexandria. They were named
after the milestone closest to the monastery.

The Pempton Monastery

Closest to Alexandria, at the fifth milestone on the way to Mareotis
(now Maryut), stood the famous Pempton. This monastery was
founded by Saint Anastasia, a virgin of Constantinople whom the
emperor Justin asked for in marriage, though his wife was still alive.
Anastasia reported this to the empress, who sent her to Alexandria and
built her a convent outside the city. Later, Anastasia retired to Scetis.

The Ennaton Monastery

The most famous of this monastery group was the Ennaton, at the
ninth milestone. The Ennaton, also known as Dair al-Hanatun or Dair
al-Zuqaq, was situated west of Dakhila. The bedouins refer to this site
as Kom al-Zuqaq, which is near Kom al-Hanatun (Ennaton). Four or
five kilometers west of Kom al-Zuqaq is a small village called al-Dair,
where there are several ruins.

By the sixth century, the Ennaton had achieved considerable importance in the life of the church. John II (505–16) and Peter IV
(567–76) had been monks in the Ennaton prior to their elections as
patriarchs. In 616, the patriarch Anastasius (605–16) was residing at
the Ennaton when he welcomed the patriarch of Antioch for a confer-

ence that resulted in the reestablishement of full communion with the Church of Antioch. At the order of Anastasius, Thomas of Harkel and Paul of Tella wrote many Syriac manuscripts at the Ennaton Monastery. The Ennaton was destroyed by the Persians during the patriarchate of Andronicus (616–23). In the days of Mark II (799–819), John the Hermit of the Ennaton prophesied the destruction of Alexandria. According to al-Maqrizi, who called the Ennaton 'al-Zuqaq,' it was the duty of the Coptic patriarch after his election in the al-Mu'allaqa Church of the Holy Virgin in Cairo to proceed to the Ennaton, but the custom fell into disuse.

Other monasteries on the road from Alexandria to the Desert of Scetis were the Dekaton, at the tenth milestone, and the Eikoston, at the twentieth milestone.

The Oktokaidekaton

The Oktokaidekaton was situated at the eighteenth milestone and known as the third monastery from Alexandria, though it was not on the road to the Desert of Scetis but on the way to the episcopal see of al-Karyun.

It has been suggested that the site called al-Dair north of the village of al-Amiriya may mark the place where this ancient monastery was situated. The monastery is said to date from the fifth century.

Here Andronicus and Anastasia of Antioch lived for twelve years. When Anastasia died at the Oktokaidekaton, her true sex was at last revealed. Anastasia was one of the numerous women-monks like Theodora and Euphrosyne, who dressed in monks' attire and joined the desert fathers. The fourth-century council of Gangra strongly condemned this practice.

Dair Qabriyus

Dair Qabriyus (the Monastery of Cyrius or Cyprius) was situated on the coast northeast of Alexandria.

By the seventh century, the monastery had acquired considerable importance. Abbot Theonas had lived at the monastery from 572 until at least 622. In 621, Benjamin I entered the monastery as a monk before he was elected to the patriarchate. The monastery escaped the Persian destructions.

The Metanoia

In the latter part of the fourth century, a monastery of the Pachomian order called the Metanoia, or the Monastery of Penitence, was built at Canobus east of Alexandria, on the site of the ancient temple of Isis and Osiris, famous for the incubation oracles.

Theophilus, who destroyed the Alexandrian Serapeum, did not spare the temples at Canobus and installed a monastery, while another monastery was set up at Menuthis in the Temple of Isis. The Metanoia attracted both Greeks and Romans, for whom Saint Jerome translated the monastic rules into Latin.

At the beginning of the fifth century, Cyril I decided to convey the bodies of Saints Cyrus and John, who had been buried in Saint Mark's Cathedral, to Menuthis in order to replace the pagan healing cult with a Christian one. Numerous miracles were soon performed, and the fame and prosperity of the new sanctuary became as great as that of the earlier pagan one.

In the sixth century, the Metanoia was considered one of the leading monasteries, and Andrew, the abbot of the monastery, appears to have been a kind of provincial superior for the Nile Delta, or perhaps for the monasteries founded by the Metanoia. By the end of the sixth century, the Metanoia was definitely in Byzantine hands, whereas the Ennaton remained a stronghold of the Copts. The Metanoia escaped the destructions that befell the Ennaton and also avoided destruction by the Persians.

The Church in the Temple of Taposiris Magna

The temple of Taposiris Magna is situated in Burg Abu Sir in the immediate vicinity of the ancient Roman lighthouse. The visitor travels thirty-five kilometers west from Alexandria along the coastal road as far as Burg al-'Arab. At Burg al-'Arab, follow the road to the village of Burg Abu Sir.

The large temple construction, known to the bedouins as Qasr al-Bardawil, stands on the summit of a hill. The temple was at one time dedicated to Osiris, as the name Abu Sir indicates.

The ruins of the ancient town cover the southern slope of the hill on which the temple was built. The space within the vast temple enclosure gives the impression of a great void. Excavations have brought to light traces of a small Christian church, the apse of which was built against the pylons at the eastern wall of the temple.

In the seventh century, the Monastery of Taposiris was an important institution. Victor, a monk of this monastery, was a candidate for the patriarchate. From the nineteenth century onward, the ruins were studied by Pacho (1819), Scholz (1820), Minutoli (1834), Robecchi-Brichetti (1890), and Breccia (1920).

The Lourdes in the Desert: Saint Menas

The Shrine of Saint Menas (Dair Abu Mina) at Mareotis (Maryut) is situated in the Western Desert fifteen kilometers southeast of Burg al-'Arab, eleven kilometers south of Bahig, and eighty-five kilometers southwest of Alexandria.

There were many martyrs' shrines in Egypt, but their popularity was generally confined to their own districts. The only two martyrs' shrines that had an international reputation were those of Saints Cyrus and John at Abu Qir and of Saint Menas at Maryut; of these, that of Saint Menas was undoubtedly the more celebrated one.

During the reign of Constantine, a small oratory, like a tetrapylon, was built over the tomb of the saint. A few years later, during the patriarchate of Athanasius, a church was built over the tomb, and bishops, priests, and laity rejoiced in the consecrations of the first Church of Saint Menas. The fame of the signs and wonders that appeared in that church through the intercession of Saint Menas the Martyr spread abroad. Soon the church became too small to accommodate all the pilgrims who came from many parts of the ancient world.

During the reign of the emperor Arcadius, the sanctuary was enlarged through the building of a great basilica, the Church of Arcadius. The emperor Zeno then constructed a large city and a palace for himself in the vicinity of the shrine.

The number of priests and monks attached to the Church of Saint Menas is difficult to estimate, though one may be justified in speaking of several hundred priests, in addition to thousands of shopkeepers, workers, etc., who inhabited the Desert of Mareotis in the fifth and sixth centuries.

Ever since the discovery of the ruins of the Saint Menas baths in 1907, the sacred shrine in the Desert of Mareotis has been compared with Lourdes, for large numbers of pilgrims go to the Shrine of Saint Menas to be healed by the waters, which has a beneficial therapeutic effect. Ampullae embossed with the effigy of the saint together with inscriptions for containing the sacred water were on sale at the site and found their way into almost every part of the ancient world.

At the beginning of the seventh century, the Shrine of Saint Menas was in the hands of the Greeks or Melkites, for we hear of the visit of the Melkite patriarch of Alexandria, Saint John the Almoner, to the Desert of Mareotis.

During the patriarchate of Kha'il (743–67) there arose the question of the jurisdiction over the Church of Saint Menas, for both the Copts and Melkites requested a decision from the government. The judge decided in favor of the Copts.

During the patriarchate of Joseph I (831–49), the churches and buildings of Saint Menas suffered considerable damage, for in 836, the caliph al-Mu'tasim decided to build his palace, Jawsaq al-Khaqani, in Samarra with the most precious marble and stones available in his empire. Thus the Church of Saint Menas was robbed of its colored marbles and its unequaled pavement. Joseph, however, rebuilt the church.

There is good reason to believe that it was customary for the patriarchs of the eighth and ninth centuries to go to the Desert of Mareotis on the Feast of Saint Menas, in order to celebrate the Divine Liturgy at the shrine of the saint. In the ninth century, the Shrine of Saint Menas was pillaged and destroyed by the Bedouins, and by the eleventh century Bedouins are reported to have hidden themselves there in order to waylay travelers. The Church of Saint Menas was still standing as late as the twelfth century, but the pilgrim city around it was in ruins.

Almost one thousand years of silence cover the remains of this once glorious Christian metropolis. In 1905, the German Kaufmann expedition rediscovered the Shrine of Saint Menas and excavated the ruins for two successive years. The remains of this shrine that have been brought to light are as follows:

The Church of Saint Menas

The Church of Saint Menas, built over the tomb of the saint, was consecrated by the patriarch Theophilus (384–412) and was built of limestone. The Church of Saint Menas had three aisles with apses. The altar, the foundations of which can still be seen, stood immediately above the tomb of the saint.

The Basilica of Arcadius

As the Church of Saint Menas became too small for the many pilgrims attracted to this holy shrine, the emperor Arcadius built an enormous basilica to the east of the Church of Saint Menas. The roof of this basilica was supported by fifty-six marble columns, the socles of which can still be seen. Like the Church of Saint Menas, the Basilica of Arcadius had three aisles. The basilica had a length of sixty meters and a width of twenty-six and a half meters. The transept had a length of fifty meters. The total length of the group of sacred buildings comprising the basilica, the first church over the tomb of the saint, and the baptistery, is as much as 120 meters.

The Baptistery

A monumental baptistery was added to the western part of the church. Its ruins are from twelve to fourteen meters high. The baptistery was a central building, square on the outside and octagonal within.

The Southern Circular Building

An expansive semicircular court extends on the southwest side of the baptistery. On the south side of the colonnade are several irregularly proportioned rooms, perhaps for the sick who wanted to be near the shrine of the saint.

The Northern Basilica

To the north of the city and near the parking lot of the new Monastery of Saint Menas are the foundations of the sixth-century northern basilica. The church has three aisles. A staircase leads to an upper gallery. The baptistery was on the southern side. A large atrium extends west of the nave.

The Eastern Church

About two kilometers east of the new Monastery of Saint Menas are the foundations of a fifth-century tetraconch church. The central part consists of a square nave with four cross-shaped columns at each corner. Beneath the foundations, remains of an older building were discovered.

The Western Church

About two kilometers west of the Great Basilica are the remains of an additional church, consisting of an altar room, nave, and baptistery. The site was discovered in 1987.

Just outside the ruins of the church is the cornerstone for the new Coptic Monastery of Saint Menas. The text on the stone reads as follows:

> The Monastery of Abu Mina Thawmaturgus. Its cornerstone was laid by the blessed hand of His Holiness, the Glorious Pope Cyril VI, Pope of Alexandria and Patriarch of the See of Mark, and this was on the blessed Friday, November 27, 1959, Hatur 17, 1676 A.M.

With the enthronement of Cyril VI to the patriarchal see of Saint Mark in 1959, a new chapter in the history of the Shrine of Saint Menas began. Both the Coptic Museum, in cooperation with the German Archaeological Institute in Cairo, and the Coptic Othodox Church have centered their attention on the ancient shrine.

On November 25, 1961, Cyril VI dedicated the first cells and the Chapel of Saint Samuel, which constitute the first part of the new Monastery of Saint Menas. The Chapel of Saint Samuel, which is part of the building in which the cells are situated, is adorned with many icons. Several of those icons have been transferred to Maryut from the Church of Saint Menas north of Old Cairo.

On February 15, 1962, some of the relics of Saint Menas were translated from the Church of Saint Menas in Fumm al-Khalig, Cairo to the Church of the Holy Virgin in Maryut. Monks of the Monastery of the Syrians, under the leadership of Abuna Mina Apa Mina, settled in the new monastery. In 1969 construction of the monumental Basilica of Saint Menas began. On March 9, 1971, Pope Cyril VI died. On November 24, 1972, his body was transferred from the Cathedral of Saint Mark in 'Abbasiya to the Desert of Mareotis, where he reposes in the crypt of the Basilica of Saint Menas. On November 26, 1976, Pope Shenuda III celebrated the Eucharist in the new basilica with its seven altars.

More than sixty monks inhabit the monastic cells. Several buildings for pilgrims can accommodate the increasing number of visitors. A retreat house for conferences, administrative buildings, and a large library were completed in the eighties. Two kiosks offer devotional materials and souvenirs. An extensive wall encloses the new spacious pilgrimage area.

Cellia

The ancient monastic site of Cellia, a name that comes from the Greek word for 'cells,' was rediscovered by Professor Antoine Guillaumont of Paris in the spring of 1964. In the following year excavations of the site were undertaken by a French-Swiss team of experts under the direction of Professor Rodolphe Kasser of Geneva. The site of Cellia is located about two kilometers south of the Nubariya Canal and twenty kilometers east of the Gianaclis vineyards. The site of Cellia comprises the zones of Qusur al-Ruba'iyat and Qusur Wadayda in Markaz Hush 'Ish, and Qusur al-'Izayla, Qusur 'Abid, and Qusur 'Isa in Markaz Dilingat, the whole of which extends over eleven kilometers in length and two kilometers in width.

Cellia is mentioned several times in early writings dealing with monasticism, such as the *Apophthegmata Patrum, the Historia monachorum in Aegypto* of Rufinus, the *Historia Lausiaca* of Palladius, and the *Collationes Patrum* of Cassianus. The origin of the new monastic settlement is related in the *Apophthegmata Patrum*, where we read that, as the monks at Nitria had become very numerous, a certain Abba Antony came to Abba Amon in Nitria to ask his advice about a suitable locality for a new colony of monks. Having partaken of a meal at the ninth hour (3:00 p.m.) Abba Amon and Abba Antony journeyed into the desert until sunset. Abba Amon then selected a suitable site for a monastic settlement and marked it with a cross. Rufinus states in his *Historia monachorum in Aegypto* that the monks at Nitria who wished for greater solitude retired to Cellia, where they constructed cells out of hearing and sight of one another.

A peculiarity of the cells excavated is that they comprise not a single room, as might be expected, but a number of rooms. Around this group of rooms are traces of a wall about one meter high.

In the walls of most of the rooms are niches, often decorated, that were destined for books and utensils. The walls of the rooms are often painted in dark red with cross designs, as well as a few inscriptions. Outside this group of rooms there appears to have been a small garden.

The Coptic Monasteries of Wadi al-Natrun

The Valley of Wadi al-Natrun

Wadi al-Natrun has a long history dating back to pharaonic times. Caravans traveled from the Bahariya and Farafra oases to the Nile Delta, passing the small depression of Wadi al-Natrun.

Three localities west of the Nile Delta are frequently referred to by the early monastic fathers. Macarius the Alexandrian, in the latter part of the fourth century, had four cells in the Western Desert: one in Scetis, the inner desert; one in Libya; one in the "Cells", and one in Mount Nitria.

Mount Nitria, a place where nitrate was found, is situated between forty and fifty kilometers north of the present Wadi al-Natrun rest house, or some fourteen kilometers southwest of Damanhur. Though still in the desert, the mountain is situated on the edge of the Delta. In this locality we find the earliest home of Christian asceticism. Palladius, who visited the monks living in Nitria in 391, met about two thousand of the great and strenuous men who were adorned with the excellence of their spiritual life.

The second settlement was Cellia, situated northeast of Scetis, the present Wadi al-Natrun. According to Palladius, this was the habitation of Macarius the Alexandrian.

The locality that concerns us here has been known by a number of names: Scetis, Scythis, al-Askit, Scitium, Shiet, Shihet, Wadi Habib, and Wadi al-Natrun. Its distance from Cellia was a journey of about sixty kilometers, and from Mount Nitria about seventy-five kilometers. While both Mount Nitria and Cellia were visited by monks and others, there is no indication that Scetis was ever inhabited until the day Saint Macarius ventured there.

This, then, was the area that became the center of Coptic monasticism, the region into which the great saints of the Egyptian Church withdrew: Saint Macarius the Great, Saint Bishoi, Saint John the Short, Saint John Kame, and many others. Here we find the 'little strangers,' Maximus and Domitius of the Monastery of the Romans (Dair al-Baramus), and Moses the Black, who, being attracted by the saints of Scetis, decided to remain in the desert and follow the ascetic life. This settlement, more remote than either Mount Nitria or Cellia, became in later years one of the foremost centers of Egyptian monasticism.

The glory of Mount Nitria passed away after the fifth century and what we know of its previous existence comes to us through the reports of visitors. The two pairs of Rufinus and Melania and Saints Jerome and Paula are said to have visited Mount Nitria, and their testimonies give us an insight into the ascetic lives of the fathers in that region. Cellia's glory also faded after a short while. Only the most remote and isolated community survived the internal and external pressures exerted on the monastic fellowships, so the Desert of Scetis, or Wadi al-Natrun, because of its isolation, became for many years the residence of the Coptic patriarchs.

Wadi al-Natrun is about fifty kilometers long, and runs southeast to northwest, with its southeastern end being seventy-five kilometers northwest of Cairo. The valley is never more than eight kilometers wide.

For centuries, the monasteries in the Desert of Scetis could enjoy the isolation that the desert provided. The building of the Cairo-Alexandria desert road in 1936 and the construction of the rest house with its General Motors beacon at Wadi al-Natrun have helped to destroy the cherished isolation of the monasteries. With this encroachment of the 'world' on the Desert of Scetis, one may well ask whether the eremitical manner of life in Wadi al-Natrun may not suffer the same fate as the eremitical settlements in Nitria and Cellia. To the desert fellowship, the 'world' is death, and the 'world' penetrates rapidly and unceasingly into the desert.

The Monastery of the Romans

The Monastery of the Romans (Dair al-Baramus) is the northernmost of the four remaining monasteries of Wadi al-Natrun. The distance from the rest house to the monastery is approximately fourteen kilometers.

Dair al-Baramus is the earliest settlement in Wadi al-Natrun. The Arabic name 'Baramus' is a transliteration of the Coptic 'Pa-Romeos,' which means 'of the Romans.' The history of its foundation is related to the two Roman saints Maximus and Domitius. According to tradition, these two young Roman princes, sons of the Roman emperor Valentinian, arrived in Wadi al-Natrun after having visited the Christian shrines of Nicea and Palestine. Here they met Saint Macarius, who served as the priest of the desert. At first, Saint Macarius tried to dissuade them. After a while, however, the 'two little strangers' had established themselves in their cell, and the older brother attained perfection before he died. Three days later, the younger brother also died. Whenever the fathers came to Saint Macarius he used to take them to the cell of those two brothers and say to them, "Behold ye the martyrdom of these little strangers." A year after their death Saint Macarius consecrated the cell of the princes and said, "Call this place the Cell of the Romans." With regard to the date of the foundation of the monastery, it is quite possible that a monastic community existed in the general location of the present Dair al-Baramus as early as 340. Archaeological discoveries in and around the Dair al-Baramus in 1994 identified the present monastery with the original Dair Anba Musa al-Aswad, or the Monastery of Saint Moses the Black, which was under the leadership of Saint Isidore the Hegumen. On account of the christological problems and divisions in the sixth century, the monastery became known as that of the Holy Virgin of al-Baramus. This is the forerunner of the present Dair al-Baramus.

All four Wadi al-Natrun monasteries suffered six sacks. The first occurred in 407, the second a few years later in 410, the third in 444, the fourth in 507, the fifth in 817, and the sixth and last in the eleventh century. In all these sacks the monastic buildings were wrecked, the churches plundered, and the monks either slain or carried off as captives.

In response to the almost continuous attacks by the Berbers and Bedouins, the ninth-century patriarch Shenute I built protecting walls around the monasteries. In 1088, 712 monks inhabited seven monasteries in Wadi al-Natrun, and twenty monks resided in Dair al-Baramus. Significant reconstructions were carried out in the thirteenth century by Patriarch Gabriel III. The most severe threat to the monasteries, however, was the Black Death in the fourteenth century, which was followed by a famine.

Dair al-Baramus, though insignificant in the early Middle Ages, supplied two monks in the seventeenth century who ascended the patriarchal throne, Matthew III (1631–46) and Matthew IV (1660–75). The monastery produced several outstanding theologians, the most important being Abuna Na'um and Abuna 'Abd al-Masih ibn Girgis al-Mas'udi, both of the nineteenth century.

The most important visitors to the monastery from the seventeenth to the nineteenth centuries were: Coppin (1638), Thevenot (1657), De Maillet (1692), Du Bernat (1710), Sicard (1712), Sonnini (1778), Lord Prudhoe (1828), Lord Curzon (1837), Tattam (1839), Tischendorf (1845), Jullien (1881), and Butler (1883).

The monastery has five churches. The Church of the Holy Virgin Mary (al-'Adhra') is so entangled in a maze of structures that it is difficult to see except for its roof. To the northwest of the nave is the entrance to the Chapel of Saint Theodore the General, and in the west end is the baptistery. From the west end of the north aisle of the Church of al-'Adhra' one can enter the Chapel of Saint George. At the north wall of the Church of al-'Adhra' is a new (1957) ivory-inlaid feretory with glass windows, which contains the bodies of Saints Moses the Black and his teacher Isidorus.

The Church of al-'Adhra' has altogether three altars, which show elements of widely different periods, some as old as the ninth century. The church is decorated with a number of icons representing Saints Antony and Paul the Theban, Saint Onuphrius, Saints Maximus and Domitius, Saints Apollo and Apip, Saint Barsum, Saint Cyril, and the Holy Virgin Mary.

The relics of the patrons of the monastery, Saints Maximus and Domitius, are believed to repose beneath the central altar. Major restorations of the Church of al-'Adhra' were carried out in 1986, and several wall paintings of the twelfth and thirteenth centuries were discovered.

The nineteenth-century Church of Saint John the Baptist is situated in the northeastern area of the monastery. The church, with its three altars, was built by the patriarch Cyril V in a modern Byzantine style.

The keep, or *qasr*, has been for centuries the abode of solitaries, the most famous of whom was Abuna Sarabamun (1920). The Church of Saint Michael is situated on the second floor of the keep. The altar is covered with a dome.

The walls around the monastery have a height of ten to eleven meters and a thickness of about two meters. As in the case of the other monasteries, one has a magnificent view from the walls of the interior of the monastery and the vastness of the desert outside. The refectory, which is not used at present, is situated parallel to the main church. The visitor should note the stone lectern with its roughly incised cross.

The guest house is a comfortably furnished nineteenth-century Levantine building and is reserved for the accommodation of visitors.

The pictures that decorate the reception hall are those of Anba Athanasius, the late metropolitan of Beni Suef; Anba Murqus, metropolitan of Abu Tig; Anba Sawirus, metropolitan of Minya; Anba Banyamin, the late metropolitan of Minufiya; Anba Tuma, the late metropolitan of Tanta; Anba Macarius, the late bishop of Dair al-Baramus; and Abuna Barnaba, at one time hegumen of Dair al-Baramus.

The library, once housed in the keep, has been transferred to a room on the first floor of the eastern part of the monastery. It contains about three thousand volumes, which are kept in several cabinets. The classification was the work of the famous Abuna 'Abd al-Masih ibn Salib al-Baramusi, who was known for his great learning.

The recent renovations and extensions were carried out under the supervision of Pope Shenuda III. These include the construction of an asphalt road to the monastery, several major cultivation projects, six water pumps, a sheepfold, a henhouse, and two generators. In addition many new cells were constructed inside and outside the monastery. A clinic and a pharmacy serve the monks. A spacious retreat center for conferences and a large two-story guesthouse were opened in January 1981.

Under the leadership of Bishop Isidore, the number of monks has steadily increased to almost one hundred desert fathers.

The limestone cave of the late pope Cyril VI, known as the Rock of Sarabamun has become a popular place of pilgrimage. The site, about two and a half kilometers northwest of the monastery, is marked by twelve wooden crosses. The interior of the spacious one-room cave is adorned with numerous pictures and icons of Cyril VI. An iron latticework in front of the entrance to the cave protects the site. In the desert around the monastery are several caves inhabited by hermits.

The Monastery of Saint Macarius

The Monastery of Saint Macarius (Dair Abu Maqar) is the southern-most monastery in Wadi al-Natrun. It can be seen to the west from the Cairo–Alexandria desert highway about 129 kilometers from Cairo, or eighty-six from Alexandria. One reaches the monastery by turning into the desert at the road sign on the desert highway that points to the monastery.

From a historical point of view, the Monastery of Saint Macarius is the most interesting monastery in Wadi al-Natrun. It has supplied more patriarchs (twenty-nine) than any other monastery. The foundation of Dair Abu Maqar is closely associated with the life of Saint

Macarius the Great (300–90). He was the son of a village priest. As a young boy he learned the Scriptures. As was the custom, his parents decided for him to be married, but Saint Macarius avoided association with his wife, because of his high esteem for virginity. One day when he as working as a camel driver, Saint Macarius saw a vision of an angel who promised him that his followers would inhabit the desert to which he had taken the camels.

Later, he withdrew to the inner desert, where, at that time, no ascetics had settled. His first settlement was in the vicinity of the present Dair al-Baramus.

After the death of Saints Maximus and Domitius, Saint Macarius was led by an angel to a certain rock, and there he was told to build a church. This church, then, with the cells around it, formed the nucleus of the present monastery. In spite of the community that grew up around him, Saint Macarius remained an anchorite throughout his life. He used to live in one of the cells, which was connected by a tunnel to a small cave. After the death of Saint Macarius, Saint Paphnutius, who is described as possessing such knowledge that he could expound the Scriptures without reading from them, became his undisputed successor.

Three times in the course of the fifth century, the monastery was sacked by Berbers. In the third sack, forty-nine monks gladly submitted themselves to the swords of the invading Berbers.

Toward the middle of the sixth century, the monastery acquired great importance when it became the official residence of the Coptic patriarchs, who were no longer permitted by the Byzantine rulers to reside in Alexandria.

In the seventh century, the monasteries, which were widely devastated by the fourth Berber attack, were rebuilt. The consecration of the new Church of Saint Macarius by Patriarch Benjamin I took place in 650.

Some of the outstanding monks of this period were Saint John the Hegumen (d.675), and Saints Abraham and George of Scetis, also of the seventh century. By the beginning of the ninth century, the Laura of Saint Macarius contained a thousand cells. The monastery was sacked again in 866. The patriarch Shenute I rebuilt the church and provided the monastery with a fortified wall.

In the beginning of the eleventh century, the Monastery of Saint Macarius gained prominence, especially during the widespread persecutions of al-Hakim (996–1021). The patriarch Zacharias and most of the bishops had found refuge in Wadi al-Natrun. It was at that time that a Turkish prince obtained the head of Saint Mark the Evangelist. On learning that the Christians would pay a large sum of money for it, he took the head to Cairo and sold it for three hundred dinars. Later, it was carried to the patriarch at the Monastery of Saint Macarius.

In the middle of the eleventh century, the Monastery of Saint Macarius claimed more than half of the total number of monks in Wadi al-Natrun.

As this monastery became the patriarchal residence, it became customary for the patriarchs to consecrate the chrism (myron) there, in a ceremony that took place on the Thursday of Holy Week.

From the middle of the fourteenth century this monastery began to deteriorate, on account of the Black Death and the subsequent famine and the political pressures exerted by the Mamluk rulers.

The monastery was visited by Josef von Ghistele (1481), who was shown a firman with the signature of the hand of the Prophet Muhammad. Arnold von Harff (1497) discovered many underground caves like chapels, and Villamont (1590) found there those aquiline stones that are helpful to women in labor. Sandys (1611), on the other hand, mentions the Rose of Jericho at the monastery, which had the same effects as Villamont's stones.

In the seventeenth century, the monastery served temporarily as a seminary for Capuchin missionaries for the study of Arabic and Coptic theology and liturgies.

From the Middle Ages onward, the monastery had sheltered a considerable library. The library remained intact until the seventeenth century, when European bibliophiles discovered the treasures. The library was successively carried off by Cassien (1631), Agathangelus (1634), Goujon (1670), Huntington (1678), Sicard (1712), Assemani (1714), Sevin (1729), Tattam (1839), Tischendorf (1844), Chester (1873), and Evelyn White (1921).

When Thevenot visited the monastery in 1656, he described it as the most dilapidated of the four monasteries of Wadi al-Natrun, and Du Bernat (1710) noticed only four monks there, while Granger (1730) found the monastery in ruins. By 1799, though, Andreossy counted twenty monks at the monastery.

The most significant building in the monastery is the Church of Saint Macarius. The present church is merely a remnant of a once beautiful building, large portions of which have been destroyed. The church has two altars, one dedicated to Saint Benjamin (south), the other to Saint John the Baptist (north). The eastern niche of the former altar was at one time the seat of the patriarch. The northern altar is interesting because of its 'inner choir' and its shrine, which was built by Mikha'il Yusuf and his brother Bishai in 1930.

South of the choir stands the feretory with the bodily remains of the three Macarii and Saint John the Short. The feretory also contains the relics of the following patriarchs: Kha'il II (849–51), Kha'il III (880–907), Gabriel I (910–20), Cosmas III (920–32), Macarius I (932–52), Christodoulus (1047–77), Cyril II (1078–92), John V (1147–66), Mark III (1166–89), and John XV (1619–29), as well as the son of Martinius, a minister in the reign of Theodosius the Younger.

The Church of Saint Iskhiron of Qallin has three altar rooms (*haikals*), though only two altars. The date of this church may well fall within the fourteenth century.

The Church of the Forty-Nine Martyrs (al-Shuyukh) is used for the Liturgy during the Fast and on the Feast of the Nativity. During this period, the relics of the three Macarii and Saint John the Short are transferred from the Church of Saint Macarius and placed at the north wall of the choir. The church is adorned with icons representing the three Macarii, Saint Macarius, Saint Mark, Saint George, and the Holy Virgin Mary. The church serves as the place of burial for the forty-nine monks who submitted to the Berber swords.

The *qasr* of the Monastery of Saint Macarius is by far the most interesting one of its kind because of its many chapels and churches. One enters the *qasr* by a narrow drawbridge that leads to the first story of the building. The interior of the tower is divided into three floors: the ground floor and the first and second stories. On the first story of the *qasr* is the Chapel of the Holy Virgin, with three *haikals*. The screen, which may be the work of a thirteenth century artist, is worth seeing.

On the second story are three churches that are remarkable for their wall paintings. The Church of Saint Michael is the northernmost church. It has one *haikal*, which has a beautiful screen. The south wall of the church is decorated with pictures representing a whole gallery of saints: Saint Eusebius, Saint Basilides, Saint Justus, Saint Apoli, and Saint Theoclia. On the north wall within the choir screen is a painting of Saint Michael, and a little further to the east is a small figure, probably that of Saint Hilaria, the daughter of the emperor Zeno. In the nave of the church are a total of nine pillars with rather interesting capitals, some Doric, others Corinthian with crosses carved among the foliage.

The Church of Saints Antony, Paul, and Pachomius is situated south of the Church of Saint Michael on the second floor. On the north wall of the chapel are paintings of the three founders of Egyptian monasticism to whom the church is dedicated.

The Church of the Hermits, or Church of the Wanderers (al-Suwwah) is the southernmost of the three churches on the second floor. The wall paintings of the church represent nine hermits: Saint Samuel, Saint John the Hegumen, Saint Onuphrius (Abu Nofr), Saint

Abraham, Saint George, Saint Apollo, Saint Apip, Saint Misael, and Saint Pidjimi.

Among the new features of the monastery are the plantations outside the original walls to the east. This garden was begun in 1925 by Anba Abra'am, who served as hegumen of the monastery and as bishop of Balyana. In 1954, a round water tower was built.

In 1969 Cyril VI ordered Abuna Matta al-Maskin and his twelve monks to leave Wadi al-Rayyan, where they had lived for ten years, and to settle at the Monastery of Saint Macarius. This was the beginning of a spiritual and architectural restoration of the monastery. Only six monks used to live at the monastery, and the historic buildings were on the point of collapse. Today more than 120 monks, many of whom are university graduates, make up the monastic community.

One of the most urgent tasks was the restoration of the old buildings, many of which were pulled down and replaced by more than 150 new cells, a refectory for the daily agape-meal, a library, a spacious guest house, several reception rooms, and visitors' quarters. The new buildings, which include a bakery, barns, and garages as well as storage and repair facilities, occupy an area of ten acres, six times that covered by the old monastery.

During the restoration of the Church of Saint Macarius in the autumn of 1978 the monks claim to have discovered the relics of Saint John the Baptist and those of the ninth-century-B.C. prophet Elisha. These were found in a crypt below the northern wall of the church. They were placed in a special reliquary in the sanctuary of Saint John the Baptist in the Church of Saint Macarius. The modern printing press, installed in 1978, produces the monthly magazine *Saint Mark* and other publications in Arabic and foreign languages. The clinic is staffed by several monks who are qualified physicians and by several pharmacists. It serves the four hundred laborers, the visitors, and the monks.

About one kilometer north of the monastery, large farm buildings have been set up to house cows, buffaloes, sheep, and poultry. Noteworthy is a new type of beet fodder, which the monks are the first to have cultivated in Egypt. In 1978 President Sadat donated two thousand feddans of desert land to the monastery, along with two tractors. A new well was drilled to obtain water.

The monastic life centers on the daily common meal, or agape, in the refectory. Once a week between 2:00 and 8:00 a.m. the Divine Liturgy is celebrated, followed by the agape. Other meals are taken by the monks in their cells, which contain small kitchens.

The monastery maintains friendly links with several other monasteries, including the Benedictine Abbey at Chevetogne, Belgium;

Solesmes Abbey and the Monastery of the Transfiguration in France; Dair al-Harf in Lebanon; and the Convent of the Incarnation in England. Several monks of these monasteries have stayed for some time at the Monastery of Saint Macarius.

The monastery is under the jurisdiction of Anba Mikha'il, the metropolitan of Asyut.

The Monastery of Saint Bishoi

As is the case with all Coptic monasteries, the foundation of the Monastery of Saint Bishoi (Dair Anba Bishai) is associated with the life of its patron saint. When an angel of God appeared to him and called him into the desert, he responded willingly and went to Scetis, where he joined Saint John the Short, who had lived by himself for many years. After a while, Saint John the Short recommended that Saint Bishoi leave him and live by himself in a cave. While observing the solitary life, Saint Bishoi had several visions in which the Lord Jesus Christ appeared to him.

On the occasion of the first sack of the monastery in 407, both Saints Bishoi and John the Short escaped. The former found refuge in a mountain near the Fayyum, where he met the anchorite Paul of Tammua, with whom he cultivated a great friendship. Saint John the Short went to the Monastery of Saint Antony. Three months after Saint Bishoi's arrival in the Fayyum, however, he died.

Like the Monastery of Saint Macarius, the Monastery of the Romans, and the Monastery of Saint John the Short, the Monastery of Saint Bishoi suffered five sacks by the Berbers. Al-Maqrizi (fifteenth century) refers especially to the fourth destruction of the monastery during the patriarchate of Andronicus (616–23). The patriarch Benjamin I (623–62), however, reconstructed it. When the time of the persecutions by the Berbers had come to an end in the ninth century, the bodies of Saints Bishoi and Paul of Tammua were returned to the Monastery of Saint Bishoi.

In 1096, the monastery suffered another pillage. At the time of the patriarch Benjamin II (1327–39), considerable restoration of this monastery was undertaken, for ants had destroyed much of the woodwork, and the buildings threatened to collapse.

The monastery was visited by Coppin (1638); Thevenot (1657), who regarded it as the best of the four Wadi al-Natrun monasteries; Wansleben (1672); Sicard (1712), who found only four monks present; Granger (1730); Sonnini (1778); Andreossy (1799); Curzon (1837); and Tattam (1839), who acquired numerous manuscripts from the monastery. Wilkinson (1843) saw thirteen monks in the monastery, and Junkers (1875) was not permitted to enter because a

European before him had stolen several manuscripts. Jullien (1881) felt that the monastery could boast of the best water, which was substantiated by Butler (1883).

The visitor to the old part of the Monastery of Saint Bishoi can see five churches: the main Church of Saint Bishoi, the Church of Saint Iskhiron, the Church of the Holy Virgin, the Church of Saint George, and the Church of Saint Michael on the roof of the keep.

The Church of Saint Bishoi has three altars, and it belongs to the most ancient part of the monastery, dating back to the ninth century. The church, which has undergone several restorations, was newly redecorated in 1957. It is used by the monks during the summer months for the celebration of the Divine Liturgy. Set in the floor at the western end of the church is the *lakan*, a marble basin used in the Maundy Thursday foot-washing rite. In the northeast corner of the choir stands the feretory, which contains the bodily remains of Saints Bishoi and Paul of Tammua. In the southwest corner of the nave stands the new, dignifed feretory of Benjamin II, which is adorned with icons of the three Macarii, Saint Matthew, Saint Thomas, and the Crucifixion. Moreover, the monks claim the relics of Saint Ephraem the Syrian. An increasing number of Copts repair to the relics of Saint Bishoi, which are believed to be incorruptible. Noteworthy is the modern altar screen in the Church of Saint Bishoi, which features paintings by Ishaq Fanus of the apostles and the desert fathers.

The Church of Saint Iskhiron is reached from the south side of the choir of the main church. To the north of its *haikal* is the baptistery.

To the northeast of the main church is the Church of the Holy Virgin. This church is used during the winter months for the Divine Liturgy. The Church of Saint George is not used now for services.

The refectory of the monastery is connected with the western end of the church. Southeast of the church is the kitchen and bakehouse.

The keep of the monastery is entered at the first floor by means of a drawbridge that rests on the roof of the gatehouse. On the second story of the keep is the Church of Saint Michael. The icons on the iconostasis, which date from the eighteenth century, have been restored. They show the twelve apostles in pontifical vestments. In no other monastery do we find the Church of Saint Michael so isolated as in the Monastery of Saint Bishoi. It is probable, therefore, that at one time the keep had an additional floor, like those of the other monasteries.

A new church dedicated to the Holy Virgin with three altars occupies the first story of the keep.

Recent installations in the monastery are a power generator to supply the monastery with electricity and a new water pump, south of the *qasr*. A second belfry was erected in 1955.

Following his enthronement in November 1971, Pope Shenuda III selected the Monastery of Saint Bishoi as his pontifical residence. Here he spent some forty months between September 1981 and January 1985 in enforced exile. During this time he ordained about one hundred young men as monks. Since his release the stream of visitors to the monastery has steadily increased.

Four hundred acres of desert land have been acquired, the greater part of which has been cultivated. Three reservoirs for drinking water, a new library, a three-story guest house, three large units of monastic cells, and lecture and conference buildings have been constructed at the rear of the old monastery. Here too is the new pontifical desert residence and the new Church of Saint Shenuda. Over the past twenty years, the number of monks at this monastery has increased to over 160. Many of these monks serve in the restored Upper Egyptian monasteries as well as in Coptic churches overseas.

The Monastery of the Syrians

The Monastery of the Syrians (Dair al-Surian) is situated five hundred meters northwest of the Monastery of Saint Bishoi. Like the Monastery of Saint Bishoi, it is easily accessible.

For many centuries the name of Saint John Kame has been closely associated with the Monastery of the Syrians, for after the destruction of the Monastery of Saint John Kame between 1330 and 1442, the monks of that monastery migrated to the Syrian Monastery, carrying with them the relics of their patron saint. This transfer of Coptic monks to the Syrian Monastery may be the explanation for the presence of the two national groups in the Syrian Monastery at the beginning of the fifteenth century.

Saint John Kame (d.859) was a native of Jebromounonson (Shubra Manethou) in the district of Saïs. At an early age he was forced into marriage, but persuaded his wife to consent to a life of virginity and permit him to live the life of a monk. Inspired by a vision, he entered Wadi al-Natrun, where he became a disciple of Saint Teroti, who inhabited a cell in the vicinity of the Monastery of Saint Macarius.

The Monastery of the Syrians was founded in the sixth century as a consequence of the Gaianite heresy. It was the duplicate of the Monastery of Saint Bishoi to which the Orthodox monks withdrew. To emphasize their orthodoxy at their new monastery, they retained the name of the patron saint and added to it the title of 'Theotokos.' The name Theotokos, or 'God-bearer,' was derived from the impor-tance with which the Orthodox monks regarded the doctrine of the Incarnation. The teachings of the Gaianites were considered by their opponents a Docetist heresy, which by denying the doctrine of the Incarnation, lowered the status of the Holy Virgin Mary. Thus, the Monastery of the Syrians was known as the Theotokos Monastery of Saint Bishoi.

The first Syrian monks associated with the monastery arrived in Wadi al-Natrun at the beginning of the ninth century. They were Matthew and Abraham of the city of Tekrit, and there is good reason to believe that they settled in the Western desert around the time of the fifth sack of the desert monasteries.

In the tenth century the Monastery of the Syrians gained prominence and importance. Incised in the altar screen of the Church of the Holy Virgin Mary is an important reference in Syriac. It speaks of the abbot Moses of Nisibis, who had the doors constructed during the patriarchates of Cosmas III of Alexandria (920–32) and Basil of Antioch (932–35). Moses is also credited with valuable additions to the monastery library.

During the patriarchate of Philotheus (979–1003), the Syrian monastery was associated with the Copts.

In the middle of the fourteenth century, the monastery suffered a most serious setback, for at this time the Black Death swept over Egypt and took a terrible toll on the monks of Wadi al-Natrun. A note in a Syriac manuscript of 1413 states that a visitor found only one monk in the Monastery of the Syrians.

By the end of the fifteenth century, the monastery seems to have recuperated, for when Ignatius XI, the patriarch of Antioch, visited Wadi al-Natrun, the monastery was inhabited by Syrian monks. In 1516, there were altogether forty-three monks, eighteen of whom were Syrians and twenty-five Egyptians. From this time on the Egyptian element was predominant. In the sixteenth century, the monastery was so strong that it could dispatch half of its monks to the Monasteries of Saint Antony and Saint Paul, which had been destroyed by the Bedouins in 1484. With the help of twenty monks of the Monastery of the Syrians, the Monastery of Saint Antony was rebuilt, and ten monks of the Syrian monastery were commissioned to assist in the reconstruction of the Monastery of Saint Paul.

Peter Heyling, the Lutheran missionary of Lübeck, was the last visitor to mention the partial occupation of the Syrian monastery by Syrian monks, in 1634.

The large collection of Syriac manuscripts attracted many European bibliophiles. No other Coptic monastery has suffered so severely from the thefts of Europeans. The most important manuscripts are either in the Vatican, the Bibliothèque Nationale in Paris, or the British Museum in London. Elias Assemani (1707) secured forty volumes from the monastery, and others were obtained for the Vatican by J.S. Assemani (1715). In 1730, Granger was refused entry to the library, and Browne found it impossible to obtain any manuscripts in 1792. Andreossy removed some manuscripts in 1799. Lord Curzon actually purchased a considerable quantity of manuscripts in 1837.

Tattam secured many manuscripts for the British Museum in 1839, while Tischendorf obtained only a few parchment sheets in 1844. In 1847, the British Museum obtained over two hundred items from Pacho. Brugsch was unable to purchase any manuscripts in 1852. Other visitors were Lansing (1862), Chester (1873), Junkers (1875), Jullien (1881), and Butler (1883).

The principal church of the monastery is that of the Holy Virgin. Because of its artistic treasures, this church has repeatedly attracted the attention of archaeologists and architects. A date around 950 is reasonable to accept for the building of the church. Almost in the middle of the nave is the basin for the Maundy Thursday foot-washing rite. At the eastern end of the north aisle stands the feretory of Saint John Kame.

In 1988 the Western apse, with its painting of the Ascension of Christ, was partially destroyed by fire. Underneath this twelfth-century Syrian painting appeared one of the earliest Coptic paintings (950) of the Annunciation. The theme of this unusual painting is the perpetual virginity of the Mother of God.

From the western end of the north aisle, one passes through a narrow passage to the cell of Saint Bishoi, a small square structure with an altar built against the east wall. The cell is roofed with a vaulted ceiling into which a hook has been driven. Supposedly, Saint Bishoi used to pray in this cell day and night, his hair tied to the hook to prevent him from falling asleep or sinking down.

The most outstanding feature of the Church of the Holy Virgin is the choir and the sanctuary doors with their ivory-inlaid panels. The sanctuary doors are the more interesting. While the choir door has only six rows of panels, the sanctuary door has seven. The first row has six figures. The two central panels (the third and the fourth) show Christ and the Holy Virgin Mary; the second and fifth panels show the Egyptian and the Syrian patriarchs, Saint Mark the Evangelist and Saint Ignatius, Bishop of Antioch. The two outer panels show the two great patriarchs Saint Dioscorus (444–54), the twenty-fifth patriarch of Alexandria, and Saint Severus I, the first Jacobite patriarch of Antioch (512–18).

The second row of panels shows a repeated pattern of circles interlaced to form crosses. In each of the six fields of the third row, six linked circles are arranged in pairs, each circle containing a cross. The fourth row, though somewhat damaged, has in each panel a cross enclosed in a four-leafed shamrock with a trefoil at the junction of each leaf. The fifth row has in each panel six swastikas, each enclosed in a circle. The sixth row is a dark grille on a white ground based on linked circles. The seventh row has a pattern of a plain cross in a double-stepped framing, the design of the cross thus filling the whole panel. This interesting piece of workmanship dates from the tenth century.

The semidomes that form part of the choir ceiling have two interesting wall paintings. The southern semidome has the Annunciation and the Nativity, and the northern semidome the Dormition of the Holy Virgin Mary.

Attached to the west wall of the choir is a marble tablet, or stele with a Coptic text commemorating Saint John Kame. The text informs us of the death of Saint John Kame in 859.

The *haikal* of the church is decorated with stucco ornaments similar to those in the Mosque of Ibn Tulun in Cairo. The altar is covered with a slab of black marble that was probably imported by the Syrians at the time of the building of the church. This church is at present used for the celebration of the Divine Liturgy during the summer months.

During the winter months, the monks hold their services in the Cave Church, or the Church of the Lady Mary (Sitt Mariam), which is situated in the northeastern part of the monastery. The church has three altars and a nave with a marble *lakan*. When this church is in use, the relics of Saint John Kame are removed from the Church of the Holy Virgin and placed north of the doorway of this church.

The Church of the Forty Martyrs of Sebaste is situated north of the Church of the Holy Virgin, adjoining the east of the porch. In this church, Christodoulus, the abuna of Ethiopia, was buried in 1624. Apart from this, the church is of little interest.

The keep of the monastery stands to the west of the northern gate and comprises a basement and three upper stories. The third story contains the Church of Saint Michael.

Around the traditional tamarind tree of Saint Ephraem a printing press—now obsolete—with a manually controlled printing machine has been built.

The water tower, which was built between 1955 and 1956, provides the monastery with running water, and it is situated in the eastern part of the monastery. It is thirteen meters high and has a capacity of forty-five cubic meters.

During the 1960s, the monastic buildings underwent major alter-ations. The guest house, including the library and museum, built in 1914 by Qummus Maksimus Salib (1895–39) was replaced by additional cells, and a special library building and museum were constructed. The well-catalogued library contains more than three thousand volumes and several hundred valuable manuscripts.

The collection of Coptica includes several very fine sixteenth- and seventeenth-century Coptic icons, several Ethiopica, a twelfth-century Nubian marble tray, fragments of a medieval *haikal* screen, and a wooden feretory. This feretory, which is said to be contemporary with the *haikal* screens of the Church of the Holy Virgin, belongs to the tenth century. Tradition asserts that it contained some relics of Saint Severus, Saint Dioscorus, Saints Cyriacus and his mother Julietta, Saint Theodore the Oriental, the Forty Martyrs of Sebaste, Saint James the Persian, Saint John the Short, Saint Moses the Black, and some hair of Saint Mary Magdalene. These relics are now preserved in a separate tube and kept together with those of Saint John Kame.

Until the middle of the twentieth century, the Monastery of the Syrians had only one gate, that is, the one in the western part of the north wall. A few years ago, the southern part of the east wall was broken through, and a new gate with an imposing staircase leads to the monastery plantation.

The monastery farm, located in the northeastern part of the plantation, has a large variety of domestic animals including camels, donkeys, cattle, goats, sheep, and poultry.

In the space between the plantation and the monastery is a retreat house, where church groups, students, and young people can spend time in study and contemplation.

Around the eastern part of the monastery large sections of desert land have been acquired and cultivated. About forty separate cells were constructed throughout the old orchard.

The Ruins of the Monastery of Saint John the Short

The annals of the desert fathers mention four original monastic settlements in the Desert of Scetis: the Cell of the Romans, later known as the Monastery of al-Baramus, and the cells of Saints Macarius, Bishoi, and John the Short. Three of these settlements survived the vicissitudes of the centuries. Only the Monastery of Saint John the Short succumbed during the troubled days of the late Mamluk period in the beginning of the sixteenth century. At that time the last monks of the monastery migrated to the nearby Monastery of Saint Macarius, taking with them the relics of their patron and their library.

Saint John the Short (Colobus), born in the beginning of the fourth century in the nome of Oxyrhynchus (al-Bahnasa), joined Anba Amoes in the Desert of Scetis at the age of eighteen. At the time of the first destruction of the monasteries by the Berbers around 407, he fled to the

Red Sea Monastery of Saint Antony, where he died. Toward the end of the eighth century, Coptic monks went to the Monastery of Saint Antony, which from the seventh to the ninth century was occupied by Melkite (Greek Orthodox) monks. Through shrewdness they succeeded in gaining possession of the relics of Saint John and deposited them in the Monastery of Saint Macarius, where they repose to this day.

In January 1992 an international team of archaeologists sponsored by two American institutions excavated some of the ruins of the monastery, including the outer walls and the church.

Christianity in the Nile Delta

The first appointment of bishops outside of Alexandria is ascribed to Demetrius I (188–230), an obvious mark of the extension of organized Christianity into Lower and Upper Egypt. However, the history of Christianity in the villages and towns of the Nile Delta is rather obscure. On the one hand, the annual inundation of the Nile has destroyed many records and remains; on the other, the very definite and successful penetration of Islam in Lower Egypt was not conducive for the preservation of Christian antiquities.

The Principal Towns and Villages

Damanhur

Damanhur, the ancient Egyptian Time-an-Hor, or the Roman Hermopolis Parva, is an important cotton center. There is little of interest in the modern town, which was founded in the middle of the nineteenth century. The Coptic Orthodox have two churches, the Church of the Archangel (1848) and the Church of Saint George (1948). The Greek Orthodox church is dedicated to Saints Constantine and Helena. The Catholic church is dedicated to the Annunciation of the Holy Virgin Mary. Moreover, there is a Coptic Evangelical church in Damanhur.

In 1957, Abuna Bulus Bulus established the first Coptic social center in Damanhur (rural diakonia), thereby initiating a movement that was to spread throughout the Delta and the Nile Valley. In March 1998, the Coptic archbishopric of Buhaira in Damanhur received some of the relics of Saint Athanasius.

Damietta

Damietta, the Thamiastis of the Romans, the Tamiati of the Copts, and the Dumyat of the Arabs, is situated on the east bank of the eastern branch of the Nile.

During the Ptolemaic period, a seaport of considerable size must have existed here. The old town probably was situated nearer to the sea than the modern town. In the Middle Ages, Damietta was a trading center for a certain linen called 'dimity,' as well as oil, coffee, dates, fish, etc. The town was attacked in 1169 by the king of Jerusalem, who set up siege towers, but Salah al-Din defended the town so successfully that the invaders were obliged to return to Palestine. In 1218 the town was besieged by King John of Jerusalem, and after a fight of twenty-five hours, Germans and Frisians succeeded in capturing the town. The success of the Christians was marred, however, by the interference of Palagius Galvani, the papal legate, and by the vigilance of Sultan Malik al-Kamil. Following the capture, the mosques were converted into churches, but in 1221, the Christians were compelled by a treaty to evacuate the town. In 1249 Louis IX landed at Damietta, the garrison fled, and the French king occupied the town without striking a blow. But in the course of the following year, the Crusaders were obliged to restore it to the Arabs as part of the ransom of Louis IX, who had been taken prisoner at Mansura. During the same year, by a resolution of the Egyptian emirs, the town was destroyed and Baibars rebuilt the city on the east bank of the river.

The Coptic Orthodox church in Damietta is dedicated to the Holy Virgin. The Catholics maintain the Church of Saint Francis of Assisi. The Greek Orthodox church is dedicated to Saint Nicholas.

On December 19, 1969, the Franciscan fathers assembled in great numbers in Damietta in order to commemorate the 750th anniversary of Saint Francis' arrival in Damietta. The memorial service was held in the old Greek Catholic church (now Coptic Orthodox) in the presence of the governor of Damietta, the principal *shaikhs*, and the orthodox priests of the city. After the service, the Franciscan fathers proceeded to the old mosque of Damietta, where Father Joseph Cisternino o.f.m. preached the sermon, which was followed by the Lord's Prayer in Latin.

Damira

The village of Damira in the district of Talkha is situated seven kilometers northwest of Mansura. In the ninth century, the fifty-fourth patriarch of Alexandria, Cosmas II (851–58) removed his residence to Damira, where "all the inhabitants were Christians. The patriarch lived here in quietness and peace while the notables of Cairo took charge of the affairs of the church." In the eleventh and twelfth centuries, Damira was known for its large Jewish settlement. Rabbi Benjamin of Tudela (twelfth century) counted seven hundred Jews there. Also Cyril II (1078–92) used to spend several months in Damira. Saint

George the New Martyr suffered martyrdom in 959 near the Church of Saint Michael in Damira. A church in his honor was built in Tabanuha, three kilometers west of Damira. From the eleventh to the fourteenth centuries, Damira was an episcopal see.

Kafr Yusuf Samri

The village of Kafr Yusuf Samri, five kilometers south of Zaqaziq, is situated in the province of Sharqiya. In the Church of Saint Michael (1887), the archangel is said to have appeared on Sunday, 28 April 1996 at 14:30, when he was seen by more than one thousand people. He reappeared in the form of a bright light on Friday, 14 June during the liturgy, which was being celebrated by the priests Samuel Zakhariah, Makar al-Antuni, and Shehata Shenuda. The light remained for one hour, filling the altar room. Some people saw the full figure of the archangel, others merely a wing outside the altar room. On 28 January 1996 he appeared as a youth in a white gallabiya, on other occasions as a priest. Among the numerous miracles associated with this angelic apparition were healings of diverse diseases, oedemas, tumors, hypertrophies, and hemorrhoids. Other miracles included the multiplication of oil and the transformation of water into oil.

Mahalla al-Kubra

With the beginning of the spinning and weaving industry in 1927, Mahalla al-Kubra has rapidly become one of the largest Egyptian towns. There are three Coptic Orthodox churches, dedicated to Saint Mary, Saint George, and Saint Damiana. The Catholics have the Church of Saint Augustine, and there is also one Coptic Evangelical church. The Greek Orthodox church is dedicated to Saint George.

Mansura

Mansura, the 'City of Victory,' is a thriving town largely on account of its cotton industry. Mansura was founded by Sultan Malik al-Kamil in 1221 as an advantageous substitute for Damietta. The town is situated on the east bank of the Damietta branch of the Nile, which is here both broad and deep.

Mansura was attacked by the Crusaders under Louis IX in 1249. After great difficulties the Crusaders succeeded in crossing the Ashmun Canal, but in the neighbourhood of Mansura they were defeated by the young Sultan al-Mu'azzam Turanshah. The Crusader fleet was destroyed. When the Crusaders attempted to escape, they were intercepted by the Mamluks. Robert, Count of Artois, three hundred of his men, and nearly all the Templars were slain. King Louis IX was captured, and a year later released on payment of a ransom of ten million francs and the surrender of Damietta.

There are five Coptic Orthodox churches in Mansura: the Church of the Archangel, the Church of Saint George, the Church of Saints Antony and Paul, the Church of the Holy Virgin, and the Church of Saint Damiana. The Greek Orthodox churches are dedicated to Saints Athanasius and Cyril and Saint Nicholas. The Catholics have three churches, a Greek Catholic church, a Maronite church, and a Coptic Catholic church. There is also a Coptic Evangelical church.

Minuf

Minuf, the Momenphis of the Greeks, is an ancient town. The Coptic Orthodox Church of Saint George was built in 1890. The Episcopal Church of Egypt maintains a school and a church in Minuf.

Sakha

The village of Sakha in the province of Gharbiya is situated about two kilometers south of the industrial and commercial center of Kafr al-Shaikh. Today insignificant, in the early Middle Ages Sakha was known as a 'Christ-loving town,' a title otherwise reserved for Alexandria. It has been suggested that "Bikha Isous," which was visited by the Holy Family on their Flight to Egypt, might be Sakha. Severus, the sixth-century patriarch of Antioch, spent the last days of his life in Sakha, where he died in 538. His relics were transferred to the Ennaton Monastery west of Alexandria. In the seventh century, Sakha was well known for the asceticism of Saint Agathon the Stylite, the only Egyptian pillar-saint. He lived altogether one hundred years, forty in the world, ten in the desert, and fifty on top of the column. One of the famous bishops of the eighth century was Saint Zachariah of Sakha, who served his diocese for thirty years. His homilies and historical books are his important literary contributions.

Samannud

The town of Samannud (Zeb-nuter) is situated on the west bank of the Damietta branch of the Nile east of Mahalla al-Kubra in the province of Gharbiya. The Church of Apa Nub with his relics is a popular pilgrimage center, especially on 31 July. Coptic tradition holds that the Holy Family visited Samannud. The water of the well in the church is said to have been blessed by Jesus. The popularity of the church is due to the young martyr Apa Nub, who suffered torture and martyrdom by Armianus, the governor of Alexandria. Local Christians report that every so often Apa Nub steps out of his icon to play with the children. His relics were taken to Samannud by Saint Julius of Aqfahs.

Shentana al-Hagar

The village of Shentana al-Hagar is situated north of Birkat al-Sab'
between Quwisna and Tanta. On the second day of the fast of the
Holy Virgin on 7 August 1997, the Holy Virgin was reported to have
appeared in the form of a "silver-colored dove-like image" on the roof
of the Church of the Holy Virgin here. On 16 August, the silver lights
on the cross took on the shape of the Holy Virgin in her long white
dress and gray headcover. On 20 August, Metropolitan Bishoi and
Bishop Benjamin witnessed the apparition: "The Virgin was bending
before the cross with her hands clasped. She turned toward the
audience and blessed them with outstretched arms." The poster of the
Holy Virgin of Zaytun in the church is said to have wept oil on 20
March 1998. In 1997 and 1998 the painting of Christ in the apse was
repeatedly illuminated. On the west wall of the narthex repose the
relics of the Fayyum martyrs and Saint Salib, which were laid down by
Bishop Benjamin in January 1993. The shrine of the apparition of the
Holy Virgin (by Atif Iskandar of Shibin al-Kom, September 1997)
stands on the north wall of the narthex.

Shibin al-Kom

Shibin al-Kom is a small town near Minuf, but it is the see of a Coptic
bishop. There is the Coptic Orthodox Church of the Holy Virgin
(1800) and the Church of Saint George (1907). The Catholics have a
church dedicated to Saint John the Baptist. There is also a Coptic
Evangelical church at Shibin al-Kom. The Greek Orthodox church is
dedicated to Saint Spyridon.

Sinbillawain

Near Sinbillawain, which is on the main line from Zaqaziq to
Mansura, is the mound the Arabs call Timai al-Amdid, which marks
the site of the classical Thmuis. There is the Coptic Church of the
Holy Virgin in Sinbillawayn.

Tanta

The capital of the large province of Gharbiya, Tanta is a great
commercial, social, and Islamic center. It is the see of the Coptic
Orthodox bishop as well as that of a Greek Orthodox bishop. There
are five Coptic Orthodox churches: one dedicated to the Holy Virgin
(1873), two dedicated to Saint George, one dedicated to the
Archangel Michael, and one dedicated to Saint Menas. The Greek
Orthodox churches are dedicated to the Presentation of the Lord,
Saint George, and the Dormition of the Holy Virgin. The Catholics

have three churches: the Church of Saint Anne, a Greek Catholic church, and a Coptic Catholic church. There are two Coptic Evangelical churches in Tanta.

Zaqaziq

Zaqaziq, the capital of the province of Sharqiya, is one of the chief centers of the Egyptian cotton and grain trade. At one time, many European merchants had their offices in Zaqaziq. Zaqaziq is the see of a Coptic Orthodox bishop. The Coptic Orthodox churches are: the Church of Saint George and the Church of Saint Takla Haymanot, the only church in Egypt dedicated to the Ethiopian national saint, constructed in 1848. Then there are the Churches of Saint Bishoi (1898) and the Archangel (1942). The Armenian Orthodox Church has the Church of the Holy Cross, and the Greek Orthodox churches are dedicated to the Three Hierarchs and the Dormition of the Holy Virgin. The Catholics have the Church of Saint Joseph. There is also a Coptic Evangelical Church of Zaqaziq.

The Coptic Pilgrimage Shrines

The Shrine of Saint Damiana

The Shrine of Saint Damiana, or Dair Sitt Dimyana, in the Nile Delta used to belong to the diocese of the metropolitan of Jerusalem and has been served from time immemorial by monks from the Monastery of Saint Antony. Since 1970, the Shrine of Saint Damiana has been incorporated into the newly formed diocese of Damietta. Moreover, instead of monks administering the shrine, the shrine has become a convent.

To reach this shrine, one proceeds from Cairo to Mansura (133 kilometers), and from Mansura one travels north along a rough agricultural road for twenty-two kilometers to the town of Bilqas. After passing through Bilqas, one turns east on the main road to Shirbin. After two kilometers, another rough agricultural road leads north to Dair Sitt Damiana.

Marcus was a Christian governor who lived in the middle of the third century. He had only one child, Damiana. When the girl grew up, her father chose a nobleman for her to marry. But Damiana refused, for she had been taught the Christian virtue of virginity. "If you really care for me," she told her father, "build me a castle where I can live and preserve my virginity and serve my Christ." And her father built her a large palace covering an area of fifteen feddans. Soon the daughters of the other noblemen followed the example of Damiana, and she and forty virgins served the Lord.

One day, Diocletian summoned all the noblemen from Egypt,

demanding that they worship the Roman gods. Those who refused to worship the gods were persecuted. Marcus, the father of Saint Damiana, had decided to give up his Christian faith. But when he returned to Egypt his daughter said, "Either you become a Christian again, or I refuse to be called your daughter." Marcus went back to Diocletian and made a Christian confession, and the king ordered that Marcus be killed. When the king discovered that Damiana had inspired her father to change his religion, he sent a statue of himself to Damiana's castle, demanding that she and her virgins worship it. They refused, and consequently they were tortured and killed.

The four churches of the convent are: the First Church of Saint Damiana, the Second Church of Saint Damiana, the Third Church of Saint Damiana, and the Church of the Holy Virgin Mary.

According to tradition, the initial development of the complex began with the building of the tomb of Saint Damiana and her forty virgins by Saint Helena, the mother of Constantine.

The first church in commemoration of the martyrdom of Saint Damiana was built by John I (496–505), the twenty-ninth patriarch of Alexandria.

This church, however, was destroyed when ocean floods covered the whole land. The tomb of Saint Damiana and her forty virgins remained under water for seventy years. Then the Christians began to pray, asking God to withdraw the waters from their holy shrine, and the waters receded. When John II camped near the original estate of the saint, he had a dream in which Saint Damiana appeared to him and ordered him to build a church. The patriarch obeyed her and built a church in her honor. This then is the first Church of Saint Damiana, which is situated in the southwestern part of the convent. There is no doubt whatsoever that this building constitutes the most ancient part of the whole complex.

The second Church of Saint Damiana, known as the Old Church, was built in the latter part of the nineteenth century by Anba Yuhanna, metropolitan of Burullus.

One reaches the church through the inner court of the convent. Apart from the wooden screen, the church is uninteresting. It has one *haikal*, which is dedicated to Saint Damiana. The *haikal* screen bears the date of 1845 and, therefore, antedates the construction of the church. North of the sanctuary is a prayer chamber with icons and paintings of Saint Damiana, Saint George, and the Holy Virgin Mary. In front of the prayer chamber is a candelabrum with an icon of Saint Damiana and her forty virgins attached to it. South of the sanctuary is the *gynaikion*, the prayer chamber for women, which has no decoration whatsoever.

In the western part of the church is the tomb of Saint Damiana. Three steps lead up to the tomb, which is enclosed by a wooden screen. Twenty-five little oval windows in the screen enable the pilgrims to view the shrine. The screen was built by Galil Ibrahim, the carpenter of Bilqas in 1887. Small rags and pieces torn from handkerchiefs are attached to the screen by pious pilgrims as votive offerings. The wooden cross that stands three feet west of the tomb bears the following inscription: "The great martyr, the virgin Damiana, 1879, made at the home of Anba Basiliyus."

The third Church of Saint Damiana, which is in the outer court of the convent, is a very recent construction. The church was built in 1932 by Bishop Peter of Mansura and was completed by Bishop Timothy. Its dimensions are forty meters by twenty meters. The church has only one *haikal*.

The fourth church is situated on the first floor of the south wing of the inner court. It is dedicated to the Holy Virgin Mary (1879).

Wansleben visited the shrine in 1672. Father C. Sicard s.j. traveled in May 1714 via Mansura and Bilqas to the shrine of "Sainte-Gemianne," where he saw a church with twenty-two domes. Sir Gardner Wilkinson (1843), mentions this shrine and the fair associated with it.

A full and rather interesting report of the celebrations in honor of Saint Damiana is also presented by Leeder:

> The moolid is still attended every year, between May 5 and May 20, by some 4,000 to 6,000 pilgrims coming from all parts of Egypt. They usually pitch a tent round the monastery, and live there for a period of not less than eight and not more than fifteen days, ending with the actual day of the celebrations. Numbers of merchants usually go and hold bazaars, in which they sell food, drink, sometimes clothing, ornaments, perfumes, rings, handkerchiefs, sticks, etc., and especially wooden and brass crosses imported from Jerusalem. They refer to Sitt Damiana for the ability to give fruitfulness to women, or long life to the children of a woman who has lost many in infancy. Therefore, many gifts of money, jewels, gold and silver are presented to her church.

The pilgrimage takes place annually on May 21, the date on which the church was dedicated by Saint Helena, and on January 20, the day of the martyrdom of Saint Damiana.

On May 7, 1975, Pope Shenuda III consecrated the new cells for the nuns and the new buildings of the convent. At the Convent of Saint Damiana, some nuns follow a strictly contemplative life, while others are engaged in social and welfare work. Still others are devoted to painting icons and embroidering liturgical textiles. A clinic serves the pilgrims, the population of the region, and the nuns.

The Churches of Saint George at Mit Damsis

The two Churches of Saint George at Mit Damsis are well known throughout Lower Egypt on account of the annual *mulid* held there from August 22 to 28. Several thousand pilgrims, including many patients suffering from various ailments, visit the ancient Church of Saint George, expecting to be cured by Saint George of their afflictions.

The Churches of Saint George are situated on the eastern bank of the Damietta branch of the Nile, approximately twenty kilometers north of Mit Ghamr.

One enters the new Church of Saint George (built about 1880) through a churchyard enclosed on three sides by hostels for pilgrims. The new Church of Saint George is situated at the eastern end of the court. Above the entrance of the church is a large circular mosaic of Saint George (1961). The new church has three *haikals*, which are dedicated to Saint Michael (north), Saint George (center), and the Holy Virgin (south). The icons on the iconostasis represent from north to south: Saint Shenute, Saint Rebecca, Saint George, the Holy Virgin, Christ, Saint Mark, Saint Damiana, Saints Constantine and Helena, and Saint Antony. The baptistery is in a separate building to the south of the church.

The ancient Church of Saint George is reached by turning to the right after entering the churchyard. One proceeds a few steps down and enters the large nave of the Church of Saint George from the north. Here, several hundred pilgrims assemble during the *mulid* in expectation of being healed by Saint George. The ancient church, which according to local tradition was built by Saint Helena, has three *haikals*, which are also dedicated to Saint Michael (north), Saint George (center), and the Holy Virgin (south). South of the *haikal* of the Holy Virgin are the tombs of several priests. This room, however, is presently used as a storage place for chairs and other furniture. The *haikal* screen is inlaid with ivory, and an icon of Christ (1900) is attached to the central *haikal*. The miraculous icon of Saint George adorns the northern wall of the nave of the ancient church.

The Church of Saint Rebecca at Sunbat

The Church of Saint Rebecca, or Sitt Rifqa, in Sunbat near Mit Damsis is the site of a prominent annual *mulid* in honor of the saint and thirteen other martyrs who died with her during the Diocletian persecution.

Sunbat, a small village on the western bank of the Damietta branch of the Nile, can be reached from Mit Damsis by taking a felucca two kilometers south and then a donkey for two and a half kilometers. The church is situated in the western part of the village of Sunbat, next to the village school. One enters the church through a spacious church-yard. The church has two *haikals*, which are dedicated to the Holy Virgin and Saint Rebecca. The southern room, at one time an altar room, contains the relics of Saint Rebecca and the thirteen martyrs.

Rebecca and her children Agathon, Amon, Peter, Simeon, Isaac, Thomas, Andrew, and John (there is no unanimity about the names of the other martyrs) were natives of the Upper Egyptian province of Qus, where Agathon was the prefect. Christ appeared to them and revealed that they would suffer martyrdom near Alexandria, and that their bodies would be carried to Lower Egypt. Rejoicing at this, they publicly confessed their faith before Dionysius, the governor. They did not recant when they were tortured. Then they were sent to Alexandria, where they were questioned by the governor Arianus; finally, after suffering torture, they were martyred. Their relics were translated to Sunbat in the thirteenth century.

Daqadus near Mit Ghamr

One of the largest *mulid*s in the Nile Delta is celebrated annually on August 22 in the Church of the Holy Virgin in the village of Daqadus, about three kilometers north of Mit Ghamr on the east bank of the Damietta branch of the Nile. According to an early medieval Coptic tradition, the holy family is said to have stopped there on their flight into Egypt.

In the twelfth century, Michael V, the seventy-first patriarch of Alexandria, was born in Daqadus. At that time the town was a dependency of the Coptic archbishopric of Jerusalem, as is attested by numerous manuscripts in the church library. The name Daqadus appears in ancient Coptic texts as 'Ti Theotokos Athokotos,' that is, 'the Mother of God of Daqadus.' 'Athokotos' is a variant of 'theotokos,' which became Daqadus in its Arabic form. Literary evidence testifies to a Church of the Holy Virgin in Daqadus existing in A.H. 626 (A.D. 1239). The church library contains several ancient dated manuscripts, among them a commentary on the doctrines of Saint Paul by Abu al-Farag ibn al-'Assal dated A.M. 1048 (A.D. 1332).

The Church of the Holy Virgin at Musturud

The Church of the Holy Virgin (al-'Adhra') is situated in the village of Musturud, 3 kilometers west of al-Matariya. Those traveling from Cairo to Ismailia and Port Said normally pass Musturud. The church lies on the left side of the road when coming from Cairo and can be easily identified by its new bell tower (1961).

The Church of the Holy Virgin is of interest because it is built over a cave that is said to have given shelter to the holy family on their flight into Egypt. Also, within the church there is a well in which the Holy Virgin is said to have washed the Christ child.

The church is entered through a door in the north wall. Almost opposite the entrance are stairs leading into the cave. Icons and candle stands adorn the small sanctuary. Another staircase leads to the eastern part of the church and the well of the Holy Virgin. Close by is the baptismal font. The church has three *haikals* dedicated to Saint John the Baptist (north), the Holy Virgin (center), and Saint George (south). On the southern wall are several icons which are noteworthy.

An annual *mulid* (August 7–22) is celebrated at the church in honor of the Assumption of the Holy Virgin.

The Monastery of Saint George at al-Khatatba

At the edge of the desert west of the town of al-Khatatba, on the banks of the Rosetta branch of the Nile, the Monastery of Saint George, or Dair Mari Girgis, was recently built in response to a definite need for an increasing number of monastic candidates. In the medieval history of the four Wadi al-Natrun monasteries, al-Khatatba in the province of Minufiya has played an important role as a place of departure for the trek across the desert. Monks and visitors to the monasteries used to sail from Cairo to al-Khatatba, where they mounted donkeys for the fifty-kilometer ride to the nearest monastery, that of Saint Macarius.

Because of its proximity to Cairo and the cities and towns of the Nile Delta, the monastery serves the Copts of the region as a center for retreats, discussions, and contemplation. The abbot of the monastery is Anba Bemwa.

Additional Coptic Pilgrimage Sites in the Delta

Several pilgrimages take place on the feast of the Archangel Saint Michael on 12 Bauna (19 June) in the village churches in Minufiya, for example in Sirbibai, four kilometers north of Tanta; in Tukh Tum-Besha near Quwisna; and in Sharqiya in Kafr al-Dair near Minya al-Qamh. Pilgrimages in honor of Saint George occur annually in Birma near Tanta but also in Minya al-Qamh. These take place on 23 Barmuda (1 May) and 3 Bauna (10 June). Another well-known pilgrimage to the Church of Saint George takes place in Mahalla Marhum in Gharbiya north of Tanta on 16 Abib (23 July). A large pilgrimage takes place annually from 19 to 26 Barmuda (27 April to 4 May) in Tukh Dalaka between Tala and Shibin al-Kom in Minufiya. Since the eighteenth century the Monastery of al-Baramus in Wadi al-

Natrun has maintained a dependency in Tukh Dalaka. Patriarchs Matthew III al-Tukhi and John XVI both came from Tukh. On 28 Hatur (7 December), a pilgrimage honoring the fourth-century bishop Sarabamun of Nikiu takes place in the Church of Saint Sarabamun in al-Batanun, northeast of Shibin al-Kom. In Zifta, almost opposite Mit Ghamr, the annual pilgrimage takes place in the new Church of Saint Mercurius (Abu al-Saifain) on 25 Abib (1 August) and 25 Hatur (4 December). Those bitten by rabid dogs still turn to the therapeutic waters of the well in the Church of Saint Philotheus in the village of Sanhira, south of Tukh in Qalyubiya.

The Coptic Churches of Old Cairo and Its Environs

The site now known as Old Cairo is mentioned by Strabo (24 B.C.) and by Ptolemy (A.D. 121–51) under the name Babylon. Through this town there ran a canal connecting the Nile with the Red Sea. The Roman emperor Trajan (98–117) reopened the canal and enlarged and fortified the fortress built at the southern end of the town. This fortress, known as the Castle of Babylon or Castle of Egypt, was further enlarged by the emperor Arcadius (395–408). This city became a bishopric in the first half of the fifth century. A certain Cyrus, bishop of Babylon, was present at the Council of Ephesus held in 449. At the time of the Arab conquest of Egypt, Babylon was a large city extending northward as far as Tendounias (Umm Dunain), the present district of al-Azbakiya, where there was a fortified outpost. This outpost was captured by the Arab general 'Amr ibn al-'As, who speedily occupied the city as far as the Castle of Babylon, to which he laid siege. On April 9, 641, this castle surrendered, and the Arabs gave it the name Qasr al-Sham'. Then the Arabs marched against Alexandria, from which the Byzantines eventually evacuated under treaty on September 29, 642.

After the Arab conquest of Egypt, the name Babylon became more and more used to denote the district immediately around Qasr al-Sham', which eventually became inhabited chiefly by Christians. Where 'Amr ibn al-'As had pitched his camp at the siege arose a new quarter called al-Fustat, from the Greek word 'fossaton,' meaning 'camp,' and populated mainly by the Arabs. As capital of Egypt and seat of the government, the city rapidly increased in size and importance, and eventually became known as Misr. Already in 743 we hear of a certain Theodore, bishop of Misr, who assisted at the election of Kha'il I to patriarch of Alexandria at the Church of Saint Shenute. The episcopal see of Misr took the place of the older See of Babylon, and its cathedral church was that of Saint Mercurius until the reign of the patriarch Christodoulos (1047–77), who transferred the seat of the patriarchate from Alexandria to the al-Mu'allaqa Church of the Holy Virgin in Cairo and made this church a patriarchal one.

As for the churches of Babylon, we possess no information about them prior to the Arab conquest of Egypt, but since there was a bishop of Babylon in the fifth century, we may assume that the cathedral was not the only church in the city.

The Coptic Churches of Babylon

The ancient Coptic Churches of Cairo are, for the most part, situated in Old Cairo, especially in the enclosure of the Roman Castle of Babylon, which is now known as Qasr al-Sham'.

The Church of the Holy Virgin Mary (al-Mu'allaqa Church)

The Church of the Holy Virgin Mary, situated facing the Metro station of Mari Girgis, owes its title of al-Mu'allaqa ('the Suspended') to the fact that its eastern and western ends rest on the two south-western bastions of the Castle of Babylon, and its nave is suspended over the passage that leads into the castle. The position of the church can be best understood by descending a flight of steps leading down from the enclosed garden of the Coptic Museum.

The church was probably built during the patriarchate of Isaac (690–92), when the recent Arab invasion made it advisable to build a church in a place difficult to access. Otherwise, the earliest reference to the church seems to be the statement in the biography of the patriarch Joseph (831–49), where we read that the governor of Egypt "came to the church which is in the Fortress of al-Sham', called the Suspended." The church was rebuilt in the reign of the patriarch Abraham (975–78). In the eleventh century it became the official residence of the Coptic patriarchs of Alexandria. During the patriarchate of Christodoulus (1047–77), a quarrel for supremacy in the Qasr al-Sham' broke out between the Church of Saints Sergius and Bacchus and al-Mu'allaqa Church because it was the practice to consecrate new patriarchs in the Church of Saints Sergius and Bacchus, but Christodoulus went to al-Mu'allaqa. Cyril II as well as Michael IV were consecrated at al-Mu'allaqa. In the course of its long history, this church has been many times restored; the last restoration was made in the latter part of the twentieth century. Objects of historical interest that were no longer of service were removed and are now preserved in the Coptic Museum.

The church is of the basilican plan. Of special interest is the timber wagon-vaulted roof and the white marble columns (and one of black basalt) that separate the nave from the aisles. The small tank sunk in the floor of the nave, now boarded over, was formerly used for the the foot-washing rite on Maundy Thursday and on the Feast of Saints Peter and Paul. The marble *ambon*, or pulpit, dates from the eleventh century. The central *haikal* screen, which is ebony inlaid with ivory, dates from the twelfth or thirteenth century. On the top of the screen are seven large icons. The altar is dedicated to the Holy Virgin Mary.

The church has three *haikals*: the central one dedicated to the Holy Virgin Mary, the northern one to Saint George, and the southern one to Saint John the Baptist. The northern *haikal* screen has a design of squares with crosses that are alternately ivory and ebony. Above the screen are seventeen icons representing scenes from the martyrdom of Saint George. The southern sanctuary screen shows a cruciform pattern and dates from the thirteenth century. On the top of the screen are seven small icons representing different periods in the life of Saint John the Baptist. All these icons are the work of the Armenian artist Orhan Karabedian, executed in 1777.

The little Church of Saint Mark occupies the floor of the bastion to the right of the gateway of the Roman castle, along with the Sanctuary of Saint Takla Haymanot, the national saint of Ethiopia. The screen dates from the thirteenth century.

On the east wall of the Sanctuary of Saint Takla Haymanot is a damaged wall painting representing the twenty-four elders of the Apocalypse. The elders are portrayed standing in a row and clothed in priestly vestments.

At one time, all of the columns of this church were adorned with paintings, but today, only the picture on the fifth column from the east in the southern row is adorned with a painting of a beardless person with a nimbus wearing a coronet. This person is a female saint, possibly a queen or a princess.

The Church of Saints Sergius and Bacchus

The Church of Saint Sergius (Abu Sarga) can be reached either by descending the flight of steps to the left of the entrance to the Greek Orthodox Church of Saint George, passing through the narrow lane, and turning to the right, or by descending the steps from the garden in front of the Coptic Museum. The Church of Saint Sergius is the most ancient church in Old Cairo. It is built over the traditional site visited by the holy family on their flight into Egypt.

In this church in 859, Shenute I, the fifty-fifth patriarch, was elected to his office. In 977, Abraham, the sixty-second patriarch, was also elected to his office in the church, after which he celebrated the Divine Liturgy first in al-Mu'allaqa and then in the Church of Saint Sergius.

The Church of Saints Sergius and Bacchus is of the basilican type. A large tank is sunk in the floor in the narthex at the western end of the church. This tank was formerly used for the service of the blessing of the water on the Feast of the Epiphany. The twelve columns around the nave are all of white marble with the exception of one, which is of granite, representing Judas Iscariot. Traces of figures can still be seen on them. The marble *ambon* rests on ten columns.

The screen of the central sanctuary dates from the thirteenth century. The upper part contains small panels of ebony inset with large crosses of solid ivory. Above the panels are icons of the Twelve Apostles and the Holy Virgin Mary. The screen is decorated with several panels from the leaves of a door, which can be assigned to the eleventh or twelfth century. Those on the right depict three warrior saints, while those on the left show the Nativity and the Last Supper. The altar stands beneath a large and lofty canopy borne on four Saracenic columns. The screens of the northern and southern sanctuary are inlaid with plain ivory.

The southern sanctuary is no longer used for services. The northern sanctuary is roofed with a large dome, and in the east wall there is a small tribune of three bow-shaped steps in the center of which is the synthronon, originally the seating arrangement for the bishop and the elders. The baptistery is situated at the western end of the northern aisle. The southern gallery has a sanctuary dedicated to Abraham, Isaac, and Jacob, while the northern gallery has a sanctuary dedicated to Saint Michael.

The Sanctuary of the Holy Family is situated in a crypt beneath the center of the choir. It is entered by a stairway leading down from the southern sanctuary. The sanctuary has an altar but no sanctuary screen. The southern aisle is used as a baptistery and has the baptismal font at its east end.

Since the fourteenth century there existed a rather intimate connection between the Church of Saints Sergius and Bacchus and western pilgrims. Few Franks who visited Cairo in the Middle Ages failed to make a pilgrimage to this church. In 1323, Willelmi Bonemayn, probably a French consul, obtained the reopening of the church from the Sultan Malik al-Nasir, for no services had been celebrated there after the disturbances in 1321, the most intensive persecutions of the Copts by the Mamluks. From the accounts of the seventeenth- and eighteenth-century travelers it emerges that the Franciscans, who for many years owned a hospice nearby, also for long periods had the right of saying Mass in the crypt of the church and for some time apparently even controlled it. (See Bremond, 1644; Wansleben, 1672; Morison, 1697; Lorenzo Cozza, 1711). On 25 April 1991, Bishop

Mattaus of Old Cairo announced the discovery of the relics of Saint Bashnuna under the pavement near the *ambon* of the church. Saint Bashnuna, a monk of the Monastery of Saint Macarius, suffered martyrdom on 19 May 1164. A shrine with his relics and an icon of the saint stand on the site of the discovery of the relics.

The Church of Saint Barbara

The visitor should now return to the lane leading past the Church of Saints Sergius and Bacchus and then continue down it and take the first turn to the left, which will bring him to the Church of Saint Barbara.

The church, originally dedicated to the Unmercenary Physicians of the Church, Saints Cyrus and John, was, according to Eutychius, built by a certain wealthy scribe in 634. Later, when the relics of Saint Barbara were translated to this church, a new sanctuary was added to house the relics. The present edifice comprises two distinct churches, one dedicated to Saint Barbara and the other to Saints Cyrus and John.

In the nave one should note the beautiful marble *ambon*, which is borne on ten columns. The screen of the central *haikal*, inlaid with ivory carved in relief, dates from the thirteenth century.

The southern sanctuary, no longer used for services, contains the shrine of Saint Barbara with her relics. The screen of the northern sanctuary dates from the Fatimid period (972–1171).

Passing through the northern transept of the Church of Saint Barbara, one enters the Church of Saints Cyrus and John.

The Church of Saints Cyrus and John

The Church of Saints Cyrus and John, almost square in shape, comprises a nave, a choir, two sanctuaries, and a baptistery. The southern sanctuary is dedicated to Saint George and the northern sanctuary to Saints Cyrus and John. At the corner of the south wall, one should note the icon of Saints Cyrus and John together with a case containing their relics.

The baptistery, which is in a line with the two sanctuaries, has a polygonal font set in a mass of masonry.

The Church of the Holy Virgin Mary

After passing the doorway in the Roman wall and following the narrow lane, the visitor will take the first turn to the left, which will lead directly to the Church of the Holy Virgin Mary, known as the Pot of Basil.

According to the *History of the Patriarchs*, the Church of the Holy Virgin Mary served as a residence for twenty-seven days for the patriarch Kha'il III (880–907) when he was released from the prison in which he had been confined by Ahmad ibn Tulun. We hear of this church again when Arsenius, a brother of the Greek concubine of al-Hakim, was elected patriarch of the Greek Orthodox Church in Egypt (c.985), and obtained possession of it for the Greek Orthodox community of Cairo. It was still in the hands of the Greek Orthodox community when Mawhub ibn Mansur compiled his part of the *History of the Patriarchs of the Egyptian Church* in 1088. In the eighteenth century this church was rebuilt.

On March 26, 1979, the church was destroyed by fire. In the same year, a temporary wooden church was built on a site southeast of the former church. The temporary wooden church continues the commemoration of the former historic church to the Holy Virgin, Saint Sarabamun, and the Archangel Michael. The name 'Pot of Basil' may date from the time when this church belonged to the Greeks, since basil is used by the Greeks for blessing the water on the first of every month. On the other hand, the 'pot' may also be a metaphor for the Holy Virgin, namely the vessel of basil with its heavenly odor, the divine child.

The Church of Saint George

In the immediate vicinity of the Church of the Holy Virgin Mary is the Church of Saint George (Mari Girgis). The original church of Saint George was built by Athanasius, the scribe who also founded the Church of Saints Cyrus and John. This church is also mentioned in the biography of Patriarch Alexander II (704–29). In the nineteenth century, this church was destroyed by a fire, and all that remains of the original edifice is a room known as the Hall of Nuptials. The modern church erected on the site of the original church is without architectural interest.

The Convent of Saint George

Near the Church of Saint George is the Convent of Saint George, which is inhabited at present by forty nuns. A door in the convent wall facing the street gives access to a small court. From within the convent we descend by a stairway to the ancient part, which dates from the tenth century. In the north, east, and west walls of this hall are doors that give access to narrow cells. There are fourteen cells in all, but six have been walled up. A door on the south side gives access to a chamber in which there is a shrine containing an icon as well as the chain of Saint George. This convent is mentioned by al-Maqrizi in the fifteenth century.

The Coptic Churches of Old Cairo

The Monastery of Saint Mercurius

The Monastery of Saint Mercurius is situated in Shari' Gami' 'Amr in Old Cairo. The former entrance was from the west side, and the ancient door of sycamore wood strengthened by iron bands is now preserved in the Coptic Museum. At one time, this monastery was close to the bank of the Nile, but the river has gradually retreated until, at present, it is six hundred meters from the monastery.

The monastery, which is surrounded by a high wall, contains three churches and a convent for nuns.

The Church of Saint Mercurius

The Church of Saint Mercurius (Abu al-Saifain) was rebuilt in the time of the patriarch Abraham (975–78), since it had been demolished and made a storehouse for sugar cane. In 1168 it was burnt by a fanatic mob, but it was rebuilt in 1176.

The church is remarkable for the number of icons on the walls and columns of the church. In the nave, one should note the very beautiful *ambon* decorated with mosaics and resting on fifteen columns. In the choir alone there are sixty-three icons by Orhan Karabedian the Armenian.

The screen of the central sanctuary is of ebony inlaid with thin plates of ivory in the form of crosses and squares.

The doorway is flanked by two Corinthian columns and has above it two icons, one of Christ and the other of the Holy Virgin. Below is a row of icons; in the center is Christ, who has on his right hand the Holy Virgin Mary, Saint Michael, and three apostles, and on his left, Saint John the Baptist, Saint Gabriel, and three more apostles.

In the central sanctuary, the fine domed altar canopy rests on woodwork with four open-pointed arches springing from four marble columns. Behind the altar is the red-and-white marble tribune, and above the niche, which contains a fresco of Christ, there are paintings of the seraphim. The southern sanctuary is now converted into a baptistery. At one time, this sanctuary was dedicated to Saint Gabriel. The northern sanctuary is dedicated to the Holy Virgin. Its wooden screen is inlaid with ivory and ebony.

In the northern aisle, a doorway opens onto a stairway leading down to a small, dark underground chamber. This low-ceilinged, vaulted chamber has an altar, and here Saint Barsum the Naked dwelt for twenty years. On the feast day of the saint, a service is held in this shrine. Saint Barsum the Naked died in 1317.

Leaving the northern aisle by a door, we enter a courtyard northeast of the Church of Saint Mercurius. On the left are the sanctuaries of Saint James the Sawn-Asunder, Saint George, and Saint Gabriel. To the right is the baptistery. These sanctuaries are no longer used for services.

From the courtyard, a stairway leads up to the roof of the Church of Saint Mercurius. Halfway up this stairway, a passage leads to a door that gives access to the galleries around the church. In these galleries are five dismantled sanctuaries. During the Middle Ages, the walls of the Upper Church of Saint Mercurius, with its numerous chapels, were either fully or partially adorned with wall paintings.

After leaving the Church of Saint Mercurius, the Church of Saint Shenute is some twenty meters on.

The Church of Saint Shenute

The Church of Saint Shenute, which is situated about two meters below the present street level, is one of the very ancient churches of Old Cairo.

The church was first mentioned in the year 743, when an assembly of bishops, clergy, and representatives of the people met to elect a new patriarch. In the time of al-Hakim (996–1021), the Muslim call to prayer was made from this church. The church was restored by Patriarch Benjamin II (1327–39).

At the west end of the nave, the visitor should note the two circular apertures covered by a stone slab in the floor. The first of these apertures is the ancient well of the church, and the second is the tank used on Maundy Thursday. The nave is separated from the aisles by ten marble columns, five on each side.

In the nave is a wood *ambon* with a design of crosses. It stands on eight wooden columns. The screen of the central sanctuary is red cedar inlaid with a plain ivory wheel-and-cross pattern. The southern sanctuary is dedicated to Saint Michael, and its screen is ebony inlaid with sculpted ivory. The screen of the northern sanctuary, which is no longer used for services, is wood inlaid with ivory. A flight of steps near the entrance leads to the upper church, in which there are three dismantled sanctuaries. At the southwest end of one of these sanctuaries is a baptistery.

In the main Church of Saint Shenute there are two columns adorned with paintings. The second column from the east in the southern row has a painting of a warrior saint or a king facing the nave. In the course of major repairs in the church, archaeologists discovered several relics between the two columns in the narthex. The identity of the relics was established through the visions of a monk; some of the relics belonged to Saints Dioscorus and Aesculapius of

Akhmim, others to Saint Julius of Aqfahs and Saint Menas. The new shrine of Saint Julius with his icon is dated 14 July 1995. A collection of relics of anonymous saints awaits identification.

The Church of the Holy Virgin

In order to reach this church, known as al-Damshiriya, one should take the first left after passing through the doorway of the monastery. According to al-Maqrizi, this church was demolished in 785 but was rebuilt in the time of the caliph Harun al-Rashid (786–809). The roof covering the nave is wagon-vaulted and lofty, whereas the one covering the west end and the northern and southern aisles is low and horizontal. The southern sanctuary is dedicated to Saint Michael, and the northern sanctuary is now converted into a shrine to the Holy Virgin Mary. The name of the church, al-Damshiriya, originates from the name of a Coptic notable of Damshir, ten kilometers north of Minya, who undertook the restoration of this church in the eighteenth century. An impressive gallery of eighteenth-century Coptic icons by Ibrahim al-Nasikh and Orhan Karabedian adorns the northern and southern walls of the nave. A nineteenth-century Ethiopian icon of the Holy Virgin and Child (Maria lactans) is a copy of the Se'el Gebsawit of the Monastery of Jāmādo Maryam in Lasta. This icon is attributed to Saint Luke. On the west wall are the relics of Saints Victor, Menas, Mercurius, and George with the identifying eighteenth-century icons.

The Convent of Saint Mercurius

In the lane a little beyond the Church of Saint Mercurius, a passage leads to the Convent of Saint Mercurius (Dair Abu Saifain lil-Rahibat). The convent has about forty-five nuns. This convent has three new churches, which are dedicated to Saint Mercurius, the Holy Virgin, and Saint Damiana. Upon entering the convent, one notices a well. The wall painting near the well is of the Samaritan woman. In the Church of Saint Mercurius are new wall paintings of the Pantocrator, the Holy Virgin, Saint Mercurius, and the Crucifixion. The relics of the patron saint are kept in this church. The Church of the Holy Virgin is adorned with wall paintings of the Annunciation, the Nativity, the Flight into Egypt, and the Twelve Apostles. The Church of Saint Damiana is not yet completed, although the mosaic of Saint Damiana and her forty virgins is already in situ. The wall paintings were executed by Isaac Fanus in 1968. A Church of Saint Joseph is under construction in the new part of the convent.

The Coptic Churches North of Old Cairo

The Monastery of Saint Menas in Old Cairo (Fumm al-Khalig)

The Monastery of Saint Menas (Dair Abu Mina) is situated in the northern part of Old Cairo, north of the Roman aqueduct, at the northernmost corner of the Christian cemetery, off Shari' al-Sadd al-Barrani in the district of Fumm al-Khalig. According to al-Maqrizi, the Church of Saint Menas was restored in 724, and it has been restored in recent times by the Committee for the Preservation of Arab Art.

To the right of the passage leading through the garden to the church, there is a wall with fifteen mosaics showing the feasts of the church, from the Annunciation to the Ascension of Christ, and two additional mosaics of Saint George and Saint Bahnam and his sister Sarah. A short flight of steps leads down to the west end of the Church of Saint Menas. On the right is a gate of iron latticework that gives access to the tomb of two former priests of this church. The nave is separated from the aisles by six square masonry pillars, three on each side, and by four piers. Against the easternmost pillar is a marble *ambon* supported on twelve columns. To the left of this sanctuary is a shrine of Saint Menas, in which an ornamented bolster containing the relics of Saint Bahnam and his sister Sarah is placed. Most of the relics of Saint Menas, which were formerly kept in this church, were returned to the desert Monastery of Saint Menas in Maryut in 1962, though some of the relics still repose in the narthex of the church. The southern sanctuary is now used as a shrine, in which there are a number of icons. The northern sanctuary is accessible only from the central sanctuary, and it is now used as a sacristy. From the south end of the choir, a door leads into a long, vaulted passage running east and west. At the east end is a baptistery. From the baptistery one passes into the Church of Saint Bahnam.

The Church of Saint Bahnam

The Church of Saint Bahnam consists of two sanctuaries, both of which are dedicated to the patron saint. The screen of the northern sanctuary, which is inlaid with ivory, is relatively modern, having the date of 1813. The screen of the southern sanctuary is somewhat older and bears the date 1775.

Saint Bahnam and his sister Sarah were of royal birth. Saint Sarah, who suffered from leprosy, was healed, converted, and baptized by Matthew the Hermit. The king, their father, persecuted and finally killed his children. Possessed of an evil spirit, the king was also healed by Matthew the Hermit. He and his wife became Christians and dedicated a church to their martyred children. The relics of this church include those of the Unmercenary Saints Cosmas and Damian, Saint George, and Saint Takla Haymanot.

The Church of Saint George

A stairway leads up to the Church of Saint George, which has two sanctuaries. The southern sanctuary is dedicated to Saint George, and its screen is dated 1747. The northern sanctuary, which contains an icon of the saint together with some of his relics, is now used as a shrine of Saint George.

The Coptic Churches South of Old Cairo

These Coptic churches to the south of Old Cairo are situated south of the village Qasr al-Sham' and also beyond the bridge across the Old Cairo-Muqattam highway.

The Church of the Holy Virgin by the Steps of Babylon

The Church of the Holy Virgin is surrounded by a gray brick wall some ten meters high. A flight of steps leads down to the enclosure, which is a sign that the surrounding ground level has risen considerably since the church's construction in the eleventh century.

From the eleventh to the fifteenth centuries several Coptic patriarchs resided at the church. According to Coptic tradition, the holy family, as well as Saints Mark and Peter, visited the site, and Peter sent his epistle from here (1 Pet. 5:13).

The plan of this church approaches a square. The church consists of a narthex, nave, choir, northern and southern aisles, and three sanctuaries. The narthex has two baptisteries, one on the left with a small font and one on the right with a very large font. The screen of the central sanctuary is wood inlaid with ivory with a cross in a square pattern. Along the top of the screen is the usual row of icons. The northern sanctuary is dedicated to the Holy Virgin. Its screen is of wood, but has no icons. The southern sanctuary is now used as a shrine. It has a lattice-work wooden screen. The shrine is adorned with several nineteenth-century icons of the Holy Virgin, Saint Damiana, Saint Stephen, Saint Antony, Saint Paul the Hermit, Saint Barbara, Saint Shenute, and Saints Peter and Paul. Two bolsters are said to contain the relics of Saint Damiana and Saint Simeon the Tanner. From the eleventh to the fifteenth centuries, seven Coptic patriarchs were buried at this church. On 4 August 1991, the relics of Saint Simeon the Tanner were discovered. Some of them repose in the new Church of Saint Simeon the Tanner on the Muqattam Hills, others in the al-Mu'allaqa Church of the Holy Virgin and the Church by the Steps of Babylon.

A street in the Monastery of Saint Antony, Red Sea
(photograph by the author)

The garden and belfries of the Monastery of Saint Antony
(photograph by the author)

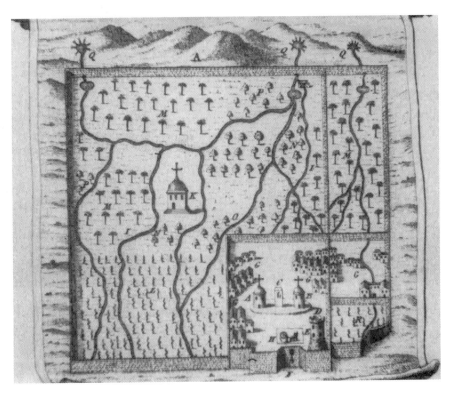

Plan of the Monastery of Saint Antony by Pococke, 1737

The Church of Saint Michael in the Monastery of Saint Paul, Red Sea
(photograph by the author)

The Monastery of Saint Paul in 1880, according to Fr. Jullien

The Monastery of the Syrians, Wadi al-Natrun
(photograph by the author)

Mural of the Nativity in the Monastery of the Syrians
(photograph courtesy of the Monastery of the Syrians)

The Monastery of the Syrians (photograph by the author)

Icons in the Monastery of Saint Bishoi, Wadi al-Natrun
(photograph by the author)

Coptic monks in front of the Church of Saint Bishoi, Monastery of Saint Bishoi
(photograph by the author)

Coptic monk in the Monastery of Saint Bishoi
(photograph by the author)

Reliquary of Saint Bishoi, Monastery of Saint Bishoi
(photograph by the author)

Modern icon of the three Macarii

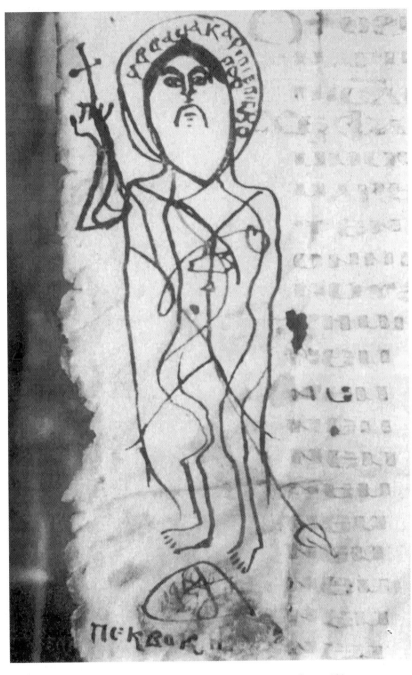

Saint Macarius the Bishop in a sketch in the margin of a twelfth-century
Bohairic text of the Exodus, Coptic Museum
(photograph by the author)

The Church of Saint Macarius, Monastery of Saint Macarius, Wadi al-Natrun
(photograph by the author)

The Church of the Holy Virgin, Monastery of Saint Samuel, Western Desert
(photograph by the author)

The belfry of the Monastery of Saint Samuel
(photograph by the author)

The ruined Monastery of Saint Simeon, Aswan
(photograph courtesy of Société d'Archéologie Copte)

Entrance to the Church of Saints Cyrus and John, Old Cairo
(photograph by the author)

Porch and entrance to the cave Church of Saint Michael, Wadi al-Rayyan
(photograph by the author)

A hermit's cave, Wadi al-Rayyan (photograph by the author)

A typical Coptic church interior: the Church of the Holy Virgin, Shentana al-Hagar
(photograph by the author)

The translation of the relics of Saint Mark from Venice to Cairo, in a modern
icon in Saint Mark's Cathedral, Cairo
(photograph by the author)

His Holiness Pope Shenouda III, 117th Pope of Alexandria and
Patriarch of the See of St. Mark
(photograph courtesy of the Coptic Patriarchate)

The Monastery of Saint Theodore the Oriental

In close proximity to the Church of the Holy Virgin by the Steps of Babylon is the Monastery of Saint Theodore the Oriental, which contains two churches, one of which is dedicated to Saints Cyrus and John and the other to Saint Theodore. Both of these churches are mentioned by Ibn Duqmaq (fourteenth century).

The Churches of Saints Cyrus and John

A door in the wall of this monastery gives access to a courtyard, whence a short passage leads into a second small courtyard. On the right is the Church of Saints Cyrus and John. The church has three *haikals*, all of which are a step higher than the choir.

The central sanctuary is covered with a dome, and in the east wall is the usual niche with a painting of the Pantocrator.

The altars are dedicated to Saint George, Saints Cyrus and John, and the Holy Virgin. The icons on the central screen show the Holy Virgin and the Twelve Apostles in the eucharistic vestments of the Coptic Church.

The northern column of the nave is enclosed in a glass case. In the dark stucco spots on the column, believers see the images of the Holy Virgin, the face of Jesus Christ, and the face of Pope Cyril VI. The relics of Saints Cyrus and John and Saint George repose in a shrine on the south side of the church.

The Church of Saint Theodore the Oriental

The Church of Saint Theodore is situated to the left of the courtyard and was redecorated in the beginning of the twentieth century. The Church of Saint Theodore has three *haikals*.

The narthex, which is separated from the nave by a wooden lattice-work screen, has at its south end the baptistery. The nave, which contains an *ambon*, is covered by three domes painted pale green. The central sanctuary, which is one step higher than the choir, has a wooden screen inlaid with ivory.

The northern sanctuary is dedicated to the Holy Virgin. The northern aisle is separated from the nave by a latticework screen adorned with numerous icons.

In the northern aisle there is a shrine with icons, beneath which an ornamented bolster contains some of the relics of Saint Theodore and Saint George.

The Church of Saint Michael al-Qibli

This church is situated within an enclosure about five hundred meters south of the Monastery of Saint Theodore. The building is discernible by a tall campanile and known as Dair Malak Mikha'il al-Qibli.

The church was built in the tenth century. In the thirteenth century, Pope Gabriel III was enthroned in this church. The building was restored several times.

The church has three *haikals* dedicated to Saint George, Saint Michael, and the Holy Virgin. The icons in this church date from the nineteenth century and represent both the Italo-Byzantine and the Nazarene style. The relics in this church belong to Saint Menas and Saint Ptolemy.

Some Coptic Churches in Greater Cairo

The Church of the Virgin in Harat Zuwayla

The Church of the Virgin in Harat Zuwayla is situated in the north-eastern district of Cairo known as Khurunfish, off Shari' Bain al-Surain. The lower church is dedicated to the Holy Virgin Mary and the upper church to Saint George. To the northwest corner of the lower church, the Church of Saint Mercurius is annexed. Close by, there is also the Convent of Nuns of the Holy Virgin Mary.

The Church of the Holy Virgin Mary was founded in the tenth century. It is mentioned in connection with the appointment of a new bishop of Cairo, which took place during the patriarchate of Macarius II (1102–28). It was also among the churches demolished in the year 1131, but was later rebuilt. From the fourteenth century to 1660, this church served as the residence of the patriarch.

The Church of the Holy Virgin Mary, or the Lower Church

The church lies about five meters below the present street level, and the entrance to it is through the southern aisle. It comprises a narthex, nave, choir, and three sanctuaries. The nave is separated from the narthex and the northern and southern aisles by three rows of ancient marble columns. The marble *ambon* is supported on four twisted columns. Across the choir there is a beam, on which there is affixed a modern painting of the Last Supper. The screen of the central sanctuary is ebony inlaid with ivory. Over the sanctuary rises a lofty dome ornamented with gated pendentives. The altar canopy is a dome supported on four marble columns. In the apse there is a fine tribune rising in six marble steps. In the center is the synthronon. The southern sanctuary is dedicated to the archangel Gabriel, and its screen is inlaid with ivory. Along the tops of this screen are seven nineteenth-century icons that represent the Annunciation, the Nativity, the Baptism, the Entry into Jerusalem, the Resurrection, the Ascension, and the Descent of the Holy Spirit.

In the floor before this sanctuary is a well, the water of which is used for healing the sick. According to tradition, the water of the well was blessed by Christ on the flight of the holy family into Egypt. Every year, Ethiopian priests come to the church to take water from this well.

A door on the right of the southern sanctuary gives access to a shrine in which there are several famous icons. On the southern side of the shrine is a fourteenth-century (?) icon of the Holy Virgin Mary. Regarding the miracles associated with this icon, it is reported that whenever Patriarch Matthew I (1378–1408) fell into temptation, he would stand in front of the icon, addressing it in supplication as if it were a person. It was then that the Holy Virgin appeared to him, and his burdens were lightened, his problems solved, and his soul comforted. Also, Saint Ruwais is said to have prayed before this icon. The icon shows the Holy Virgin Mary seated on a tree that shoots forth from the back of Jesse (Isa. 11:1–10). Around her are the four major and the twelve minor prophets, and above them are two angels.

At the east end of the northern aisle are two sanctuaries, the screens of which are inlaid with ivory. The first sanctuary is dedicated to the archangel Michael, and its screen is dated A.M. 1495 (A.D. 1778–79). The second sanctuary is dedicated to Saint John the Baptist.

At the west end of the church is a shrine. In the center there is an icon of the Crucifixion; on the right, the Baptism of Christ; and on the left, the Holy Virgin. A doorway in the northwest corner of the northern aisle gives access to the Church of Saint Mercurius.

The Church of Saint Mercurius

This church was built by al-Mu'allim Ibrahim al-Gawhari in the year A.M. 1490 (A.D. 1773–74). It comprises a nave, choir, northern and southern aisles, three sanctuaries, and a baptistery. The nave is covered with a dome and the central sanctuary with a semidome. In the nave there is an *ambon* supported on six wooden columns.

The aisles are separated from the nave by six columns, three on each side. The screen of the central sanctuary is wood inlaid with ivory, and along the top of it is a row of icons.

The Church of Saint George, or the Upper Church

The upper church is dedicated to Saint George. It is small and comprises a nave and three sanctuaries. Outside this church there is a small chamber that contains a shrine of the Holy Virgin Mary. Behind the latticed screen is an icon of the Holy Virgin Mary together with icons of saints.

The Convent of Nuns of the Holy Virgin Mary

Annexed to the Church of the Holy Virgin Mary of Harat Zuwayla is a convent that was built by the patriarch Cyril IV (1854–61). The nuns have a chapel in the gallery on the north side of the Church of the Holy Virgin Mary.

The Churches of the Holy Virgin and of Saint George in Harat al-Rum

The Church of the Holy Virgin Mary is situated at the end of a lane leading off Shari' Sukkariya in the Muski district in the vicinity of al-Azhar University.

It was founded in the tenth century, but it has been several times demolished and rebuilt. The church was among those closed or demolished in the reign of al-Hakim (996–1021). From 1660 to 1799, this church was the seat of the patriarch in Cairo. The present edifices date from the time of Muhammad 'Ali.

On entering this church, one should note the roof, which is formed of twelve domes: one over each of the three sanctuaries and nine over the rest of the church. The choir is separated from the nave by five piers. To the northern pier of the choir is attached a wooden *ambon*. The screen of the central sanctuary is inlaid with ivory. Along the top is the usual row of icons. The altar is marble. The southern sanctuary is dedicated to the four bodiless living creatures of the Apocalypse and the northern sanctuary to Saint Marina. A door to the right of the southern sanctuary gives access to a long passage. In a recess to the left is the ancient baptistery, and at the end of the passage is the modern baptistery. One floor above the ground and close to the Church of the Holy Virgin Mary, but not directly over it, is the Church of Saint George, which has the same twelve-domed roofing as the Church of the Holy Virgin Mary.

Close by the Church of the Holy Virgin Mary is the Convent of Nuns of Saint Theodore, which has three shrines and a very fine reception room.

The Old Cathedral of Saint Mark at Azbakiya

The old Cathedral of Saint Mark is situated at Shari' al-Kanisa al-Murqusiya in the Azbakiya district of Cairo. One approaches the cathedral through a courtyard, which is flanked by the Coptic College on the north and the former patriarchal residence and offices on the south.

The first church was erected in this place in the year 1800, when the seat of the patriarch was transferred here by the patriarch Mark VIII (1796–1809) from the Church of the Holy Virgin Mary at Harat al-

Rum. The present building was begun by the patriarch Cyril IV (1854–61) and was finished during the pontificate of the patriarch Demetrius II (1861–70).

The church is built in the style of Greek Orthodox churches of the period, and its interior decoration resembles that of a Greek Orthodox church. The northern and southern aisles are separated from the nave by lofty marble columns. The *ambon*, which is attached to one of these columns on the north side, is reached by a spiral staircase. The sanctuary screen is decorated with an iconostasis. Behind the square altar of the sanctuary is a tribune with a synthronon.

The superb ancient lectern belonged to the Church of Saints Sergius and Bacchus in Babylon, Old Cairo.

The Church of Saint Stephen

To the north of the patriarchal Church of Saint Mark is the Church of Saint Stephen. It was built during the pontificate of the patriarch Mark VIII (1796–1809).

The church comprises a nave, a choir, and one sanctuary. The sanctuary screen is wood inlaid with plain ivory. Along the top of the screen is a row of icons, in the center of which is the Crucifixion.

On the south side of this church is a door that gives access to a mortuary chapel in which the bodies of the following patriarchs are interred: Cyril IV (110th patriarch), Demetrius II (111th patriarch), Cyril V (112th patriarch), John XIX (113th patriarch), Macarius III (114th patriarch), and Joseph II (115th patriarch).

On the north side of this church a door opens into the baptistery, in which there are two fonts. The basin of the larger font is used for adult baptisms.

The Church of Saints Peter and Paul in 'Abbasiya

The Church of Saints Peter and Paul in 'Abbasiya is situated at Shari' Ramsis next to the Coptic Archaeological Society and near the Coptic Institute and the Coptic Theological Seminary.

The church was built in 1911 over the tomb of Butrus Ghali Pasha, the former prime minister, by the members of his family. It is one of the finest examples of modern Coptic ecclesiastical architecture. Constructed entirely of dressed stone, it boasts mural paintings by Primo Pancirolli of Rome and mosaics by Angelo of Venice.

This church comprises a nave, a choir, northern and southern aisles, a confessional, two sanctuaries, and a baptistery. The aisles are separated from the nave by ten marble columns, five on each side. There are three entrance doors at the west end, and three entrance doors on both the north and south sides of the church.

In the nave, one should note the mural paintings above the arches. They represent, from west to east: Saint Matthew, the Annunciation, the Nativity, the Flight into Egypt, the Multiplication of Loaves and Fishes, the Entry into Jerusalem, Saint Luke, Saint Mark, the Last Supper, the Crucifixion, the Resurrection, the Ascension, the Descent of the Holy Spirit, and Saint John.

Against the pier on the north of the sanctuary is a fine marble *ambon*, and before the sanctuary there is the confessional. Above the door that gives access to the tomb of Butrus Ghali Pasha, the dates of the deceased are inscribed in Arabic and French: May 12, 1846–February 21, 1910. Within the crypt there is a granite sarcophagus mounted on a base of black granite, which contains the remains of Butrus Ghali Pasha, and to the left of it are the tombs of his eldest son, Nagib Ghali Pasha, and his widow. On the north and south sides of the sarcophagus the last words of the deceased are written in Arabic and French: "God knows that I did no harm to my country."

The altar of the sanctuary is marble and supported on four white marble columns.

Around the border of the semidome above the sanctuary there is inscribed in Coptic and Arabic, "Glory to God in the heights," and in the semidome itself there is a beautiful mosaic depicting Christ as Pantocrator, seated on a throne with the Holy Virgin Mary on his right and Saint Mark on his left. Below is Saint Paul the Hermit, Saint Cyril, Saint Athanasius, and Saint Antony.

On the walls of the southern and northern aisles are two rows of mural paintings.

At the east end of the northern aisle is the sanctuary of the Holy Virgin Mary. Behind the altar is a mosaic of the Holy Virgin Mary and the Christ child. On the north wall is a painting of Saint Paul, and on the south wall is a painting depicting the widow of Butrus Ghali Pasha presenting the church through an angel to the Mother of God, with Saint Anne on one side and Saint Elizabeth on the other. Further on, there are paintings of Saint Barbara and Saint Mary the Egyptian. Over the door is a painting of King David.

The Church of Saint Ruwais in 'Abbasiya

The Church of Saint Ruwais (Dair Anba Ruwais) comprises a nave, a choir, and two sanctuaries, which are covered by two domes.

Saint Ruwais was a contemporary of Matthew I (1378–1408). From his youth he practiced an extreme asceticism. He settled at the Monastery of al-Khandaq, healed the sick, predicted the future, and assisted the imprisoned patriarch. The church was built on the site of the former Church of Saint Mercurius in al-Khandaq, which existed in the fourteenth century. Eight steps lead to the crypt with the tombs of Saints Sulaiman and Ruwais. The forearm and hand of Saint Ruwais repose in a bolster in the southern *haikal*.

At the bottom of the steps on the left, there is the tomb of Saint Sulaiman, a companion of Saint Ruwais. Opposite this tomb is a doorway that gives access to a crypt directly beneath the central sanctuary of the church above. On the right of this doorway is a modern icon of Saint Ruwais and his companion Saint Sulaiman. Within the crypt, which was restored in 1949, is the tomb of Saint Ruwais.

On the sarcophagus there is inscribed in Arabic: "Here reposeth in the Lord the Saint, the righteous Anba Farig, known as Anba Ruwais. He fell asleep on Friday the 21st of Baba in the year A.M. 1121, which corresponds to the 18th of October, 1404."

In this crypt there are also buried the following patriarchs: Matthew I, eighty-seventh patriarch (1378–1408), John XI, eighty-ninth patriarch (1427–52), Matthew II, ninetieth patriarch (1453–65), and Gabriel VI, ninety-first patriarch (1466–74).

The New Cathedral of Saint Mark

On July 24, 1965, President Gamal Abd al-Nasser laid the cornerstone of the new Cathedral of Saint Mark at Shari' Ramsis in 'Abbasiya. On the occasion of the 1,900th anniversary of the martyrdom of Saint Mark the Evangelist and the translation of his relics from Venice to Cairo, the new cathedral was inaugurated. The cathedral is one of the largest churches in Africa and measures one hundred meters in length and thirty-six meters in width. The central dome has a height of fifty-five meters. The two bell towers are eighty-five meters high. The seating capacity is five thousand people.

The upper church has three *haikals* dedicated to Saint Menas, Saint Mark, and the Holy Virgin. The center altar is a gift of the Russian Orthodox Church. The other two altars are made of Egyptian alabaster. The eastern part of the ground floor is occupied by the crypt of Saint Mark. On July 26, 1968, the relics of the Evangelist were placed into a cavity of a block of solid Aswan granite in this crypt. To the west of the crypt are the two churches of the Holy Virgin and Saint Bishoi and the Holy Virgin and Saint Ruwais. Since 1973 the relics of Saint Athanasius have reposed on the ground floor of the cathedral. Also the tomb of Bishop Samuel, who served as bishop for ecumenical and social affairs from 1962 to 1981, is on the ground floor. He was assassinated on 6 October 1981.

The Church of Saint Michael in al-Khandaq

The Church of Saint Michael, known also as the Monastery of Saint Michael the Northern, was rebuilt in 1894 by Ibrahim Bey Malaka al-Wahhabi on the site of the ancient Coptic Monastery of Saint George in al-Khandaq. Al-Khandaq ('the drain' or 'the ditch') was situated outside the city walls of medieval Cairo. Nowadays, the church occupies a site near Shari' Misr wa-l-Sudan in the district of 'Abbasiya, at some distance behind the Coptic Orthodox Theological Seminary.

The Church of Saint Michael with its two belfries has one central *haikal* dedicated to the Archangel; the southern and the northern *haikal*s have no altars. The iconostasis is of the Syro-Byzantine type. The baptistery is situated to the south of the church. During the patriarchate of Christodoulus (1047–77), the monastery at al-Khandaq was an episcopal see of some importance. Solomon, the king of Nubia, visited Cairo in 1080 and was buried in the Monastery of Saint George at al-Khandaq. During the patriarchate of Cyril II (1078–92), there were numerous churches at al-Khandaq.

Al-Khandaq remained an episcopal see until the fourteenth century. It is said that at least twelve churches were situated there. The only archaeological remains of this distinguished Christian site are a red granite column, a capital, and fragments of a pillar. These objects are in the northern part of the churchyard.

The Church of the Holy Virgin in Zamalek

The Church of the Holy Virgin (al-'Adhra') at Shari' Mar'ashli and Shari' Muhammad Habib Pasha in Zamalek is one of the modern Coptic Churches in Egypt. The architect, Mr. Ramsis Wisa Wasif, designed the church in a modernist Coptic style. The church, which was completed in 1960, has three *haikal*s. The central *haikal* is dedicated to the Holy Virgin, the northern *haikal* to Saint Michael, and the southern *haikal* to Saint George. The stained-glass windows represent the miracles of Christ.

The Church of Saint George in Heliopolis

The Church of Saint George in Heliopolis is situated at Shari' 'Abd al-'Aziz Fahmi. The church, which is built in Byzantine style according to the model of the Hagia Sophia in Istanbul, has a large dome surmounting the nave. There are twelve stained-glass windows in the dome showing among other themes the Annunciation, the Nativity, the Crucifixion, the Resurrection, the Ascension, Pentecost, the Holy Virgin and Child, and Saint Mark. Above the entrance is a stained-glass window portraying Saint George.

The church, which was also constructed by Wisa Wasif, has three *haikals*, which are dedicated to the Holy Virgin (north), Saint George (center) and Saint Menas (south). The baptistery is situated in a separate room in the southern part of the church, and the baptismal font is constructed of alabaster. The stained-glass window shows the Baptism of Christ.

The Church of the Holy Virgin at Zaytun

This church, built in 1925 by Khalil Ibrahim Pasha for his family, has attracted large numbers of pilgrims, both Christian and Muslim, ever since the first apparition of the Holy Virgin on April 2, 1968. For several weeks in 1968 and 1969 thousands of pilgrims assembled every night in front of this church in anticipation of the apparition of the Holy Virgin in bright blue or orange light on the dome or in one of the windows of the northeastern cupola of the church. Many healing miracles are said to have taken place in conjunction with the apparition.

The church is situated at Shari' Tuman Bey, Zaytun. Following the apparitions, the church has been renovated and enlarged in order to serve as a pilgrimage center. To the west of the church, a new roofed hall adorned with wall paintings of the Holy Virgin, Cyril VI, the Flight into Egypt, the Via Dolorosa, the Ascension, the Holy Virgin of Zaytun, and Christ healing the blind (painted by S. Antun in 1970) provides shelter for pilgrims.

The Church of the Apparition of the Holy Virgin

In commemoration of the apparition of the Holy Virgin at Zaytun on April 2, 1968, Pope Cyril VI laid the cornerstone for this monumental building in 1970. The church is situated opposite the old church of the Holy Virgin at Shari' Tuman Bey in Zaytun. The church includes a spacious ground-floor hall. The upper church has three *haikals*. The western end of the nave is covered by a large gallery. The episcopal throne is decorated with a relief of the *Mater Dolorosa* by the Florentine master Carlo Dolci (1616–86).

The Church of Saint Simeon the Tanner in al-Muqattam

The Church of Saint Simeon the Tanner is situated at the foot of the Muqattam Hills east of Cairo within the district of the *zabbalin*, the garbage collectors of greater Cairo. The church was built amidst the dwellings of the *zabbalin* in 1977. Pope Shenuda III has visited the church and the general area several times since 1977. Some of the relics of Saint Simeon, which were discovered on 4 August 1994 in the Church of the Holy Virgin by the Steps of Babylon repose on the northern wall of the nave. The paintings on the western wall of the nave depict the miracle of the moving of the Muqattam Hills by the prayers of Saint Simeon the Tanner and Pope Abraham (975–78) at the time of the caliph al-Mu'izz. This occurred as a witness to the biblical injunction: "If ye have faith as a grain of mustard seed, ye shall say unto this mountain, Remove hence to yonder place; and it shall remove" (Matt. 17:20).

The general area belonging to the church includes a vast garden with impressive reliefs showing biblical themes, a spacious retreat house, and nestled within the mountain face, the Church of Saint Paul. The conference hall is built into one of the caves of the Muqattam Hills and can hold several thousand people.

The Other Coptic Churches in Greater Cairo

'Abdin
The Church of Saint Gabriel (1855), Harat al-Saqqayin (built by Mikha'il Bey Sharubim, Sa'd Bey 'Abduh, Shenuda Bey Bakhum, Shenuda Bey Bulus, Qummus Girgis Butrus, and Qummus Bulus Girgis).

'Ain Shams
The Church of Saint George (1936), al-Matariya.

al-Azbakiya
The Church of Saint George (1924), Shari' al-Qulali; the Church of the Holy Virgin (1884), Shari' al-Wazir 'Ala' al-Din (built by Yuhanna Gad, Damian Bey Gad, and Mikha'il Gad).

al-Wayli
The Church of Saint George (1926), Manshiyat al-Sadr (built by Qummus Kirillus Matta); the Church of the Holy Virgin (1940); the Church of Saint Mercurius (1955), 'Izbat Mansur; the Church of Saint Michael (1892), Hadayiq al-Qubba; the Church of Saint John the Baptist (1948), Shari' al-Gabal al-Ahmar (built by Nicholas Greiss); the Church of the Holy Virgin, 'Izbat al-Qusayyarin; the Church of Saint George, al-Zawiya al-Hamra'; the Church of the Holy Virgin, 'Amiriya.

al-Sahl
The Church of Saint George (1935), Shari' Khumarawayh; the Church of Saints Mercurius and Damiana (1936), Ard Rif; the Church of Saint Damiana (1950), Ard Baba Dublu (built by Qummus 'Abd al-Masih Shirbini, Dr. Hilmi Makari, Joseph Makari, and Wisa Dimitriyus); the Church of the Holy Virgin and the Angel (1956),

Ard Sharif; the Church of Saint Mark (1953), Minyat al-Shiriq (built by the Coptic Orthodox Society for the Propagation of the Holy Scriptures).

Bab al-Sha'riya
The Church of Saint George (1939), 31 Sikkat al-Dahir (built by Anba Yu'annis XIX and Anba Tuma, bishop of Tanta).

Bulaq
The Church of Saint Damiana (1910), Shari' al-'Adawiya.

Heliopolis
The Church of Saint Mark (1925), Shari' Cleopatra; the Church of Saint George (1935), Almaza; the Church of Saint Menas, Shari' Ibrahim Luqa; the Church of Saint George, Shari' Sa'ud; the Church of Saint George, Shari' al-Alf Maskin; the Church of the Holy Virgin, Madinat Nasr.

Ma'adi
The Church of Saint Mark; the Church of the Holy Virgin; the Church of Saint Raphael; the Church of Saint George, Tura.

Helwan
The Church of Saint George; the Church of the Holy Virgin.

Faggala
The Church of the Holy Virgin, Shari' Kamil Sidqi.

Zahir
The Church of Saint Michael; the Church of Saint George.

Matariya
The Church of the Holy Virgin (1950), 'Izbat al-Nakhl; the Church of Saint George (1957), Manshiyat al-Tahrir; the Church of the Holy Virgin (1952), 4 Shari' al-Muq'ad; the Church of Saint George (1957), Shari' al-Masakin al-Sha'biya.

Rawd al-Farag
The Church of Saint George (1936), 58 Shari' Gazirat Badran; the Church of the Holy Virgin (1941), Shari' 'Ayyad Bey; the Church of Saint Michael (1956), Shari' 'Ayyad Bey (built by Mr. Yunan Nakhla of al-Mahabba); the Church of the Holy Virgin (1942), Shari' Masarra; the Church of Saint Michael (1952), Shari' Tusun; the Church of the Holy Virgin (1948), Shari' al-Karki; the Church of Saint Michael (1953), Shari' Ghali; the Church of Saint Shenute, Shari' 'Ayyad Bey; the Church of the Holy Virgin, Rawd al-Farag; the Church of Saint Mark, Rawd al-Farag.

Shubra

The Church of Saint Menas, 37 Shari' al-Tur'a al-Bulaqiya; the Church of Saint Antony, Shari' al-Khargi; the Church of Saint George (1938), Shari' al-Guyush; the Church of the Holy Virgin (1944), Shari' al-Wuguh; the Church of the Holy Virgin (1924), Shari' Mahmasha; the Church of Saint Barbara (1943), Shari' al-Sharabiya; the Church of Saints George and Sarabamun (1948), 'Izbat al-Ward; the Church of the Holy Virgin, Shari' Hafiziya, the Church of Saint George, Shari' Abu Taqiya; the Church of Saint Mark, Shari' al-Guyush; the Church of Saint Mark, Khumarawayh; the Church of Saint George, Wayli al-Kabir, Abu Layla.

Zaytun

The Church of Saint George, 'Ain Shams; the Church of the Holy Virgin, Matariya; the Church of the Holy Virgin, Midan al-Tahrir, Matariya; the Church of Saint Damiana, Matariya; the Church of Saint George, Madinat al-Nut, Matariya; the Church of Saint Timothy (1957), Zaytun; the Church of Saint John (1940), Hilmiyat al-Zaytun.

The Cathedral of Saint George in Giza

The diocese of Giza includes thirty churches, the most important of which is the Cathedral of Saint George, which was dedicated in 1956. The central altar is dedicated to the equestrian warrior saint, the northern altar to the Holy Virgin. To the south of the main altar is a prayer chapel.

The wall paintings in this cathedral were executed by E.R. 'Ayyad. The central apse is adorned with a large painting of the twenty-four elders of the Apocalypse and the Pantocrator. The northern wall has paintings representing Saints Michael, Gabriel, Raphael, and Suriel, as well as Saints Mark, George, Menas, and Theodore. On the southern wall are paintings of Saints John the Baptist, Antony, Paul the Theban, Macarius, Pachomius, Domitius, Maximus, Cyril I, and Athanasius. On the west wall, there are paintings of Saints Damiana and Barbara. Noteworthy is the beautifully carved iconostasis, a copy of a fifth-century model in the Coptic Museum. The stained-glass windows represent themes from the Old and New Testaments.

The Churches and Monasteries between Cairo and Suhag

Between Cairo and Minya

The Monastery of Saint Mercurius at Tammua

Those on their way to Memphis, Saqqara, or Dahshur may want to stop at the village of Tammua, eleven kilometers south of Giza, to visit the ancient Monastery of Saint Mercurius, or Dair Abu Saifain. Coming from Cairo, one should turn left (east) and follow the road through the village for about one and a half kilometers. The monastery is situated north of the village on the bank of the Nile.

Since 1967, the monastery buildings have been used as a training center for the rural diakonia of the Coptic Church. South of the present buildings, one can still see the remains of the ancient wall that enclosed the monastery. Visitors should not fail to enter the keep (*qasr*). From the second floor of the keep, one has a magnificent view of Tura, Ma'adi, and Cairo.

The church has three sanctuaries, which are dedicated to Saint Damiana (north), Saint Mercurius (center), and Saint John the Baptist (south). The wooden *haikal* screen is adorned with twenty-seven icons representing the apostles and Egyptian saints. The baptistery is situated in the north corner of the church. The shrine of Saint Mercurius on the north wall holds a bolster that contains the relics of Saint Mercurius or Saint Paphnutius.

Abu al-Makarim (thirteenth century) gives the following account:

> The monastery is surrounded by an enclosing wall. Its church is named after Saint Mercurius and overlooks the river, to which it is close. Contiguous to the monastery there is a keep, entered from the church; and in its upper story there are fine manzarahs. The monastery was restored by the shaikh Abu al-Yumn Wazir, leader of the Diwan of Lower Egypt in the caliphate of al-Amir [1101–30]. In the church lies the body of Saint Paphnutius, the superior of this monastery. The monastery contains a painting of the Lady, the pure Virgin Mary. Al-Afdal [twelfth century] took pleasure in sitting in his place in the upper story of the building. The shaikh Abu al-Yumn provided for this church vessels of gold and silver.

The Church of Saints Cosmas and Damian in Manyal Shiha

Situated in the western section of the village on the west bank of the Nile opposite Tura, the church belongs to the diocese of Giza. The annual pilgrimage to the Unmercenary Physicians Cosmas and Damian, whose relics repose in the sanctuary, takes place from 27 to

29 May. Epileptics and those suffering from nervous disorders especially repair to this church. In 1985 a shrine for the twelve-year-old virgin-martyr Saint Mohrail of Tammua (d.305) was erected in the western part of the church. The former Church of Saint Mohrail, built by Bishop Tsadi of Memphis, existed until the fourteenth century. Her relics and those of her brother Saint Hor were venerated in Cairo in the eleventh century. Today, Saints Mohrail and Hor have become popular youth-saints.

The Church of the Holy Virgin at Ma'adi

The Church of the Holy Virgin is situated at one of the most beautiful sites on the banks of the Nile in Ma'adi. Proceed thirteen kilometers from Cairo along the corniche to the suburb of Ma'adi. The Church of the Holy Virgin, known as Dair al-'Adhra', is situated three hundred meters south of the Ma'adi Yacht Club. The church, with its three Coptic domes, is seen from a distance.

According to an oral tradition, the church was built on the site of a synagogue. It was from this site that the holy family traveled by boat to Upper Egypt, and the stairs leading down to the Nile, fifty meters north of the church, were used by the holy family.

On March 12, 1976, an Arabic Protestant pulpit Bible (Smith–Van Dyck version, nineteenth century) floated down the Nile. The book was saved by a Coptic deacon who descended the historic steps leading to the river. Since that time the Bible has been exhibited in the northwestern chapel of the church.

The present church building dates back to the eighteenth century. The church is entered through an outer and an inner court. The three *haikals* are dedicated to the Holy virgin (center), Saint Michael (north), and Saint George (south). The baptistery is situated in the southwest corner of the narthex (1958). The northern sanctuary is presently used as a storage place for candles.

The church is noteworthy on account of its many good icons, though most of them date from only the nineteenth century. In the small womens' chamber on the south side of the sanctuary, there are two bolsters with relics of unknown saints.

The Ruins of the Monastery of Saint Arsenius on Gabal Tura

South of Wadi al-Tih on a terrace overlooking the Nile Valley are the ruins of the Monastery of Saint Arsenius, known also as Dair al-Qusayr (the Monastery of the Little Castle) or Dair al-Baghl (the Monastery of the Mule), because a mule used to carry water from the Nile to the monastery.

The ruins of the monastery are impressive. A small chapel, the niche of which is still preserved, is of interest because of the Coptic writing and drawings of animals on the wall of the niche. In one of the subterranean churches, one can observe the remains of polychrome wall paintings on plaster. The dimensions of the monastery can be seen from the remaining walls. The fireplace is situated on the north side of the enclosure, the oil press on the west, and the cemetery on the south.

Saint Arsenius was a native of Rome and a teacher of the two princes, Arcadius and Honorius, the sons of Theodosius the Great. Arsenius fled from the royal palace around 394 and went to the Desert of Scetis, where he became a disciple of Saint John the Short. After the raid on Scetis in 408, Saint Arsenius fled to Tura, where he spent altogether twelve years. He died in 449. Abu al-Makarim (thirteenth century) refers to the Monastery of Saint Arsenius:

> The [Melkite] patriarch Eustathius founded in this monastery the Church of the Apostles, and he founded a cell for the bishops. The monastery is in the possession of the Melkites, and contains a body of their monks. In this monastery there are eight churches, and they are enclosed within a wall. The Church of the Apostles was destroyed by al-Hakim in 1010, and a band of the common people came here and seized the coffins of the dead and the timbers from the ruins. Afterward it was decreed that the monks should restore the ruined building, and al-Yasal assigned to the monastery sixteen feddans of land. On one occasion, a mob of Muslims went up, and by a ruse induced the monks to open the gate to them, whereupon they entered and sacked the monastery, and killed some of the monks.

He also mentions a great festival at which many people assembled.

In the thirteenth century the monastery contained only five monks in poor circumstances. In former times, however, there were six thousand monks in the monastery and the caves nearby. But in the fourteenth century, the monastery was still occupied by monks.

In the proximity of the ruins of the monastery, about 2,500 pages of Greek manuscripts were discovered when in August 1941 the British Army cleaned a large cave at the foot of the mountain for use as an ammunition depot. More or less complete, these manuscripts represent eight books that were until then almost entirely unknown.

The Church of Saint Barsum the Naked at Ma'sara

The Church of Saint Barsum the Naked (Barsum al-'Aryan) is situated between Tura and Helwan. Before crossing the Ma'sara canal, turn to the left and follow the canal for five hundred meters up to a small mosque on the right. Here, turn sharply to the left, and after three hundred meters, the church comes into sight.

The Church of Saint Barsum has three *haikals*, of which, however, only the central one is being used. South of the nave is the shrine of the saint, the object of the annual pilgrimages. The shrine contains the tomb of Saint Barsum as well as several icons.

Saint Barsum, son of al-Wagi Mufaddal of Cairo, was defrauded by his uncle of his patrimony and so became a monk and entered the solitary life in the crypt of the Church of Saint Mercurius in Old Cairo, where there was a serpent the people feared. The saint overcame this reptile and lived in the crypt for twenty years, practicing many austerities. During periods of oppression, Saint Barsum ascended to the roof of the church and there openly offered intercessions. Thereupon, he was arrested and carried off to prison. Then he was sent to the Monastery of Shahran at Ma'sara, where he dwelt in the courtyard on a heap of dust and ashes. Many miracles are recorded of him, and Sultan al-Nasir (1310–41) figures in some of them. Saint Barsum died in 1317. The mulid of Saint Barsum takes place annually on September 27 in the village of Ma'sara.

The site of the Church of Saint Barsum can be identified with the ancient Monastery of Saint Mercurius, or Dair Shahran, which is mentioned by Abu al-Makarim and was built by Abba Poemen in the days of al-Hakim. It is said that the caliph often visited this monastery. Under the leadership of Bishop Pisentius, a hospital and a social center were established near the Church of Saint Barsum.

The Ruins of the Monastery of Saint Jeremiah at Saqqara

Coming from Badrashayn, one follows the road to the Pyramid of Unis (Onnos) and the Mastaba of Mereruka. After ascending the hill for about 150 meters, it is advisable to park the car near the first guard house. From there, one proceeds south on foot for another 150 meters. Though many of the ruins are covered by sand, the remains of the three churches, the oil press, and numerous cells can still be seen. Beware of the deep shaft in the southern part of the monastery; this leads to the Tomb of Nesitahuti.

The Monastery of Saint Jeremiah was built in the first half of the sixth century. The columns and bases of the main church were of Proconnesian marble and probably imported ready-made. For a century and a half the monks enjoyed a peaceful time, and some expansion of buildings and many repairs took place. During disturbances in the latter half of the seventh century, the sculptures representing living creatures were excised or hidden. Some rebuilding activity took place, and the great church was shortened and its floor raised. Much was saved from the ruins and utilized in the new fabric, but new stone was needed as well, and this was taken from the Temple of Nectanebo. About one hundred years later, around 750, some attempt was made to rebuild the monastery, but the community was dwindling away and several buildings were deserted and had become covered with sand. From coins discovered at the Monastery of Saint Jeremiah, it is believed that the site was inhabited from the end of the fifth century until the middle of the ninth century.

The monastery was excavated in 1908–10 by J.E. Quibell. The *ambon*, niches, capitals, and friezes have been removed to the Coptic Museum in Old Cairo.

Qimn al-'Arus

The village of Qimn al-'Arus, where Saint Antony the Great was born in 251, is situated ninety-four kilometers south of Cairo on the west bank of the Nile and west of the Cairo–Aswan railroad. The village is surrounded by cultivated land. The people of the village, though today entirely Muslim, are still conscious of the fact that Saint Antony was born there. In the center of the village is a large rectangular mosque, at one time a church. In the courtyard of the mosque are a few ancient columns, which, according to the testimony of the villagers, belonged to the ancient Church of Saint Antony in Qimn al-'Arus.

The Dependency of the Monastery of Saint Antony

The dependency of the Monastery of Saint Antony (Dair Anba Antonius) is situated in the town of Bush on the west bank of the Nile, 120 kilometers south of Cairo. The present buildings date from the year 1880, when they were erected under the supervision of Abuna Yusab al-Antuni. According to tradition, the original property of the monastery consisted of fifty-two feddans owned by the father of Saint Antony in Qimn al-'Arus in the vicinity of al-Wasta. The dependency was visited by Wansleben (1672) and Granger (1730). The Church of Saint Antony was built by Abuna Basilius. The church has three *haikals*. The southern *haikal* is dedicated to Saint Michael, the central *haikal* to Saint Antony, and the northern *haikal* to Saint George.

The Dependency of the Monastery of Saint Paul the Theban

Situated in the vicinity of about two hundred meters northwest of the dependency of the Monastery of Saint Antony is the dependency of the Monastery of Saint Paul the Theban (Dair Anba Bula). Compared with the dependency of the Monastery of Saint Antony, that of Saint Paul is unpretentious. In every aspect, the dependency of the Monastery of Saint Paul does not display the prosperity of its neighboring monastery.

The present buildings, comprising the episcopal residence and a few cells, were erected around 1875, though the present Church of Saint Paul was already in existence in 1870.

The Church of Saint Antony at Dair al-Maymun

At one time a monastery, today Dair al-Maymun (the Monastery of the Blessed) is a small village situated in a palm grove on the east bank of the Nile. It can be reached from Cairo via the road from Helwan al-Saff to Kuraymat (108 kilometers).

At the beginning of the thirteenth century the monastery was still inhabited, and Abu al-Makarim mentions the keep, a garden, a mill, and a wine press. In the fifteenth century, al-Maqrizi identified it as the Monastery of al-Gummayza. Dair al-Maymun was visited by Wansleben (1673), Norden (eighteenth century), Russegger (1836), and Giamberardini (1955). Two churches, the Church of Saint Antony and the Church of Saint Mercurius, are the only remnants of a once distinguished monastic settlement.

The Church of Saint Antony has two *haikal*s: the center one is dedicated to Saint Antony, the northern one to Saint George. The *haikal* screen shows the date of A.M. 1264 (A.D. 1529–30). The church is built above the cave in which Saint Antony is said to have lived prior to the establishment of the monastery. The cave, in the south side of the church, is about 1.95 meters in depth, 1.75 meters in length, and 0.8 meters in width and is covered by a wooden door placed into the floor.

The Church of Saint Mercurius is much older than the present building of its neighboring church. A stone *haikal* screen divides the sanctuary from the choir. To the north of the *haikal* is a staircase leading to a bell tower.

The Monastery of the Holy Virgin at Bayad al-Nasara

The Monastery of the Holy Virgin Mary (Dair al-'Adhra') at Bayad al-Nasara is situated on the east bank of the Nile, almost opposite the town of Beni Suef.

The monastery is beautifully located immediately on the east bank of the Nile. It is enclosed by a high wall. The cells, at one time occupied by monks, are arranged back along the wall. The old church has been completely torn down, and a new church dedicated to the Holy Virgin has been built. The new Church of the Holy Virgin Mary has two *haikal*s, which are dedicated to the Holy Virgin Mary and Saint Damiana. The new church was consecrated by Bishop Athanasius in January 1963.

In 1965, Bishop Athanasius of Beni Suef established at the former monastery a retreat house for the Coptic Order of the Daughters of Saint Mary. Also, Bayad al-Nasara serves as a training center of the rural diakonia, where artisans, Sunday School teachers, and cantors are trained.

A large *mulid* is held annually from August 7 to August 23 in honor of the Assumption of the Holy Virgin Mary.

The Coptic Cathedral in Beni Suef

The Coptic Orthodox Cathedral of the Holy Virgin has three altars dedicated to Saint George, the Holy Virgin, and Saint Mercurius. Nearby is a large multipurpose community center, which can claim to be the best and most efficient center in Egypt. In addition to the training center for girls in Beni Suef, the diocese of Beni Suef operates a training center in the village of Bani Bakhit.

The Church of Saint George at Biba

The town of Biba is situated twenty-two kilometers south of Beni Suef. The Church of Saint George, which attracts large numbers of pilgrims for the annual *mulid* of Saint George, is situated on the banks of the Nile in the eastern part of the town.

The church is situated in a large enclosure. An outer and an inner court provide for the pilgrims at the time of the *mulid*. A Coptic school is situated north of the church.

The Church of Saint George is a nineteenth-century construction with modern wall paintings. The church has one altar, which is dedicated to Saint George. North of the sanctuary is a prayer chamber for men dedicated to the Holy Virgin. South of the sanctuary is a prayer chamber for women dedicated to Saint Antony.

The remains of a medieval ivory-inlaid *haikal* screen are incorporated into the modern and artistically inferior screen. Two seventeenth-century icons of the Resurrection and the Crucifixion can be seen on the inner walls of the sanctuary.

The *mulid* in honor of Saint George is observed annually, a week prior to the Feast of the Ascension, normally in May.

The Church of Apa Klog at al-Fant

Al-Fant is situated on the west bank of the Nile between al-Fashn and Maghagha. In the center of the village is the Church of Apa Klog, or Saint Colluthus, the only exclusively Coptic unmercenary physician. As such, he followed the biblical order "Freely ye have received, freely give" (Matt 10:8). His relics repose in the church. Twice a year on 14 June and 28 January the Copts gather to commemorate the blessings of their patron-saint. The present church was visited by Wansleben in 1672.

The Church of Saint Theodore at al-Bahnasa

The town of al-Bahnasa, the ancient Oxyrhynchus, today predominantly Muslim, is situated at the edge of the desert on the west bank of the Bahr Yusuf canal, about twenty-two kilometers west of Bani Mazar. Only a very few architectural fragments point to the distinguished history and tradition of this important cultural and early ecclesiastical center.

The principal church of al-Bahnasa is dedicated to Saint Theodore, who is highly venerated in this section of the country (cf. the *mulid* of Amir Tadrus at Dair al-Sanquriya, eight kilometers south of al-Bahnasa). The church, which was built in 1923 by Ibrahim Ghattas and Abuna Butrus Ishaq, is of little interest, except for the modern Byzantine iconostasis. The church has three *haikals*, which are dedicated to the Holy Virgin, Saint Theodore, and the Archangel. A small modern necropolis is found in the churchyard north of the sanctuary.

The inhabitants of al-Bahnasa believe that the holy family visited their village on their flight into Egypt. In the fourth century, Oxyrhynchus, where the fish formerly had been worshiped, served as one of the principal monastic settlements. The author of the *Historia Monachorum* speaks of ten thousand monks and twenty thousand virgins under the bishop of Oxyrhynchus.

Al-Bahnasa reached international fame on account of the expeditions of Drs. B.P. Grenfell and A.S. Hunt of the Egypt Exploration Fund. Among the earliest discoveries were the two series of the *Sayings of Jesus,* or *Logia Jesu,* which were published in 1897 and 1904. For the Bible scholar, perhaps the most noteworthy material constitutes the third-century fragments of Matthew, chapter 1, verses 1–9, 12, and 14–20 (Oxyrh. Pap. 2) and the fragments of chapters 1, 15, 16, and 20 of John (Oxyrh. Pap. 208 and 1228).

In addition to the Christian material, Oxyrhynchus yielded a wealth of pre-Christian manuscripts, such as poems of Pindar; fragments of Sappho and Alcaeus; substantial pieces of Alcman, Ibycus, and Corinna; the greater part of the *Ichneutae* of Sophocles; extensive remains of the *Hypsipyle* of Euripides; and large portions of several plays of Menander. Important also is the so-called *Hellenica Oxyrhynchus,* the author of which is not determined with certainty, but is most likely Ephorus. A *vita* of Euripides by Satyrus, written in the form of a dialogue, is an interesting specimen of popular biography. An epitome of some of the lost books of Livy constitute the chief literary find in Latin.

The Church of Saint Theodore at Dair al-Sanquriya

Dair al-Sanquriya is on the eastern bank of the Bahr Yusuf canal, approximately twenty kilometers west of Bani Mazar.

The Church of Saint Theodore is situated in the southeastern part of the enclosure and built on the site of an ancient monastery. Noteworthy are the fourteen red granite columns, three of which have acanthus-leaf capitals. The columns support the roof of the northern and western porches.

The church has three *haikals*, which are dedicated to the Holy Virgin (north), Saint Theodore (center), and Saint George (south). The *haikal* screen is noteworthy for its ivory inlaid designs.

The *ambon*, which is decorated with icons of the Twelve Apostles, is attached to the northwestern column. The baptistery is situated in the northeastern part of the church.

West of the church is an enclosed necropolis with eight tombs belonging to the family of Mikha'il Athanasius, the restorer of the church.

The Basilica at Kom al-Namrud

About twenty-five kilometers west of Samalut, near the village of Shusha, are the extensive monastic ruins and the basilica at Kom al-Namrud. The site was visited by Palladius in the fourth century and was once inhabited by thirty thousand monks and nuns. The basilica measures thirty by seventeen meters.

The Church of Saint Iskhirun in Bayahu

Every year during Ascensiontide, Coptic pilgrims gather at the Church of Saint Iskhirun of Killin, a fourth-century military saint and martyr. The village is situated on the west bank of the Nile five kilometers south of Samalut. Fragments of capitals and columns of the old church are still seen in the streets and in the courtyard of the church. The well with the therapeutical water in the church is believed to have been miraculously transported from the ancient original church of Saint Iskhirun in Killin near Kafr al-Shaikh in the Nile Delta.

The Church of the Holy Virgin at Gabal al-Tayr

One of the most beautiful churches in Egypt is the Church of the Holy Virgin (Dair al-'Adhra') at Gabal al-Tayr, known also as the Convent of the Pulley. One can cross the Nile from Bayahu to Gabal al-Tayr by felucca (no regular service), though one should allow a maximum of two hours, for the crossing depends on the wind. Having reached the east bank of the Nile, one climbs the cliff (166 stairs) and reaches the ancient Church of the Holy Virgin, which is reputed to have been built by the empress Helena. A memorial tablet on the west wall of the church indicates that the first church was built in the year A.M. 44 (A.D. 328) and that it was repaired by Severus, the bishop of Minya, in 1938.

The Church of the Holy Virgin is mentioned by Abu al-Makarim:

> This church is hewn out of the mountain side, and in the rock is the mark of the palm of the hand of the Lord Christ which was made when he touched the mountain. . . . He grasped the mountain, when it worshiped before him, and restored it to its place with his hand, so that the mark of his palm remains impressed upon the mountain.

Dair al-'Adhra' was inhabited by monks until the middle of the nineteenth century. This is substantiated by Wansleben (1672), F.L. Norden (1740), Richardson (1816), Henniker (1819), and Lord Curzon (1838).

The *haikal* and choir of the Church of the Holy Virgin are cut out of solid rock and may be regarded as subterranean. The choir, raised about one meter above the nave, is approached by a double flight of steps. The deeply recessed niches are characteristic of ancient Upper Egyptian churches. The most ancient part of the church is probably the narthex.

The Church of the Holy Virgin attracts annually tens of thousands of pilgrims who come by feluccas from as far as Minya, Asyut, and even from Cairo for the Feast of the Assumption of the Holy Virgin (August 22).

Between Minya and Asyut

The Coptic Churches of Minya

Minya is the episcopal see of the Coptic Orthodox bishop of Minya and al-Ashmunain. The Coptic Orthodox Cathedral is dedicated to Saint Mark. In addition, there are the following Coptic Orthodox Churches in Minya: the Church of Saint Theodore, the Church of the Holy Virgin, the Church of Saint George, and the Church of Saint Menas.

The Ruins of the Monastery of Abu Fanah

The ruins of the Monastery of Abu Fanah, or the Monastery of the Cross, are situated at the edge of the desert near Qasr Hor. From the railway station at Itlidim, one proceeds west to Qasr Hor, where one crosses the Bahr Yusuf canal. Continue for another two kilometers toward the edge of the desert, and the monastery is situated about one kilometer in the desert.

The ruins of the monastery extend over a wide area, which is covered with potsherds and bricks. Pieces of gray granite, which are spread about in considerable quantity, may lead one to conclude that this was the site of an ancient temple. On a small hill, not far from the entrance, are the ruins of a square building that at one time served as the *qasr*.

The church is the only building to have survived the destruction of the monastery. The three naves are separated by twelve pillars. The semicircular apsis is adorned with small pillars. Moreover, there are two side chapels. The church is decorated with numerous wall paintings of crosses, small and large and of various designs. Attached to the church was a bakery. The baptistery was situated on the south side.

The Cave of Abu Fanah is situated about eighty meters to the right of the ruined monastery.

Abu Fanah, known as Apa Bane (fourth to fifth centuries), was inspired to the anchoritic life by the hermits he visited in the Western Desert. Following their example, he entered the wilderness near al-Ashmunain. Apart from his ascetic exercises, he is known for his concern for the sick and the poor and his many miracles. It is said that he predicted the date of the death of Theodosius the Great. The monastery was built in his memory.

Abu al-Makarim mentions the Church of Abu Fanah, which was restored by al-Rashid Abu al-Fadl. Al-Maqrizi speaks of a monastery of Abu Fanah with fine stone architecture. The patriarch Theodosius II (thirteenth century) used to be a monk at Abu Fanah. In former times, there were a thousand monks here, but the first monastic community had already disintegrated prior to the Arab conquest in the seventh century, and in the fifteenth century only two monks survived.

In the course of excavations by the Austrian Archaeological Institute, the tomb of Apa Bane was discovered in 1992.

The Church of Apa Hor at Sawada

The Church of Apa Hor, known as Dair Apa Hor or Dair al-Sawada, is situated in the village of Dair Apa Hor, four kilometers south of Minya on the east bank of the Nile opposite Maqusa and one kilometer east of Sawada at the foot of the mountain range.

The Church of Apa Hor, which is subterranean and cut into the rock, is entered through a narrow tunnel. Having passed through the tunnel, one descends several steps and reaches the nave, which is almost completely dark. Four pillars divide the central nave from the narrower side naves. A dome surmounts the nave. The church has two *haikal*s, which are dedicated to Apa Hor (north) and to the Holy

Virgin (south). The wooden *haikal* screen is noteworthy because of the beautiful ivory work. The upper east wall above the *haikal* screen is adorned with a cross and two birds. The tomb of Apa Hor is said to be situated above the *haikal* of Apa Hor.

The Church of Saint Damiana is situated above the cave church. At one time, the church had three altars, though now only the central altar dedicated to Saint Damiana is being used. The *haikal* screen is inferior to that of the cave church, yet interesting on account of the inlaid smoked wood.

Apa Hor, a young monk who lived during the latter part of the third century, desired martyrdom and went to Pelusium to make his public confession of faith. The governor inflicted many tortures upon him, but at length, the saint's steadfastness caused the governor and his family to embrace the Christian faith. Later, another governor sent Apa Hor to Antinoe, where, after much torture and suffering, he was beheaded.

The Eastern Laurae South of Minya

At least seven monastic centers are known on the east bank of the Nile south of Minya: the tombs of Bani Hasan, the quarries of Manhari, the caves of Speos Artemidos, and the quarries of Dair al-Dik, Shaikh 'Abada, Abu Hinnis, and al-Barsha.

From the fifth century onward large numbers of monks settled around the city of Antinoe. Abu al-Makarim and al-Maqrizi mention five monasteries east of Antinoe, and in addition they refer to numerous churches in this region. The northernmost settlement included Dair Sunbat, which was studied and described by Cledat. A little further to the south and situated at the very edge of the cliffs is Dair al-Nasara. Still further to the south is Dair al-Dik, an extensive laura as well as a monastery.

The Hermitages of Bani Hasan

The famous tombs of Bani Hasan are situated about three kilometers south of Abu Qurqas on the east bank of the Nile. Hewn out of the rock and situated high up in the mountain, they can be assigned to the Eleventh and Twelfth Dynasties. Of the many tombs inhabited by Christian anchorites from the fourth to the sixth centuries, tomb 23, that of Nouternekht, might be the best example. On the east wall of the tomb are Coptic inscriptions and a Coptic alphabet. It has been suggested that this tomb served as a school. Other tombs in which we discover Coptic graffiti are numbers 2, 3, 13, 14, 15, 17, 18, 19, 21, 22, 24, 32, and 33.

The Valley of the Anchorites near Speos Artemidos

Passing Speos Artemidos, a temple built by Thutmosis III and Hatshepsut, and continuing for one and a half kilometers southeast, one will approach the Valley of the Anchorites. Here, several caves were inhabited by monks and hermits, as can be seen from the crosses engraved on the walls. The remains of mud-brick walls in the caves lead one to believe that a sizable community of hermits resided here.

Dair al-Dik

The monastery, which is built of crude bricks, is situated near the banks of the Nile opposite the Island of Shiba. The measurements of the ruins are 146 by 92 meters. The Laura of Dair al-Dik extends for over one and a half kilometers north of the monastery. This laura consists of at least sixteen cells and a cave church more or less in the center of the laura. In addition, there is a two-story cave monastery hewn in the rock. The church is noteworthy because of its numerous wall paintings of crosses.

The laura of Dair al-Dik, like the other laurae in this vicinity, may date back to the fifth or sixth century. The founder of this settlement was Abba Apollo. The monastery, on the other hand, may not have been built until the tenth century.

The Ancient Churches East of Shaikh 'Abada

About eighteen kilometers south of the famous tombs of Bani Hasan, opposite the town of al-Rawda on the east bank of the Nile is the village of Shaikh 'Abada. To the east of the village, which is beautifully located amidst palm trees, are the ruins of the ancient Antinoopolis, or Antinoe, the town established by Emperor Hadrian in A.D. 130 in honor of his favorite, Antinous, who died there.

To the northeast of Shaikh 'Abada in the mountain are several quarries which form a semicircle. In the center of the semicircle are the remains of a Christian monastery, the walls of which were built with crude bricks. At least nine cells are situated in the vicinity of the monastery, especially on the slopes to the south of the ruins. Some of the cells are adorned with graffiti of crosses or the 'alpha and omega.'

Around the semicircle are the ruins of two ancient churches.The one in the center was attached to a monastery behind the church. A part of the building was cut into the rock, whereas the other part was enclosed with a brick wall. Some of the cells are still visible. The walls of the central church show several paintings. The niche is surmounted by a dome. This niche, in turn, contains three small niches separated from one another by columns. A small door gives access to the court of the monastery, where the remains of the cells around the court can be seen.

In the church further to the south are the remains of wall paintings of saints and some Coptic graffiti, as well as a cross enclosed by a double circle.

The Mortuary Chapel of the Holy Virgin in the Necropolis

The Church of the Holy Virgin is situated approximately two kilometers east of the village of Shaikh 'Abada.

At one time a sizable building at the eastern edge of the ancient town, the Church of the Holy Virgin was partially restored in 1934. The altar room is locked with an iron gate. The paintings on the eastern and southern walls are badly damaged. On the southern wall, one can still see traces of a painting of Theodosia between Saint Colluthus and the Holy Virgin. Stored in the altar room are three socles and one column.

The Monastery of Saint John at Dair Abu Hinnis

A few kilometers south of Shaikh 'Abada and the ruins of Antinoe is the village of Dair Abu Hinnis, with the Church of Saint John the Short.

From an architectural point of view, this church has attracted considerable attention because it shows most clearly the changes that were made from a church of the basilican style to one roofed with domes and obstructed by clumsy masses of brickwork to support them. The church consists of a narthex, a nave, and the sanctuaries. The nave, which is divided into three bays, is covered by three domes. The piers supporting these domes are so large that they completely block the interior, which is quite dark. The southern part of the nave is the *gynaikion*, or women's chamber; the central part is reserved for men and the eastern part for the choir.

The church has two *haikal*s, which are dedicated to the Holy Virgin and to Saint John the Short. The icons in the *haikal* of the Holy Virgin (north) represent Saints John the Short and Macarius. The nineteenth-century icon of Saint John the Short was a gift of Demetrius, 111th patriarch of Alexandria. The icons in the *haikal* of Saint John the Short show the Holy Virgin (seventeenth century), Saint John the Short (1837), and a Greek Jerusalem proskynitarion, a nineteenth-century souvenir picture that provided orthodox pilgrims with most of the hagiotopographical sites and hagiological commemorations in the Holy Land. They were produced by Greek arabophone artists in Jerusalem. Attached to the *haikal* screen is a modern print of the Sacred Heart of Jesus. West of the northern *haikal* is the baptistery. The apsis walls are ornamented with three niches. Note the twenty columns with acanthus-leaf capitals and the temple fragments used in the construction of the church.

Tradition asserts, as is the case with so many churches in the Nile Valley, that the church was built during the reign of Saint Helena. Al-Maqrizi refers to the Monastery of Abu al-Na'na', which stands near Ansina (Antinoe) and is one of the oldest buildings of that city. Its church is in a tower, not on the ground, and the monastery bears the name of Saint John the Short.

The Cave Church of Saint John

The cave church is part of an extensive laura of at least thirty-seven caves extending over a distance of more than two kilometers. Many of these caves are adorned with Christian graffiti.

The cave Church of Saint John the Short is situated behind the village of Dair Abu Hinnis, about three kilometers to the southeast. After passing through the village, one enters the desert with its many cemeteries and follows the path leading east to the mountain.

This church was built into two or three ancient caves. The narthex of the church is unusually large and has a fine western entrance approached by a flight of steps from above. The church is rich in wall paintings and thus has attracted many archaeologists. These paintings are all of the same style and are from the sixth or seventh century. Unfortunately, all the paintings are seriously damaged, as the faces of the persons have all been purposely destroyed.

The themes of the wall paintings in the room to the right include the Massacre of the Innocents, with King Herod sitting on his throne in the temple and assisting in the massacre. At the end of the wall are representations of Zachariah and Elizabeth, which may belong to the Massacre of the Innocents. The subsequent scenes show the Apparition of the Angel Gabriel to Saint Joseph, and the Flight into Egypt with the Holy Virgin and the Christ child on an ass, and Saint Joseph. The wall paintings decorating the niche represent five persons, including Christ and the Holy Virgin at the wedding at Cana, where Christ changed the water into wine with a stick.

The room to the left has a wall painting of the Resurrection of Lazarus. Other paintings show the life of Zachariah with the angel Gabriel in the temple. In addition to the major themes, there are numerous Coptic inscriptions on the walls.

The Monastery of Saint Bishoi at Dair al-Barsha

The Monastery of Saint Bishoi (Dair Anba Bishai) is situated on the east bank of the Nile in the village of Dair al-Barsha about four kilometers south of Dair Anba Hinnis. The monastery consists of the Church of Saint Bishoi, situated in the northeastern part of the monastery, the ruins of monastic buildings west of the church, and the well to the north of the church.

The Monastery of Saint Bishoi has an upper and a lower church. The lower church, known as the Church of Saint Bishoi, has three *haikals* dedicated to Saint Bishoi, Saint George, and the Holy Virgin. The *haikal* screen, which is constructed of burnt brick, shows definite signs of antiquity. The screen is adorned with icons of Saint Bishoi, Saint George, and the Holy Virgin. North of the *haikal* of Saint Bishoi is a small *gynaikion*, and next to it the staircase leading to the upper church. The bakery for the *qurban*, or Eucharist, is situated in the southwest corner, and the baptistery is in the northwest corner of the church.

The upper church, which is doubtless older, has two *haikals*, the walls of which show several layers of wall paintings. The stone *haikal* screen shows the date of A.M. 1582 (A.D. 1866). The five domes of the upper church form the sign of a cross and are beautifully decorated with stars, crosses, and other geometrical designs. Tradition relates that the upper church served the local population as a place of refuge in times of danger and persecution.

According to a local oral tradition, the monastery was founded by Saint Bishoi, who settled in the Nile Valley following the sack of the Monastery of Saint Bishoi in Wadi al-Natrun. In the sixth and seventh centuries, the monastic community is said to have numbered over one thousand monks.

The Church of Saint Bishoi was used regularly until a few years ago, but now only on special occasions. Until very recently, the church was used for weddings on Saturday afternoons. Following the ceremony, the bride and the groom would spend the wedding night in the sanctuary. After the celebration of the Divine Liturgy on Sunday morning, the newly married couple would return to their home.

The Hermitages at al-Barsha

Al-Barsha, also known as Dair al-Nakhla, is a small village with a largely Christian population about eight kilometers south of al-Rawda on the east bank of the Nile. The hermitages, which are situated in ancient tombs, are located about one kilometer in the mountains behind the village. The tombs are scattered at all levels on both sides of the wadi. Just beyond tomb 7, on the north side of the wadi, are several small quarries with Coptic graffiti. The quarries on the south side of the wadi contain tombs decorated with Coptic crosses and the 'alpha and omega.' Whether a few solitaries or a colony of monks resided here is difficult to determine.

The Church in the Tomb of Urarna at Gabal Shaikh Sa'id

The rock tombs of Gabal Shaikh Sa'id are situated south of the village of al-Barsha on the east bank of the Nile, almost opposite Mallawi. These tombs are also known as the Tombs of al-Barsha, or Dair Abu Fam.

The Tomb of Urarna was greatly wrecked by the Christians, who covered the walls with plaster. The tomb was transformed into a Christian place for worship by making the two chambers of the tomb into one, destroying the reliefs, decorating the walls with Christian paintings, and finally, constructing an apse at the back of the tomb. The walls are covered with sketches of Saint George and the dragon, Coptic graffiti, and a Coptic cross.

The Ruins of the Basilica of Hermopolis Magna

The ruins of the Basilica of Hermopolis Magna are situated just outside the village of al-Ashmunain, eight kilometers northwest of Mallawi.

The columns and capitals of the ruined basilica lead one to believe that, at one time, this building served as a Greek temple, which may have been partially converted into a church during the Christian era.

Hermopolis, an ancient bishopric, is often mentioned in the annals of the Egyptian Church. In the third century, Conon, bishop of Hermopolis, received a letter from the patriarch Dionysius allowing the lapsed believers to be readmitted to his church.

The Ruins of the Monastery of Saint Apollo at Bawit

The ancient site of the famous Monastery of Saint Apollo (Dair Anba Abulu) at Bawit is situated about thirteen kilometers west of Dairut and three kilometers southwest of Dashlut and about one kilometer into the desert.

At one time, this large monastery included several smaller monasteries with individual chapels. The monastery, which was founded in the fifth or sixth century, was inhabited until the eleventh century.

Several objects from the Monastery of Saint Apollo are exhibited in the Louvre and in the Coptic Museum in Old Cairo. The famous polychrome painting of early Christianity is also exhibited in the Coptic Museum. It represents Christ enthroned and supported by the four creatures of the Apocalypse (Apoc. 4:6–7), and the Holy Virgin flanked by the apostles and two local saints.

The Monastery of the Holy Virgin at al-Qusiya (Qusqam)

Historically speaking, the Monastery of the Holy Virgin (Dair al-Muharraq) belongs to the group of monasteries established by Saint Pachomius (Anba Bakhum) or his immediate successors. The location of the monastery, as well as the type of monastic life practiced by the monks, suggests a Pachomian origin. The history of the foundation of the Monastery of the Holy Virgin is closely interwoven with the story of the flight of the holy family into Egypt. Near Qusqam (now al-Qusiya), Joseph built a small house of bricks and covered it with palm leaves, and the holy family stayed there for three years, six months, and ten days. This is the site of Dair al-Muharraq.

About the history of the monastery very little is known, and of the 117 patriarchs who have sat on the throne of Saint Mark, only four have come from Dair al-Muharraq. A thirteenth-century historian writes about the monastery that pilgrimages had been made by many multitudes from all districts to this church since ancient times because it has been celebrated for its signs and wonders and healing various diseases.

The monks of Dair al-Muharraq who have left the strongest impressions on the Coptic Church are Mikha'il al-Buhayri (d.1923) and Anba Abra'am of the Fayyum (d.1914).

Dair al-Muharraq can be conveniently divided into two main sections, the outer and the inner court. A large wall with an irregular trapezoidal outline encloses the monastery building. The dimensions of the monastery are 275 meters by 155 meters. In the inner court, we clearly see the ancient and the modern part of the monastery. The ancient structures of the monastery, situated in the western part, have attracted the interest of architects and historians. Here we find the Church of the Holy Virgin Mary, the keep, and the small tower.

The Church of the Holy Virgin Mary claims to be the oldest church in the world. The altar stone in the shape of a stele, which is dated December 11, 747, is of interest. The Church of Saint Michael is situated on the second story of the keep. The church is said to have been built by Gabriel VII (1525–70), patriarch of Alexandria.

The largest church within the inner court of the monastery is the Church of Saint George (1888). The building incorporates modern Byzantine features. The altar and the *haikal* screen are built of marble. Beneath the altar are the tombs of three monks, Qummus Salib (d.1905), Qummus Bakhum I (d.1928), and Severus, bishop of Dairut and Sanabu (d.1927).

South of the sanctuary is the baptistery, where up to five hundred children are baptized during the annual *mulid* in honor of the Holy Virgin Mary.

The new Church of the Holy Virgin in the outer court of the monastery was dedicated in 1964. This church was built especially for the increasing number of pilgrims who attend the annual *mulid*. The church has three altars, which are dedicated to Saint Takla Haymanot (north), the Holy Virgin (center), and Saint George (south).

The outer west wall has two niches. In the northern niche is a painting showing Mikha'il al-Buhayri, and in the southern niche is a painting showing Anba Abra'am, bishop of the Fayyum. Above the entrance to the church is a painting of the flight of the holy family.

Dair al-Muharraq is a unique monastic institution. Its location on the edge of the desert has greatly influenced the neighboring Coptic community. It is, therefore, not a desert monastery like those of Wadi al-Natrun or the Eastern Desert. In many ways it resembles a large estate administered by the church. The wealth of the monastery is seen in the splendor of its modern buildings, the most notable being the Pachomian Castle. This building reveals all the elegance of nineteenth-century Levantine style.

The Theological Seminary at Dair al-Muharraq was founded by Qummus Bakhum I in 1905. The new seminary building, completed in 1937, is situated in the outer court.

The fact that the monastery is dedicated to the Holy Virgin Mary attracts pilgrims for the various *mulids* in honor of her. During the week of June 21–28, about fifty thousand pilgrims journey to the monastery for the Feast of the Consecration of the Church of the Holy Virgin Mary. At the time of the *mulid* in June 1988, forty-seven pilgrims were killed because of a panic due to a fire that broke out among the tents. Through a miracle—as the monks see it—the monastery did not burn down.

The Monastery of Saint Mercurius near al-Hawatka

The ruins of the Monastery of Saint Mercurius (Dair Abu Saifain) are situated almost two kilometers south of al-Hawatka on the southern edge of the village of al-Gawli. The monastery, which is almost hidden by a group of large trees, is surrounded by a Christian necropolis.

A new construction is built on the ruins of the ancient monastery. There is one altar, which is dedicated to Saint Mercurius. The baptistery is in the northeastern corner of the church. The remains of the old wooden *haikal* screens can be seen inside and in front of the church. Fragments of granite columns are used as thresholds. The fragment of the column built into the baptistery belonged to a temple.

East of Asyut

The Monastery of Saint Victor

The Monastery of Saint Victor (Dair Abu Buqtur al-Gabrawi) is situated on the edge of the desert in the village of Dair al-Gabrawi. The monastery can be reached from Abnub by traveling seven kilometers northwest toward Bani Ibrahim.

The new church of Saint Victor was built on the site of an ancient church, of which there are no traces. The church, which is situated near a Christian necropolis, has three *haikal*s dedicated to Saint Victor, the Archangel, and the Holy Virgin.

The Monastery of Saint Victor at Shu

The Monastery of Saint Victor at Shu, also known as the Church of Buqtur Shu, can be easily approached from Abnub. Buqtur Shu is a small village approximately five kilometers from Abnub, within the agricultural area between Abnub and Dair al-Gabrawi. At one time a large and important town, Buqtur Shu is today a small and insignificant village.

The church is situated on the eastern edge of the village. The new church was built on the site of an older church, and the ancient well in the inner court is the only remaining part of the older structure. The new church has one *haikal* dedicated to Saint Victor of Shu.

The *Confession of Faith*, in which Patriarch Gabriel VIII (1587–1603) recognized the supremacy of the Roman papacy, was written in the Monastery of Saint Victor at Abnub in January, 1590. This confession was addressed to Pope Sixtus V (1585–90) and contained the willingness of the Coptic patriarch to unite with the See of Rome. The document was submitted in Rome by Ghubriyal al-Muharraqi, Archdeacon Barsuma of the Church of Saint Mark in Alexandria, and Ghubriyal, a monk of the Monastery of the Holy Virgin at Gabal al-Tayr.

The Monastery of the Holy Virgin in Bani Rizah

The village of Bani Rizah adjoins Abnub, and it is difficult to determine where the town ends and the village begins.

The Monastery of the Holy Virgin (Dair al-'Adhra') was rebuilt in 1955 by Abuna Musa Sama'an. Except for the well in the inner court, there are no remains of the older church. The new brick church, which has three *haikal*s, can be entered through two doors. The *haikal*s are dedicated to the archangel Michael, the Holy Virgin, and Saint George. An old icon of the Crucifixion is attached above the left door. According to tradition, the old church was built in the time of the Romans.

It is advisable to obtain the key for the church from the priest of the Church of Saint Abi Fam in Abnub (see below).

Once a year, during the Feast of the Holy Virgin (August 15–22), a large *mulid* is held at Dair al-'Adhra'.

The Church of Abi Fam (Phoebammon) in Abnub

The Church of Abi Fam is the largest of the Coptic churches in Abnub. Built on the site of an ancient church, the new church was erected in 1880. The church has three *haikals*, which are dedicated to the archangel Michael (north), Abi Fam (center), and Saint George (south). The baptistery is situated on the southeast corner of the church, and the *gynaikion* occupies the westernmost part of the church. Noteworthy is an eighteenth-century icon of Abi Fam, one of the very few iconographical representations of the saint.

The Monastery of Saint Isaac

The Monastery of Saint Isaac (Dair Abu Ishaq), south of 'Arab al-'Awamir, can be reached from Abnub. The monastery, which is situated on the edge of the desert, is located between 'Arab Mitayr and 'Arab al-'Awamir. The monastery is built of mud bricks and is crowned by a large dome and several small ones.

The interior of the church is very plain. The church has three *haikals* dedicated to the Holy Virgin (north), Saint Isaac (center), and Saint Mercurius (south).

The Church of Saint George in Bani Murr

On 23 Barmuda (1 May), the Coptic pilgrims of the region around Abnub on the east bank of the Nile gather in the Church of Saint George in Bani Murr, eight kilometers north of Asyut. The small church has two altars, dedicated to Saint George and the Holy Virgin. On 15 January 1918, President Gamal Abd al-Nasser was born in Bani Murr.

Between Asyut and Suhag

The Coptic Churches of Asyut

Asyut, or Siyut, the name which is still preserved in the Coptic Syout, has always enjoyed considerable importance, even in antiquity, because of its favorable location on an extensive, fertile plain.

Of the numerous Coptic Orthodox churches in Asyut, the Church of Saint Apater is the most significant one. The church is situated in the old district of the city. One enters the church, which was built toward the end of the eighteenth century, through a large courtyard. The Church of Saint Apater has three sanctuaries on the ground floor, dedicated to Saint Michael (north), Saint Apater (center), and Saints Peter and Paul (north). On the first floor, above the Church of Saint Apater, is the Church of Saint Theodore the Warrior. A third church north of the Church of Saint Apater is dedicated to the Holy Virgin. North of the sanctuary is the baptistery.

Saint Apater, or Shahid Abadir, the son of Basilides and Eirene, was deputy governor of Alexandria. During the Diocletian persecution he sought the crown of martrydom, but wishing to spare his mother's feelings, he went to Upper Egypt. Arianus, the governor, believing him to be a native of al-Ashmunain, addressed him in Coptic, but Saint Apater replied in Greek and thus was betrayed. After suffering many tortures, he was beheaded.

Dair al-Muttin on Stable 'Antar

Dair al-Muttin is situated on a mountain about one and a half kilometers west of Asyut known as Istabl 'Antar, or the Stable of 'Antar.

Soon after Saint Antony began to teach the ascetic life, Christian hermits began to inhabit the large rock-hewn tombs in the hills west of Asyut (Lycopolis). The monks destroyed the statues in the tombs and defaced the pictures of the gods on the walls. One of the most famous Christian teachers of this place was Saint John of Lycopolis (d.394), who attained great celebrity as a prophet and was occasionally consulted by the emperor Theodosius. He is said to have declared that the emperor was to conquer Maximus the rebel and defeat Eugenius, and both events took place.

Dair al-Muttin consists of two chapels built into the tombs of the pharaonic necropolis. The tombs are situated to the north of the necropolis between the Tomb of Emsa and that of Shaikh Abu Tuq.

The Church of the Angel at Durunka

The village of Durunka is situated about four kilometers south of Asyut, at the foot of the long line of frowning cliffs. The Church of the Angel (al-Malak) and the village lie on the slope at the foot of the cliff.

The church has two *haikals*; the northern *haikal* is dedicated to Saint Bishoi and the central *haikal* to the angel. South of the central *haikal* is the sacristy. The baptistery is situated in the southern part of the *gynaikion*.

The six eastern bays of the church are covered with brick domes, while the western part of the church is roofed with beams covered with reeds and a flat mud-brick roof.

The Church of the Holy Virgin Mary at Dair Durunka

The village of Dair Durunka is situated about ten kilometers south of Asyut at the foot of the mountain range that extends west of Asyut. The Church of the Holy Virgin Mary is situated on a shelf of the cliff, facing to the west the large caves, which at one time were inhabited by hermits and later by Christians escaping persecution. The ruins of the cave village and the ancient cave Church of the Holy Virgin Mary are still visible. During the annual *mulid* (August 7–22) in commemoration of the visit of the holy family to Asyut, thousands of pilgrims inhabit the caves. According to a local oral tradition, the holy family rested in one of the caves. On the slope, many new buildings have been established for the accommodation of pilgrims. Numerous apparitions of the Holy Virgin are reported to have occurred at the time of the annual *mulid.*The episcopal residence of Bishop Michael is situated north of the church.

The Church of the Holy Virgin Mary and Saint Theodore

The village of Dair Rifa is situated on the slope of the mountain range that extends south from Asyut. Coming from Asyut, one first passes Dair Durunka. After another five kilometers, one approaches Dair Rifa. The ascent to Dair Rifa is by a steep climb, following some well-worn steps cut into the hard limestone.

One enters the Church of the Holy Virgin Mary through a massive doorway. The church, which is built into the rock, is divided into four sections, the *gynaikion* being the most western part. The church is lighted by a hole in the roof just in front of the *haikal*. The altar is dedicated to the Holy Virgin Mary. The church is adorned with several good icons; the most ancient one depicts the Holy Virgin Mary. Within the great tomb is the Church of Saint Theodore, a small mud-brick structure roofed with a little dome. The church has one *haikal*, which is dedicated to Saint Theodore.

The new Church of the Holy Virgin Mary and Saint Theodore, built in 1950 by Habib Rizq of Asyut, is situated in the cultivated land. The church has three *haikals* and is adorned with modern religious paintings. Special celebrations are held annually in the new church, as well as in the ancient ones, on the Feast of Saint Theodore on April 15.

The Village of al-Zawya

During the Middle Ages to the nineteenth century, the Coptic village of al-Zawya, also known as Zawyat al-Dair, fifteen kilometers south of Asyut on the edge of the Western Desert, was the site where thousands of African slaves were castrated before being transported from Asyut to Cairo and from there to the harems of the Ottoman empire. The Coptic Church in al-Zawya is dedicated to Abu Tarbu, or Saint Therapon, the patron saint of healing.

The Monastery of the Holy Virgin at Dair al-Ganadla

The Monastery of the Holy Virgin is situated about two kilometers west of Dair al-Ganadla, almost directly west of the town of Sidfa, and thirty-six kilometers south of Asyut.

The monastery is enclosed by walls on the north, east, and south sides, while the west wall is formed by a frowning cliff. The monastery is entered through a doorway in the north wall of the enclosure.

The new Church of the Apostles, built in 1865, stands in the north-west part of the enclosure, a little south of the north wall, thus leaving a space for a door to an ancient tomb. This passage now leads to the *gynaikion*. The church, the three domes of which can be seen from a distance, has three *haikals* dedicated to Saint Macrobius (north), Saints Peter and Paul (center), and Saint George (south).

The ancient cave Church of the Holy Virgin is situated west of the new church. This church is built in the mouth of an ancient quarry that extends into the cliff. At the westernmost end of the cave are numerous wall paintings.

According to a local tradition, this church marks the site of a famous anchorite's dwelling place. Another local tradition associates the cave with the visit of the holy family to Egypt. It is in this cave that the holy family is said to have rested.

Pope Shenuda III has established a center for spiritual retreats, to be administered by a monk, at the Monastery of the Holy Virgin.

The Church of Saint Mercurius at Shutb

The village of Shutb, in the Middle Ages the site of the Monastery of Abu al-Sari where the relics of Saint Theodore reposed, is eight kilometers south of Asyut on the road to Abu Tig. According to the Synaxarion, Saint Theodore was a native of Shutb. In the eleventh century, Abraham, bishop of Shutb, attended the episcopal synod in Cairo, and in 1320 and 1330, Athanasius, bishop of Shutb, is mentioned among those who attended the services of the consecration of the holy myron. The memory of Saint Theodore of Shutb has been forgotten, although the villagers maintain that, once upon a time, twenty-four churches were situated in Shutb. The new Church of Saint Mercurius (1940) was built on the site of one of these churches.

The Churches and Monasteries between Suhag and Aswan

West of Suhag

The Churches of Suhag

Suhag, a very handsome and clean Upper Egyptian town, is the episcopal see of the Coptic Orthodox bishop of Suhag. The diocese comprises all the churches in the district of Suhag.

There are two Coptic Orthodox churches in Suhag, the Church of the Holy Virgin and the Church of Saint George.

The Monastery of Saint Shenute

A banked road leads west from the southern part of Suhag via the village of Mazalwa to the early Christian settlement of the White Monastery (al-Dair al-Abyad), which is dedicated to Saint Shenute. The distance from Suhag to the White Monastery, on the edge of the desert, is about four and a half kilometers. The monastery is surrounded on its north, west, and south sides by a large amount of of both burnt and crude brick debris. The monastery once included not only the present stone structures, but also cells, kitchens, and store-houses, the ruins of which can still be seen.

The original settlement was founded by Saint Bigoul. After his father's death, Saint Shenute became a monk in the monastery of Saint Bigoul, who was his maternal uncle. Before long, Saint Shenute's administrative gifts led him to important offices in the monastic community and in the church. At his uncle's death in 385 Saint Shenute became the hegumen of the monastery. In the monastery, the rule was based on the precepts of Saint Bigoul, which were similar to those of Saint Pachomius. In 431 Saint Shenute attended the Ecumenical Council of Ephesus, where he opposed Nestorius, patriarch of Constantinople. The date of his death seems to have been about 449. He was a religious reformer who was ready to employ physical force in dealing with disobedient monks.

Following the death of Saint Shenute, the community continued under the leadership of Besa, who was succeeded by Zenobius. Some inscriptions on the wall paintings of the central apse of the sanctuary furnish us with some historical information of the period from 1076 to 1124. Those who engraved their names were Armenians who had established themselves in the White Monastery.

Major restorations of the monastery took place between 1202 and 1259. In the latter part of the eighteenth century, the southwest corner of the enclosing wall had collapsed, but was rebuilt under the direction of Muhammad 'Ali.

The appearance of the monastery from the outside shows a striking resemblance to an ancient Egyptian temple. The monastery is entered through a gate in the southern wall that leads to the great hall parallel to the nave of the Church of Saint Shenute.

The Church of Saint Shenute occupies the major part of the monastery. The church has three apses at the east end, which are vaulted with burnt brick. The walls of the apses are decorated with columns in two ranges, each surmounted by architraves, and between the columns are niches. The semidomes are decorated with paintings representing the Dormition of the Holy Virgin Mary (north), the Pantocrator and the four Evangelists (center), and the Resurrection with the two women and two angels (south). The church has three sanctuaries, which are dedicated to Saint George (north), Saint Shenute (center), and the Holy Virgin Mary (south). Since 1975 the monastery has been occupied by several monks. On June 14, 1997, the Holy Synod of the Coptic Church officially acknowledged this monastery.

The Monastery of Saint Bishoi

The Red Monastery (al-Dair al-Ahmar), or the Monastery of Saint Bishoi (Dair Anba Bishai), is about three kilometers north of the White Monastery at the extreme western edge of the cultivated land.

Unlike the White Monastery, the Red Monastery is situated within a village, and some houses lie to the south and to the east. The area to the north and west of the monastery is mainly covered with debris.

The monastery received its name from the burnt red bricks of its outside walls, which are considerably thicker at the base than at the top. The historical data on this monastery are very scarce, and it seems that the Red Monastery existed in the shadow of the nearby White Monastery.

The Church of Saint Bishoi is situated in the northeastern corner of the monastery. The original plan of this church is almost the same as that of the Church of Saint Shenute. The church has one *haikal*. Icons of Saints Shenute, Bishoi, and Bigoul are attached to the *haikal* screen. The north and south apses are without altars. The area of the original nave and aisles of the church are largely occupied with buildings.

The Church of the Holy Virgin Mary is situated in the southwestern corner of the monastery. This church seems to be of great antiquity. Immediately west of the church is the well.

This monastery has also been reoccupied by several monks.

East of Akhmim

The Monastery of Saint Pachomius

The Monastery of Saint Pachomius (Dair Anba Bakhum) is situated in the village of Sawama'a Sharq, about eight kilometers north of Akhmim. To reach the monastery, proceed northeast from Akhmim for two and a half kilometers. At the fork, follow the Akhmim al-Sharqiya canal for another three kilometers northwest to 'Ubur al-Waqf. Turn right on the road to Sawama'a Sharq. The village of Sawma'a Sharq is situated on the edge of the desert, and the Monastery of Saint Pachomius lies in the northern part of the village.

The Church of Saint Pachomius is the only construction that has survived the destruction of the monastery. The church, which has five *haikals*, is situated within a courtyard.

The Monastery of Saint Michael

The Monastery of the Archangel Michael (Dair al-Malak) is situated on the edge of the desert near the village of al-Salamuni, about two kilometers north of al-Hawawish. On the feasts of the archangel Michael on November 21 and June 19, special services are celebrated.

The Church of Saint Michael has three *haikals*, which are dedicated to the Holy Virgin (south), Saint Michael (center), and Saint George (north). According to tradition, the monastery was built in the thirteenth century. At least one monk stays at the monastery.

The Monastery of the Martyrs

The Monastery of the Martyrs (Dair al-Shuhada') is situated in a cemetery on a slight elevation.

The monastery can be visited without a key, since the key seems to be lost, but a large stone is rolled against the entrance door from within. The Church of the Martyrs has altogether seven *haikals*, though the original church had only three *haikals*. Three *haikals* were added on the south side, and one *haikal* was added on the north. The three central *haikals* are dedicated to the Holy Virgin (south), the Holy Martyrs (center), and Saint Michael (north).

Special services are conducted by the priests of Akhmim on January 10 and July 9.

From this monastery comes the now-famous *Book of Proverbs*, which is one of the earliest complete papyrus manuscripts in existence. It contains a translation of the Proverbs of Solomon into the Akhmim dialect. The book was probably written in the fourth century. It has one of the longest texts in this dialect ever preserved.

The Monastery of the Holy Virgin

The Monastery of the Holy Virgin (Dair al-'Adhra') east of Akhmim can be reached by following the road parallel the Sahil al-Hawawish canal toward al-Hawawish for six kilometers.

The Church of the Holy Virgin is situated in the eastern part of the monastery. The original church had three *haikals* dedicated to Saint George (south), the Holy Virgin (center), and Saint Michael (north). North of the main church we find two additional *haikals* that are more recent. These two *haikals* are dedicated to Saint Paul the Hermit and Saint Antony. At least one monk stays at the monastery.

The Monastery of Saint George

The Monastery of Saint George (Dair Mari Girgis al-Hadidi) is on the east bank of the Nile, about eight kilometers south of Akhmim. The complex is south of the village of Dair al-Hadid and situated on an elevation that is easily accessible.

Inside the enclosure are several small houses and huts inhabited by Coptic families. The Church of Saint George stands against the eastern wall of the enclosure and has three *haikals*, which are dedicated to Saint Michael (south), Saint George (center), and the Holy Virgin (north). The church is well preserved and offers a very good example of Upper Egyptian Coptic church architecture. The nave consists of five bays from east to west and is roofed with domes supported by pillars set in squares.

The Monastery of Saint Pisada

The Monastery of Saint Pisada (Dair Apa Bisada) is on the east bank of the Nile in the small village of al-Ahaiwa Sharq opposite the town of al-Manshah, the ancient Ptolemaïs Hermiou, about eighteen kilometers south of Suhag. The Monastery of Saint Pisada was formerly a large and beautiful monastery, if one judges by the few remaining ruins of the first building, which have been used in the construction of the present one. The Church of Saint Pisada is situated within an enclosure.

According to tradition, the monastery was built in the thirteenth century.

Saint Pisada, who was employed by his father as a shepherd, had as his companion a boy named Agripidos, who herded goats. While Pisada grew in piety, Agripidos grew in worldliness. Eventually, by coincidence, Agripidos married the daughter of Emperor Numerian, and after the emperor's death, he became the emperor known as Diocletian. During the Diocletian persecution, which was carried out in Upper Egypt by the governor Arianus, Saint Pisada suffered martyrdom.

Between Girga and Nagʿ Hammadi

The Monastery of Saint Michael

The Monastery of Saint Michael (Dair al-Malak Mikha'il) is situated on the east bank of the Nile, almost opposite Girga, near Nagʿ al-Dair.

There is good evidence that the monastery was established gradually. The Church of the Angel, which has altogether five *haikals*, shows this gradual development in that the two northern *haikals* are obviously an addition. Each *haikal* is covered by a dome. The altar of the central sanctuary, which is dedicated to Saint Michael, is covered with a beautiful wooden canopy. The ceiling is adorned with geometrical patterns.

The Monastery of Saint Moses

Abydos, eleven kilometers west of al-Balyana, was one of the most renowned cities of ancient Egypt. It was famous as the chief seat of worship of Osiris, the god of the underworld in Upper Egypt.

The Monastery of Saint Moses (Dair Abu Musa), also known as the Monastery of Saint Damiana (Dair Sitt Damiana), is situated three kilometers north of the Temple of Ramses II.

The church has seven *haikals* with artistically carved screens. Above the individual *haikal* doors, icons of the respective patron saints indicate their dedication. From north to south, the *haikals* are dedicated to Saint Antony, the Holy Virgin, Saint Moses, Saint Michael, Saint Damiana, Saint George, and Saint John the Baptist. Eleven domes cover the church. The body of Saint Moses, a native of al-Balyana, is said to have been buried there. Al-Maqrizi merely states that this is a large monastery. In 1590, the monastery was reconstructed.

Between Nag' Hammadi and Luxor

The Monastery of Saint Bidaba

The Monastery of Saint Bidaba (Dair Anba Bidaba) is situated in the cultivated land about two kilometers southwest of the railway station of Nag' Hammadi.

Inside the surrounding wall, the buildings are constructed on various levels. The monastery has three adjoining churches that look like dark cellars. The churches are dedicated to the Holy Virgin, Saint Bidaba, and Saint Sidarus. Divine services are provided by the priest of the town of Bahgura al-Gharbi. According to tradition, the monastery was founded by Saint Helena. Saint Bidaba, bishop of Qift, suffered martyrdom at Isna under Emperor Claudius.

The Church of Saint Menas

The Church of Saint Menas the Wonderworker (Dair Mari Mina al-'Agaybi) is situated about one kilometer south of the village of Hiw on the edge of the desert, but still in the cultivated land. The church has five *haikals*, which are dedicated from north to south to Saint Sidarus, the Holy Virgin, Saint Menas, Saint George, and Saint Victor. The central altar of Saint Menas is surmounted by a wooden dome. The western part of the church is early twentieth century. The screen of the *haikal* of Saint Victor is the oldest one, dating from 1729. The other screens belong to the first decade of the twentieth century.

The Monastery of Saint Palemon

The Monastery of Saint Palemon (Dair Anba Balamun), also known as the Monastery of Saint Mercurius (Dair Abu Saifain), is situated on the Asyut–Luxor road, about one kilometer beyond Qasr al-Sayyad on the lefthand side.

One enters the monastery yard through a gate in the eastern wall. The church immediately to the right is the Church of Saint Mercurius (Abu Saifain). The church has three *haikals*: the central one is dedicated to the Holy Virgin Mary, the northern one to Saint Macarius, and the southern one to Saint Mercurius. Abutting the southern part of the church are two rooms that may have once served as *haikals*.

The second church is dedicated to Saint Palemon. Built in 1925, it was renovated in 1940. The church is decorated with numerous modern Byzantine wall paintings showing biblical scenes. The church has altogether five *haikals*, which are dedicated from north to south to Saint Gregory, Saint Palemon, Saint Antony, Saint Mercurius, and Saint Damiana.

The third church, dedicated to Saint Damiana, is the most ancient building of the monastery. It is situated about one and a half meters below the level of the rest of the monastery. The church has one *haikal*; its screen, however, is modern (1907).

Saint Palemon, a hermit of Upper Egypt, lived during the reign of Saint Constantine. He was the leader of a group of ascetics when Saint Pachomius joined him. After being Saint Palemon's disciple, Saint Pachomius left him in order to found a community of his own at nearby Tabennese.

In the beginning of the fifteenth century, Qummus Murqus of the Monastery of Saint Palemon experienced a vision of the translation of the relics of Saint George to the Church of Saint George in Old Cairo.

The Monastery of the Angel

Situated about one kilometer west of the Monastery of Saint Palemon is the Monastery of the Angel (Dair al-Malak), on the east side of the village of al-Dabba. The monastery is built in the same style as the Monastery of Saint Palemon, especially so far as its main dome is concerned.

The Cave of Saint Palemon

Between the Monastery of Saint Palemon and the nearby Monastery of the Angel stretches an isolated desert that was the site of the first monastic endeavors of Saint Palemon. About three hundred meters from the Monastery of the Angel, in a rock face in a little wadi, are two cavities that are almost completely obstructed by rubbish. According to tradition, these are supposed to have been a hermitage.

In this immediate vicinity, near the cliff of the Gabal al-Tarf, the famous Gnostic papyri of Chenoboskion were discovered. The Coptic priest of the Monastery of the Angel was one of the first people to have handled this precious treasure. This library was hidden in a cemetery and dates from the fifth century, the time when the Pachomian monasteries finally extended their influence throughout this region.

The Ruins of the Basilica of Dandara

A short distance from the west bank of the river and a little to the north of the village of Dandara, near Qina, stands the Temple of Dandara, where the goddess Hathor was worshipped. The basilica was built in the immediate vicinity of the Mammisium, or the 'house of giving birth,' which was built by Caesar Augustus.

The basilica, constructed of unusually good masonry, is built of sandstone taken from the Mammisium. The carved details of the ruins correspond in many ways to those discovered at the White and Red Monasteries at Suhag. Only of the western and northern parts are there any remains.

The Monastery of Saint Mercurius

The Monastery of Saint Mercurius (Dair Abu Saifain) is situated in the eastern part of the village of Higaza on the very edge of the desert.

In the center of the monastery is the Church of Saint Mercurius, which is still used on Sundays for the celebration of the Divine Liturgy. According to a local oral tradition, the church was built by Saint Helena in the fourth century. The Church of Saint Mercurius has three *haikals* dedicated to Saint Pachomius (north), Saint Mercurius (center), and Saint George (south). The *haikal* screen is adorned with an icon of Saint Mercurius. The baptistery is situated in the southwestern corner of the church. The church measures thirteen meters from east to west, and ten meters from north to south. It was restored in 1911.

East of the Church of Saint Mercurius is a second inner court that leads to the Church of the Holy Virgin. The church is not in use. In the northeastern part of the monastery is the Church of Saint Bidaba, which is not used either. Adjoining this church is the Church of Saint Victor (Mari Buqtur), with its three *haikals*. This church was recently restored. The churches of the Holy Virgin, Saint Bidaba, and Saint Victor are of similar structural design. In general, the monastery is in good condition.

The Monastery of Saint Pachomius at Minshat al-ʿAmmari

The Monastery of Saint Pachomius, or Dair Anba Bakhum, is situated on the edge of the desert about eight kilometers northeast of the ruins of the Temple of Karnak, not far from the Luxor airport. The Church of Saint Pachomius, which has five *haikals*, is located in a rectangular enclosure of considerable size. The main entrance to the church is through the northern gate of the walls and then passing through the churchyard. The women, however, have their own entrance from the south side of the church. The *gynaikion* is the southernmost part of the church, in which the baptistery is also situated. The monastery is occupied by several monks. It was officially recognized by the Holy Synod of the Coptic Church in 1997.

Between Naqada and Qamula

The six monasteries on the edge of the ancient desert of Gabal al-Asas, on the west bank of the Nile between the villages of Naqada and Qamula, are of interest to students of Christian antiquities.

At one time, this desert was inhabited by famous anchorites like Elias of Mount Bishwaw and Samuel of Mount Banhadab. In the thirteenth century, there were numerous churches and monasteries around Qamula, the most famous being the Churches of Saint Theodore, Saint Mercurius, Saint George, and Saint Victor. There were also the two Churches of Saint Shenute and Saint John, and the Monasteries of Saint Nub and Saint Theodore.

In addition to the desert monasteries, there is near Qamula the famous church of Saint Mercurius, which claims the tomb of the patron. A large *mulid* is held annually on August 1 in commemoration of the dedication of the Church of Saint Mercurius.

The Monastery of Saint Michael

The Monastery of Saint Michael, or Dair al-Malak Mikha'il, is the southernmost monastery between Qamula and Naqada. This monastery was also known as the Monastery of the Well, because of its excellent well water. The monastery contained a keep and was surrounded by walls. It is said to have possessed the body of Saint Pisentius, the hegumen of the monasteries of Upper Egypt.

The monastery is entered through a gate in the east wall. There are two churches in the monastery, both of which are sadly ruined. In the southern church one can still identify three *haikals*. The northern church is entirely ruined and much imagination is required to reconstruct it.

The Monastery of Saint Victor

About two kilometers north of the Monastery of Saint Michael and one kilometer northwest of the village Qamula al-Awsat, there is the Monastery of Saint Victor, or Dair Mari Buqtur.

The outer court of the monastery is entered through a gate in the east wall. In the southwestern corner of the court is the tomb of Basiliyus Ghali (1938). The ancient mud-brick church has four *haikals* dedicated to Saint Victor, Saint Michael, the Holy Virgin Mary, and Saint Menas. The wall paintings in the *haikals* have almost entirely disappeared. Situated south of the monastery is the new Church of Saint Victor, with its entrance facing the west. Note the Coptic cross above the entrance. At least one monk occupies the monastery.

The Monastery of Saint George

The Monastery of Saint George, or Dair Mari Girgis, also known as Dair al-Magma', is west of Qamula al-Bahri and about five hundred meters west of the edge of the desert on a slight elevation. It is the largest and most significant of the monasteries between Qamula and Naqada.

The monastery, which is enclosed by a high wall, consists of a group of four churches, in which three are all attached and the fourth stands by itself in the debris of the surrounding buildings, west of the others and more or less ruined. The entrance to the monastery is through a gate in the north wall. The three churches standing together are dedicated to Saint Michael (northern church), Saint George (central church), and Saint John (southern church). All three churches differ considerably in their construction and were built at different times.

The Church of Saint Michael is entered through a hole in the north wall of the nave of the adjoining Church of Saint George. The main apse, the one furthest to the north, was decorated with beautiful wall paintings representing Christ surrounded by angels, which unfortunately are now ruined.

The Church of Saint George is of the basilican type, though also ruined. The wall paintings that once adorned the *haikal* are also largely destroyed. South of the Church of Saint George is the Church of Saint John, which belongs to a later period than the other two churches. This church has been entirely rebuilt.

The Monastery of the Holy Cross

Situated exactly on the edge of the desert in the small villages of

Hagar Danfiq is the small Monastery of the Holy Cross, or Dair al-Salib.

The monastery has two churches. The ancient church, situated in the western part of the monastery, is in a state of ruin. The new church, situated in the eastern part of the monastery, has three *haikals*.

The Monastery of Saint Michael near Naqada

The Monastery of Saint Michael, or Dair Malak Mikha'il, is about four kilometers southwest of Naqada and surrounded by a large desert necropolis.

The monastery, which is situated on a slight elevation, can be entered through gates in the northern and southern walls. The Church of Saint Michael lies in the eastern part of the enclosure and is roofed with numerous domes. Another church, completely ruined, is situated in the southwest corner of the enclosure.

About fifty meters north of the monastery is a new church with one *haikal*.

The Churches and Monasteries of Thebes

Madinat Habu

The center of the Christian community of Thebes (modern-day Luxor) was the town of Jeme, which may have extended from Dair al-Madina to Madinat Habu. With the end of paganism, and before the Temple of Madinat Habu was buried in the sand, a church that some called the Cathedral of Saint Athanasius was built in the second court of the Temple of Ramses III. On the columns of the church many Christians scribbled their names, while others wrote short prayers. The remains of the church, however, were cleared in 1895 by the Service des Antiquités.

Dair al-Rumi

Up on the hill that divides the Valley of the Queens into two branches are the remains of a small monastery, known to some as Dair al-Rumi.

Dair al-Madina

More important than the settlement in the Valley of the Queens was Dair al-Madina. The little Ptolemaic temple, begun by Ptolemy IV, is now called Dair al-Madina. It owes its name to a Christian monastery, the church of which may have been dedicated to Saint Isidorus.

Dair al-Bahri

One of the most splendid temples of Thebes is the Temple of Queen Hatshepsut at Dair al-Bahri, or the Northern Monastery. This temple was built by Queen Hatshepsut, the sister, wife, and co-regent of Thutmosis III. Christian monks settled here on the upper terrace. Today, all traces of the monastery once situated in the large hypostyle hall of the upper terrace have been cleared away. The monastery had a square brick tower nearly eight meters high, and the buildings were made of mud bricks and stones taken from the Eighteenth Dynasty walls.

The Monasteries of Saints Cyriacus and Epiphanius

The Monastery of Cyriacus extended roughly from tomb 65 (Nebamon) to tomb 67 (Hapuseneb) of the noblemen's tombs on the eastern slope of the hill of Shaikh 'Abd al-Qurna. From the Monastery of Cyriacus one can easily reach the Monastery of Epiphanius, which is about twenty meters above the road to Dair al-Bahri.

The Monastery of Epiphanius, which was excavated in 1912 by the Metropolitan Museum of Art Egyptian expedition, was built on the site of the Eleventh Dynasty tomb of the vizier Daga, about four hundred meters south of Dair al-Bahri. Only a few remains of the monastery can be seen today. The monastery is first mentioned in a will of the seventh-century monks Jacob and Elias.

The Monastery of Phoebammon

The Monastery of Phoebammon (Dair Abi Fam), excavated in 1948 by the Coptic Archaeological Society, is situated about eight kilometers west of the Valley of the Queens. It can be reached only with considerable difficulty by crossing the desert of al-Kula in al-Hamra', and it is advisable to employ the services of a competent guide. This monastery, possibly of the fourth century, was built presumably with one or two floors against the mountain cliffs. It has yielded a wealth of Coptic graffiti.

Other Hermitages

Other Christian monasteries and cells of anchorites existed on the hilltop of Qurnat Murrat, in the Ramesseum, and on the hillside of Shaikh 'Abd al-Qurna.

Of special interest is the Tomb of Ramses IV (No. 2), which is one of the finest examples of the royal tombs of the Twentieth Dynasty. This tomb shows the most evident signs of actual occupation by early Christian anchorites, as seen by the large number of Coptic graffiti scribbled all over the walls, including a number of Coptic inscriptions written in red paint. One of the two saints praying with arms upraised is Apa Ammonius the Martyr, probably the bishop of Isna. Another anchorite has drawn up a list of seven famous Coptic hermits: Apa Paul, Apa Antony, Apa Pachom, Apa Palemon, Apa Petronius, Apa Theodore, and Apa Horsiese. On the left wall is a Coptic cross.

The Churches in the Temples in and around Luxor

The Church in the Temple of Luxor

The Temple of Luxor was built by Amenophis III (Eighteenth Dynasty) on the site of an older sandstone sanctuary and was dedicated to Amon, Mut, and Khonsu. During the religious revolution of Amenophis IV, the representations and the name of Amon were obliterated, and a sanctuary of the sun was built beside it.

During the Byzantine period five churches were built within the area of the Temple of Luxor. There was the large basilica with a baptistery northwest of the nave, southeast of the eastern pylon. The Mosque of Abu al-Haggag was constructed upon the site of a church. Another church was built in the court of Ramses II, and a smaller church existed in the southwestern section of the temple area. Finally, there are the remains of an apse with wall paintings at the southwestern end of the narthex with its thirty-two columns.

There are altogether twelve socles belonging to columns or statues with fourth-century Latin dedicatory texts. West of the temple are four socles of columns with dedications to the emperors Diocletian and Maximian and the caesars Constantius and Galerius. Another socle for a statue of the caesar Galerius (before 305) was donated by a certain Valerius. East of the temple are four socles belonging to columns with dedications to the emperors Licinius and Galerius and the caesars Constantine and Maximinus Daia. Within the temple are three socles of statues dedicated to Emperor Constantine, Duke of Egypt, the Thebaid, and the two realms of Libya (324). All of these socles were erected prior to the promulgation of Christianity as the religion of the state.

The Church in the Temple of Karnak

The ruins of the great temple at Karnak are perhaps the most wonderful of any in Egypt, and they certainly merit many visits. The visitor to the ancient Christian church in the Temple of Karnak will pass through the Great Court, the Great Hypostyle Hall, and then through the Central Court and the courts of Thutmosis I, Amenophis II, and Thutmosis III to the remains of the Temple of the Middle

Kingdom. From here, one enters the Great Festival Hall of Thutmosis III, where in the fourth century the Christians established a church.

In the Festival Hall of Thutmosis III, the paintings of saints can be clearly identified on six columns, for the heads of these figures are relatively well preserved. The space between the central columns was used for worship. Unfortunately, it is impossible to reconstruct the ancient church.

The Church in the Temple of Madamut

The Temple of Menthu is situated at the outskirts of the village of Luxor. It was founded by Amenhotep II (Eighteenth Dynasty).

A small church was built into the temple, and its ruins are still traceable. The church must have had three naves, and the remains of the pillars can still be identified. As in the case of the churches in the temples of Luxor and Karnak, this church ought to be assigned to the fourth or fifth century.

The Church in the Temple of Tud

The village of Tud, the ancient Tuphium, is situated twenty-five kilometers south of Luxor, on the east bank of the Nile opposite Armant. The temple belongs to the Fifth Dynasty, but was reconstructed in the Eleventh Dynasty. The temple is dedicated to Mont.

The church is situated in the northeastern corner of the large temple area. Apart from the apse, which is relatively well preserved, numerous stones with Coptic decorations have been discovered.

The church was destroyed in the Middle Ages. Later, another church was built on the edge of the desert. The church is dedicated to Saint Abshai. The Christian cemetery in the immediate vicinity was explored by Maspero, where the corpse of a bishop and pieces of his vestments were discovered.

Saint Abshai al-Qabrin was a devout ascete of Tud. He is said to have read through the whole book of Jeremiah, and when he finished, Jeremiah appeared and embraced him.

Between Luxor and Aswan

The Convent of Saint Theodore

The Convent of Saint Theodore the Warrior (Dair al-Shahid Tadrus al-Muharib) is situated in the desert about five hundred meters southwest of the Temple of Madinat Habu.

After entering the convent, one passes through a small courtyard to the church. The Church of Saint Theodore is divided into five sections from east to west, the most eastern being the *haikals*, the most western being the new *gynaikion*. The church has four *haikals*, which are dedicated from north to south to the Holy Virgin Mary, Saint Claudius, Saint Theodore, and Saint Michael. The *haikal* screens are adorned with modern religious pictures. The roof consists of seventeen domes resting on arches. The church is illuminated through small holes in the domes. The baptistery is situated at the southern end of the church.

Saint Theodore is one of the most popular Egyptian warrior saints. In Euchaites, Persia, he fought and defeated a dragon. The Saint was tortured and suffered martyrdom during the Diocletian persecution.

During the first years of the pontificate of Shenuda III, the convent was repopulated with several nuns. The patrons of the convent are Saints Theodore and Claudius. The tomb of the internationally known Egyptologist Labib Habashi (1905–84) is in the convent.

The Ruins of the Monasteries near Armant

The region around the town of Armant was one of the prominent monastic centers. Significant collections of Christian papyri and ostraka have come from this area, and many Christian stelae now exhibited in various museums have their origin in this general area.

The Ruins of the Monastery of the Waterwheel

The Monastery of the Waterwheel, or Dair al-Saqiya, is fifteen kilometers north of Armant in a large wadi that opens into a stony desert. At the foot of a high, overhanging cliff is a rectangular enclosure of sixty meters by eighty meters. Within this enclosure on a rock rise the remains of the crude brick monastic buildings. At the foot of the cliffs are two caves, and in front of them the church was built. The remains of small columns and capitals substantiate this.

The Monastery of al-Misaykra

About nine kilometers northwest of Armant in the stony desert is a vast field of ruins known as Dair al-Misaykra or Dair al-Namus. From the rubbish heaps emerge the remains of several large buildings, some of which had more than one story. The crude brick walls are pierced with little ogival windows. Here and there one discovers a capital. Nearby are the remains of a large cemetery from which many of the stelae that are now in museums came.

The Monastery of the Christians

A short distance (one kilometer) north of Dair al-Misaykra are the ruined walls of a multi-storied square tower surrounded by the remains of enclosure walls. These ruins are situated on the slope of a hill. The Monastery of the Christians, or Dair al-Nasara, may have been considered a stage between the cultivated land and the hermitages of the inner desert. West of Dair al-Nasara are the remains of the Monastery of Saint Posidonius and numerous hermitages.

The Convent of Saint Pisentius and Abshai at Tud

Tud, on the eastern bank of the Nile is known on account of its temple. The convent, inhabited by fifteen nuns, is situated in the eastern part of Tud at the edge of the desert. The convent, with a small inner court, has two churches: the church of Saint Pisentius with three *haikal*s (Saint Palamon, Saint Pisentius, and the Holy Virgin) and, to the south, the second church with four altars (Saint Victor, the Holy Virgin, Saint George, and Saint Pisentius). The annual feast is held on Kiyahk 15 (January 3).

The Monastery of Saint George at al-Rizaiqat

Dair Mari Girgis is situated on the edge of the desert near al-Rizaiqat, west of Dimuqrat and southwest of Armant. It is within the diocese of Luxor. The large church of Saint George has twenty-one domes and six *haikal*s (Saint Matthew the Potter, Saint Antony, the Holy Virgin, Saint George, Saint Michael, and Saint Ammonius of Isna). The wonder-working icon of Saint George is attached to the southern wall of the nave. The modern icons were executed by Filib Riyad of Isna in 1972. The monastery, which has served for many centuries as a pilgrimage center, was reoccupied by monks in 1976. The monastery is officially recognized by the Holy Synod. The popular *mulid* commemorating the consecration of the Church of Saint George takes place November 10–16.

The Monastery of Saint Matthew the Potter at Nag' al-Zinaiqa

The distance from Asfun to the monastery is about seven kilometers. The monastery, which is enclosed by a high wall, is situated in the desert. In front of the monastery are several Christian tombs that are interesting because of their picturesque cupolas and crosses. These tombs are said to date from the fourteenth and fifteenth centuries.

Saint Matthew the Potter was a native of Bishnai. He became a monk in the Church of the Holy Virgin of al-Maqbabat and later went to Isna, and from there to Asfun, where he founded the above-mentioned monastery in the eighth century.

The *History of the Patriarchs* records that Matthew the Priest, who was also a fisherman, built the monastery in the days of the patriarch Alexander II (704–29) and that many became monks with him there.

Al-Maqrizi (fifteenth century) writes, "At Asfun there was a large monastery, and Asfun was one of the finest towns in Egypt, and the monks of the monastery there were famous for their learning and intelligence. With Asfun, its monastery was also destroyed, and this was the most remote of the monasteries in Upper Egypt."

The beautiful wall paintings in the Church of Saint Matthew the Potter are from the eleventh to the thirteenth centuries. They represent Christ and the Twelve Apostles as well as other saints. The church has three *haikal*s adorned with paintings of the seraphim and saints. During the past forty years a great deal of vandalism has destroyed many of the paintings. Lefort, who visited the site in 1939, considered this monastery one of the finest testimonies of ancient monastic life in the Nile Valley. The tomb of Saint Matthew the Potter is situated in the church. According to tradition, this saint was buried in a clay casket.

Since 1975 the monastery has been occupied by several monks.

The Convent of Saint Ammonius and the 3,600 Martyrs of Isna

Isna, known to the ancient Egyptians as Sent and to the Greeks as Latopolis, has been the home of Christian monks and anchorites from the fourth century onward. Coptic records frequently refer to monks who lived in and around Isna. In the reign of Decius (249–51), the last of the Roman emperors whose name appears on the walls of the Temple of Isna in the middle of the town, it was decreed that every Christian should offer sacrifices to the Roman gods. Those who complied received certificates from the magistrates, while those who refused suffered death.

The Convent of the 3,600 Holy Martyrs (Dair Manaws wa-l-Shuhada') is situated about six kilometers southwest of Isna on the edge of the desert.

The convent, which is enclosed by a wall, contains two churches, the Church of the Holy Virgin Mary (built about 1931) and the ancient Church of the Holy Martyrs.

The old Church of the Holy Martyrs is one of the most beautiful churches in Upper Egypt. On one of the wall paintings in the church one finds the date A.M. 502 (A.D. 786). The consecration of the Church of the Holy Martyrs is mentioned in the Coptic Synaxarion on Tuba 19 (January 27). Because of alterations and additions to it, the church actually comprises two churches. The three *haikal*s in the eastern part of the church are dedicated, from north to south, to Saint George, the Holy Virgin Mary, and the Holy Martyrs of Isna. Numerous well-preserved wall paintings adorn the Sanctuary of the Holy Martyrs. Two additional *haikal*s are situated in the northwestern corner of the church. In addition, five tombs are situated in the church.

The new Church of the Holy Virgin Mary is situated south of the Church of the Holy Martyrs. The church has three *haikals* dedicated to Saint George, the Holy Virgin Mary, and Saint Michael. The baptistery is in the southwestern corner. The church is decorated with numerous paintings executed in a primitive manner, which are the religious expression of the many pilgrims who annually come to the monastery for the *mulid* of Saint Ammonius, bishop of Isna, on December 23.

Saint Ammonius was consecrated bishop to the See of Isna by Patriarch Peter I (301–10). Tradition asserts that he built the monastery, residing there Tuesday through Friday of each week and coming back to Isna to spend Saturday to Monday among his people.

The convent is occupied by twenty nuns who pay special veneration to Saint Dulagi and her four sons Surus, Harman, Banufa and Shatayasi. They suffered martyrdom in Isna during the Decian persecution (250).

The Monastery of Saint Pachomius at Idfu

The Monastery of Saint Pachomius, or Dair Anba Bakhum, is situated on the edge of the desert five kilometers west of Idfu. About its history nothing is known. The abandoned monastery, rebuilt by Bishop Hadra of Aswan, was reoccupied in 1975. The consecration took place in 1980. The church of Saint Pachomius has four *haikals* (Saint Pachomius, the Holy Virgin, Saint George, and Saint Michael). About thirty new cells and fifteen rooms for guests have been built. The monastery belongs to the diocese of Aswan. The annual *mulid* is on the Bashans 14 (May 22).

The Monastery of Saint Simeon

The Monastery of Saint Simeon (Dair Anba Sim'an) is situated on the west bank of the Nile, at about the same latitude as the southern point of Elephantine Island.

The Monastery of Saint Simeon was originally dedicated to Anba Hadra of Aswan. Anba Hadra married at the age of eighteen, but preserved his chastity and later became a disciple of Saint Baiman. After eight years of ascetic practices under the supervision of his teacher, he retired to the desert and applied himself to the study of the life of Saint Antony. Later he was consecrated bishop of Aswan by Patriarch Theophilus (384–412).

The monastery was built in the seventh century and reconstructed in the tenth century, but destroyed in 1173. In the thirteenth century, the monastery was in ruin.

The Monastery of Saint Simeon is of considerable architectural interest, and though it is ruined, its main features are well preserved. The monastery is surrounded by a wall more than six meters high, the lower part of which is built of rough stone, the upper part of mud bricks. One enters the monastery through the gate of a small tower in the east wall. Within the enclosure are two main groups of buildings. At the lower level lies the church, which consists of a nave, the aisles, the choir, and the sacristies. The dome of the choir was adorned with a beautiful Byzantine painting of the twenty-four elders of the Apocalypse, and opposite the choir was another representation of Christ with two angels bowing before him. There are numerous Coptic inscriptions in the sacristies. The monks lived in the northern section of the monastery, a two-story building. The second story had a large central vaulted hall with cells opening on each side of the long corridor. Each cell had two or more stone benches for the monks to sleep on. At the northwest angle was the refectory. Below the main building are several rock-hewn cells and a rock chapel with a painted ceiling and pictures of saints. In the monastery were found numerous stone slabs giving the history of many of the monks.

The Churches and Monasteries of the Fayyum

Christianity found its way into the Fayyum at the same time it entered the Nile Delta, or Lower Egypt, and the desert around the Fayyum oasis, especially Mount Qalamun, was inhabited by monks as early as the fourth century. Of the thirty-five monasteries in the greater Fayyum region in the early Middle Ages, only five can now be visited.

The capital of the oasis, Madinat al-Fayyum, is the episcopal see of the Coptic Orthodox bishop of the Fayyum. There are four Coptic Orthodox churches in Madinat al-Fayyum: the Church of the Holy Virgin (1850), the Church of Saint George, the Church of the Archangel (1800), and the Church of Abu Saifain al-'Azab (1800).

Dair al-'Azab

Dair al-'Azab is six kilometers south of Madinat al-Fayyum on the road to Beni Suef.

Dair al-'Azab was founded by Peter, twelfth-century bishop of the Fayyum, or by the thirteenth-century patriarch Cyril III. Since the eighteenth century, no monks have inhabited the monastery. The old church in the southeastern corner of the courtyard is dedicated to the Holy Virgin Mary. The church has three *haikals*, which are dedicated to Saint Antony (north), the Holy Virgin Mary (center), and Saint Michael (south). The new church, dedicated to Saint Mercurius or

Abu Saifain, is situated west of the old church. An annual *mulid*, held August 15–22 in commemoration of the Assumption of the Holy Virgin Mary, is attended by more than ten thousand pilgrims.

In the course of the expansion of the pilgrimage center, the relics of Saint Abra'am of the Fayyum (1829–1914) were transferred on May 6, 1987 from the Church of Saint Mercurius to a new Saint Abra'am Memorial Center east of the church. The festive translation was carried out by seven bishops.

The Monastery of the Archangel Gabriel at Naqlun

The Monastery of the Archangel Gabriel, or Dair al-Malak Ghubriyal, is one of the oldest Coptic monasteries in the Fayyum and dates from the sixth or seventh century. In the history of the Fayyum monasteries, it is referred to as the Monastery of Naqlun. The monastery is situated thirteen kilometers south of Madinat al-Fayyum on an elevation, so it can be seen from a distance.

The Church of Saint Gabriel has three *haikals*: the central one is dedicated to the Archangel, and the other two are dedicated to Saint George and the Holy Virgin. Wooden screens with a wicker design divide the church from east to west into four sections: the *haikals*, the choir, the section for the faithful, and the narthex.

From the architectural evidence of the present church we may surmise that it was largely rebuilt and completely redecorated during the latter part of the nineteenth or the beginning of the twentieth century, under the episcopacy of Anba Abra'am, though using materials from the two former churches at Naqlun.

The walls of the inner and outer courts of the ancient monastery are still discernible. Remains of the cells and their respective niches can be seen from the roof of the Church of Saint Gabriel. The small houses in the southwestern part of the monastery and those inside the monastery south of the church, as well as the small chalet west of the church, are used by the pilgrims to the *mulid* of Saint Gabriel.

With the emergence of the monastery at al-Qalamun under the dynamic leadership of Saint Samuel, the Monastery of Naqlun was gradually but steadily pushed into the background. On the approach of the Melkite patriarch Cyrus, Saint Samuel, who had stayed for three and a half years at Naqlun, persuaded the two hundred lay members and 120 monks of Naqlun to flee to the mountains. After the release of Saint Samuel from his imprisonment by the Byzantines, he set about establishing his monastery at al-Qalamun, and two years later, the group consisted of forty-one monks, fourteen of whom had come from the Monastery of Naqlun. Thus, from the middle of the seventh century onward, the Monastery of Saint Samuel at al-Qalamun began to surpass the Monastery of Saint Gabriel at Naqlun in importance and position.

It is said that the mountain called Naqlun contained the place where Jacob, son of Isaac, son of Abraham, enjoyed the shade and worshiped, and sacrifices were offered to God in the days of Joseph, the son of Jacob, when Joseph superintended the building of Fayyum and Hagar al-Lahun. The Ethiopian Synaxarion informs us that "at the present day" the body of Abba Kaw is at the Monastery of Naqlun. This means that between the latter part of the twelfth century and the beginning of the fifteenth century the Monastery of Naqlun was not just one of several monasteries in the Fayyum, but also contained the relics of one of the foremost martyrs of the oasis. By the middle of the fifteenth century, however, the importance of the monastery had declined.

On August 19, 1672, Johann Michael Wansleben visited the Fayyum and found the Monastery of Naqlun almost completely ruined, though its two churches (presumably Saints Michael and Gabriel) seem still to have been standing. One church, probably the Church of Saint Michael, Wansleben could not enter because the monks used it as a storage place for their provisions. The Church of Saint Gabriel he describes as being very beautiful, all painted within with pictures of stories of the holy scriptures, and having a nave supported by slender columns of several stone drums each.

Today the Church of Saint Gabriel serves as parish church for the region of Qalamshah, south of Madinat al-Fayyum. Two monks reside in the once-abandoned monastery. At the time of the annual *mulid* large numbers of pilgrims from the Fayyum and Beni Suef assemble at the monastery and occupy the numerous dwelling places built for this purpose.

In July 1991 twelve skeletons were discovered some 150 meters southwest of the monastery. They showed signs of severe mutilation. The Coptic Church declared them martyrs. Parts of the relics have been distributed to many Coptic churches in Egypt and overseas.

In the course of restoration of the Church of Saint Gabriel in 1997, several eleventh-century paintings depicting the Archangel Gabriel, Saint Mercurius, and Saint George were discovered. The central apse was adorned with a painting of the Holy Virgin and the Apostles. Some of the art work could be assigned to an even earlier period. Other recently revealed paintings include the Holy Virgin, Christ, Saint Bisada, and Saint Simeon the Stylite. East of the monastery, archaeologists discovered in the hills eighty-nine two-room rock-hewn hermitages. In addition, more than one thousand manuscripts, some on parchment, were found. Apart from the discovery of the 'Twelve

Naqlun Martyrs,' who are widely venerated all over Egypt, the region has become one of the famous archaeological sites in the Fayyum.

The Monastery of the Holy Virgin and the Dove at al-Lahun

The Monastery of the Dove, or Dair al-Hamam, is the most picturesque monastery in the Fayyum. It is beautifully situated in the desert on the edges of the Nile Valley. The distance from the village of al-Lahun to Dair al-Hamam is about eight kilometers, five of which follow a desert track. The monastery, with its three white domes, can be seen shortly after passing the brick pyramid.

The Church of the Holy Virgin Mary has two *haikals*. The center one is dedicated to the Virgin Mary and the southern one to Saint George. The baptismal font is situated to the north of the center *haikal*. Some of the icons in the church are of recent make. The many potsherds around the monastery lead one to believe that it was once of considerable importance.

The small chapel is dedicated to Saint Isaac of Tiphre, who is considered the patron of the monastery. In the inner court Abuna Zosimus Anba Bishai built a model of Golgotha and the Via Dolorosa.

In 1985 the monastery was placed under the direct authority of Pope Shenuda III, and in May 1987 major renovations of the church and the monastery were begun. The eastern wall of the monastery is covered with a layer of mud that the wasps produce annually between January 10 and March 10. A kiosk offers souvenirs and devotional literature.

The Monastery of Saint George at Sidmant

The Monastery of Saint George, or Dair Mari Girgis, is the most recent of the Coptic monasteries in the Fayyum region, and the Church of Saint George and the cells attached to it were built in 1914. The monastery is situated about twenty-five kilometers south of Madinat al-Fayyum.

In the thirteenth century, a monastery of Saint George was situated in Sidmant. In 1260, Butrus al-Sidmanti, a Coptic theologian of distinction, served as a monk in the Monastery of Saint George. A monastery dedicated to Saint George at Sidmant is also mentioned by al-Maqrizi. In the fifteenth century, the monastery was deserted.

The monastic life at Sidmant was reestablished in the first half of this century by monks from the Monastery of Saint Antony. The monastery belongs to the diocese of Beni Suef and al-Bahnasa. Large numbers of pilgrims from Beni Suef and the Fayyum attend the annual *mulid* a week prior to the Feast of the Ascension.

Dair Abu Lifa at Gabal Qatrani

The ruins of Dair Abu Lifa are situated two kilometers northwest of Qasr al-Sagha on the southeastern spur of the Qatrani mountain chain, approximately thirteen kilometers north of Lake Qarun.

For the period from the seventh to the ninth centuries, we have definite evidence of the monastery's occupancy by monks. Apart from this, the first reference to this monastery is found in a fifteenth-century manuscript published by Ahmed Bey Kamal under the title *Le livre des perles enfouiés*. For the treasure seeker, the author gives the following directions:

> When you go in the Fayyum, direct your way to the Monastery of Abu Lifa, otherwise known as the Monastery of Abu Banukh. This monastery, which is situated above the first mountain of Abu Qatran, is well known and cut in the rock. When you are there, leave it behind you and continue three miles in a westerly direction. . . .

The only remains of the monastery are now two caves cut into the rock. Either earthquakes or rain must have caused the collapse of the southern section of the monastery, entailing a considerable fall of rock and leaving no more than the northernmost caves in situ.

The remaining part of the upper story of the monastery consists of a cave with five rooms, the largest of which has in its southern part a round cistern with an outer diameter of 1.7 meters and a depth of 0.7 meters. On either side to the east and west is a round room. North of the principal room is a small passage leading to two additional rooms, which have a height of 0.8 meters.

The second cave can be reached from the foot of the mountain by climbing a sand dune that approaches almost to the entrance of the cave.

The Ruins of the Monastery of the Archangel Michael at al-Hamuli

The ruins of the Monastery of the Archangel Michael are situated in the desert three kilometers southwest of the village of al-Hamuli.

An elevation can be seen from a distance. This mound marks the site of the ruined monastery. An area of 150 meters by fifty meters is covered with potsherds, mud bricks, and small fragments of pillars and socles. Numerous small pieces of plaster can be found, some of which show polychrome designs.

In 1910, a party of Bedouins digging for *sabakh* (a kind of fertilizer obtained from ruins) discovered a library of numerous Coptic manuscripts, known today as the Hamuli Manuscripts of the Pierpont

Morgan Library. The copyists' notes, with which many of the Hamuli manuscripts terminate, inform us that they were either written for the Monastery of the Archangel Michael or transferred to it from some other Fayyumic monastery. The dates given fall into the period between 823 and 914.

The Churches and Monasteries of the Western Desert

The Monastery of Saint Samuel at al-Qalamun

The Monastery of Saint Samuel (Dair Anba Samuel) at al-Qalamun belongs, historically speaking, to the Fayyum monastery group. The monastery is situated near the northern end of Wadi al-Mawalih, which is a continuation of the great depression comprising the Fayyum Province and Wadi al-Rayyan. It is built near two springs in Wadi al-Mawalih, 'Ain al-Samar and 'Ain al-Burdi.

Saint Samuel was born in 598 in the village of Pelkip and joined the ascetic life at al-Qalamun at a very early age. From there he went to Wadi al-Natrun, where under the care and supervision of Saint Agathon he learned the angelic life. During his lifetime, the Coptic Christians underwent several severe persecutions by the Persians and the Byzantine authorities. Saint Samuel was imprisoned and beaten and, after severe questioning, was about to be publicly flogged when the civic authorities saved his life. The Hermit of al-Qalamun lived fifty-seven years in his monastery, and his powers of spiritual and administrative leadership earned him a place among the monastic stars of the first magnitude.

The date of the monastery's foundation should be placed in the fourth or fifth century. The monastery was destroyed in the ninth century during the patriarchate of Shenute I. By the twelfth century, the monastery had recovered, and we hear of large walls, flourishing gardens, twelve churches, and four large towers. At that time, the monastery was inhabited by 130 monks, and it was considered one of the important monastic institutions in Egypt. Yaqut al-Rumi (thirteenth century) mentions that Dair al-Qalamun is famous to the people and is well known. By the fifteenth century it was abandoned. The Monastery of Saint Samuel was reinhabited in 1898 by Abuna Ishaq al-Baramusi and ten monks who had left the monasteries of Wadi al-Natrun.

The remains of the ancient monastery are still partly visible. The monastery must have covered an area of about twelve acres enclosed by a thick wall, the foundations of which are still recognizable north of the present monastery. Northwest of the monastery, the old wall appears to have had a width of eight meters and was probably one of the keeps mentioned by the medieval writers. The large amount of glass fragments and broken pottery leads one to believe that the number of monks who once inhabited the monastery was considerable.

The Monastery of Saint Samuel has three churches: the Catacomb Church of Saint Samuel, the New Church of Saint Misael, and the Church of the Holy Virgin Mary.

The Catacomb Church is a subterranean sanctuary belonging to the fifth century, making it the oldest part of the present monastery, situated in the *qasr*. Marks on the stone *haikal* screen indicate that six icons once decorated the church. Two steps lead up to the *haikal*, to the east end of which there stands a marble column 1.25 meters high. At the time of the return of the monks, at the end of the nineteenth century, the Catacomb Church served at first as living quarters.

The New Church of Saint Misael is situated on the top story of the *qasr*. It has one *haikal* and was built by Abuna Ishaq around 1905. The two feretories standing at the north wall of the church contain the relics of Saint Bisada and Saint Domitius (Dumadius). There is a tradition that says that the relics of Saint George were concealed in the monastery during the days of the persecutions.

The new Church of the Holy Virgin Mary, with its nine domes, was recently dedicated. The church was designed by the monks of the monastery, three of whom are civil engineers. The relics of Saint Samuel and Saint Apollo are kept in this church.

The Monastery of Saint Samuel has benefited significantly from the recent monastic renaissance. The churches have been renovated and adorned with numerous neo-Coptic paintings. Several agricultural projects around the monastery provide the necessary supply for the steadily increasing number of monks.

The Cave of Saint Samuel

Prior to the establishment of the first monastery in the region of al-Qalamun, the monks lived in caves. These caves are found around the natural elevations in Wadi al-Mawalih and the Bahr bi-la Ma'. The most important cave in this area is the Cave of Saint Samuel, situated four to five kilometers east of the monastery in Mount Qalamun. The cave is situated at an altitude of about 160 meters, some fifteen meters below the mountain top. The entrance to the cave faces west, and the passage of the cave extends for some thirty meters into the rock.

According to tradition, Saint Samuel lived here during the last years of his life, visiting the monastery at intervals.

The Caves of Wadi al-Rayyan

In this chapter we hope to show that the ideal of the Egyptian anchoritic life not only had a distinguished past, but was also lived for a decade in the twentieth century. Following their reconciliation with the late pope and patriarch Cyril VI in May 1970, the hermits of Wadi al-Rayyan established themselves in and around the Monastery of Saint Macarius in Wadi al-Natrun.

Anchorite life in the twentieth century is a rare phenomenon, both in the east and in the west. In Egypt, the anchoritic ideal was revived in the 1950s when several monks withdrew from the Monastery of the Syrians (Dair al-Surian) in Wadi al-Natrun and, following the example of Abuna 'Abd al-Masih al-Habashi, settled around the Rock of Sarabamun and in Wadi al-Farigh.

In the beginning of 1958, while living at the Monastery of Saint Samuel (Dair Anba Samuel), Abuna Matta al-Maskin visited Wadi al-Rayyan, where he stayed for one week, sleeping at night under a palm tree. One night, Abuna Matta al-Maskin saw a vision:

> Walking along the wadi, I saw an old man sitting in front of the door of a cave, and as I approached the old man, he rejoiced, saying, "I have waited here for thee for many years. Come, come along." And the old man arose and took my hand and said, "I shall give unto thee this mountain." Then, one of the fathers standing near me went to the old man, and as he was about to touch him, the old man disappeared.

After a few days in the wadi, Abuna Matta al-Maskin returned to the Monastery of Saint Samuel.

Then, in the autumn of 1960, just prior to the official suspension of Abuna Matta al-Maskin and his disciples by the patriarch, he went again to Wadi al-Rayyan. This time, Abuna Matta al-Maskin and his disciples arrived in two jeeps at 'Ain al-Rayyan al-Bahariya, where they stayed for some time. While they were living near the well, some Bedouins approached them, asking them whether they were mere visitors or whether this was to be their homeland. Then Abuna Matta al-Maskin remembered the vision and the charge of the old man, who had entrusted the wadi to him. At first, the Bedouins mocked them; however, when they realized that Abuna Matta and his disciples were determined to remain in the wadi, they offered their help. One of the Bedouins said to Abuna Matta al-Maskin, "When I was a youth, some forty years ago, I used to enter this wadi to search and dig for treasures, and at that time, I discovered a cave which is fit for you." Although afraid of being led astray, Abuna Matta al-Maskin and his disciples departed from the well and went along with the Bedouins, and after a walk of almost two hours, they arrived at the cave, which was filled with sand. Abuna Matta al-Maskin and his disciples remained at this cave, however, assured that it was the will and the design of God for them to live there.

The requirements for joining the anchoritic life at Wadi al-Rayyan were the same as those stipulated by the early desert fathers: complete renunciation of the world, its pleasures, and concerns; separation from the family; and renunciation of all property. The hermits of Wadi al-Rayyan were serious in their attempt to emulate the fourth- to sixth-century anchoritic life of the Egyptian deserts, which they considered central to the 'Golden Age' of the Christian Church. They followed strictly the pattern of the ascetic life set forth by the Egyptian desert fathers, and according to Abuna Matta al-Maskin, Saint Macarius of Scetis was regarded as their prototype. Normally, the hermits stayed in their caves throughout the week, except for Saturday afternoon and Sunday, when they gathered for the weekly assembly in the cave Church of Saint Michael. This weekly assembly, which in the fifth and sixth centuries was an integral part of the monastic life at Nitria, Cellia, and Scetis, was also considered an important part of the life in Wadi al-Rayyan. On Saturday afternoons at 3:00, the hermits assembled in the cave church for the canonical hours, which were followed by the evening offering of incense. Afterward, they returned immediately to their caves. On Sunday mornings at 5:00 in summer, 6:00 in winter, they assembled again in the cave church for the canonical hours, the morning offering of incense, and the celebration of the Divine Liturgy.

The hermits of Wadi al-Rayyan maintained a high degree of individualistic piety. In fact, it is held that the hermits remained always in their cells, lest the most ordinary sights and sounds of the world should distract them from their continuous pursuit of the angelic life. Abuna Matta al-Maskin was the spiritual head of the hermits, and he was referred to by his disciples as 'our father.' He was regarded as endowed with charismatic qualities; moreover, he was the father confessor of all hermits. If he was ever absent, no one took his place. The hermits spent most of their time in contemplation and copying spiritual texts. Thus, for example, the hermits copied the spiritual writings of Isaac of Nineveh, the Nestorian bishop of the latter part of the sixth century. Several hermits copied in Arabic the *Ladder of Paradise* by John Climacus (570–649), which treats the monastic virtues and vices, and the complete 'apatheia,' which is upheld as the ideal of Christian perfection.

The hermits did not wear a uniform garb, though all of them wore sandals and a black robe without a belt or a leather girdle. On their heads, they wore either a woolen cap or a *taqiya*, the brown cap normally worn by the *fellahin*. Some wore a cowl that covered the head and neck. They inhabited a number of caves hewn out of a shaly limestone and marl on the northern slope of Wadi al-Rayyan. The settlement was divided into two groups of caves: the eastern group consisting of five caves and the western group of seven caves, including the cave church. The distance from the easternmost cave to the westernmost cave is approximately two kilometers, and though the distances between each cave varies considerably, on the average the caves are approximately 150 meters apart. There were two basic types of caves, the one-room and the two-room cave, although there was no particular significance attached to the fact that hermits occupied one or the other kind. At the same time, there were certain similarities of construction that pertained to all caves. Thus, for example, all caves had a small 'balcony' in front of the entrance. Moreover, the entrance and the windows of all caves faced the south. In all instances, the stone bed was situated in the easternmost part of the cave. The height of the caves, as well as the cave church, which were roofed by massive limestone, was approximately 1.9 meters. All caves had wooden doors that could be locked.

The largest cave, which measures about eleven meters by six meters, is occupied by the Church of Saint Michael. The cave church is divided into three parts: an apse, a nave, and a narthex. Four steps lead down into the nave. On the north side of the nave, there is a stone bench with space for four people. East of the stone bench is a small library for the community. The hermits grew several kinds of vegetables in their garden, including tomatoes, watercress, *mulukhiya* (Jew's mallow), spinach, carrots, radishes, and some small date palms. The garden was tended by the hermits on a rotating basis. By 1970 the monks had left Wadi al-Rayyan and moved to the Monastery of Saint Macarius in Wadi al-Natrun.

The Christian Remains in Kharga Oasis

The Christian Necropolis of al-Bagawat

The Christian necropolis of al-Bagawat is situated in the eastern part of Kharga Oasis, on the slopes of Gabal al-Tayr, about one and a half kilometers from the Persian Temple of Hibis.

The necropolis covers an area about five hundred meters long and two hundred meters wide. The main entrance to the necropolis is at the south side, in the direction of the town. The church of the necropolis occupies a central place. There are altogether 263 chapels or shrines, which have been arranged in eight groups.

The necropolis of al-Bagawat was used as a burial site prior to the introduction of Christianity into the oasis. Consequently, there are chapels at al-Bagawat that belong to both the pre-Christian and Christian eras. Archaeological discoveries confirm that Christianity was introduced in Kharga in the latter half of the third or in the beginning of the fourth century. Only the remains of decorations, architecture, etc. will enlighten us as to what era the chapels are from.

From ancient times, the oasis served as a place for banishment. Some of the great Christian theologians of the fourth and fifth centuries like Saint Athanasius and Nestorius were banished to Kharga, where they lived for many years.

The Chapel of the Exodus
The Chapel of the Exodus is situated behind the group of chapels that occupies the central ridge in the northern part of the necropolis.

The chapel belongs to the oldest type and can be considered one of the earliest chapels in the necropolis. Its paintings may be attributed to the first half of the fourth century. The Chapel of the Exodus is unique in the necropolis insofar as the whole interior is painted with different scenes from the Old Testament and a few scenes referring to Christian subjects.

The Chapel of Peace
The Chapel of Peace is situated near the entrance to the necropolis on the western slope. The chapel stands by itself and is generally known as the Byzantine Tomb. The walls of the chapel are covered with Coptic, Greek, and Arabic graffiti.

The paintings in this chapel are of purely Byzantine style, and the subjects represented are those found in the catacombs in Rome and in many early churches in Egypt and elsewhere. There is one typical Egyptian subject in this chapel, the representation of Saints Paul and Thecla, who seem to have been popular saints in Kharga. The wall paintings may be attributed to the fifth and sixth centuries.

In five other chapels are still a few remains of paintings, including the themes of Saints Paul and Thecla, the Sacrifice of Abraham, and the Phoenix.

The Church
The Church of the Necropolis is built at the northern edge and commands a magnificent view. It is the largest building, and is situated in the middle of the cemetery.

The church may be assigned to the fifth century, and thus it can be considered one of the most ancient churches of Egypt.

Besides the Necropolis of al-Bagawat, there are two other Christian sites in Kharga. The walls of Dair Ghanaym are covered with many Christian texts, and on the summit of one of the hills of Gabal al-Tayr there lived some hermits, as evidenced by the Coptic texts on the walls.

The Monastery of Mustafa Kashif

The Monastery of Mustafa Kashif is situated two kilometers west of the Christian Necropolis of al-Bagawat.

The monastery had three floors. That this building was used by Christians is evident from the remains of a church, the apse of which is still visible. Moreover, one can still see the ruins of several cells constructed around the tomb of a hermit or a local saint. Inscriptions in the cells, probably just names, may belong to the fifth or sixth century.

The Church in the Temple of Hibis

In the vicinity of the Christian Necropolis of al-Bagawat is situated the Temple of Hibis, which was built by Darius I (521 B.C.), added to by Darius II, and restored by Nectanebo (378–60 B.C.). This is the only Persian temple in Egypt.

Soon after the abandonment of the Temple of Hibis by the pagan priests, a Christian church was erected against the north side of the portico.

The church was built in the first part of the fourth century. Its destruction may well have coincided with the invasion of the Blemmyes in 450, who sacked Hibis and carried away large numbers of prisoners, including Nestorius.

Of the many inscriptions found on the walls of the temple, only two refer to the church.

The Christian Remains in Dakhla Oasis

Dakhla Oasis, or the Inner Oasis, is situated 120 kilometers west of Kharga Oasis and three hundred kilometers west of Armant. Like Kharga Oasis, Dakhla was inhabited by Christians, as one can see from the few remains that have survived complete obliteration. At one time, Dakhla was part of the Oasis Magna of the Romans.

The Ruins of Dair al-Hagar

Traveling northwest from Mut, the capital of Dakhla Oasis, to Dair al-Hagar, one passes the ruins of Dair Aba 'Uthman. This may have been a church, for in the eastern part of the ruins are the remains of an apse. North of Mut is the Temple of Dair al-Hagar. The temple is enclosed by a crude brick wall, and between the entrance and the temple court are the remains of a basilica with three naves. Six socles in the central nave are still discernible.

The Christian Remains in Bahariya Oasis

The Church of Saint George at al-Haiz

The small oasis of al-Haiz is situated forty-seven kilometers southwest of the village of al-Bawiti in the oasis of Bahariya. Al-Haiz has always been an important station for the caravans between Bahariya and Farafra.

The Church of Saint George is situated southeast of al-Haiz. In many ways, this church can be compared with the Basilica of Dandara, one of the oldest churches in the Nile Valley. The Church of Saint George is mentioned as the place where the relics of Saint George, except his head, were contained. During the reign of al-Hafiz, the body of Saint George disappeared, but it was later returned. The church is of the basilican type with two entrances. The south entrance led to the church, while the entrance at the northwest corner led first to the baptistery. The ceiling has fallen down and the upper parts of the walls are destroyed.

The Temple of Alexander, 'Ain al-Tibaniya

In the course of excavations in 1997 in the Temple of Alexander (Qasr al-Magisba) of 'Ain al-Tibaniya, the foundations of a small church with three altar rooms were discovered. This building belongs to the eighth century, the period in which the Christian faith was introduced to the oases of Bahariya and Farafra.

The Ruins of the Monastery at al-Ris

The ruins of the monastery at al-Ris are situated about five hundred meters south of the ruins of the Church of Saint George at al-Haiz. Two sections of mud-brick walls are still visible, the extension of which indicates that the site was occupied by a large building.

The Coptic Ruins of Qasr Muharib

The ruins of Qasr Muharib are situated ten and a half kilometers east of Bawit and four and a half kilometers east of Mandisha. The ruins consist of the remains of a church and nearby to the west, the remains of several aqueducts.

The Churches and Monasteries of the Eastern Desert

The Monastery of Saint Antony at Mount Clysma

A monastic settlement was established in the reign of Julian the Apostate, that is between 361 and 363. A few years after the death of Saint Antony, his followers settled and organized themselves where their master had lived and died. The original settlement included only the most necessary buildings.

The Monastery of Saint Antony, or Dair Anba Antonius, served as a place of refuge for some monks of Wadi al-Natrun when the monasteries there underwent several sacks during the fifth century and Saint John the Short escaped to the Red Sea.

In the seventh century, the Monastery of Saint Antony was occupied by Melkite monks, for Saint John the Almoner, Melkite patriarch of Alexandria (609–20), supplied a certain Anastasius, hegumen of Saint Antony's Monastery, with large sums of money and ordered him to buy up captives taken by the Persians. This was in the latter half of 615. The Melkite occupation lasted until the eighth century. Around 790 some Coptic monks disguised as Bedouins entered the monastery to steal the bodily remains of Saint John the Short.

During disturbances in the eleventh century, the Monasteries of Saint Antony and Saint Paul were badly damaged and many of the monks lost their lives. The extent of the devastation is not known to us. About one hundred years later, the Monastery of Saint Antony was restored and in Coptic hands.

During the patriarchate of John VI (1189–1216), the monastery was inhabited by Coptic monks and even supplied candidates for the Ethiopian abunate.

The monastery was included among the many renovation projects executed by the Coptic Church during the twelfth and thirteenth centuries. The wall paintings in the Church of Saint Antony belong to the thirteenth century and are the work of the sons of Ghalib (1232–33).

In the latter part of the fifteenth century the monastery and its library were destroyed by the Bedouins who lived in the monastery as servants of the monks. One night, the Bedouins, desiring to become the masters of the monastery, indiscriminately killed all the monks and took possession of the monastery. The smoke stains in the Church of Saint Antony still remain as a solemn reminder of this desolation.

In the history of the Monastery of the Syrians we read that Patriarch Gabriel VII (1525–70) assisted in rebuilding the monastery. At that time, sixty-three monks inhabited Dair al-Surian, and of these, twenty were sent to Dair Anba Antonius, while another group of ten monks helped in the reconstruction of Dair Anba Bula.

After the restoration of the monastery, an Ethiopian community lived for some time with the Egyptians in the Monastery of Saint Antony. In the seventeenth century, the Monastery of Saint Antony was used by the Capuchin missionaries to the east as a language school for the preparation of their priests.

The eighteenth-century travelers provide much information. Lucas (1714), was sent by Louis XIV for study purposes; an anonymous traveler (1716) sketched the monastery; and Sicard and J.S. Assemani (1716) secured some volumes for the Vatican library. De Granger (1730) noted twenty-five monks, and Sarqis of Hadjen (1765) scratched his name in Armenian on the north wall of the Church of the Holy Virgin Mary.

The nineteenth-century travelers who recorded their observations at Saint Antony's Monastery are: Tattam (1839), who examined the library; Wilkinson (1843); and the Russian archimandrite Uspensky (1850), who scratched his name on the west wall of the Church of Saint Antony. Cardinal Massaia (1851) entered the monastery under the name of G. Bartorelli and abducted Michelangelo, a Coptic Catholic priest. Callinicus, Greek Orthodox patriarch (1859), scratched his name on the north wall of the Church of Saint Antony.

That the monastery has played an important part in the general history of the Coptic Church can be seen from the large number of patriarchs that come from Mount Clysma. The leadership of Saint Antony's Monastery became especially noticeable during the seventeenth, eighteenth, and nineteenth centuries. Twelve Antonian monks ascended the patriarchal throne, and for almost three hundred years, they determined the history of the church.

The Church of Saint Antony and the old south wall are the few remains that date prior to the rebuilding of the present monastery in the sixteenth century. The present church existed in the fifteenth century, as the smoke stains caused by the occupation of the Bedouins indicate. The graffiti on the walls of the church testify to sometime between the fifteenth and sixteenth centuries. The paintings of the warrior saints fall into the period of the restoration of the church by the sons of Ghalib in 1232–33.

From April to October, the Divine Liturgy is celebrated in the Church of the Apostles or the Church of Saints Peter and Paul. This church is to the east of the Church of Saint Antony. It is much more recent than the former. The Church of the Apostles contains three *haikals*. The northern *haikal* is dedicated to Saint George, the central *haikal* to the Twelve Apostles, and the southern *haikal* to Sitt Damiana.

In the passage leading from the Church of Saint Antony to the Church of the Holy Apostles is the new feretory with the relics of Saint Yustus al-Antuni (1910–76). The relics of Saint Yusab ibn al-Abahh (1735–1826) repose in the reliquary in the Church of the Holy Apostles.

During Lent, the monks celebrate the Divine Liturgy in the Church of Saint Mark. The twelve-domed church, dating from 1766, has three *haikals*. The southern *haikal* is dedicated to Saint Mercurius, the central *haikal* to Saint Mark, and the northern *haikal* to Saint Theodore.

For many centuries this church has attracted the piety of the Bedouins and the peasant pilgrims because of the miracles associated with the relics of Saint Mark that are kept in the wooden feretory on the north wall of the church.

The Church of the Holy Virgin Mary is used only during the fifteen-day period of fasting before the Feast of the Assumption of the Holy Virgin on August 22. The church, which is located in the same building as the refectory, has only one *haikal*.

The Chapel of Saint Michael is located, as in the Wadi al-Natrun monasteries, on the top floor of the keep. The *haikal* screen bears a date of the seventeenth century, though the church is much older.

In addition to these five churches, there are two churches named after Saint Paul the Theban. Neither of these churches are in use. The 'old' Church of Saint Paul was built by the patriarch Cyril IV (1854–61). The church has three *haikals*. The 'new' Church of Saint Paul was built by Anba Tawfilus in 1930.

The spring of Saint Antony supplies the monastic community with sufficient water. Situated in the southern part of the monastery, it provides about one hundred cubic meters daily.

The Cave of Saint Antony

We know from the *Vita Antonii* that the great hermit, when he withdrew from his original cell at Pispir, did not stay in the desert. He went up to Mount Clysma, where he discovered a natural cave that was invisible from the wadi.

As one climbs the mountain to which Saint Antony withdrew, one passes the cave of Saint Paul the Simple. The cave is about two kilometers southeast of the monastery, 680 meters above the Red Sea and 276 meters above the monastery, and lies at 28° 55' latitude and 30° 3' longitude. A wooden table now serves as an altar.

The cave of Saint Antony comprises four parts: the terrace, the tunnel, the cave, and the balcony. The tunnel (thirty-four centimeters wide at ground level and ninety-eight centimeters wide at chest height) connects the terrace with the cave. The balcony of Saint Antony's cave is located about three meters below the terrace. It is here the saint used to make his palm-leaf baskets.

The Hermitages in Wadi 'Araba

In addition to the cave of Saint Antony, there are numerous cells in Wadi Natfah and Wadi Bakhit, about thirty-six kilometers north of the Monastery of Saint Antony. Wadi 'Araba is deeply cut by gorges, and the hermitages are situated in these gorges. The dimension of a cell here is about two meters by two and a half meters. A little niche cut in the rock served as a cupboard. At one side a small opening provided some daylight. The entrances to the hermitages are rarely more than seventy centimeters high and fifty centimeters wide.

The Monastery of Saint Paul the Theban

At the south wall of the cave Church of Saint Paul stands a modern marble feretory. The inscription on the tomb reads, "Born in Alexandria in the year 228, died in the year 343."

At the age of sixteen, Saint Paul fled into the desert to escape the persecution of Decius. For some time he dwelt in a cave in front of which a palm tree grew, but later he went to the Eastern Desert. Before his death he was visited by Saint Antony, to whom he gave his tunic made of palm leaves.

Though the monastery of Saint Paul the Theban, or Dair Anba Bula, may not be the oldest Coptic monastery, it was founded in memory of the first hermit of whom we have any knowledge.

The monastery was well known by the sixth century, for Antoninus Martyr, a native of Placentia, visited the shrine between 560 and 570. An isolated Ethiopian reference informs us that Gabriel II (1131–45), the seventieth patriarch, lived for three years in banishment in the Monastery of Saint Paul.

In the last decade of the fifteenth century, the Monastery of Saint Antony suffered severely from the revolt of the Bedouins and their subsequent occupation of the monastery. It is quite likely that the Monastery of Saint Paul experienced a similar fate, for we read in the history of the Monastery of the Syrians that patriarch Gabriel VII (1525–70) assisted in rebuilding this monastery as well. Of the thirty monks he commissioned for the task of reconstructing the monasteries in the Thebaid, ten were sent to the Monastery of Saint Paul.

For several centuries, the administration of the Monastery of Saint Paul was entrusted to the hegumen of the Monastery of Saint Antony, a situation that prevailed until the nineteenth century.

The Monastery of Saint Paul has altogether four churches, three of which are situated in the ancient part of the monastery.

The Church of Saint Paul, or the Cave Church, is the spiritual center of the monastery. The sanctuary was originally built into the rock cave where Saint Paul used to live. It is here that the bodily remains of Saint Paul are preserved.

The walls of the church are covered with paintings that are, generally speaking, in better condition, though of inferior artistic quality than those of the Church of Saint Antony in the monastery at Mount Clysma.

The new marble feretory of Saint Paul stands at the south wall of the church. The Divine Liturgy is celebrated in this church during January, February, and March, and the three *haikals* are used interchangeably during this season.

Almost above the Church of Saint Paul is the Church of Saint Mercurius, which was constructed in the latter part of the eighteenth century. It is only used once a year during the week prior to Lent.

On the third floor of the *qasr* is the Church of the Holy Virgin Mary.

The Church of Saint Michael is the largest church in the monastery. Situated southwest of the Cave Church, it serves as the main church for services. Before entering the church, one passes through the bell tower just outside the main church. The Church of Saint Michael has two sanctuaries: the northern *haikal* is dedicated to Saint Michael and the southern *haikal* to Saint John the Baptist.

The water at Dair Anba Bula is supplied by two wells. The Spring of Anba Bula is situated in the western part of the monastery. The water issuing from the mountain crevices flows into a cemented reservoir tank and is used for drinking and cooking. A small drain leads the surplus water into a second reservoir, which is used by the monks for washing. A further drain carries off the water into a larger basin, where it is distributed for irrigation. The other spring is traditionally associated with Miriam, the musician, prophetess, and sister of Moses and Aaron. New guest quarters for men and women and a kiosk have been built outside the monastery.

The Christian Ruins at Qattar

The Qattar mountain range is situated between Qina on the Nile and al-Ghardaqa at the Red Sea coast. There are several Christian sites in the general Qattar region. The Umm Sidri Monastery is situated about thirty-five kilometers southwest of al-Ghardaqa on the Red Sea coast. This region was a retreat for ascetics during the fourth and fifth centuries.

The Christian church at Qattar is situated in the Nagat gorge of the Qattar mountains, between Mons Porphyrites to the north and Mons Claudianus to the south. One reaches the church by traveling from Qina along Wadi Qina for about forty kilometers, where one turns to the east into Wadi al-Atrash and continues past al-Saqiya and Dair al-Atrash. This church was built in the middle of the fourth century, according to an inscription discovered there.

APPENDIX A
Marks of Identification:
Tattoo and Name

Whereas at certain periods in the early Middle Ages Egyptian Christians were forced to identify themselves as believers in Jesus Christ by wearing heavy wooden crosses around their necks, the Copts of today carry less obvious and less burdensome labels to mark their identity. Now many Copts still point with pride to the crosses tattooed on the insides of their right wrists. Similarly, their names still often carry a testimony to their apostolic faith. This means that to this day, tattoo and name are the two distinguishing marks of the Coptic minority in the Nile Valley, whether they happen to be Orthodox, Catholic, or Evangelical Copts.

The use of tattoos by Copts principally serves their religious and ethnic identification in a predominantly Muslim and Arab society. In addition, however, we must recognize that the Coptic fellahin in particular also consider the sign of the cross a kind of phylactery, a protective device against evil spirits, the *jinni*, and diseases. "Where the seal of the cross is, the wickedness of Satan hath no power to do harm," said one of the early fathers. When Saint Antony made the sign of the cross, the devil trembled. At the same time, the tattoo of the cross is often thought of as a permanent reminder of certain blessings received or certain vows which have been made. And in some instances, the Coptic tattoo may serve purely decorative purposes.

Many Copts visit a tattooer at a Coptic *mulid* (the annual feasts in honor of the Holy Virgin or a saint) or while on a pilgrimage to Jerusalem. At the occasion of every Coptic *mulid*, one notices at least one tattooer's booth, with numerous cross and other designs hung all around it, set up near the church of the patron saint.

In Egypt, the tattooer either copies the design of the cross by eye or composes and draws the design directly on the skin. In Jerusalem, on the other hand, the tattooer uses designs carved on blocks to transfer the design to the skin. Nowadays, almost all tattooers employ an electric needle by which the design is pricked into the skin. In Upper Egypt, however, I have seen the old method still used, which consists of a set of needles, generally seven, tied together, with which the skin is pricked in the desired pattern; the pigment is a mixture of lampblack and oil or water.

In the past few years, however, there has been a noticeable decrease in the practice of tattooing among the Copts, especially among the educated classes. In some instances, especially in the cities, Copts tend to camouflage their religious identity. Others dismiss the custom as belonging to a superstitious past. In Upper Egyptian villages, however, Christians are still deeply conscious of their religious heritage and show the tattooed cross with pride.

In addition to the cross tattooed on the inside of the right wrist, the name is still a distinctive mark by which Copts can be identified. Indeed, the majority of Copts are easily recognizable on account of their names, for in Egypt, more than in any of the other Middle Eastern countries, the name of a person betrays his religious and ethnic identity.

Coptic names are inclusive rather than exclusive, and in addition to the ancient pharaonic names, the Copts have borrowed and transformed Greek, Latin, Hebrew-Aramaic, Ethiopian, Arabic, Syrian, French, and English names. The names used by the Copts show traces of all the nations that have successively dominated Egypt. After the introduction of Christianity into Egypt, Egyptians who had accepted the Christian faith selected Christian names, that is, names of biblical personages, church fathers, saints, monks, and hermits, with the idea that these distinguished personages would serve as protectors for the newly baptized. Thus many Hebrew-Aramaic, Greek, and Latin names were introduced into Egypt. At the same time, many pre-Christian names were preserved because their bearers, who were martyrs, saints, or monks, had been canonized.

During the Hellenistic, Roman, and Byzantine eras, Greek and Latin names were so widely adopted by the Copts that many of the Coptic saints and monks from this period bear purely Greek and Latin names.

After the Arab conquest, Coptic and Greek names were often translated into Arabic, such as Christodoulus into 'Abd al-Masih. During the French and particularly the English occupations, numerous Copts gave their children western names like Cromer, Kitchener, Henry, William, etc. In recent years, the trend toward religiously neutral names has become more and more pronounced. In order to avoid immediate identification as Christians, some Copts have given their children Arabic names, which do not necessarily reveal their faith. This means that nowadays there are many Copts known by names that could be used by Christians and Muslims alike.

The following list of Coptic names represents the most widely used names in the twentieth century. The names are divided into two groups, those used only by Copts and those used by both Copts and Muslims. The letters following the names indicate the linguistic origin of the word:

A=Arabic; C=Coptic; E=English; F=French; G=Greek; H=Hebrew-Aramaic; L=Latin, P=Pharaonic; S=Syriac. Synchretistic names are given two letters: CA=Coptic–Arabic; CG=Coptic–Greek; CL=Coptic–Latin; CP=Coptic–Pharaonic.

Names Used by the Copts

 Abadir (CA)–Apater
 'Abd al-Malak (A)–'servant of the angel'
 'Abd al-Masih (A)–'servant of Christ'
 'Abd al-Nur (A)–'servant of the light'
 'Abd al-Sayyid (A)–'servant of the master'
 'Abd al-Shahid (A)–'servant of the martyr'

'Abd al-Thuluth (A)–'servant of the Trinity'
Abiskhayrun (CA)–Apa Iskhiron
'Ammanuwil (H)–Immanuel, 'God with us'
Amun (CP)–Amon
Andarawus (CG)–Andrew, 'manhood'
Antonius (CL)–Antonius
Anubis (P)–Anubis
Armaniyus (CL)–Armenius
Arsaniyus (CL)–Arsenius
'Aryan (A)–'the naked one'
Athanasiyus (G)–'immortal'
'Awni (A)–'my help'
'Azir (H)–Eleazer, 'court of my God'
Bakhum (CP)–Pachomius
Banyamin (H)–Benjamin, 'son of the right hand'
Barnaba (H)–Barnabas, 'son of consolation'
Barsum (S)–'son of the flesh'
Basali, Basili (G)–'king'
Bisada (C)–Pisada
Bishai, Bishoi (C)–Pishoi
Bishara (A)– 'annunciation'
Bistawrus (CG)– 'belonging to the cross (*stauros*)'
Bulus (CG)–Paul
Buqtur (CA)–'victorious'
Bushra (A)–'good news'
Butrus (CG)–Peter
Dimitri (G)–Demetrius
Dimyan, Dimyanus (G)–Damian
Diyusqurus (G)–Dioscorus
Doss (CG)–Theodore, 'gift of God'
Fakhuri (A)–'the potter'
Faltas (CG)–Philotheus, 'friend of God'
Fanus (CG)–Epiphanius, 'lantern'
Fara'un (CA)–Pharaoh
Farah (A)–'pleasure'
Farangi (CL)–Frank
Fiktur (L)–'victorious'
Filistin (HA)–Palestinian
Filubus (CG)–Philip, 'lover of horses'
Gabra (H)–'strong man'
Garas (A)–'bell'
Garays (CG)–'grace'
Gayyid (A)–'good,' 'generous'
Ghali (A)–'dear,' 'costly'
Gharghuri (G)–'wakeful man'
Ghattas (A)–'diver,' 'baptized one'
Ghubriyal (H)–Gabriel, 'man of God'

Girgis, Gawrgis, Gurgi (G)–George
Habashi (A)–Ethiopian
Hakim (A)–'physician,' 'wise man'
Ham (H)–Ham
Hanna (H)–John, 'mercy of the Lord'
Hazkiyal (H)–Ezekiel, 'strength of God'
Hinayn (HC)–John
Ilya (H)–Elijah, 'the strong Lord'
Iqladiyus (CL)–Claudius
Isha'iya (H)–Isaiah, 'salvation of the Lord'
Iskandar (GA)–Alexander
Istafanus (GA)–Stephen, 'crown'
Istafarus (CG)–Christophorus, 'Christbearer'
Istawrus (G)–'cross'
Kirillus (GA)–Cyril
Lawandi (CL)–Laurentius
Luqa (CL)–Luke, 'luminous'
Malak (A)–'angel'
Manassa (H)–Manasseh, 'he who is forgotten'
Manqariyus (CP)–Menkure
Mansi (A)–'forgotten'
Maqar, Maqariyus (G)–'blessed'
Mashriqi (A)–'my dayspring'
Masih (HA)–Christ, 'anointed one'
Matta (H)–Matthew, 'given,' 'reward'
Mikha'il (H)–Michael
Milad (A)–'nativity'
Mina (CP)–Menas
Misa'il (H)–Misael, 'he who is asked for'
Mitri (G)–Demetrius
Muftah (A)–'key'
Murqus (L)–Mark
Nakhla (A)–'palm tree'
Nasif (A)–'veil or equitable'
Nasri (A)–'my vow,' 'my victory'
Niqula (G)–Nicholas, 'conquerer of people'
Qaldas (CL)–Claudius
Qassis (A)–'priest'
Qaysar (CL)–Caesar, 'cut out of the womb'
Qibti (A)–'Egyptian'
Qiddis (A)–'saint'
Qilada (CL)–Claudius; (A)–'necklace'
Qiryaqus (GA)–Cyriacus
Qudsi (A)–'holy'
Qulta (CA)–Colluthus
Qustus, Qustandi, Qustandinus (GA)–Constantine
Quzman (GA)–Cosmas

Rahib (A)–'monk'
Ramsis (CP)–Ramses
Rizq Allah (A)–'fortune bestowed by God'
Rufayil (H)–Raphael
Sahyun (H)–Zion, 'monument'
Salib (A)–'cross'
Sam (H)–Shem
Samuel (H)–Samuel, 'asked of God'
Sarabamun (CP)–Serapis Amon
Sawirus (CL)–Severus
Shanuda (CP)–Shenute
Sharubim (H)–Seraphim, 'fiery serpent'
Shuhdi (A)–'martyr'
Sidarus (CG)–'gift of Isis'
Sidrak (H)–Shadrach, 'tender,' 'nipple'
Sim'an (H)–Simeon, 'he who obeys'
Sulwanis (CL)–Silvanus
Suryal (H)–Suriel
Tadrus, Tawadrus (CG)–Theodore, God's gift
Tubiya (H)–Tobias, 'the Lord is good'
Tuma (H)–Thomas, Didymus, 'twin'
Wadi' (A)–'decent'
Wahba (A)–'gift'
Wahib (A)–'one who is given'
Wanis (H)–John
Wisa (CP)–Besa
Ya'qub (H)–Jacob, James, 'that which supplants'
Yafith (H)–Japheth
Yanni (H)–John
Yassa (H)–Jesse
Yuhanna (H)–John
Yunan (H)–Jonah
Yustus (L)–'righteous'
Yuwaqim (H)–Joachim

Names Used by Copts and Muslims

'Abd al-Malik (A)–'servant of the king'
'Abd al-Quddus (A)–'servant of the Holy One'
'Abd Allah (A)–'servant of God'
'Abduh (A)–'his servant'
'Adil (A)–'just'
Amin (A)–'faithful'
Anwar (A)–'most illuminated'
As'ad (A)–'the happier one'
'Ata Allah (A)–'gift of God'

'Atiya (A)–'gift'
'Awad (A)–'gift'
'Awad Allah (A)–'gift of God'
'Ayyad (A)–'the feasting one'
Ayyub (H)–Job, 'the assailed one'
'Aziz (A)–'dear'
'Azmi (A)–'my determination'
Badi' (A)–'excellent'
Bahig (A)–'delightful'
Bitar (A)–'farrier,' 'veterinarian'
Dawud (H)–David, 'well-beloved'
Fa'iz (A)–'the winning one'
Fahim (A)–'the intelligent one'
Fakhri (A)–'my pride'
Farag (A)–'release,' 'relief'
Farhat (A)–'gay,' 'happy'
Farid (A)–'unique'
Fath Allah (A)–'triumph of God'
Fathi (A)–'my triumph'
Fawzi (A)–'my victory'
Fayiz (A)–'triumphant'
Fikri (A)–'my mind'
Fu'ad (A)–'essence,' 'heart'
Gad (A)–'generous'
Gamal (A)–'beauty'
Gamil (A)–'beautiful'
Habib (A)–'friend'
Hafiz (A)–'keeping,' 'maintaining'
Halim (A)–'clement,' 'patient'
Hani (A)–'the happy one'
Hazim (A)–'strict,' 'resolute'
Hilal (A)–'crescent'
Hilmi (A)–'my patience'
Ibrahim (H)–Abraham, 'father of a great multitude'
'Id (A)–'feast'
Ishaq (H)–Isaac, 'laughter'
Kahil (A)–'horse of noble breed'
Kamal (A)–'completeness'
Kamil (A)–'complete'
Karam (A)–'generosity'
Karim (A)–'generous'
Labib (A)–'intelligent'
Latif (A)–'pleasant,' 'nice'
Lutfi (A)–'my pleasantness'
Magdi (A)–'my glory'
Magid (A)–'the one who advances'
Mahanni (A)–'the pleasing one'

Mahir (A)–'the competent one'
Makram (A)–'generous'
Mansur (A)–'the victorious one'
Mas'ud (A)–'the happy one'
Mufid (A)–'the useful one'
Murad (A)–'the desired one'
Na'im (A)–'delight'
Nabih (A)–'discerning,' 'eminent'
Nabil (A)–'noble'
Nadir (A)–'rare,' 'seldom'
Nagi (A)–'the saved one'
Nagib (A)–'intelligent'
Nash'at (A)–'beginning'
Nasim (A)–'breath'
Nasr (A)–'victory'
Nasri (A)–'my victory'
Nazih (A)–'pure,' 'blameless'
Nazim (A)–'one who is orderly'
Nazir (A)–'equal'
Nimr (A)–'tiger'
Ra'fat (A)–'compassion'
Ra'uf (A)–'kind'
Radi (A)–'satisfied one'
Rafiq (A)–'the kind one,' 'companion'
Raghib (A)–'one who desires'
Ramzi (A)–'my symbol'
Rashad (A)–'integrity'
Rasmi (A)– 'my plan,' 'my design'
Ratib (A)–'regularizer'
Rif'at (A)–'high rank'
Riyad (A)–'garden'
Rizq (A)–'fortune'
Rushdi (A)–'my maturity'
Sa'd (A)–'happiness'
Sa'id (A)–'the fortunate one'
Sabri (A)–'my patience'
Sadiq (A)–'the truthful one'
Salama (H)–'peace'
Salim (A)–'correct,' 'sound'
Sami (A)–'growing superior'
Samir (A)–'companion'
Shafiq (A)–'kind'
Shakir (A)–'thanking'
Sharif (A)–'honorable'
Shawqi (A)–'my strong desire'
Shukri (A)–'my thanks'
Sidqi (A)–'my truth'

Subhi (A)–'my sunrise'
Sulaiman (H)–Solomon, 'peaceable'
Tal'at (A)–'appearance'
Tawfiq (A)–'reconciliation,' 'prosperity'
Thabit (A)–'steady'
Wagdi (A)–'my passion'
Wagih (A)–'handsome,' 'distinguished'
Wahid (A)–'lonely'
Yusri (A)–'my fortune'
Yusuf (H)–Joseph, 'increase'
Zachariah (H)–'the Lord remembereth'
Zaki (A)–'intelligent'

APPENDIX B

The Patriarchs of the Coptic Church and the Rulers of Egypt

No.	Name	Year	Monastery	Ruler	Year
1.	Mark	d. 68	–	Nero	54–68
2.	Anianus	d. 83	–	Nero	54–68
				Galba	68–69
				Otho	69
				Vitellius	69
				Vespasian	69–79
				Titus	79–81
				Domitian	81–96
3.	Abilius	d. 95	–	Domitian	81–96
4.	Cerdon	d. 106	–	Nerva	96–98
				Trajan	98–117
5.	Primus	d. 118	–	Trajan	98–117
				Hadrian	117–138
6.	Justus	d. 129	–	Hadrian	117–138
7.	Eumenius	d. 141	–	Hadrian	117–138
				Antoninus Pius	138–161
8.	Marcianus	d. 152	–	Antoninus Pius	138–161
9.	Celadion	d. 166	–	Antoninus Pius	138–161
10.	Agrippinus	d. 178	–	Marcus Aurelius	161–180
11.	Julian	d. 188	–	Marcus Aurelius	161–180
				Commodus	180–192
12.	Demetrius I	d. 230	–	Commodus	180–192
				Pertinax	193
				Didius Julianus	193
				Septimius Severus	193–211
				Caracalla	211–17
				Macrinus	217–18
				Heliogabalus	218–22
				Alexander Severus	222–35
13.	Heracles	d. 246	–	Alexander Severus	222–35
				Maximinus	235–38
				Pupienus	238
				Gordianus	238–44
				Philippus	244–49
14.	Dionysius	d. 264	–	Philippus	244–49
				Decius	249–51
				Gallus	251–53
				Valerianus	253–60
				Gallienus	260–68

No.	Name	Year	Monastery	Ruler	Year
15.	Maximus	d. 282	–	Gallienus	260–68
				Claudius II	268–70
				Aurelianus	270–75
				Tacitus	275–76
				Florianus	276
				Probus	276–82
16.	Theonas	d. 300	–	Carus	282–83
				Numerianus	283–84
				Diocletian	284–305
17.	Peter I	d. 310	–	Diocletian	284–305
				Galerius	305–11
18.	Achillas	d. 311	–	Galerius	305–11
				Licinius	308–24
19.	Alexander I	d. 328	–	Licinius	308–24
				Constantine I	306–37
20.	Athanasius I	328–73	–	Constantine I	306–37
				Constantius II	337–61
				Julian	361–63
				Jovian	363–64
				Valens	364–78
21.	Peter II	373–78	–	Valens	364–78
				Gratian	367–83
				Valentinian	375–92
22.	Timothy I	378–84	–	Theodosius I	379–95
23.	Theophilus	384–412	–	Theodosius I	379–95
				Arcadius	395–408
				Theodosius II	408–50
24.	Cyril I	412–44	Abu Maqar	Theodosius II	408–50
25.	Dioscorus	444–54	–	Theodosius II	408–50
				Marcian	450–57
26.	Timothy II	457–77	–	Marcian	450–57
				Leo I	457–74
				Zeno	474–91
27.	Peter III	477–89	–	Zeno	474–91
28.	Athanasius II	489–96	–	Zeno	474–91
				Anastasius I	491–518
29.	John I	496–505	Abu Maqar	Anastasius I	491–518
30.	John II	505–16	Zugag (Ennaton)	Anastasius I	491–518
31.	Dioscorus II	516–18	–	Anastasius I	491–518
				Justin I	518–27
32.	Timothy III	518–36	–	Justin I	518–27
				Justinian I	527–65
33.	Theodosius I	536–67	–	Justinian I	527–65
				Justin II	565–78
34.	Peter IV	567–76	Zugag (Ennaton)	Justin II	565–78
35.	Damian	576–605	Abu Yuhinnis	Justin II	565–78
				Tiberius II	578–82
				Maurice	582–602

No.	Name	Year	Monastery	Ruler	Year
				Phocas	602–10
36.	Anastasius	605–16	–	Phocas	602–10
				Heraclius	610–34
37.	Andronicus	616–23	–	Heraclius	610–34
38.	Benjamin I	623–62	Qibriyus	Heraclius	610–34
				'Umar	634–44
				'Uthman	644–56
				'Ali	656–61
				Hasan ibn 'Ali	661
				Mu'awiya I	661–80
39.	Agathon	662–80	–	Mu'awiya I	661–80
40.	John III	680–89	Abu Maqar	Yazid I	680–85
				'Abd al-Malik	685–705
41.	Isaac	690–92	Abu Maqar	'Abd al-Malik	685–705
42.	Simon I	692–700	Zugag (Ennaton)	'Abd al-Malik	685–705
43.	Alexander II	704–29	Zugag (Ennaton)	'Abd al-Malik	685–705
				al-Walid ibn 'Abd al-Malik	705–15
				Sulaiman	715–17
				'Umar ibn 'Abd al-'Aziz	717–20
				Yazid II	720–24
				Hisham	724–43
44.	Cosmas I	729–30	Abu Maqar	Hisham	724–43
45.	Theodore	730–42	Tamnura (Mareotis)	Hisham	724–43
46.	Kha'il I	743–67	Abu Maqar	al-Walid ibn Yazid	743–44
				Yazid III	744
				Ibrahim	744
				Marwan II	744–50
				al-Saffah	750–54
				al-Mansur	754–75
47.	Menas I	767–76	Abu Maqar	al-Mansur	754–75
				al-Mahdi	775–85
48.	John IV	777–99	Abu Maqar	al-Mahdi	775–85
				al-Hadi	785–86
				Harun al-Rashid	786–809
49.	Mark II	799–819	Abu Maqar	Harun al-Rashid	786–809
				al-Amin	809–13
				al-Ma'mun	813–33
50.	James	819–30	Abu Maqar	al-Ma'mun	813–33
51.	Simon II	830	Abu Maqar	al-Ma'mun	813–33
52.	Joseph	831–49	Abu Maqar	al-Ma'mun	813–33
				al-Mu'tasim	833–42
				al-Wathiq	842–47
				al-Mutawakkil	847–61
53.	Kha'il II	849–51	Abu Yuhinnis	al-Mutawakkil	847–61
54.	Cosmas II	851–58	Abu Maqar	al-Mutawakkil	847–61
55.	Shenute I	859–80	Abu Maqar	al-Mutawakkil	847–61
				al-Muntasir	861–62
				al-Musta'in	862–66

No.	Name	Year	Monastery	Ruler	Year
				al-Mu'tazz	866–69
				al-Muhtadi	869–70
				Ahmad ibn Tulun	870–81
56.	Kha'il III	880–907	Abu Maqar	Ahmad ibn Tulun	870–81
				Khumarawayh	881–96
				Gaysh ibn Khumarawayh	896
				Harun ibn Khumarawayh	896–904
				Shayban ibn Ahmad	904
				al-Muqtafi	904–08
				al-Muqtadir	908–32
57.	Gabriel I	910–20	Abu Maqar	al-Muqtadir	908–32
58.	Cosmas III	920–32	–	al-Muqtadir	908–32
59.	Macarius I	932–52	Abu Maqar	al-Muhtadi	932–34
				al-Radi	935
				al-Ikhshid	936–46
				Abu al-Qasim Unjur	946–60
60.	Theophanes	952–56	Abu Maqar	Abu al-Qasim Unjur	946–60
61.	Menas II	956–74	Abu Maqar	Abu al-Qasim Unjur	946–60
				Abu al-Hasan 'Ali	960–66
				Kafur	966–68
				Abu al-Fawaris ibn 'Ali	968–69
				al-Mu'izz	972–75
62.	Abraham	975–78	Layman	al-Mu'izz	972–75
				al-'Aziz	975–96
63.	Philotheus	979–1003	Abu Maqar	al-'Aziz	975–96
				al-Hakim	996–1021
64.	Zacharias	1004–32	–	al-Hakim	996–1021
				al-Zahir	1021–36
65.	Shenute II	1032–46	Abu Maqar	al-Zahir	1021–36
				al-Mustansir	1036–94
66.	Christodoulos	1047–77	al-Baramus	al-Mustansir	1036–94
67.	Cyril II	1078–92	Abu Maqar	al-Mustansir	1036–94
68.	Michael IV	1092–1102	Abu Maqar & Singar	al-Mustansir	1036–94
				al-Musta'li	1094–1102
				al-Amir	1102–30
69.	Macarius II	1102–28	Abu Maqar	al-Amir	1102–30
70.	Gabriel II	1131–45	Layman	al-Hafiz	1130–49
71.	Michael V	1145–46	Abu Maqar	al-Hafiz	1130–49
72.	John V	1147–66	Abu Yuhinnis	al-Hafiz	1130–49
				al-Zafir	1149–54
				al-Fa'iz	1154–60
				al-'Adid	1160–71
73.	Mark III	1166–89	Layman	al-'Adid	1160–71
				Salah al-Din	1171–93
74.	John VI	1189–1216	Layman	Salah al-Din	1171–93
				al-'Aziz 'Imad al-Din	1193–98
				al-Mansur Muhammad	1198–1200
				al-'Adil I	1200–18
75.	Cyril III	1235–43	–	al-Kamil	1218–38
				al-'Adil II	1238–39

No.	Name	Year	Monastery	Ruler	Year
				al-Salih Nagm al-Din	1239–49
76.	Athanasius III	1250–61	Abu Maqar	Shagarat al-Durr	1250
				al-Ashraf Musa	1250–54
				'Izz al-Din Aybak	1254–57
				Nur al-Din 'Ali	1257–59
				Sayf al-Din Qutuz	1260
				al-Zahir Baybars	1260–77
77.	John VII	1262–68	–	al-Zahir Baybars	1260–77
		1271–93			
78.	Gabriel III	1268–71	–	al-Zahir Baybars	1260–77
				Baraka Khan	1277–79
				Salamish	1279
				Qalawun	1279–90
				al-Ashraf Khalil	1290–93
79.	Theodosius II	1294–1300	Abu Fanah	al-Nasir Muhammad	1294
				al-'Adil Kitbugha	1294–96
				Husam al-Din Lagin	1296–99
				al-Nasir Muhammad	1299–1309
80.	John VIII	1300–1320	Shahran	al-Nasir Muhammad	1299–1309
				Baybars Jashankir	1309–10
				al-Nasir Muhammad	1310–41
81.	John IX	1320–27	–	al-Nasir Muhammad	1310–41
82.	Benjamin II	1327–39	Saint Arsenius	al-Nasir Muhammad	1310–41
83.	Peter V	1340–48	Abu Maqar	Sayf al-Din Abu Bakr	1341
				al-Ashraf Qujuq	1342
				al-Nasir Ahmad	1342
				al-Salih Isma'il	1342–45
				al-Kamil Sha'ban	1346
				al-Muzaffar Haggi	1347
				al-Nasir Hasan	1347–50
84.	Mark IV	1348–63	Shahran	al-Nasir Hasan	1347–50
				al-Salih Salih	1350–54
				al-Nasir Hasan	1354–61
				Salah al-Din Muhammad	1361–63
85.	John X	1363–69	–	al-Ashraf Sha'ban	1363–77
86.	Gabriel IV	1370–78	al-Muharraq	al-Ashraf Sha'ban	1363–77
				'Ala' al-Din 'Ali	1377–81
87.	Matthew I	1378–1408	al-Muharraq	'Ala' al-Din 'Ali	1377–81
				Salah al-Din Haggi	1382
				Barquq	1382–88
				al-Nasir Farag	1388–1405
				'Izz al-Din 'Abd al-'Aziz	1405
				al-Nasir Farag	1405–12
88.	Gabriel V	1409–27	Saint Samuel	al-Nasir Farag	1405–12
				al-Musta'in	1412
				al-'Adil al-Mu'ayyad Shaikh	1412–21
				al-Muzaffar Ahmad	1421
				Sayf al-Din Tatar	1421
				Nasir al-Din Muhammad	1421–22
				al-Ashraf Barsbay	1422–38

No.	Name	Year	Monastery	Ruler	Year
89.	John XI	1427–52	–	al-Ashraf Barsbay	1422–38
				Gamal al-Din Yusuf	1438
				Jaqmaq	1438–53
90.	Matthew II	1452–65	al-Muharraq	Jaqmaq	1438–53
				Fakhr al-Din 'Uthman	1453
				Sayf al-Din Inal	1453–60
				Shihab al-Din Ahmad	1460
				Sayf al-Din Khushqadam	1460–67
91.	Gabriel VI	1466–74	Antonius	Sayf al-Din Khushqadam	1460–67
				Sayf al-Din Yalbay	1467
				Timurbugha	1467
				Qaytbay	1467–96
92.	Michael III	1477–78	–	Qaytbay	1467–96
93.	John XII	1480–83	al-Muharraq	Qaytbay	1467–96
94.	John XIII	1484–1524	al-Muharraq	Qaytbay	1467–96
				al-Nasir Muhammad	1497–98
				al-Zahir Qansuh	1500
				al-Ashraf Janbalat	1501
				Qansuh al-Ghuri	1501–16
				Tuman Bey	1517
				Salim I	1517–20
				Sulaiman I	1522–66
95.	Gabriel VII	1525–70	al-Surian	Sulaiman I	1522–66
				Salim II	1566–74
96.	John XIV	1571–86	al-Baramus	Salim II	1566–74
				Murad III	1574–95
97.	Gabriel VIII	1587–1603	Bishoi	Murad III	1574–95
				Muhammad III	1595–1603
98.	Mark V	1603–19	Abu Maqar	Ahmad I	1603–17
				Mustafa I	1617–18
				'Uthman II	1618–20
99.	John XV	1619–29	Antonius	'Uthman II	1618–20
				Mustafa I	1620–23
				Murad IV	1623–40
100.	Matthew III	1631–46	al-Baramus, Abu Maqar	Murad IV	1623–40
				Ibrahim I	1640–48
101.	Mark VI	1646–56	Antonius	Ibrahim I	1640–48
				Muhammad IV	1648–87
102.	Matthew IV	1660–75	al-Baramus	Muhammad IV	1648–87
103.	John XVI	1676–1718	Antonius	Muhammad IV	1648–87
				Sulaiman II	1687–91
				Ahmad II	1691–95
				Mustafa II	1695–1703
				Ahmad III	1703–30
104.	Peter VI	1718–26	Antonius	Ahmad III	1703–30
105.	John XVII	1727–45	Antonius, Bula	Ahmad III	1703–30
				Mahmud I	1730–54
106.	Mark VII	1745–69	Antonius	Mahmud I	1730–54
				'Uthman III	1754–57
				Mustafa III	1757–73

No.	Name	Year	Monastery	Ruler	Year
107.	John XVIII	1769–96	Antonius	Mustafa III	1757–73
				'Abd al-Hamid I	1773–89
				Salim III	1789–1805
108.	Mark VIII	1796–1809	Antonius	Salim III	1789–1805
				Muhammad 'Ali	1805–48
109.	Peter VII	1809–52	Antonius	Muhammad 'Ali	1805–48
				Ibrahim	1848
				'Abbas I	1848–54
110.	Cyril IV	1854–61	Antonius	'Abbas I	1848–54
				Sa'id	1854–63
111.	Demetrius II	1861–70	Abu Maqar	Sa'id	1854–63
				Isma'il	1863–82
112.	Cyril V	1874–1927	al-Baramus	Isma'il	1863–82
				Tawfiq	1882–92
				'Abbas II	1892–1914
				Husayn Kamil	1914–17
				Fu'ad	1917–36
113.	John XIX	1928–42	al-Baramus	Fu'ad	1917–36
				Faruq	1936–52
114.	Macarius III	1942–45	Bishoi	Faruq	1936–52
115.	Joseph II	1946–56	Antunius	Faruq	1936–52
				Muhammad Nagib	1952–54
				Gamal Abd al-Nasser	1954–70
116.	Cyril VI	1959–71	al-Baramus	Gamal Abd al-Nasser	1954–70
				Anwar Sadat	1970–81
117.	Shenuda III	1971–	Surian	Anwar Sadat	1970–81
				Hosni Mubarak	1981–

Burial Places of Coptic Patriarchs of the See of Alexandria According to Coptic Tradition

No.	Name	Place of Burial
1	Saint Mark	Bucolia, Alexandria
2	Anianus	Bucolia, Alexandria
3	Abilius	Bucolia, Alexandria
4	Cerdon	Bucolia, Alexandria
5	Primus	Bucolia, Alexandria
6	Justus	Bucolia, Alexandria
7	Eumenius	Bucolia, Alexandria
8	Marcianus	Bucolia, Alexandria
9	Celadion	Bucolia, Alexandria
10	Agrippinus	Bucolia, Alexandria
11	Julian	Bucolia, Alexandria
12	Demetrius I	Bucolia, Alexandria
13	Heracles	Church of the Cave, Alexandria
14	Dionysius	Church of the Cave, Alexandria

No.	Name	Place of Burial
15	Maximus	Church of the Cave, Alexandria
16	Theonas	Church of the Cave, Alexandria
17	Peter I	Church of the Cave, Alexandria
18	Achillas	Church of the Cave, Alexandria
19	Alexander I	Church of the Cave, Alexandria
20	Athanasius I	Dominicium, Alexandria
21	Peter II	Dominicium, Alexandria
22	Timothy I	Dominicium, Alexandria
23	Theophilus	Dominicium, Alexandria
24	Cyril I	Church of the Cave, Alexandria
25	Dioscorus	Island of Gangra, Paphlagonia
26	Timothy II	Church of Saint Mark, Alexandria
27	Peter III	Church of Saint Mark, Alexandria
28	Athanasius II	Church of Saint Mark, Alexandria
29	John I	Church of Saint Mark, Alexandria
30	John II	Church of Saint Mark, Alexandria
31	Dioscorus II	Church of Saint Mark, Alexandria
32	Timothy III	Church of Saint Mark, Alexandria
33	Theodosius I	Church of Saint Mark, Alexandria
34	Peter IV	Ennaton Monastery near Alexandria
35	Damian	Ennaton Monastery near Alexandria
36	Anastasius	Ennaton Monastery near Alexandria
37	Andronicus	Church of Saint Mark, Alexandria
38	Benjamin I	Church of Saint Mark, Alexandria
39	Agathon	Church of Saint Mark, Alexandria
40	John III	Church of Saint Mark, Alexandria
41	Isaac	Church of Saint Mark, Alexandria
42	Simon I	Church of Saint Mark, Alexandria
43	Alexander II	Church of Saint Mark, Alexandria
44	Cosmas I	Church of Saint Mark, Alexandria
45	Theodore	Church of Saint Mark, Alexandria
46	Kha'il I	Church of Saint Mark, Alexandria
47	Menas I	Church of Saint Mark, Alexandria
48	John IV	Church of Saint Mark, Alexandria
49	Mark II	Church of Saint Mark, Alexandria
50	James	Tanda
51	Simon II	Church of Saint Mark, Alexandria
52	Joseph	Church of Saint Mark, Alexandria
53	Kha'il II	Monastery of Saint Macarius
54	Cosmas II	Church of Saint Bartholomew, Danush
55	Shenute I	Church of Saint Mark, Alexandria
56	Kha'il III	Monastery of Saint Macarius
57	Gabriel I	Monastery of Saint Macarius
58	Cosmas III	Monastery of Saint Macarius
59	Macarius I	Monastery of Saint Macarius

No.	Name	Place of Burial
60	Theophanes	Thrown into the river
61	Menas II	Mahallat Danyal, Gharbiya
62	Abraham	Al-Mu'allaqa Church, Old Cairo
63	Philotheus	Damrua
64	Zacharias	Church of the Virgin by the Steps of Babylon
65	Shenute II	Damrua
66	Christodoulus	Monastery of Saint Macarius
67	Cyril II	Monastery of Saint Macarius
68	Michael IV	Monastery of Saint Macarius
69	Macarius II	Monastery of Saint Macarius
70	Gabriel II	Monastery of Saint Macarius
71	Michael V	Monastery of Saint Macarius
72	John V	Monastery of Saint Macarius
73	Mark III	Monastery of Saint Macarius
74	John VI	Church of the Virgin by the Steps of Babylon
75	Cyril III	Dair al-Sham'
76	Athanasius III	Church of Saint Mercurius, Old Cairo
77	John VII	Church of Saint Mercurius, Old Cairo
78	Gabriel III	Dair al-Nastur, al-Basatin
79	Theodosius II	Dair al-Nastur, al-Basatin
80	John VIII	Dair al-Shahran
81	John IX	Dair al-Nastur, al-Basatin
82	Benjamin II	Dair al-Shahran
83	Peter V	Church of the Virgin by the Steps of Babylon
84	Mark IV	Dair al-Shahran
85	John X	Church of the Virgin by the Steps of Babylon
86	Gabriel IV	Church of the Virgin by the Steps of Babylon
87	Matthew I	Church of Saint Ruwais, Khandaq
88	Gabriel V	Church of the Virgin by the Steps of Babylon
89	John XI	Church of Saint Ruwais, Khandaq
90	Matthew II	Church of Saint Ruwais, Khandaq
91	Gabriel VI	Church of Saint Ruwais, Khandaq
92	Michael III	Church of the Virgin by the Steps of Babylon
93	John XII	Church of the Virgin by the Steps of Babylon
94	John XIII	Church of the Virgin, Harat Zuwayla
95	Gabriel VII	Church of Saint Mercurius, Old Cairo
96	John XIV	Monastery of the Syrians
97	Gabriel VIII	Monastery of the Syrians
98	Mark V	Monastery of Saint Macarius
99	John XV	Dair Bishih, al-Bayadia
100	Matthew III	Church in Tukh
101	Mark VI	Church of Saint Mercurius, Old Cairo
102	Matthew IV	Church of Saint Mercurius, Old Cairo
103	John XVI	Church of Saint Mercurius, Old Cairo
104	Peter VI	Church of Saint Mercurius, Old Cairo

No.	Name	Place of Burial
105	John XVII	Church of Saint Mercurius, Old Cairo
106	Mark VII	Church of Saint Mercurius, Old Cairo
107	John XVIII	Church of Saint Mercurius, Old Cairo
108	Mark VIII	Church of Saint Mark, Azbakiya
109	Peter VII	Church of Saint Mark, Azbakiya
110	Cyril IV	Church of Saint Mark, Azbakiya
111	Demetrius II	Church of Saint Mark, Azbakiya
112	Cyril V	Church of Saint Mark, Azbakiya
113	John XIX	Church of Saint Mark, Azbakiya
114	Macarius III	Church of Saint Mark, Azbakiya
115	Joseph II	Church of Saint Mark, Azbakiya
116	Cyril VI	Monastery of Saint Menas, Maryut

APPENDIX C
Language, Architecture, and Calendar

The Coptic Language

The scribes of pharaonic Egypt used hieroglyphic characters to write on the walls of temples and tombs, yet those symbols did not actually represent the phonetic form of the language. The hieroglyphs were partly phonetic and partly descriptive. Later, an abridged cursive form of writing known as Hieratic was introduced. This form of writing still followed the archaic and conventional system until a third form emerged, which was used for secular purposes only and became known as Demotic.

Following the conquest of Egypt by Alexander the Great, Greek became the official language and remained so until well after the Arab conquest in 640. Greek was the language spoken in the famous Catechetical School of Alexandria, and it was the medium of communication among the patriarchs and bishops of the early church. It remained the official language until the days of the governor 'Abd Allah ibn Marwan (705–709) who tried to use Arabic in public affairs.

The Coptic language was the Egyptian vernacular language expressed in Greek characters with the addition of seven letters to represent those sounds that were unknown to the Greeks. These letters were taken over from Demotic. Our earliest examples of Coptic are the London Horoscope of 100 and the two second-century mummy labels from Akhmim.

Coptic has five dialects: Sa'idic, Bohairic, Fayyumic, Akhmimic, and Subakhmimic. Of these dialects only Bohairic is in use, as the liturgical language of the Coptic Church. Sa'idic may be considered the classical dialect, and it was widespread in Egypt. The other three dialects were limited to the districts of which they bear the names.

Though Sa'idic was the general Coptic language until the ninth century, Bohairic replaced Sa'idic, partly on account of ecclesiastical influence, and a good deal of the Sa'idic literature then extant was translated into Bohairic. During the reign of al-Hakim (996–1021) Christians still spoke Coptic among themselves, and Muslims would not know what was being said. Within one hundred years, however, there were many changes.

In 1131, the patriarch Gabriel II admonished the priests to explain the Lord's Prayer in the vernacular Arabic. This meant that even at this early date Coptic was little understood by the people. In the thirteenth and fourteenth centuries, Coptic liturgical books began to have Arabic translations side by side with the Coptic. Yet in Upper Egypt, Coptic seems to have prevailed much longer. Al-Maqrizi implies that Coptic was still spoken in the monasteries around Asyut in the fifteenth century. It is generally believed that

Coptic ceased to be a spoken language in the seventeenth century. Today, Pope Shenuda III has ordered that Coptic be taught in all Coptic colleges and seminaries.

The Plan of a Coptic Church

Early Coptic churches were usually built on the plan of a basilica, but in the case of the ancient churches of Cairo, rebuilding, additions, and alterations have often considerably modified the original plan. A Coptic church comprises four distinct parts: from the west end is the narthex, then the nave, then the choir, and finally the sanctuary.

In the narthex of some of the ancient churches there is a deep oblong tank sunk in the floor, now usually covered over with boards. This tank was formerly used for the service of blessing the water on the Feast of the Epiphany; now, however, a portable basin is used for this service.

The nave is normally divided into three parts by a double colonnade, the northern aisle being reserved for women. At the western end of the nave in the ancient churches there is usually the mandatum tank, a shallow rectangular basin sunk in the floor, also covered over by boards now. This tank was formerly used for the service of foot-washing on Maundy Thursday and on the Feast of Saints Peter and Paul. Nowadays, a small portable basin is used for this service. Near the eastern end of the nave is the *ambon*, or pulpit, which is usually set against the colonnade of the northern aisle.

At the east end of the nave is the choir, which was formerly separated from the nave by a screen. The choir extends the whole breadth of the church. It contains seats for the singers as well as two candelabra and lecterns from which the lessons are read.

One or more steps lead from the chancel into the sanctuary or *haikal*. The sanctuary, into which only men are allowed to enter, and then only after having removed their shoes, is separated from the rest of the church by a solid wooden screen with a central door covered by a curtain. Along the top of this screen there is usually a row of icons. In the medieval churches these screens are beautifully carved and inlaid with ebony, ivory, and cedar. On each side of the door are two small windows. In some churches, sanctuary lamps are hung before this screen, and sometimes ostrich eggs are suspended between them. In front of the sanctuary door, which is opened for services, hangs a richly embroidered curtain. Almost all churches have three sanctuaries, each with its own altar. The central sanctuary is dedicated to the saint after whom the church is called and contains the main altar. The northern and southern sanctuaries are used on the feast day of the saints to whom they are dedicated, or whenever there is more than one celebration of the Divine Liturgy on the same day, since according to the canon law of the Coptic Church, neither the altar nor the eucharistic vessels and vestments may be used twice on the same day.

Behind the main altar there is a tribune with a throne for the bishop and seats for the officiating clergy. In the niche behind the throne there is usually a sanctuary lamp known as the perpetual lamp. The altar, which is invariably free-standing in the middle of the sanctuary, is a four-sided mass of either brickwork or stone. Above the altar is a lofty wooden canopy upheld by pillars. Beneath the dome of this canopy there is usually a painting of Christ as Pantokrator, surrounded by the cherubim and seraphim. The altar is covered with three coverings: the first is a tight-fitting case of linen or cotton reaching down to the ground; the second a red silk covering with a cross embroidered on each side, likewise reaching to the ground; and the third a white linen cloth placed on the table of the altar. At each of the four corners of the altar is a candlestick; those on the west side are shorter than the ones on the east side. In the middle of the altar is the ark, a box about twenty-eight centimeters in height and twenty-five centimeters in width, the top of which is closed with hinged flaps. On the sides of this ark are paintings, the usual subjects being the Last Supper, the Holy Virgin, an angel, and the saint to whom the church is dedicated. In this ark the chalice is placed from the beginning of the Divine Liturgy until the time of the Holy Communion.

The baptistery is normally situated at the upper end of the northern aisle, but this rule does not apply to all of the ancient Coptic churches. The font is a circular basin sufficiently deep to allow the priest to immerse the infant in the water while pronouncing the baptismal formula. The exteriors of the ancient Coptic churches are always unimposing, and the entrances to them are often through small side doors.

The Calendar of the Coptic Church

The development of the Christian Calendar in general, and of the Coptic martyrology in particular, was a reflection of the historical atmosphere in which the Christian Church lived during its first four centuries. The successive persecutions of the Christians produced an ever increasing number of martyrs whose steadfastness and perseverance was considered an inspiration and whose death for the faith called for an annual commemoration by the Church.

The earliest instance of such a commemoration comes from Asia Minor in a letter written in 156 by the Christians of Smyrna to the neighboring Church of Philomelium in Phrygia. This epistle, of which Eusebius has preserved the greater part, is important because we derive from it all our information on Saint Polycarp's martyrdom.

The Alexandrian martyrology, or Coptic Synaxarion, evolved from a local martyrology toward a more general calendar, only to return later to its local tradition. This process is evident from its inclusion of Greek, Syrian, Armenian, Roman, and Persian bishops, saints, and martyrs, who were added during the second stage of its evolution.

The first Arabic recension is attributed to Peter Severus al-Gamil, bishop of Malig (twelfth–thirteenth centuries). This was followed by a recension by Michael, bishop of Atrib and Malig (1243–47). This evolution of the Synaxarion has continued to the present day. The Coptic Church considers its patriarchs to be saints, and ninety-seven of the 116 patriarchs are commemorated in the Coptic Synaxarion.

Coptic	Julian	Gregorian	Commemorations
Tut	August	September	
1	29	11	1. New Year's Day (Nawruz) 2. Job took a bath and was healed 3. Bartholomew the Apostle 4. Milius, fourth patriarch
2	30	12	1. John the Baptist, martyr 2. Dasius, the soldier of Tanda, martyr
3	31	13	1. Assembly of the Holy Synod at Alexandria under Dionysius, fourteenth patriarch, in 243 2. Great Earthquake in Old Cairo (Misr al-Qadima) and Cairo (al-Qahira) in 1112
	September		
4	1	14	1. Macarius, sixty-ninth patriarch
5	2	15	1. Sophia, martyr 2. Mama
6	3	16	1. Isaiah, prophet, martyr 2. Basilissa, martyr
7	4	17	1. Dioscorus, twenty-fifth patriarch 2. Agathon, Peter, John, Amon, Amona, and their mother Rebecca, martyrs 3. Severianus of Gabala, bishop
8	5	18	1. Zachariah, prophet. 2. Moses, prophet 3. Diomedes, martyr
9	6	19	1. Pisora, bishop and martyr; Syra, martyr 2. Miracle of Colossae in Phrygia
10	7	20	1. Matrona, martyr 2. Basin and her three children 3. Abu Maqar 4. The Nativity of the Holy Virgin Mary
11	8	21	1. Basilides, martyr 2. Cornelius the Centurion 3. Theodora
12	9	22	1. Assembly of the Third Council at Ephesus in 431 2. Translation of the relics of Clement and his companions, martyrs 3. Saint Maurice 4. Saint Michael
13	10	23	1. Matthew II, ninetieth patriarch 2. Miracle worked by Saint Basil
14	11	24	1. Agathon the Stylite
15	12	25	1. Translation of the relics of Stephen, archdeacon 2. Leontius of Syria
16	13	26	1. Consecration of the Church of the Resurrection (Holy Sepulcher) 2. Translation of the relics of John Chrysostom

Coptic	Julian	Gregorian	Commemorations
17	14	27	1. Exaltation of the Holy Cross
			2. Theognosta, nun
18	15	28	1. Porphyrius, martyr
			2. Stephen and Niceta, martyrs
			3. Mercurius, martyr
19	16	29	1. Gregory, patriarch of Armenia
20	17	30	1. Athanasius, twenty-eighth patriarch
			2. Melitina, virgin martyr
			3. Theopista, nun
		October	
21	18	1	1. Monthly commemoration of the Holy Virgin Mary
			2. Cyprian, bishop of Carthage, and Justina, nun
22	19	2	1. Cotylas, his sister Axuwa, and their friend Tatus, martyrs
			2. Julius of Aqfahs, martyr
23	20	3	1. Eunapius and Andrew, martyrs
			2. Thecla, martyr
			3. Reopening of the Church of the Holy Virgin in the Harat al-Rum (Cairo)
24	21	4	1. Gregory, monk
			2. Quadratus, one of the seventy disciples
25	22	5	1. Jonah, prophet
26	23	6	1. The Angel's annunciation to Zachariah of the birth of John the Baptist
27	24	7	1. Eustathius and his two sons, martyrs
28	25	8	1. Apater and his sister Eirene, martyrs
29	26	9	1. Repsima, Gaiana, and her virgin sisters, martyrs
			2. Commemoration of the Birth and Resurrection of Christ
30	27	10	1. The great miracle the Lord performed with Athanasius the Apostolic
Baba			
1	28	11	1. Anastasia, virgin martyr
2	29	12	1. Arrival of Severus, patriarch of Antioch, at the Egyptian Monasteries
3	30	13	1. Simon II, fifty-first patriarch
			2. Theodora, daughter of Arcadius
			3. John the soldier, martyr
			4. Gregory, bishop of Armenia
	October		
4	1	14	1. Bacchus, companion of Sergius, martyr
5	2	15	1. Paul, patriarch of Constantinople, martyr
6	3	16	1. Hannah, prophetess and mother of Samuel the prophet
			2. Antony, bishop of Bana, martyr
7	4	17	1. Paul of Tammua, Conf.

Coptic	Julian	Gregorian	Commemorations
			2. Menas and Hasina, martyrs
8	5	18	1. Matra, martyr
			2. Hor, Susanna, and her children, martyrs
			3. Agathon, hermit
9	6	19	1. Eumenius, seventh patriarch
			2. Eclipse of the sun in the year 1242
			3. Simeon, bishop
			4. Liberius, pope of Rome
10	7	20	1. Sergius, companion of Bacchus, martyr
11	8	21	1. James, patriarch of Antioch, Conf.
			2. Pelagia, virgin martyr
12	9	22	1. Demetrius I, twelfth patriarch
			2. Matthew the Evangelist, martyr
			3. Monthly commemoration of Michael, archangel
13	10	23	1. Zacharias, monk
			2. Abtalamon and his brothers
14	11	24	1. Philip of Caesarea, one of the seven deacons
			2. Philas of Caesarea
15	12	25	1. Pantaleon, martyr
16	13	26	1. Agathon, thirty-ninth patriarch
			2. Carpus, Apollus, Peter, disciples of Isaiah the Hermit
			3. Achillas, eighteenth patriarch
17	14	27	1. Dioscorus II, thirty-first patriarch
			2. Gregory of Nyssa
18	15	28	1. Theophilus, twenty-third patriarch
			2. Heracles, thirteenth patriarch
19	16	29	1. Council at Antioch in 280 against Paul of Samosata
			2. Theophilus and his wife, martyrs
			3. Bartholomew
20	17	30	1. John the Short, Conf.
21	18	31	1. Monthly commemoration of the Holy Virgin Mary
			2. Translation of the relics of Lazarus
			3. Joel, prophet
			4. Farig (Anba Ruwais), 1404
			5. Enthronement of Cyril V
		November	
22	19	1	1. Luke the Evangelist, martyr
23	20	2	1. Joseph, fifty-second patriarch
			2. Dionysius, bishop of Corinth, martyr
24	21	3	1. Hilarion, who introduced monasticism into Palestine
			2. Paul, Longinus, and Dinah, martyrs
			3. Martha
			4. Eirene
25	22	4	1. Apip and Apollo, martyrs

Coptic	Julian	Gregorian	Commemorations
			2. Consecration of the Church of Saint Julius of Aqfahs in Alexandria
26	23	5	1. Timon, one of the seventy disciples
			2. The Seven Martyrs of Dair Anba Antonius
			3. James, brother of Christ
27	24	6	1. Macarius, bishop of Tkow, martyr
28	25	7	1. Marcianus and Mercurius, martyrs
29	26	8	1. Demetrius of Thessalonica, martyr
			2. Nativity of Jesus Christ
30	27	9	1. Consecration of the Church of Saint Mark the Evangelist and the apparition of his head
			2. Abraham, the hermit of Memphis
Hatur			
1	28	10	1. Maximus, Numitius, Victor, and Philip, martyrs
			2. Cleopas the Apostle and his companion
2	29	11	1. Peter III, twenty-seventh patriarch
3	30	12	1. Cyriacus, ascete
			2. Athanasius and his sister Eirene
4	31	13	1. John and James, bishops of Persia, martyrs
			2. Epimachus, Gordianus, and Adrianus of Rome, martyrs
			3. Thomas of Damascus, martyr
	November		
5	1	14	1. Manifestation of the head of Longinus the Soldier
			2. Timothy (Thomasius), martyr
			3. Translation of the body of Theodore the General to Shutb
6	2	15	1. Felix, pope of Rome
			2. Consecration of the Church of the Holy Virgin Mary in Dair al-Muharraq
7	3	16	1. George of Alexandria, martyr
			2. Nehroua of the Fayyum, martyr
			3. Menas, bishop of Thmoui
			4. Consecration of the Church of Saint George of Cappadocia
			5. Lucius
8	4	17	1. The Four Bodiless Living Creatures of the Apocalypse
9	5	18	1. Isaac, forty-first patriarch
			2. Assembly of the Council of Nicea in 325
			3. Anonymous saint of the desert
10	6	19	1. Fifty virgins and their mother Sophia, martyrs

Coptic	Julian	Gregorian	Commemorations
			2. Assembly of the Holy Synod at Rome on account of Epiphany and Lent
			3. Markya of Alexandria
11	7	20	1. Anne, mother of the Holy Virgin Mary
			2. Archelaus, hegumen, and Elisha, prophet
			3. Amonius, bishop of Aswan
12	8	21	1. Monthly commemoration of Michael, archangel
13	9	22	1. Timothy, bishop of Antinoe
			2. Zacharias, sixty-fourth patriarch
			3. Gabriel, archangel
			4. Joseph of Mount Asas
14	10	23	1. Martin, bishop of Tours
			2. Hanania, Azaria, Mezak
			3. Matrona
			4. Michael, archangel
15	11	24	1. Menas Thaumaturgus, martyr
			2. Autumna, martyr
			3. Menas II, sixty-first patriarch
			4. Cyril VI, 116th patriarch, enthroned at Dair Mari Mina, 1959
16	12	25	1. Feast of the Nativity
			2. Consecration of the Church of Saint Onuphrius
			3. Justus, bishop, martyr
			4. Houb of Tukh
17	13	26	1. John Chrysostom
			2. Paul, monk
			3. Coordination of Alexandrian calendars
18	14	27	1. Atrasis and Juanna, martyrs
			2. Philip the Apostle, martyr
19	15	28	1. Consecration of the Church of Saints Sergius and Bacchus
			2. Commemoration of the Preaching of Saint Bartholomew the Apostle
			3. Anonymous old saint of Upper Egypt
			4. Xenophon, John, Arcadius, and Matthias
			1. Anianus, second patriarch
20	16	29	2. Consecration of the Church of Theodore the General, son of John al-Shutbi
			3. Sophronius and Shanazhum, martyrs
			4. Matthew, apostle
			5. Athanasius I, twentieth patriarch
			1. Monthly Commemation of the Holy Virgin Mary
21	17	30	2. Gregory Thaumaturgus

Coptic	Julian	Gregorian	Commemorations
			3. Cosmas II, forty-fifth patriarch
			4. Alphaeus, Zacchaeus, Romanus, and John, martyrs
			5. Victor, Thomas, and Isaac of al-Ashmunain
			6. John of Asyut
		December	
22	18	1	1. Cosmas and Damian, their brothers Antimus, Leontius, Euprapius, and their mother Theodota, martyrs
23	19	2	1. Cornelius the Centurion
			2. Translation of the relics of Saint Marina to the Church of the Holy Virgin Mary, Harat al-Rum
			3. Joel, prophet
24	20	3	1. The twenty-four elders of the Apocalypse
25	21	4	1. Mercurius, martyr
26	22	5	1. Valerianus and his brother Thiburin, martyr
			2. Gregory of Nyssa
27	23	6	1. James the Sawn-Asunder, martyr
			2. Consecration of the Church of Saint Victor
			3. Philemon
28	24	7	1. Sarabamun, bishop of Nikiu, martyr
29	25	8	1. Peter I, seventeenth patriarch, martyr
			2. Clement of Rome, martyr
			3. Annunciation, Nativity, and Resurrection of Jesus Christ
30	26	9	1. Acacius, patriarch of Constantinople
			2. Macarius, martyr
			3. Consecration of the Church of Saints Cosmas and Damian, their Sister, and their Mother
			4. Victor, martyr
Kiyahk			
1	27	10	1. Peter of Edessa, bishop
			2. Consecration of the Church of Saint Shenuda
2	28	11	1. Apa Hor, monk
			2. Harman, bishop of Qaw
3	29	12	1. Presentation of the Holy Virgin Mary in the temple in Jerusalem
4	30	13	1. Andrew the Apostle and brother of Peter, martyr
			2. Translation of the relics of Saint Bishoi from Upper Egypt to Wadi al-Natrun
	December		
5	1	14	1. Nahum, prophet

Coptic	Julian	Gregorian	Commemorations
			2. Victor of Asyut, martyr
			3. Isidore, martyr
6	2	15	1. Batalus, martyr
			2. Abraham, sixty-second patriarch
			3. Anatolus, martyr
			4. Anonymous female saint
7	3	16	1. Matthew the Poor of Aswan
			2. Enthronement of John XIX, 113th patriarch
			3. Banina and Banau, martyrs
			4. Dermataus of al-Bahnasa
			5. John, bishop of Ermont
8	4	17	1. Heracles, thirteenth patriarch
			2. Barbara and Juliana, martyrs
			3. Paisus and his sister Thecla, martyrs
			4. Samuel, hegumen of Dair al-Qalamun
9	5	18	1. Pimen, Conf.
			2. Namin
10	6	19	1. Translation of the relics of Severus, patriarch of Antioch, to Dair al-Zugag (the Ennaton)
			2. Nicholas, bishop of Myra, Conf.
			3. Shura of Shinshif, martyr
			4. Theophanes, sixtieth patriarch
11	7	20	1. Pidjimi, ascete
			2. Consecration of the Church of Saint Claudius
			3. Benjamin of Phasia
			4. Ptolemaeus, martyr
12	8	21	1. Monthly commemoration of Michael, Archangel
			2. Hadra, bishop of Aswan
			3. John, Conf.
			4. Assembly of the Council at Rome against Novatus
13	9	22	1. Barsanuphius, martyr
			2. Apraxius, ascete
			3. Consecration of the Church of Saint Misael
			4. Elias of Samhud
			5. Mari Zali, disciple of Mari Matta
14	10	23	1. Bahnam and his sister Sarah, martyrs
			2. Christodoulus of Heliopolis
			3. Apa Hor and Apa Mena the Elders, martyrs
			4. Amonius, bishop of Esna
			5. Christodoulus, sixty-sixth patriarch
			6. Ezekiel, ascete
			7. Simeon, new martyr
			8. Bahnam and Sarah

Coptic	Julian	Gregorian	Commemorations
15	11	24	1. Gregory, patriarch of Armenia, Conf. 2. Luke the Stylite 3. Amsah al-Qifti, martyr 4. Asbah, martyr
16	12	25	1. Gideon, one of the judges 2. Harwaj, Ananiyas, and Khusi of Akhmim, martyrs 3. Consecration of the Church of Saint James the Persian 4. Eulogius and Arsenius, martyrs
17	13	26	1. Luke the Stylite of Persia and the translation of his relics 2. Elias, ascete 3. Sarabamun
18	14	27	1. Translation of the relics of Titus from Crete to Constantinople 2. Heracleas, martyr, and Philemon, priest 3. Anonymous desert monk
19	15	28	1. John, bishop of Burullus
20	16	29	1. Haggai, prophet 2. Elias, bishop of al-Muharraq 3. Pisentius
21	17	30	1. Monthly commemoration of the Holy Virgin Mary 2. Barnabas, one of the seventy disciples, martyr 3. Samuel
22	18	31	1. Gabriel and the consecration of his church in Danah 2. Anastasius, thirty-sixth patriarch 3. Barnabas, bishop of Aydab 4. Macarius II, sixty-ninth patriarch
		January	
23	19	1	1. David, prophet 2. Timothy, hermit 3. Nephew of the king of Nubia
24	20	2	1. Ignatius, patriarch of Antioch, martyr 2. Philogonius, patriarch of Antioch 3. Nativity of Takla Haymanot the Ethiopian 4. Martyrs of Bula and Salfana 5. John Kame, ascete
25	21	3	1. Bishai of al-Qabrin
26	22	4	1. Anastasia, martyr 2. Juliana, martyr 3. Consecration of the Church of Saint Bishoi 4. Heraklion, bishop
27	23	5	1. Bisada, bishop of Psoi, martyr

Coptic	Julian	Gregorian	Commemorations
28	24	6	1. Martyrdom of 150 men and twenty-four women of Antinoe
			2. The Glorious Birth of the Lord Jesus Christ
29	25	7	1. Feast of the Glorious Nativity
30	26	8	1. John, hegumen of Scetis
			2. The Adoration of the Magi
			3. Arrival of Arianus the Governor in Akhmim
			4. David and James, bishops of Jerusalem
Tuba			
1	27	9	1. Stephen, archdeacon, martyr
			2. Leontius, martyr
			3. Macarius I, fifty-ninth patriarch
			4. Dioscorus and Aesculapius, martyrs
			5. Discovery of the relics of Saint Stephen
			6. The 8,140 Martyrs of Akhmim
2	28	10	1. Theonas, sixteenth patriarch
			2. Callinicus, bishop of Ausim
			3. Yuna of Hermontis
3	29	11	1. Massacre of the 144,000 Innocents of Bethlehem
4	30	12	1. John the Evangelist
5	31	13	1. Eugenius the Soldier, martyr
			2. Banikarus, martyr
	January		
6	1	14	1. Circumcision of the Lord Christ
			2. Translation of Elijah, prophet
			3. Marcianus, eighth patriarch
			4. Basil the Great, bishop of Caesarea
			5. Mark, seventy-third patriarch
7	2	15	1. Sylvester, pope of Rome
			2. Victor
8	3	16	1. Consecration of the Church of Saint Macarius
			2. Andronicus, thirty-seventh patriarch
			3. Benjamin I, thirty-eighth patriarch
			4. Zacharias, sixty-fourth patriarch
			5. Malachi, prophet
9	4	17	1. Abraham, companion of George
			2. Anatolius, martyr
10	5	18	1. Vigil of the Feast of the Baptism of Christ
			2. Collection in Christian churches to cover what was taken from the holy fathers
			3. Justus, disciple of Saint Samuel
			4. Phocas, martyr
11	6	19	1. Feast of the Epiphany of the Divinity, the Baptism

Coptic	Julian	Gregorian	Commemorations
			2. John VI, seventy-fourth patriarch
			3. Anatolius, martyr
			4. Homily of the Holy Eucharist
12	7	20	1. Monthly commemoration of Saint Michael the Archangel
			2. Theodore the Oriental, martyr
			3. Anonymous female saint
			4. Anatolus, the Persian martyr
13	8	21	1. Miracle of the Marriage Feast at Cana, Galilee
			2. Theophilus, monk
			3. Damiana, martyr
			4. Archelides the Roman
14	9	22	1. Archelides of Rome
			2. Maximus and Domitius
			3. Theophilus, monk
			4. Maharati
15	10	23	1. Obadiah, prophet
			2. Gregory of Nyssa
			3. Homily of one of the fathers
16	11	24	1. Philotheus, martyr
			2. John IV, forty-eighth patriarch
17	12	25	1. Maximus and Domitius
			2. Joseph, bishop of Girga and Akhmim, known as al-Abahh
			3. John of the Golden Gospel
18	13	26	1. James, bishop of Nisibis
			2. Mary and Martha
19	14	27	1. Discovery of the relics of Saints Apa Hor, Pisoura, Shenuda, and their mother Ambira
20	15	28	1. Prochorus, one of the seventy disciples
			2. Consecration of the Church of Saint John of the Golden Gospel and the translation of his relics to the church
			3. Bahna, martyr; Kalug, priest
			4. Bebnuva, martyr
21	16	29	1. Dormition of the Holy Virgin Mary
			2. Hilaria, daughter of the emperor Zeno
			3. Gregory, brother of Saint Basil the Great
			4. Sophia
			5. Bartanuba
22	17	30	1. Antony the Great, ascete
23	18	31	1. Timothy the Apostle, martyr
			2. Cyril IV, 110th patriarch
			3. Badasyus of Faw
24	19	February 1	1. Mary the Alexandrian, ascete
			2. Bisada, priest

Coptic	Julian	Gregorian	Commemorations
			3. Ephraem of Fargut
25	20	2	1. Peter the Pious
			2. Askala, martyr
			3. Abadius, martyr
26	21	3	1. Martyrdom of the forty-nine martyrs of Scetis
			2. Anastasia
			3. Bagush, martyr
27	22	4	1. Sarapion, martyr
			2. Suriel, archangel
			3. Translation of the relics of Saint Timothy from Ephesus to Constantinople
			4. Phoebammon the Soldier, martyr
28	23	5	1. Clement of Rome, martyr
			2. Kaou, martyr
			3. Elias of al-Bahnasa, martyr
			4. Babylas, martyr
29	24	6	1. Xenia, martyr
			2. Cyriacus, martyr
			3. Annunciation, Nativity, and Resurrection of Jesus Christ
30	25	7	1. Pistis ('Faith'), Elpis ('Hope'), Agape ('Charity'), and their mother Sophia ('Wisdom')
			2. Palemon, hermit
Amshir			
1	26	8	1. The Second Ecumenical Council of Constantinople, 381
			2. Consecration of the first church of Saint Peter, 'Seal of the Martyrs,' seventeenth patriarch
			3. Abadius, martyr
2	27	9	1. Paul, the first hermit
			2. Longinus, hegumen of the Ennaton
3	28	10	1. James, monk
			2. Ephraem the Syrian
			3. Hadra of Banhadab, monk
4	29	11	1. Agapus, one of the seventy disciples, martyr
			2. Eucharistus
5	30	12	1. Agrippinus, tenth patriarch
			2. Bishoi, of the Monastery of Akhmim and Apa Nub
			3. Apollo, friend of Apip
			4. Translation of the relics of the forty-nine martyrs of Scetis to the Church of Saint Macarius at Dair Abu Maqar
6	31	13	1. Discovery of the relics of Saint Hipploytus of Rome

Coptic	Julian	Gregorian	Commemorations
			2. Cyrus and John, three virgins and their mother, martyrs
			3. Zanufius
	February		
7	1	14	1. Alexander II, forty-third patriarch
			2. Theodore, forty-fifth patriarch
			3. Cyrus and John, martyrs
			4. Alexandra
8	2	15	1. Presentation of Christ in the temple
			2. Dormition of Saint Simeon
9	3	16	1. Barsum, father of the Syrian monks
			2. Paul the Syrian, martyr
10	4	17	1. James the Apostle and son of Alphaeus
			2. Justus, son of King Numerianus, martyr
			3. Isidore of Pelusium
			4. Philo, bishop of Persia, martyr
11	5	18	1. Fabianus, bishop of Rome, martyr
			2. Valentianus, bishop of Rome
12	6	19	1. Monthly commemoration of Saint Michael, archangel
			2. Gelasius, monk
13	7	20	1. Sergius of Atrib with his father, mother, sister, and many others, martyrs
			2. Timothy III, thirty-second patriarch
14	8	21	1. Severus, patriarch of Antioch
			2. James, fiftieth patriarch
15	9	22	1. Zachariah, prophet
			2. Consecration of the first Church of the Forty Martyrs of Sebaste by Saint Basil the Great
			3. Paphnutius, ascete
16	10	23	1. Elizabeth, mother of Saint John the Baptist
17	11	24	1. Menas, monk of Akhmim, martyr
			2. Abraham al-Qaddis
18	12	25	1. Meletius, patriarch of Antioch
			2. James the Apostle
19	13	26	1. Translation of the relics of Saint Martianus the Monk from Athens to Antioch
			2. Peter II, twenty-first patriarch
20	14	27	1. Peter II, twenty-first patriarch
			2. Basil, Theodore, and Timothy, martyrs
21	15	28	1. Monthly commemoration of the Holy Virgin Mary
			2. Onesimus, disciple of Saint Paul, martyr
			3. Gabriel I, fifty-seventh patriarch
			4. Zacharias, bishop of Sakha
			5. Batros, metropolitan of Damascus
			6. Peter II, twenty-first patriarch

Coptic	Julian	Gregorian	Commemorations
		March	
22	16	1	1. Maruta, bishop of Martyropolis, martyr
23	17	2	1. Eusebius, son of Basilides, martyr
24	18	3	1. Agapetus, bishop
			2. Timothy of Gaza
			3. Matthias of Qus, martyr
25	19	4	1. Archippus, Philemon, and Abfiah the Virgin, martyrs
			2. Kona of Rome and Menas, martyrs
			3. Cosmas, martyr
26	20	5	1. Hosea, prophet
			2. Zadok and the 128 martyrs
27	21	6	1. Eustathius, patriarch of Antioch
28	22	7	1. Theodore the Greek, martyr
			2. Translation of the relics of Saint Theodore the General from Emesa to Nyssa
29	23	8	1. Polycarp, bishop of Smyrna, martyr
			2. Annunciation, Nativity, and Resurrection of Christ
30	24	9	1. Discovery of the head of Saint John the Baptist
Baramhat			
1	25	10	1. Narcissus, bishop of Jerusalem
			2. Alexander, soldier of Rome, martyr
			3. Mercurius, bishop
2	26	11	1. Macrobius, bishop of Nikiu
3	27	12	1. Cosmas III, fifty-eighth patriarch
			2. Porphyrius, martyr
			3. Hadid, priest
			4. Barqonias
			5. Macrobius
4	28	13	1. Council on the Island of Bani 'Amr
			2. Habulyus of Perga, martyr
			3. Porphyrius, martyr
	March		
5	1	14	1. Sarabamun, hegumen of Dair Abu Yuhannis
			2. Eudoxia, martyr
			3. Peter, ascete
6	2	15	1. Dioscorus, new martyr
			2. Theodotus, bishop of Kyrenia, Cyprus
			3. Occupation of the western part of Egypt by the Ethiopians
			4. Theodosius, Emperor
7	3	16	1. Philemon and Apollonius, martyrs
			2. Mary, martyr
			3. Menas, new martyr
8	4	17	1. Matthias the Apostle, martyr
			2. Julian, eleventh patriarch

Coptic	Julian	Gregorian	Commemorations
			3. Arianus, governor of Antinoe, martyr
9	5	18	1. Konon the Syrian, hermit
			2. Andrianus, his wife Martha, Eusebius, Arma, and forty other martyrs
			3. Philemon and Apollonius, martyrs
10	6	19	1. Apparition of the Holy Cross to Saint Helena and its recovery from the Persians by the Roman emperor Heraclius
11	7	20	1. Basil, bishop of Jerusalem
12	8	21	1. Monthly commemoration of Saint Michael, archangel
			2. Manifestation of the virginity of Demetrius, twelfth patriarch
			3. Malachias, martyr
			4. Gelasius, martyr
13	9	22	1. Dionysius, fourteenth patriarch
			2. Macarius the Great and Macarius of Alexandria returned from exile
			3. The Forty martyrs of Sebaste
14	10	23	1. Cyril III, seventy-fifth patriarch
			2. Shenute of al-Bahnasa, martyr
			3. Eugenius, Agathodorus, and Valentinus, martyrs
			4. Euchanus, Galidrus, and Elpidius, martyrs
15	11	24	1. Sarah, nun of Upper Egypt
			2. Elias of Ahnas, martyr
16	12	25	1. Kha'il I, forty-sixth patriarch
17	13	26	1. Lazarus, the beloved of the Lord
			2. George the Pious, ascete; Belasius, martyr; and Joseph, bishop
			3. Basilius, metropolitan of Jerusalem
			4. Sidhum Bishoi of Damietta
18	14	27	1. Isidorus, companion of Sana the Soldier
19	15	28	1. Aristobulus, one of the seventy disciples
			2. Six saints of Alexandria, Agapius, Thimolaus, Dionysius, Blasius, Romolus, and their companion, martyrs
20	16	29	1. Kha'il III, fifty-sixth patriarch
			2. Raising of Lazarus from the tomb
			3. Consecration of the Church of Saint Iskhiron
21	17	30	1. Monthly commemoration of the Holy Virgin Mary
			2. Presence of the Lord in Bethany
			3. Order of the high priest to kill Lazarus
			4. Theodore and Timothy, martyrs
			5. Thausta, martyr
22	18	31	1. Cyril, bishop of Jerusalem

Coptic	Julian	Gregorian	Commemorations
			2. Michael, bishop of Naqada
		April	
23	19	1	1. Daniel, prophet
24	20	2	1. Macarius I, fifty-ninth patriarch
			2. Apparition of the Holy Virgin in Zaytun, April 2, 1968
25	21	3	1. Onesiphorus, one of the seventy disciples
			2. Matthew III, 100th patriarch
26	22	4	1. Euphrasia, virgin martyr
			2. Peter VI, 104th patriarch
27	23	5	1. Crucifixion of the Lord
			2. Macarius the Great
28	24	6	1. Constantine the Great, emperor
			2. Peter VII, 109th patriarch
29	25	7	1. Annunciation to the Holy Virgin Mary
			2. Resurrection of Christ from the dead
			3. Eutychia
30	26	8	1. Gabriel, archangel
			2. Translation of the relics of James the Sawn-Asunder
			3. Samson, judge
Baramuda			
1	27	9	1. Silvanus, ascete of Scetis
			2. Berber attack on Dair Abu Maqar
			3. Aaron, priest
			4. Discussion regarding the feast of Aaron
2	28	10	1. Christophorus, martyr
			2. John IX, eighty-first patriarch
3	29	11	1. John, bishop of Jerusalem under the emperor Hadrian
			2. Michael V, seventy-first patriarch
			3. Theodorus, martyr
4	30	12	1. Victor, Decius, Eirene the Virgin, and those with them, martyrs
5	31	13	1. Ezekiel, son of Boaz, prophet
6	April 1	14	1. Appearance of the Lord to Thomas
			2. Mary the Egyptian
7	2	15	1. Joachim, the maternal grandfather of Christ
			2. Macrobius, ascete
			3. Agapius and Theodore, martyrs
8	3	16	1. Agape, Eirene, and Sionia, martyrs
			2. The 150 Persian martyrs
9	4	17	1. Zosimus, hermit in Palestine
			2. Miracle performed by Shenute I, fifty-fifth patriarch
10	5	18	1. Isaac, disciple of Apollo
			2. Gabriel II, seventieth patriarch

Coptic	Julian	Gregorian	Commemorations
11	6	19	1. Theodora of Alexandria
			2. John, bishop of Gaza
12	7	20	1. Alexander, bishop of Jerusalem
			2. Antony, bishop of Tammua
			3. Michael, archangel
13	8	21	1. Joshua and Joseph, martyrs
			2. Dionysa the Deaconess
			3. John XVII, 105th patriarch
			4. Midius, martyr
14	9	22	1. Maximus, fifteenth patriarch
15	10	23	1. Consecration of the first Jacobite Christian sanctuary
			2. Agapius, one of the seventy disciples
			3. Alexandra, wife of Diocletian
			4. Mark VI, 101st patriarch
			5. Nicolas, bishop of Myra
16	11	24	1. Antipas, bishop of Pergamon, disciple of Saint John the Evangelist, martyr
17	12	25	1. James the Apostle, martyr
18	13	26	1. Arsenius, slave of Saint Susinius, martyr
			2. Eustathius
19	14	27	1. Simeon the Armenian, bishop of Persia, and 150 with him, martyrs
			2. David, monk, new martyr
			3. Yu'annis Abu Naga al-Kabir (eleventh century)
			4. Abu 'Ala' Fahd ibn Ibrahim
20	15	28	1. Paphnutius of Dandara, martyr
21	16	29	1. Monthly commemoration of the Holy Virgin Mary
			2. Hierotheus, philosopher of Athens and convert of Saint Paul
22	17	30	1. Isaac of Hurin
			2. Alexander I, nineteenth patriarch
			3. Mark II, forty-ninth patriarch
			4. Kha'il II, fifty-third patriarch
		May	
23	18	1	1. George of Lydda, martyr
			2. Kom
24	19	2	1. Shenute I, fifty-fifth patriarch
			2. Sina
25	20	3	1. Sarah of Antioch and her two sons, martyrs
			2. Wife of Sacratus
			3. Paphnutius and Theodorus and one hundred other martyrs
			4. Young men of Ephesus
26	21	4	1. Susinius, martyr
27	22	5	1. Victor, martyr
28	23	6	1. Milius the ascete, martyr

Coptic	Julian	Gregorian	Commemorations
29	24	7	1. Eurastus, one of the seventy disciples
			2. Decius (Acacius), bishop of Jerusalem
30 Bashans	25	8	1. Mark the Evangelist, martyr
1	26	9	1. Nativity of the Holy Virgin Mary
			2. Job the Righteous
2	27	10	1. Theodore, disciple of Saint Pachomius
			2. Job the Righteous
			3. Simeon the Apostle
			4. Philotheus
3	28	11	1. Jason, one of the seventy disciples
			2. Euthymius of Fu'a, martyr
			3. Gabriel IV, eighty-sixth patriarch
4	29	12	1. John I, twenty-ninth patriarch
			2. John V, seventy-second patriarch
5	30	13	1. Jeremiah, prophet, martyr
6	May 1	14	1. Isaac of Tiphre
			2. Macarius of Alexandria
			3. Paphnutius of Dandara
7	2	15	1. Athanasius I, twentieth patriarch
			2. Nativity of Saint Shenute
8	3	16	1. John of Sanhut
			2. Daniel, hegumen of Scetis
			3. Ascension of the Lord to heaven
			4. Bakhbas of Senhum, son of Macarba
9	4	17	1. Helena, queen
			2. Gabriel VIII, ninety-seventh patriarch
			3. John XI, eighty-ninth patriarch
10	5	18	1. The three children in the furnace: Ananias, Azarias, and Misael
11	6	19	1. Theoclia, wife of Saint Justus, martyr
			2. Paphnutius, bishop
			3. Nichomius
12	7	20	1. Consecration of the Church of Saint Damiana
			2. Translation of the relics of Saint John Chrysostom from Koma to Constantinople
			3. Appearance of a cross of fire over Golgotha in 351.
			4. Mu'allim Malati
			5. Mark VII, 106th patriarch
13	8	21	1. Arsenius, tutor of Arcadius and Honorius, the sons of Theodosius the Great
14	9	22	1. Pachomius, father of Eastern monasticism
			2. Epimachus of Pelusium
15	10	23	1. Simon the Zealot

Coptic	Julian	Gregorian	Commemorations
			2. Four hundred martyrs of Dandara
			3. Menas, deacon
			4. Sidrach
16	11	24	1. John the Evangelist
17	12	25	1. Epiphanius, bishop of Cyprus
18	13	26	1. George, friend of Abraham of Scetis
			2. Consecration of the Church of Saint Paul at Alexandria
			3. Descent of the Holy Spirit
			4. Shenute
19	14	27	1. Isaac al-Qulali
			2. Isidorus of Antioch, martyr
20	15	28	1. Ammonius, hermit
21	16	29	1. Monthly commemoration of the Holy Virgin Mary
			2. Martinianus of Caesarea
22	17	30	1. Andronicus, one of the seventy disciples
23	18	31	1. Junia, one of the seventy disciples
			2. Julianus and his mother
		June	
24	19	1	1. Coming of Christ into Egypt
			2. Habbakuk, prophet, and consecration of a church in his name
			3. Bashnuna of Saint Macarius Monastery
25	20	2	1. Colluthus of Antinoe, martyr
			2. Hirutas, martyr
			3. Ibrahim al-Gawhari
26	21	3	1. Thomas the Apostle, martyr
27	22	4	1. John, thirtieth patriarch
			2. Lazarus, friend of Christ
28	23	5	1. Translation of the relics of Saint Epiphanius to Cyprus
29	24	6	1. Simon the Stylite
30	25	7	1. Michael IV, sixty-eighth patriarch
			2. Phoras, one of the seventy disciples
			3. Dumadius and Simon the Little
Ba'una			
1	26	8	1. Consecration of the Church of Saint Leontius the Syrian
			2. Cosmas of Taha and his companions, martyrs
			3. Abi Fam the Soldier, martyr
			4. Zikam, martyr
2	27	9	1. Discovery of the relics of Saint John the Baptist and Elisha the Prophet at Alexandria
			2. John XVIII, 107th patriarch
3	28	10	1. Building of the first Church of Saint George in Egypt
			2. Martha of Egypt

Coptic	Julian	Gregorian	Commemorations
			3. Alladius, bishop, martyr
			4. Cosmas I, forty-fourth patriarch
			5. Abra'am, bishop (d.1914)
4	29	11	1. Synesius of Balqim, martyr
			2. Amon and Sophia, martyrs
			3. John of Heraclia, martyr
			4. Apa Hor
			5. John VIII, eightieth patriarch
5	30	12	1. James the Oriental
			2. Bishoi and Peter, martyrs
			3. Consecration of the Church of Saint Victor at Shu
			4. Macarius of Minuf, martyr
6	31 June	13	1. Theodore, monk of Alexandria, martyr
7	1	14	1. Iskhiron of Qallin, martyr
8	2	15	1. Consecration of the Church of the Holy Virgin Mary in al-Mahamma (Musturud)
			2. Amadah and her sons, Armanius and Amah
			3. George, new martyr (d.1387)
9	3	16	1. Samuel, prophet
			2. Lucilianus and four others, martyrs
			3. Translation of the relics of Saint Mercurius to Cairo
10	4	17	1. Eudaemon, Epistemon, and Sophia, martyrs
			2. Commemoration of the closing of the temples and the opening of the churches by Saint Constantine
			3. John XVI, 103rd patriarch
			4. Enthronement of Anba Demetrius II, 111th patriarch
			5. Barsanuphius
11	5	18	1. Claudius, brother of King Numerianus, martyr
			2. Consecration of the Church of the Forty Martyrs in Alexandria
12	6	19	1. Justus, sixth patriarch
			2. Cyril II, sixty-seventh patriarch
			3. Euphemia
			4. Michael, archangel
13	7	20	1. John II, bishop of Jerusalem
			2. Gabriel, archangel
14	8	21	1. Cyrus and John, and Ptolemaeus and Philip, martyrs
			2. John XIX, 113th patriarch
15	9	22	1. Consecration of the Church of Saint Menas at Maryut

Coptic	Julian	Gregorian	Commemorations
			2. Reception of Saint Mark's relics in Rome and presentation to the Coptic delegation
16	10	23	1. Onuphrius, hermit
			2. Latsun of al-Bahnasa
			3. Palemon
17	11	24	1. Latsun of al-Bahnasa
			2. Arrival of Saint Mark's relics in Cairo, 1968
18	12	25	1. Damian, thirty-fifth patriarch
			2. Dedication of Saint Mark's Cathedral in Cairo, 1968
19	13	26	1. George, martyr
			2. Bishoi and Anoub, martyrs
			3. Achillas, eighteenth patriarch
			4. Translation of Saint Mark's relics to Saint Mark's Cathedral, 1968
20	14	27	1. Elisha, prophet
21	15	28	1. Commemoration of the building of the first church dedicated to the Holy Virgin Mary at Philippi
			2. Timotheus the Egyptian, martyr
			3. Cerdon, fourth patriarch
22	16	29	1. Consecration of the Church of Saints Cosmas and Damian, their Brothers, and their Mother
			2. Cerdon, fourth patriarch
23	17	30	1. Apa Nub, hermit
		July	
24	18	1	1. Moses the Black of Scetis, martyr
25	19	2	1. Jude, one of the seventy disciples, martyr
			2. Peter IV, thirty-fourth patriarch
			3. Bishoi and Peter, martyrs
26	20	3	1. Joshua, prophet
			2. Consecration of the Church of Saint Gabriel, Naqlun
27	21	4	1. Ananias, one of the seventy disciples, martyr
			2. Thomas of Shandalat, martyr
28	22	5	1. Theodosius, thirty-third patriarch
			2. Consecration of the Church of Saint Sarabamun, bishop of Nikiu
29	23	6	1. The seven hermits of Mt. Tuna, martyrs
			2. Hor, Bishoi, Theodora, and their mother, martyrs
			3. Consecration of the Church of Saint Suriel the Angel
30	24	7	1. Nativity of Saint John the Baptist

Coptic	Julian	Gregorian	Commemorations
Abib			
1	25	8	1. Febronia, martyr
			2. Biukha and Banain, martyrs
2	26	9	1. Thaddaeus the Apostle
			2. Benufa and Benaben, martyrs
3	27	10	1. Cyril I, twenty-fourth patriarch
			2. Celestinus, pope of Rome
4	28	11	1. Translation of the relics of Saints Cyrus and John to the Church of Saint Mark the Evangelist, Alexandria
5	29	12	1. Peter and Paul, apostles and martyrs
6	30	13	1. Aulibas, one of the seventy disciples, martyr
			2. Theodosia and those with her, martyrs
			3. Bartholomew of Rashid
	July		
7	1	14	1. Shenute, head of the solitaries
			2. Ignatius, bishop of Antioch, martyr
8	2	15	1. Bishoi
			2. Piroun and Atom of Sunbat (Mit Damsis), martyrs
			3. Balana the priest, martyrs
			4. Poemen, martyr
			5. Karas, brother of Emperor Theodosius the Great
			6. Marcus of Dair Anba Antonius
9	3	16	1. Simeon the Apostle, martyr
			2. Celadion, ninth patriarch
			3. Aaron, martyr
10	4	17	1. Theodorus, bishop of the Pentapolis, martyr
			2. Theodorus, bishop of Corinth, and those with him, martyrs
			3. Gabriel VII, ninety-fifth patriarch
11	5	18	1. John and Simon, martyrs
			2. Isaiah, hermit
12	6	19	1. Monthly commemoration of Saint Michael
			2. Apa Hor of Syracuse, martyr
13	7	20	1. Pisentius, bishop of Qift
			2. Apa Hor of Tukh, martyr
			3. Shenute, new martyr
			4. Amon of Tukh, martyr
14	8	21	1. Procopius, martyr
			2. Peter V, eighty-third patriarch
15	9	22	1. Ephraem the Syrian
			2. Cyriacus and Julietta his mother, martyrs
			3. Horasius, martyr
16	10	23	1. John of the Golden Gospel

Coptic	Julian	Gregorian	Commemorations
			2. Translation of the relics of Saint George from al-Qalamun to the church in Old Cairo
			3. Consecration of the Church of Saint Philotheus
			4. Isidore of Heliopolis
17	11	24	1. Euphemia, martyr
18	12	25	1. James the Apostle, martyr
			2. Athanasius of Clysma
19	13	26	1. Pantaleon, martyr
			2. Bebdhaba, bishop of Qift, martyr
			3. Antony, bishop
			4. John X, eighty-fifth patriarch
20	14	27	1. Theodorus of Shutb, martyr
21	15	28	1. Susinius, eunuch
			2. Holy Virgin Mary
			3. Simode
22	16	29	1. Macarius, son of Basilides
			2. Leontius of Tripoli
23	17	30	1. Longinus the Centurion, martyr
			2. Marina, martyr
24	18	31	1. Apa Nub, martyr
			2. Simon I, forty-second patriarch
			3. Ascension of Enoch
		August	
25	19	1	1. Thecla
			2. Isaac of Shama, martyr
			3. Hilaria of Damira, martyr
			4. Thecla and Mouji, martyrs
			5. Antony of Biba, martyr
			6. Apa Karagun, martyr
			7. Dometius the Syrian, martyr
			8. Consecration of the Church of Abu Saifain
			9. Palamon
26	20	2	1. Joseph the Just, the Carpenter, father to Christ
			2. Timothy I, twenty-second patriarch
27	21	3	1. Amon, martyr
			2. Consecration of the Church of Saint Abi Fam the Soldier
			3. Vision of Ezekiel
28	22	4	1. Mary Magdalene
29	23	5	1. Translation of the relics of Saint Andrew from Syria to Constantinople
			2. Barsanuphius, martyr
			3. Translation of the relics of Thaddaeus
			4. Commemoration of the Holy Gospel, the Nativity, and Resurrection of Christ

Coptic	Julian	Gregorian	Commemorations
30 Misra	24	6	1. Mercurius and Ephraem, martyrs
1	25	7	1. Apoli, martyr 2. Cyril V, 112th patriarch
2	26	8	1. Ba'issa of Minuf 2. Menas, martyr
3	27	9	1. Simon the Stylite 2. Isidorus
4	28	10	1. Hezekiah, king 2. Consecration of the Church of Saint Antony of the Monastery of Saint Antony 3. David of Sinjar and his brothers, martyrs
5	29	11	1. John the Soldier, martyr 2. James the Sawn-Asunder, martyr
6	30	12	1. Julietta, martyr 2. Besa, disciple of Shenute
7	31	13	1. Annunciation to Joachim of the birth of the Holy Virgin Mary 2. Timothy II, twenty-sixth patriarch 3. Confession of Saint Peter at Caesarea Philippi 4. Isidorus, martyr
	August		
8	1	14	1. Eleazar, his wife Salome, and their children, martyrs
9	2	15	1. Auri of Shatanuf, martyr
10	3	16	1. Matra, martyr 2. Pihebs of Ashmun Tanah, martyr 3. Yuhannis, martyr
11	4	17	1. Moses, bishop of Ausim 2. Ptolemaeus
12	5	18	1. Commemoration of the archangel Michael 2. Enthronement of Saint Constantine
13	6	19	1. Transfiguration of Christ
14	7	20	1. Commemoration of the great miracle performed by God at the time of Theophilus, twenty-third patriarch
15	8	21	1. Marina
16	9	22	1. Assumption of the Holy Virgin Mary
17	10	23	1. James the Soldier, martyr
18	11	24	1. Alexander, patriarch of Constantinople 3. Eudemon of Armant, martyr
19	12	25	1. Return of the relics of Saint Macarius to his monastery in Scetis
20	13	26	1. The seven sleepers of Ephesus
21	14	27	1. Monthly commemoration of the Holy Virgin Mary 2. Eirene

Coptic	Julian	Gregorian	Commemorations
22	15	28	1. Micah, prophet
			2. Hadid of Giza, martyr
23	16	29	1. The thirty thousand martyrs of Alexandria
			2. Damianus of Antioch, martyr
24	17	30	1. Takla Haymanot
			2. Thomas, bishop of Mar'ash
25	18	31	1. Besarion, disciple of Saint Antony
			2. Macarius III, 114th patriarch
		September	
26	19	1	1. Moses and his sister Sarah
			2. Agapius the Soldier and his sister Thacla, martyrs
			3. Verena of the Theban Legion
			4. Martyrs of Naqlun
27	20	2	1. Benjamin and Eudoxia, martyrs
			2. Mary the Armenian, new martyr
28	21	3	1. Abraham, Isaac, and Jacob
			2. Assumption of Isaac, son of Abraham
			3. Assumption of Jacob
29	22	4	1. Athanasius the Bishop, Gerasimus, and Theodotus, martyrs
			2. The arrival of the relics of Saint John the Short in the Desert of Scetis
			3. Nativity of Jesus Christ
30 Nasi	23	5	1. Malachi, prophet
1	24	6	1. Eutychius, one of the seventy disciples
			2. Bishoi of Antioch, martyr
2	25	7	1. Titus the Apostle
			2. Isaiah, brother of Apa Hor, martyr
3	26	8	1. Raphael, archangel.
			2. Andrianus, martyr
			3. John XIV, ninety-sixth patriarch
4	27	9	1. Poemen, hermit
			2. Liberius, pope of Rome.
			3. Inianamon
5	28	10	1. James, bishop of Cairo
			2. Amos, prophet.
			3. Barsum the Naked
			4. John XV, ninety-ninth patriarch
6	29	11	1. Thanksgiving to God the Exalted

APPENDIX D
The Relics of Coptic Saints

The first extensive list of the relics in the Coptic churches in Egypt was established in the latter part of the eleventh century by Mawhub ibn al-Mufarrig al-Iskandarani, a deacon in Alexandria who visited many churches in Egypt. His long list of relics appears in the biography of Cyril II (1078–92), the sixty-seventh patriarch of Alexandria.

Approximately 120 years later, during the patriarchate of John VI (1189–1216), Abu al-Makarim, known as Abu Salih the Armenian, wrote his famous study on the churches and monasteries of Egypt, in which he provides a great deal of information on the relics venerated in those Coptic churches that he describes.

The third medieval source that contributes to our knowledge of relics in the Coptic churches is the Arabic synaxarion of the Coptic Church, the first recension of which is attributed to Peter Severus al-Gamil, bishop of Malig (twelfth–thirteenth centuries), and the second to Michael, bishop of Atrib and Malig (1243–47).

The following inventory does not claim to be a complete listing of all the relics in Egypt. While I have visited a large number of Coptic churches in the Nile Delta, the Nile Valley, and in Cairo, as well as all the Coptic monasteries in the Eastern and Western Deserts, I must admit that I was unable to visit all of the approximately one thousand Coptic churches in Egypt. At the same time, it can be justifiably assumed that the following inventory includes the majority of the relics in the Coptic churches in Egypt.

'Abd al-Masih al-Makari al-Manahri (Baramuda 6/April 14)

Abuna 'Abd al-Masih (1892–1963) was widely venerated as a wonderworker by the Copts and Muslims around Minya and Maghagha. His monastic garments are venerated in the Church of the Holy Virgin in Manahra.

Abra'am of the Fayyum (Ba'una 3/June 10)

The relics of Anba Abra'am, bishop of the Fayyum (1829–1914), reposed under the southern altar in the Church of Saint Mercurius, Dair al-'Azab, Fayyum. On March 6, 1987 they were transferred to a special mausoleum east of the church in Dair al-'Azab.

Aesculapius and Dioscorus (Tuba 1/January 9)

The relics of these fourth-century ascetes and martyrs of Akhmim repose in the Cathedral of Saint Mark in Alexandria, the Church of Saint Shenuda in Old Cairo, and the Church of the Holy Virgin, Shentana al-Hagar.

Anianus (Hatur 20/November 29)

The relics of the second patriarch (d.83) repose in the Cathedral of Saint Mark in Alexandria.

Antony the Great (Tuba 22/January 30)

The Coptic Synaxarion informs us that the body of Saint Antony was buried in a place made known only to Saints Athanasius and Sarapion. Mawhub did not mention the relics of Saint Antony, though Abu al-Makarim states that "the pure body lies at his monastery, buried in his cave in which he used to pray; the body is walled up within." At the time of Mark III (1166–89), the seventy-third patriarch of Alexandria, the relics of Saint Antony were still believed to be in the Monastery of Saint Antony near Itfih. Mark ibn al-Qanbar was taken to this monastery, where he was required to swear upon the body of Saint Antony that he would not return to his former ways of sin. On the other hand, the relics of Saint Antony were also believed to have been in Constantinople. On his return from a pilgrimage to Jerusalem, Count Jocelin of Dauphiné, France, stopped in Constantinople, where he received authorization from the emperor to translate the relics to his property at La Motte Saint-Didier near Vienne in Dauphiné. They remained there some time, and when about the year 1090 a terrible epidemic known as 'Saint Antony's Fire' spread throughout the West of Europe, the belief was cherished that the relics had the power to deliver the sick. The Church of Saint Antony in Vienne, however, cannot claim to possess all the relics of the hermit. In 1231, Saint Antony's arm arrived from Constantinople in Bruges, which explains the veneration of the saint in Flanders. Tournay, Antwerp, and Arles also came to possess several relics. The cilice, or hair shirt, of the hermit is shown in Rome, and his beard is found in the Church of Saint Cunibert in Cologne, where once a year some miraculous manifestations are observed. There are no relics of Saint Antony in the Monastery of Saint Antony.

Athanasius (Bashans 7/May 15)

Athanasius was a fourth-century church father and theologian and the twentieth patriarch of the See of Alexandria. Some of his relics were translated from Rome to Cairo in May 1973. They repose in the Cathedral of Saint Mark in 'Abbasiya and in the Cathedral of Damanhur.

Bahnam (Kiyahk 14/December 23)

In the Church of Saint Menas, Dair Mari Mina, Fumm al-Khalig, Cairo, to the left of the screen of the central sanctuary, is a shrine with three bolsters. The bolster in the center contains the relics of Saint Bahnam.

Apa Bane (Amshir 25/February 4)

In 1992 the relics of Apa Bane (Abu Fana, fourth century) were discovered by an international team of archaeologists at the site of Abu Fana. They repose now in the Cathedral of Mallawi.

Barbara (Kiyahk 8/December 17)

The Coptic Synaxarion states that the relics of Saint Barbara are preserved in the Church of Saint Cyrus (Abu Qir) in Cairo, although for some time, they were in a church outside the town of Ghalalya. Mawhub saw the relics in Cairo. The Church of Saint Barbara, Old Cairo, may have been built to receive her relics. Also, in the Church of the Holy Virgin, Harat al-Rum, Cairo, on the north wall beneath the icon of Saint Marina is a bolster with some of the relics of Saint Barbara.

Barsum the Naked (Nasi 5/September 10)

For twenty years he lived in the dark crypt of the Church of Saint Mercurius, Old Cairo. Later he was sent to the Monastery of Shahran at Ma'sara, where he dwelt on a heap of dust and ashes. Many miracles are recorded of him. He died in 1317. His relics repose in the Church of Saint Barsum the Naked at Ma'sara.

Bartholomew (Tut 1/September 11)

According to Coptic and Ethiopian tradition, Saint Bartholomew the Apostle preached in the western oases, where he suffered martyrdom. Mawhub saw his relics in the Monastery of Saint Shenute in Suhag, which is also substantiated by Abu al-Makarim. Some other relics of Saint Bartholomew were preserved in the Church of Karbil in the oasis of al-Bahnasa. The relics of Saint Bartholomew have now disappeared.

Bashnuna (Bashans 24/June 1)

In the conflicts between Shawar, the governor of Upper Egypt, and the Lakhmi Arab Dirgham in 1164, the monk Bashnuna suffered martyrdom. His relics were transferred to the Church of Saints Sergius and Bacchus, Old Cairo. On April 25, 1991, during the restorations of the sanctuary the relics were discovered underneath the *ambon*.

Besa (Misra 6/August 12)

He was a disciple of Saint Shenute and served as his successor in the White Monastery at Suhag. Some of his relics repose in the Church of Saint Shenuda, Old Cairo.

Bisada (Tuba 24/February 1)

Bisada married the daughter of the emperor Numerian. He suffered martyrdom during the Diocletian persecution in the third and fourth centuries. His relics together with those of his brother and sister repose in a small chamber in the Church of Saint Bisada, al-Abaiwa Sharq, south of Suhag, and in the Church of Saint Misael, Monastery of Saint Samuel, Qalamun.

Bishoi (Abib 8/July 15)

According to the Coptic Synaxarion, Saint Bishoi died in the vicinity of

Antinoe. The first translation of his relics occurred soon after his death, when they were taken to the Monastery of Saint Shenute in Antinoe. During the patriarchate of Joseph (831–49), the relics of Saint Bishoi were translated again to the Monastery of Saint Bishoi in Wadi al-Natrun.

Cassius and Florentius

These two fourth-century Theban soldiers suffered martyrdom in the Rhine Valley at Bonn. Some of their relics were translated from Bonn to Cairo on November 5, 1991, where they repose in the pontifical chapel.

Cosmas and Damian (Hatur 22/December 1)

Relics of these two unmercenary physicians of the fourth century repose in their church in Manyal Shiha in the diocese of Giza.

Cyriacus (Abib 15/July 22)

Some relics of Saint Cyriacus were kept in the tenth-century feretory of the Monastery of the Syrians in Wadi al-Natrun. They are now preserved in a bolster together with other relics. I have seen the bolster in the Church of the Forty Martyrs of Sebaste in the Monastery of the Syrians.

Cyrus (Ba'una 14/June 21)

The relics of Saint Cyrus were placed in the Church of Saint Mark south of Alexandria, but Saint Cyril removed them to the Church of Saint Mark near the seashore, and there built a church in honor of the relics. The relics of Saint Cyrus are now in Cairo:

a) the Church of Saints Cyrus and John, Dair Tadrus, Old Cairo. On the south wall of the church is a shelf with two bolsters, the larger one of which contains some relics of Saint Cyrus.

b) the Church of Saint Barbara, Old Cairo. In the northern transept of the church is a table with a bolster containing some relics of Saint Cyrus.

Damiana (Bashans 12/May 20)

The tomb of Saint Damiana is situated in the western part of the old church of Saint Damiana in the Monastery of Saint Damiana near Bilqas in the Nile Delta. Some relics of the saint are in Cairo:

a) the al-Mu'allaqa Church of the Holy Virgin, Old Cairo
b) the Church of the Holy Virgin, Qasriyat al-Rihan, Old Cairo
c) the Church of Saint Barbara, Old Cairo
d) the Church of the Holy Virgin, Harat Zuwayla, Cairo
e) the Church of the Holy Virgin by the Steps of Babylon, Old Cairo

Dioscorus (Tut 7/September 17)

Some relics of Saint Dioscorus the patriarch have been kept in the tenth-century feretory of the Monastery of the Syrians in Wadi al-Natrun. They are now preserved in a bolster together with other relics.

Elisha (Ba'una 20/June 27)

Relics of the ninth-century-B.C. Old Testament prophet were discovered in the sanctuary of Benjamin in the Monastery of Saint Macarius in Lent 1976. They still repose there.

Ephraem Syrus (Abib 15/July 22)

The bolster containing some of the relics of Saint Ephraem the Syrian is in a feretory on the north wall of the choir of the Church of Saint Bishoi in the Monastery of Saint Bishoi in Wadi al-Natrun.

George (Baramuda 23/May 1)

Saint George is the most popular saint in Egypt. In Coptic churches I have seen eighteen bolsters containing relics of Saint George:

- a) the al-Mu'allaqa Church of the Holy Virgin, Old Cairo
- b) the Church of Saint Barbara, Old Cairo
- c) the Church of Saint George, Old Cairo
- d) the Church of the Holy Virgin, Qasriyat al-Rihan, Old Cairo
- e) the Shrine of Saint George in the Convent of Saint George, Old Cairo. The small bolster with the alleged right arm of the saint is placed on a table beneath the icon of Saint George in the inner chamber.
- f) the Church of Saint Theodore the Oriental, Dair Tadrus, Old Cairo
- g) the Church of the Holy Virgin, al-Damshiriya, Old Cairo
- h) the upper Church of Saint George, Dair Mari Mina, Fumm al-Khalig, Cairo
- i) the Church of the Holy Virgin, Harat Zuwayla, Cairo
- j) the upper Church of Saint George, Harat Zuwayla, Cairo
- k) the upper Church of Saint George, Harat al-Rum, Cairo
- l) Church of the Holy Virgin, Harat al-Rum, Cairo
- m) the Convent of Saint Theodore, Harat al-Rum, Cairo
- n) the Church of Saint George at Mit Damsis, Mit Ghamr, Nile Delta
- o) the Church of Saint George, Biba, south of Beni Suef

George the New Martyr (Ba'una 19/June 26)

As a convert from Islam, George was beheaded in front of the Church of Saint Michael at Damira in 959. His relics repose in the Church of Apa Nub in Sammanud.

Isaac of Tiphre (Bashans 6/May 14)

Mawhub mentioned that in Difra (Tiphre) there are the relics of Abu Ishaq (Abba Isaac) the martyr, and Abu al-Makarim stated that at al-Qays there is a church that contains the body of the martyr Saint Isaac. In the reliquary in al-Mu'allaqa Church, Old Cairo, there is one bolster containing some of the relics of Saint Isaac of Tiphre.

Isidore (Ba'una 24/July 1)

Isidore the Presbyter took Moses the Black to Saint Macarius. His relics repose with those of Saint Moses the Robber or Moses the Black in the Monastery of the Romans.

Iskhiron of Qallin (Ba'una 7/June 14)

On Tuba 7, A.M. 1049 (January 2, A.D. 1333) the relics of Saint Iskhiron of Qallin were translated from the Church of Our Lady the Virgin in the Monastery of Saint Samuel at al-Qalamun to the al-Mu'allaqa Church of the Holy Virgin in Old Cairo, and from there to the Monastery of Saint Bishoi in Wadi al-Natrun. Although there is a church in the Monastery of Saint Bishoi dedicated to Saint Iskhiron of Qallin, the relics of the saint are not there.

Some of the relics of Saint Iskhiron of Qallin are in the reliquary in the al-Mu'allaqa Church of the Holy Virgin in Old Cairo. And on the north wall of the Church of the Holy Virgin, Harat al-Rum, Cairo, there is a shelf beneath the icon of Saint Mark. On this shelf is a small bolster with some of the relics of Saint Iskhiron of Qallin.

James the Sawn-Asunder (Hatur 27/December 6)

According to the Coptic Synaxarion, the relics of Saint James the Sawn-Asunder used to be at al-Bahnasa in the province of Beni Suef. Mawhub saw some of the relics of the saint in Wadi al-Natrun. They were kept in the tenth-century feretory of the Monastery of the Syrians in Wadi al-Natrun, and they are now preserved there in a bolster together with other relics.

John the Baptist (Tut 2/September 12)

In Lent 1976, relics of the precursor of Jesus Christ were discovered in the sanctuary of Benjamin in the Monastery of Saint Macarius, where they now repose.

John Kame (Kiyahk 25/January 3)

When Mawhub visited the churches and monasteries in 1088, he saw the relics of Saint John Kame in the Monastery of Saint John Kame in Wadi al-Natrun. In the latter part of the fifteenth century, after the destruction of the monastery, the monks translated the relics of their patron saint to the Monastery of the Syrians in Wadi al-Natrun.

John the Short (Baba 20/October 30)

Saint John the Short (Colobos), a desert father of Wadi al-Natrun, died in the Monastery of Saint Antony. In the eighth century, monks of the Monastery of Saint Macarius stole the relics of Saint John the Short and transferred them to their monastery. Eventually they were taken to the Monastery of Saint John the Short. When the latter fell into ruin, the relics were taken to the Monastery of Saint Macarius. Some relics of Saint John the Short repose in the Monastery of the Syrians.

John, the companion of Saint Cyrus (Ba'una 14/June 21)

The relics of Saint John were placed with those of Saint Cyrus in the Church of Saint Mark south of Alexandria, but Saint Cyril removed them to the

Church of Saint Mark near the seashore. The relics of Saint John are now in Cairo:

a) the Church of Saints Cyrus and John, Dair Tadrus, Old Cairo
b) the Church of Saint Barbara, Old Cairo.

Julietta (Abib 15/July 22)

Some relics of Saint Julietta were kept in the tenth-century feretory of the Monastery of the Syrians in Wadi al-Natrun. They are now there preserved in a bolster together with other relics.

Julius of Aqfahs (Tut 22/October 2)

Author of a Coptic martyrology, Julius suffered martyrdom in Sammanud during the Diocletian persecution. His relics were discovered in 1993 and identified through a vision of a monk. They repose in the Church of Saint Shenuda, Old Cairo.

Justus (Tuba 10/January 18)

The relics of Saint Justus repose in the smaller of the two bolsters on the north wall of the new Church of Saint Samuel in the Monastery of Saint Samuel at al-Qalamun.

Klog (Ba'una 20/June 17)

Apa Klog (Colluthus), a fourth-century physician, ascete, and priest, suffered martyrdom during the Diocletian persecution. His relics repose in the Church of Apa Klog in al-Fant, south of Beni Suef.

Macarius the Great (Baramhat 27/April 5)

Saint Macarius had bidden his disciples to hide his body. During the patriarchate of John IV (777–99) the relics of Saint Macarius were returned to Wadi al-Natrun.

In the latter part of the ninth century, the caliph Khumarawayh (881–96) visited the Church of Saint Macarius and saw the body of Saint Macarius.

The relics of Saint Macarius the Great are now preserved in a long bolster in the reliquary, which stands in the southern section of the choir of the Church of Saint Macarius in the Monastery of Saint Macarius. Whenever the monks move to the Church of the Forty-Nine Martyrs for the celebration of the Divine Liturgy, they carry these relics with them and place them into the reliquary on the north side of the choir of said church.

Macarius of Alexandria (Bashans 6/May 14)

Mawhub mentioned that in the Monasteries of Wadi Habib (Wadi al-Natrun) there are the relics of the three Macarii. One of these undoubtedly was Saint Macarius of Alexandria, whose relics are preserved in a long bolster in the same reliquary, which also contains the relics of Saint Macarius of Tkow. The three bolsters with the relics of the three Macarii have the same unusual length.

Macarius of Tkow (Baba 27/November 6)

The relics of this saint repose with those of the other two Macarii in the reliquary in the Church of Saint Macarius in the Monastery of Saint Macarius in Wadi al-Natrun.

Marina (Abib 23/July 30)

On Hatur 23 (December 2), the Coptic Church commemorates the translation of the relics of Saint Marina to the Church of the Holy Virgin in the Harat al-Rum in Cairo. Her relics can also be found at the Convent of Saint Theodore, Harat al-Rum, Cairo.

Mary Magdalene (Abib 28/August 4)

Some of the hair of Saint Mary Magdalene, with which she wiped the feet of Christ, was kept in the tenth-century feretory of the Monastery of the Syrians in Wadi al-Natrun. It is now preserved in a bolster together with other relics.

Maurice (Tut 12/September 22)

Maurice was the commander of the Theban Legion who suffered martyrdom in the fourth century at Agaunum, the present St. Moritz, Switzerland. Some of his relics were translated from the Benedictine Abbey of Saint Maurice, Tholey, Saar, Germany, to Cairo on April 14, 1989. They repose in the pontifical chapel in 'Abbasiya.

Maximus and Domitius (Tuba 17/January 25)

The relics of these two sons of Valentinian are claimed by the monks of the Monastery of the Romans (Dair al-Baramus).

Mikha'il al-Buhayri

Next to Anba Abra'am of the Fayyum (1847–1923), Saint Mikha'il is the most popular saint among the monks of Dair al-Muharraq. On February 23, 1991 his relics were transferred from their location underneath the central altar of the Church of Saint George to a new reliquary. Some relics of Mikha'il repose in the Church of the Holy Virgin, Dair al-'Azab, Fayyum, the Church of Saint George, Ishnin al-Nasara, and in the Monastery of Saint Menas, Maryut.

Moses the Robber (Ba'una 24/July 1)

Mawhub mentioned the relics of Saint Moses, which he saw in Wadi al-Natrun. Standing at the north wall of the choir of the Church of the Holy Virgin in the Monastery of the Romans is a new (1957) ivory-inlaid reliquary with glass windows, which contains the relics of Saint Moses the Robber and those of Saint Isidore. Some of the relics of Saint Moses the Robber repose in the reliquary in the Monastery of the Syrians in Wadi al-Natrun and in the Church of Apa Nub, Sammanud.

Menas (Hatur 15/November 24)

In the latter part of the third century, the relics of Saint Menas were translated from Cotyaeum, the modern Kütahya southwest of Eskisehir in Anatolia, to Egypt. Once in Egypt, at the first stopping place in Maryut, the camel carrying the saint's body refused to advance any further, and thus Saint Menas was buried in the Western Desert in the vicinity of Lake Mareotis.

The translation of the relics of Saint Menas from the Desert of Mareotis to his church in Old Cairo occured during the patriarchate of Benjamin II (1327–39), the eighty-second patriarch of Alexandria. The relics remained in the Church of Saint Menas of Dair Mari Mina in Fumm al-Khalig, Cairo, until February 15, 1962, when most of the relics were returned to the Desert of Mareotis. Here Cyril VI, the 116th patriarch of Alexandria, had built a new Monastery of Saint Menas. Some of the relics of Saint Menas, however, are still claimed by at least four churches in Cairo:

    a) the Church of Saint Menas, Dair Mari Mina, Fumm al-Khalig, Cairo
    b) the Church of the Holy Virgin, al-Damshiriya, Old Cairo
    c) the Church of the Holy Virgin, Harat al-Rum, Cairo
    d) the Church of Saint Shenuda, Old Cairo

Mercurius (Hatur 25/December 4)

According to the Coptic Synaxarion, the relics of Saint Mercurius were translated to the Church of Saint Mercurius in Old Cairo during the patriarchate of John VI (1189–1216), the seventy-fourth patriarch of Alexandria, where there is now in the southern nave the shrine of Saint Mercurius. His relics can also be found in:

    a) the Church of the Holy Virgin, Qasriyat al-Rihan, Old Cairo
    b) the Church of the Holy Virgin, al-Damshiriya, Old Cairo
    c) the Church of Saint Mercurius, Harat Zuwayla, Cairo
    d) the Church of Saint George, Harat al-Rum, Cairo
    e) the Church of Saint Mercurius, Tammua
    f) the Church of Saint Mercurius, Meir, Asyut Province

The Naqlun Martyrs (Misra 26/September 1)

In the summer of 1991 the skeletons of twelve persons were discovered in the vicinity of the Monastery of Saint Gabriel, Naqlun, al-Fayyum. They had been tortured and assassinated, though circumstances and dates are not known. The Coptic Church of the Fayyum declared them martyrs, and their relics repose in three parish churches in the Fayyum, in Dair al-'Azab, and in the Monastery of Saint Gabriel. Large numbers of fragments of these persons were distributed among the Coptic dioceses in Egypt and in Coptic churches in the emigration.

Nub (Abib 24/July 31)

A native of Nahisa, Apa Nub suffered martyrdom as a youth. His relics repose in the Church of Apa Nub in Sammanud, Sharqiya.

Onuphrius (Hatur 16/November 25)

An ascete of the inner desert, he was discovered by Paphnutius. His relics repose in the Convent of Saint Theodore in the Harat al-Rum, Cairo.

Paul of Tammua (Baba 7/October 17)

The relics of Saint Paul of Tammua are in the feretory on the north wall of the choir of the Church of Saint Bishoi in the Monastery of Saint Bishoi in Wadi al-Natrun.

Paul the Theban (Amshir 2/February 9)

The relics of Saint Paul the Theban are kept in the new marble feretory on the south wall of the subterranean Church of Saint Paul in the Monastery of Saint Paul the Theban in the Eastern Desert.

Peter the Martyr (Hatur 29/December 8)

Some of his relics repose in the Church of Apa Nub, Sammanud.

Rebecca and her children (Tut 7/September 17)

In the southern chamber (at one time an altar room) of the Church of Saint Rebecca (Sitt Rifqa) at Sumbat near Mit Damsis in the Nile Delta are the relics of Saint Rebecca and her five children. The relics were translated to Sumbat during the thirteenth century.

Ruwais (Baba 21/October 31)

In the southern sanctuary of the Church of Saint Ruwais (Anba Farig) in 'Abbassiya, Cairo, there is an ornamented bolster containing the forearm and the hand of the saint, who suffered martyrdom in 1404. On the north wall of the Church of the Holy Virgin in Harat al-Rum, Cairo, beneath the icon of Saints Abraham, Isaac, and James, there is a bolster with some of the relics of Saint Ruwais.

Samuel of al-Qalamun (Kiyahk 8/December 17)

The relics of Saint Samuel are preserved in the large bolster on the north wall of the new Church of Saint Samuel in the Monastery of Saint Samuel at al-Qalamun.

Sarabamun of Nikiu (Hatur 28/December 7)

The relics of Saint Sarabamun are preserved in a bolster in the Church of Saint Sarabamun in the village of al-Batanun near Shibin al-Kom in the Province of Minufiya. Some relics of the saint are also in one of the five small bolsters in the Shrine of the Holy Virgin in the Church of the Holy Virgin, Qasriyat al-Rihan, Old Cairo.

Salib (Kiyahk 3/December 12)

The relics of this new martyr repose in the Church of the Holy Virgin in Shentana al-Hagar.

Sarah (Kiyahk 14/December 23)

In the Church of Saint Menas, Dair Mari Mina, Fumm al-Khalig, Cairo, to the left of the *haikal* screen of the central sanctuary, there is a shrine with three bolsters, the smallest of which contains some of the relics of Saint Sarah.

Sergius and Bacchus (Baba 4/October 14 and Baba 10/October 20)

According to the Coptic Synaxarion, the bodies of Saints Sergius and Bacchus were buried in the Fort of Rusafa, thirteen kilometers from Tetrapyrgium in Syria. Some of the relics of the two saints are in two bolsters, a large one and a smaller one, which are kept in the sanctuary of the Church of Saints Sergius and Bacchus in Old Cairo.

Severus of Antioch (Amshir 14/February 21)

The Coptic Synaxarion commemorates the translation of the relics of Saint Severus from Sakha to the Monastery of al-Zugag (the Ennaton), west of Alexandria. Some of the relics of Saint Severus were kept in the tenth-century feretory of the Monastery of the Syrians in Wadi al-Natrun. They are now preserved there in a bolster together with other relics.

Shenute (Abib 7/July 14)

The relics of Saint Shenute reposed in the Monastery of Saint Shenute in Upper Egypt until the invasion of Egypt by Shirkuh, who broke open the chest that contained them. The body of the saint was taken out and concealed in the ground in an unconsecrated chamber near the altar.

Some of the relics of the saint are in a bolster beneath an icon of Saints Shenute and Besa in the Church of Saint Shenute, Dair Abu Saifain, Old Cairo.

Sidhum Bishai (Baramhat 17/March 26)

Sidhum Bishai (1804–44) served as clerk at the port of Damietta when a Muslim-instigated revolt erupted. Accused of insulting Islam, Sidhum Bishai suffered martyrdom in Midan Mikha'il Surur in Damietta on March 26, 1844. His incorruptible body reposes in the Church of the Holy Virgin in Damietta.

Simeon the Tanner (Abib 28/August 4)

During the reign of al-Mu'izz (tenth century) Saint Simeon (Sama'an) advised Pope Abraham the Syrian to pray that the mountain of Muqattam be moved to its present location (Matt. 17:20). His relics were discovered in the Church of the Holy Virgin by the Steps of Babylon on August 4, 1991. Some were kept there, and some were transferred to the al-Mu'allaqa Church of the Holy Virgin and the Church of Simeon the Tanner in Muqattam.

Takla Haymanot (Misra 24/August 30)

In the southern section of the narthex of the Church of Saint Barbara in Old Cairo, there is a bolster with some relics, which I was repeatedly told are those of Saint Takla Haymanot the Ethiopian.

Theodore Stratelates (Abib 20/July 27)

His relics repose in:

a) the Church of the Holy Virgin, Harat al-Rum, Cairo
b) the Church of the Holy Virgin, Harat Zuwayla, Cairo
c) the Convent of Saint Theodore, Harat al-Rum, Cairo

In the Shrine of Saint Theodore are four bolsters, two of which contain some of the relics of Saint Theodore.

Theodore the Oriental (Tuba 12/January 20)

In the Church of Saint Theodore the Oriental, Dair Tadrus, Old Cairo, in the shrine on the north wall of the *gynaikion*, there is a bolster beneath the icon of Saint Theodore with some of his relics. Some of the relics of Saint Theodore also repose in the bolster together with other relics in the Church of the Forty Martyrs of Sebaste in the Monastery of the Syrians, Wadi al-Natrun.

Verena (Misra 26/September 1)

Verena of Thebes accompanied the Theban Legion and suffered martyrdom in the fourth century in Zurzach, Switzerland. Some of her relics were transferred in October 1986 from Zurzach to Cairo, where they repose in the pontifical chapel in 'Abbasiya.

Victor Stratelates (Baramuda 27/May 4)

His relics repose in the Church of the Holy Virgin al-Damshiriya, Old Cairo.

Yusab ibn al-Abahh (Tuba 16/January 24)

The relics of this eminent theologian and bishop of Girga and Akhmim (d. 1826) repose in the Church of the Holy Apostles, Monastery of Saint Antony, Red Sea.

Yustus al-Antuni (Kiyahk 8/December 17)

Born as Nagib M. Shihata (1910–76) in Sarawa, he joined the Monastery of Saint Antony in 1941. He had the charismatic gifts of prophecy and excelled in asceticism. His relics repose in the passage between the Churches of the Holy Apostles and Saint Antony in the Monastery of Saint Antony, Red Sea.

Bibliography

General History

Abudacnus, Josephus. *Historia Jacobitarum seu Coptorum in Aegypto, Lybia, Nubia, Aethiopia tota, & parte Cypri insulae habitantium.* Lubecae, 1733.

Amélineau, Emile Clement. *La Géographie de l'Egypte à l'époque copte.* Paris, 1893.

Atiya, Aziz S. *The Crusade in the Later Middle Ages.* London, 1938.

————. *A History of Eastern Christianity.* London, 1968.

Badawy, Alexandre. *Guide de l'Egypte chrétienne.* Cairo, n.d.

Basset, René. "Le synaxaire arabe jacobite." Parts 1–5. *Patrologia Orientalis* 1, 3, 11, 16, 17.

Bell, H. Idris. *Egypt from Alexander the Great to the Arab Conquest: A Study in the Diffusion and Decay of Hellenism.* Oxford, 1948.

Beth, Karl. *Die Orientalische Christenheit der Mittelmeerländer.* Berlin, 1902.

Brunner-Traut, Emma. *Die Kopten: Leben und Lehre der frühen Christen in Ägypten.* Cologne, 1982.

Burmester, O.H.E. Khs-. *Notice on the Map of Christian Egypt.* Cairo, 1955.

Burmester, O.H.E. Khs-. *The Egyptian or Coptic Church: A Detailed Description of Her Liturgical Services and the Rites and Ceremonies Observed in the Administration of Her Sacraments.* Cairo, 1967.

Burmester, O.H.E.Khs-, and Yassa 'Abd al-Masih. *A History of the Patriarchs of the Egyptian Church.* Vol. 2:1. Cairo, 1943.

Burmester, O.H.E. Khs-, A.S. Atiya, and Yassa 'Abd al-Masih. *History of the Patriarchs of the Egyptian Church.* Vol. 2:2–3. Cairo, 1948–59.

Burmester, O.H.E. Khs-, and Antoine Khater. *History of the Patriarchs of the Egyptian Church.* Vol. 3:1–3. Cairo, 1968–70.

Butcher, Edith Louisa. *The Story of the Church of Egypt.* 2 vols. London, 1897.

Butler, Alfred J. *The Arab Conquest of Egypt and the Last Thirty Years of the Roman Dominion.* Oxford, 1902.

Calderini, Aristide. *Dizionario dei nomi geografici e topografici dell'Egitto greco-romano.* Cairo, 1935.

Cramer, Maria. *Das Christlich-koptische Ägypten einst und heute: eine Orientierung.* Wiesbaden, 1959.

Evagrius, Scholasticus. *The History of the Church from A.D. 431 to A.D. 594.* London, 1854.

Fowler, Montagne. *Christian Egypt: Past, Present, and Future.* London, 1902.

Gregorius, Bishop, ed. *Saint Mark and the Coptic Church.* Cairo, 1968.

Hahn-Hahn, Ida Marie. *Lives of the Fathers of the Desert.* London, 1867.

Heckel, Andreas. *Die Kirche von Ägypten.* Strassburg, 1918.

Ibn al-Muqaffa', Sawirus. "The History of the Patriarchs," ed. and trans. B.T.A. Evetts. *Patrologia Orientalis* 2, 5, 10.

Jullien, Michel. *L'Egypte: Souvenirs bibliques et chrétiens.* Lille, 1891.

Kadloubovsky, E., and G.E.H. Palmer. *Early Fathers from the Philokalia.* London, 1954.

Karas, Shawky F. *The Copts since the Arab Invasion: Strangers in Their Land.* Jersey City, NJ, 1986.

Kolta, Kamal Sabri. *Christentum im Land der Pharaonen.* Munich, 1985.

———. *Von Echnaton zu Jesus.* Munich, 1993.

Lane, Edward William. *The Manners and Customs of the Modern Egyptians.* London, 1908.

Lane-Poole, Stanley. *Cairo: Sketches of Its History, Monuments, and Social Life.* London, 1898.

———. *A History of Egypt in the Middle Ages.* London, 1901.

Lansing, Gulian. *Egypt's Princess: A Narrative of Missionary Labour in the Valley of the Nile.* Philadelphia, 1864.

Leeder, S.H. *The Modern Sons of the Pharoahs.* London, 1918.

Malan, S.C. (transl.) *A Short History of the Copts and Their Church.* London, 1873.

el-Masri, Iris Habib. *The Story of the Copts.* Cairo, 1978.

Meinardus, Otto. *Christian Egypt: Ancient and Modern.* Cairo, 1977.

———. *Christian Egypt: Faith and Life.* Cairo, 1970.

Mingana, Alphonse. "The Vision of Theophilus, or the Book of the Flight of the Holy Family into Egypt." *Bulletin of the John Rylands Library* (Manchester) 13, no. 2 (1929): 383–425.

Motzki, Harald. *Dimma und Egalité: Die nichtmuslimischen Minderheiten Ägyptens in der zweiten Hälfte des 18. Jahrhunderts und die Expedition Bonapartes.* Bonn, 1979.

Neale, John Mason. *A History of the Holy Eastern Church.* 2 vols. London, 1847.

O'Leary, de Lacy. *The Saints of Egypt.* New York, 1937.

Palladius. *The Paradise or Garden of the Holy Fathers, being Histories of the Anchorites Recluses Monks Coenobites and Ascetic Fathers of the Desert of Egypt between A.D. 250 and 400 circiter compiled by Athanasius Archbishop of Alexandria: Palladius Bishop of Helenopolis, Saint Jerome and others,* trans. E.A.W. Budge. London, 1907.

Partrick, T. H. *Traditional Egyptian Christianity: A History of the Coptic Orthodox Church.* Greensboro, NC, 1996.

Philostorgius. *The Ecclesiastical History.* trans. E. Wilford, London, 1875.

Quatremère, M. *Memoires géographiques et historiques sur l'Egypte.* Paris, 1811.

Reiss, Wolfram. *Erneuerung in der koptisch-orthodoxen Kirche. Die Geschichte der koptisch-orthodoxen Sonntagsschulbewegung, etc.* Hamburg, 1998.

Renaudotius, Eusebius. *Historia Patriarcharum Alexandrinorum Jacobitarum ab Marco usque ad finem saeculi XIII.* Paris, 1713.

Richter, Julius. *A History of Protestant Missions in the Near East.* Edinburgh, 1910.

Rocco da Cesinale. *Storia delle Missioni dei Cappucini.* Vol. 3. Rome, 1873.

Roncaglia, Martiniano. *Histoire de l'Eglise copte.* 3 vols. Beirut, 1966–69.

Sharpe, Samuel. *The History of Egypt From the Earliest Times Till the Conquest by the Arabs.* 2 vols. London, 1876.

Sobhy, George. "Education in Egypt during the Christian Period and among the Copts." *Bulletin de la Societé d'Archéologie Copte* 9 (1943): 104–22.

Socrates. *The Ecclesiastical History of Socrates.* London, 1914.

Spuler, Bertold. *Die Morgenländischen Kirchen.* Leiden, 1961.

Stock, Eugene. *The History of the Church Missionary Society.* 3 vols. London, 1910.

Strothmann, R. *Die Koptische Kirche in der Neuzeit.* Tübingen, 1932.

Theodoret. *History of the Church from A.D. 322 to A.D. 427.* London, 1854.

Van Doorn-Harder and Karin-Vogt, eds. *Between Desert and City: The Coptic Orthodox Church Today.* Oslo, 1997.

Vansleb, J.M.[Johann Michael Wansleben]. *Histoire de l'Eglise d'Alexandrie.* Paris, 1677.

de Vlieger, A. *The Origin and Early History of the Coptic Church.* Lausanne, 1900.

Wadell, Helen. *The Desert Fathers.* London, 1936.

Wakin, Edward. *A Lonely Minority: The Modern Story of Egypt's Copts.* New York, 1963.

Watson, Andrew. *The American Mission in Egypt, 1854–1896.* Pittsburgh, 1904.

Winkler, W. Dietmar. *Koptische Kirche und Reichskirche. Altes Schisma und neuer Dialog.* Innsbruck, 1997.

Worrell, William H. *A Short Account of the Copts.* Ann Arbor, 1945.

Wüstenfeld, Ferdinand. *Makrizi's Geschichte der Copten.* Göttingen, 1845.

———. *Al-Sinaksari: Das Synaxarium, das ist Heiligen-Kalender der coptischen Christen aus dem Arabischen übersetzt.* Gotha, 1879.

Archaeology

Atiya, Aziz S. *The Arabic Manuscripts of Mount Sinai.* Baltimore, 1955.

Cramer, Maria. *Koptische Buchmalerei.* Recklinghausen, 1964.

Doresse, Jean. "Monastères coptes aux environs d'Armant en Thebaide." *Analecta Bollandiana* 67: 327–49.

Drescher, James. *Apa Mena: A Selection of Coptic Texts Relating to Saint Menas.* Cairo, 1946.

Fakhry, Ahmed. *Siwa Oasis: Its History and Antiquities.* Cairo, 1944.

———. "Wadi el Natroun." *Annales du Service des Antiquités d'Egypte* 40: 839–48.

Flury, Samuel. "Die Gipsornamente des Der es Surjani." *Der Islam* 6: 71–87.

Gayet, A. *L'art copte.* Paris, 1902.

Hatch, William Henry Paine. "A Visit to the Coptic convents in Nitria." *American School of Oriental Research Annual* 6 (1924): 93–107.

Hondelink, H., ed. *Coptic Art and Culture.* Cairo, 1990.

Kaufmann, C.M. *Die Ausgrabung der Menas-Heiligtümer in der Mareotiswüste.* Cairo, 1906–1908.

————. *Der Menastempel und die Heiligtumer von Karm Abu Mina in der Mariutwüste: Ein Führer durch die Ausgrabungen der Frankfurter Expedition.* Frankfurt, 1909.

————. *Die Menasstadt und das National-Heiligtum der altchristlichen Ägypter in der Westalexandrinischen Wüste: Ausgrabungen der Frankfurter Expedition am Karm Abu Mena 1905–1907.* Leipzig, 1910.

————. *Die Heilige Stadt der Wüste: Unsere Entdeckungen, Grabungen, und Funde in der altchristlichen Menasstadt und weiteren Kreisen in Wort und Bild geschildert.* Kempt, 1921.

Labib, Pahor. "Fouilles du Musée Copte à Saint-Menas." *Bulletin de l'Institut d'Egypte* 34 (1951–52): 133–138.

Larsow, F., ed. *Die Festbriefe des heiligen Athanasius von Alexandrien (Klöster der Nitrischen Wüste).* Leipzig and Göttingen, 1852.

Lewis, Agnes Smith. "A Visit to the Coptic Monasteries of Egypt." *Cambridge Antiquarian Society* 10 (1898–1900): 210–15.

————. "Hidden Egypt." *Century Magazine* 68 (1904): 745–58.

Moritz, B. *Beitrage zur Geschichte des Sinaiklosters im Mittelalter nach Arabischen Quellen.* Berlin, 1918.

Murray, G.W. "The Christian Settlement at Qattar." *Bulletin de la Société de Géographie d'Egypte* 24: 107–14.

Pauty, Edmond. "L'archéologie copte et l'oeuvre du Comité de Conservation des Monuments de l'Art Arabe, de 1933 à 1935." *Bulletin de la Société d'Archéologie Copte* 7: 81–86.

Platt. *Journal of a Tour through Egypt, the Peninsula of Sinai, and the Holy Land in 1838 and 1839,* 2 vols. London, 1841.

Strzygowsky, Joseph. *Koptische Kunst.* Vienna, 1904.

von Tischendorf, Konstantin. *Travels in the East.* transl. W.E. Schukard. London, 1847.

Tregenza, L.A. *The Red Sea Mountains of Egypt.* London, 1955.

Ward-Perkins, J.B. "The Shrine of Saint Menas." *British School of Archaeology in Rome* 17 (1949).

Wessel, Klaus. *Koptische Kunst. Die Spätantike in Ägypten.* Recklinghausen, 1963.

Wessel, Klaus, ed. *Christentum am Nil.* Recklinghausen, 1964.

Monasticism

Abbott, Nabia. *The Monasteries of the Fayyum.* Chicago, 1937.

Abu Salih. *The Churches and Monasteries of Egypt and Some Neighbouring Countries, attributed to Abu Salih the Armenian,* ed. and trans. B.T.A. Evetts. Oxford, 1895.

Amélineau, Emile Clement. *Histoire des monastères de la Basse-Egypte, vies des Saints Paul, Antoine, Macaire, Maxime et Domèce, et Jean le Nain.* Paris, 1895.

Becquet, T. "Les monastères du Ouadi Natroun." *Irenikon* 12: 351–71.

du Bourguet, Pierre. "Saint-Antoine et Saint-Paul du désert." *Bulletin de la Société Française d'Egyptologie* 7 (June 1951): 41.

Bousset, Wilhelm. "Das Mönchtum der sketischen Wüste." *Kirchengeschichte* 5 (1923): 1–41.

Bremond, Jean. *Pèlerinage au Ouadi Natroun: Une oasis du désert monastique.* n.p., n.d.

———. *Les pères du désert.* 2 vols. Paris, 1927.

Brugsch, Heinrich Karl. *Wanderung nach den Natronklöstern in Ägypten.* Berlin, 1855.

Burmester, O.H.E. Khs-. *A Guide to the Monasteries of Wadi 'n-Natrun.* Cairo, 1955.

Cauwenbergh, Paul V. *Etudes sur les moines d'Egypte depuis le concile de Chalcedoine.* Paris, 1914.

Chauleur, Sylvestre. "Le Culte de Saint Antoine." *Bulletin de l'Institut des Etudes Coptes* (1958): 3–41.

Cheneau, R.P. Paul. *Les saints de l'église.* Jerusalem, 1923.

Chester, Greville J. "Notes on the Coptic Dairs of the Wady Natroun and on the Dair Antonios in the Eastern Desert." *Archaeological Journal* 30 (1873): 105–106.

Curzon, Robert. *Visits to the Monasteries in the Levant.* London, 1847.

Evelyn-White, Hugh G. *The History of the Monasteries of Nitria and of Scetis.* New York, 1932.

———. *The Monasteries of Wadi 'n-Natrun.* New York, 1933.

Fakhry, Ahmed. "The Monastery of Kalamoun." *Annales du Service des Antiquités de l'Egypte* 46 (1947): 63–83.

Falls, J.C. Ewald. "Ein Besuch in den Natronklöstern der sketischen Wüste." *Frankfurter zeitgemässe Broschüren* 25 (1905): 61–85.

Fedden, Henry Romilly. "A Study of the Monastery of Saint Anthony in the Eastern Desert." *University of Egypt Faculty of Arts Bulletin* 5 (1937): 1–60.

Giamberardini, Gabriele. "Il Convento dell'Anba Samuel e i miracoli della Vergine." *La Voce del Nilo* 27, no. 5 (1955): 140–55.

———. *S. Antonio Abate: Astro del deserto.* Cairo, 1957.

Jullien, Michel. *Voyage aux déserts de Scete et de Nitrie.* Lyon, 1882.

———. *Voyage dans le désert de la Basse-Thebaide aux couvents de Saint Antoine et de Saint Paul.* Lyon, 1884.

Kammerer, Albert. "Les couvents coptes du Wadi Natroun." *L'illustration* 21 (March 1925): 264–67.

Keimer, Louis. "Les prosternations pénitentiaires des moines du couvent de Saint Paul dans le désert de l'Est." *Les cahiers coptes* 21 (1965).

Kersting, A.E. "The Coptic Monasteries of Wadi Natrun." *The Bulletin,* July 1949, 9–15.

Lefort, L. T. "Les premiers monastères pachomiens." *Muséon* 52: 9–15.

Leroy, Jules. *Moines et monastères du Proche Orient.* Paris, 1957.

Mackean, W.H. *Christian Monasticism in Egypt.* London, 1920.

Martin, Charles. "Les monastères du Wadi Natroun." *Nouvelle revue theologique* 62 (1935): 113–43, 238–52.

Meinardus, Otto. *The Copts in Jerusalem.* Cairo, 1960.

———. *Monks and Monasteries of the Egyptian Deserts.* Cairo, 1961, 1989, 1992.

Morton, H.V. *Through Lands of the Bible.* London, 1938.

Munier, H. "Les monuments coptes d'après les explorations du Père Michel Jullien." *Bulletin de la Societé d'Archéologie Copte* 6 (1940): 141f.

Piankoff, Alexandre. "Two Descriptions by Russian Travellers of the Monasteries of Saint Antony and Saint Paul." *Bulletin de la Societé Royale de Géographie d'Egypte* 21 (1943): 61–66.

———. "Les peintures de la Petite Chapelle au Monastère de Saint Antoine." *Les cahiers coptes* 12 (1956): 7–26.

Preuschen, Erwin. *Mönchtum und Serapisdienst.* Giessen, 1903.

Queffelec, Henri. *Saint Anthony of the Desert.* New York, 1954.

Rabino, Hyacinth Louis. *Le Monastère de Sainte-Catherine du Mont Sinai.* Cairo, 1938.

Rohlfs, Gerhard. *Drei Monate in der Libyschen Wüste.* Cassel, 1875.

Samuel al-Syriany, Badii Habib. *Guide to Ancient Coptic Churches and Monasteries in Upper Egypt.* Cairo, 1990.

———. *Ancient Coptic Churches and Monasteries in the Delta, Sinai, and Cairo.* Cairo, 1996.

Schmitz, Alfred Ludwig. "Die Welt der ägyptischen Einsiedler und Mönche." *Römische Quartalschrift für christliche Altertumskunde* 37 (1929): 189–243.

Schweinfurth, Georg August. *Auf unbetretenen Wegen in Ägypten.* Hamburg, 1922.

Schwitz, Stephan. "Geschichte und Organisation der pachomischen Klöster im 4. Jahrhundert." *Archiv für katholisches Kirchenrecht* 81 (1901): 3, 5, 461–90, 630–49.

Segny, Jean. *Le monachisme copte.* Cairo, 1954.

Sicard, Claude. "Brief des Pater Sicard an den P. Fleurian über eine Reise in die Wüste von Thebais und die dortigen Klöster." Paulus, *Sammlung* 5: 126–57.

Smolenski, Thadée. "Le couvent copte de Saint Samuel à Galamoun." *Annales du Service des Antiquités de l'Egypte* 9 (1908): 204–207.

Steindorff, Georg. "Das Kloster des Heiligen Makarios." *Velhagen und Klasings Monatshefte* 202 (1905-1906): 78–85.

Toussoun, Omar. *Etude sur le Wadi Natroun, ses moines, et ses couvents.* Alexandria, 1931.

———. *Cellia et ses couvents.* Alexandria, 1935.

Volbach, Wolfgang Fritz. "Die Koptischen Klöster in der nitrischen Wüste." *Atlantis* 1 (1929): 566–69.

Churches

Badawy, Alexandre. "Les premières églises d'Egypte jusqu'au siècle de Saint Cyrille." *Kyrilliana* (Cairo), 1947.

du Bourguet, Pierre. *Die Kopten,* trans. Eva Rapsilber. Baden-Baden, 1967.

Burmester, O.H.E. Khs-. *A Guide to the Ancient Coptic Churches of Cairo.* Cairo, 1955.

Butler, Alfred J. *The Ancient Coptic Churches of Egypt.* 2 vols. Oxford, 1884.

Clarke, Somers. *Christian Antiquities in the Nile Valley: A Contribution towards the Study of the Ancient Churches.* Oxford, 1912.

Coquin, Charalambia. *Les édifices chrétiens du Vieux-Caire.* Bibl. d'Etudes Coptes vol. 11, Cairo, 1974.

Debanne, Nicolas J. "Le mouled de Sitti Damiana." *Bulletin de la Societé Royale du Géographie d'Egypte* 8 (1917): 75–78.

Gerhards, Albert, and H. Brakmann. *Die koptische Kirche. Einführung in das ägyptische Christentum.* Stuttgart, 1994.

Habib, Raouf. *The Ancient Coptic Churches of Cairo.* Cairo, 1979.

Johann Georg, Herzog zu Sachsen. *Streifzüge durch die Kirchen und Klöster Ägyptens.* Berlin, 1914.

———. *Koptische Klöster der Gegenwart.* Aachen, 1918.

———. *Neue Streifzüge durch die Kirchen und Klöster Ägyptens.* Berlin, 1930.

———. *Neueste Streifzüge durch die Kirchen und Klöster Ägyptens.* Berlin, 1931.

Jullien, Michel. "Traditions et légendes coptes sur le voyage de la Sainte Famille en Egypte." *Missions Catholiques* 19 (1886): 9–12.

Meinardus, Otto. *The Historic Coptic Churches of Cairo.* Cairo, 1994.

Middleton, J. Henry. "The Copts and their Churches." *The Academy* 22 (1882): 248–49, 266–67, 285–86, 318.

Miedema, R. *Koptische Kunst.* Amsterdam, 1929.

Parry, E.G. *Some Ancient and Younger Churches in Egypt.* Cairo, 1952.

Sidawi, Elie. "Moeurs et traditions de l'Egypte moderne: Sitti Damiana, sa legende, son mouled." *Bulletin de la Societé Royale de Géographie d'Egypte* 8 (1917): 79–99.

Simaika, Marcus. *The Guide of the Coptic Museum.* Cairo, 1932.

de Villard, Ugo Monneret. *Les églises du monastère des Syriens au Wadi el Natroun.* Milan, 1928.

Wansleben, Johann Michael. *Nouvelle relation en forme de journal d'un voyage fait en Egypte en 1672 et 1673.* Paris, 1677.

Index

The following abbreviations have been used to distinguish personal names:
(B) = bishop, (H) = hermit, (M) = metropolitan, (P) = patriarch, (S) = saint.